Get the eBook FREE!

(PDF, ePub, Kindle, and liveBook all included)

We believe that once you buy a book from us, you should be able to read it in any format we have available. To get electronic versions of this book at no additional cost to you, purchase and then register this book at the Manning website.

Go to https://www.manning.com/freebook and follow the instructions to complete your pBook registration.

That's it!
Thanks from Manning!

Machine Learning System Design

Machine Learning
System Design
WITH END-TO-END EXAMPLES

VALERII BABUSHKIN
ARSENY KRAVCHENKO

MANNING
SHELTER ISLAND

For online information and ordering of this and other Manning books, please visit
www.manning.com. The publisher offers discounts on this book when ordered in quantity.
For more information, please contact

    Special Sales Department
    Manning Publications Co.
    20 Baldwin Road
    PO Box 761
    Shelter Island, NY 11964
    Email: orders@manning.com

Manning Publications Co.
20 Baldwin Road
PO Box 761
Shelter Island, NY 11964

Development editor:	Doug Rudder
Technical editor:	Ioannis Atsonios
Review editor:	Kishor Rit
Production editor:	Andy Marinkovich
Copy editor:	Kari Lucke
Proofreader:	Tiffany Taylor
Typesetter and cover designer:	Marija Tudor

ISBN 9781633438750
Printed in the United States of America

brief contents

v

contents

Neither Arseny's (online marketing) nor Valerii's (chemometrics) early careers had much to do with machine learning (ML). However, it was the mathematical tools of our trades like regression models and principal component analysis that sparked our obsession with extracting maximum value from data. Each of us started our journey in the early 2010s, with Valerii ultimately taking on corporate leadership roles in data science at companies such as Facebook, Alibaba, Blockchain.com, and BP, and Arseny honing his engineering skills within deep-tech startups at various stages of growth.

Before joining efforts in writing this book, the only shared piece of our careers was related to ML competitions, when we sharpened our skills on Kaggle. Valerii has reached Grandmaster status and was formerly ranked in the Top 30 globally. Arseny is a Kaggle Master with vast expertise in competitive ML, while both authors strive to share their knowledge and experience as public speakers on ML-related topics.

Our collaboration blends Arseny's hands-on experience with building and optimizing ML systems with Valerii's strategic vision and leadership in data-driven enterprises. From real-time video processing and retail optimization to financial transactions analysis, we have tried to distill our combined expertise into the essential principles for building functional ML systems.

Despite the difference in our career paths, we both discovered a gap between knowing ML algorithms and understanding how to effectively apply them in real-world scenarios. We saw brilliant minds struggling to connect the dots and combine fragmented knowledge into a coherent picture. It was this challenge that inspired us to write this book.

acknowledgments

This book would never have been brought to life without the active support of our friends and colleagues.

We would like to express our gratitude to Bogdan Pechenkin for his direct contribution to preparing draft chapters and to Igor Kotenkov, Rustem Feyzkhanov, Evgenii Makarov, and Adam Eldarov for conducting the review during the work-in-progress stages.

We would like to thank Simon Kozlov and Sam Weiss, whose approach to problem-solving inspired many pieces of this book; Sergey Foris for his contribution as an editor; and Tatyana Putilova for enlivening the book with beautiful yet informative illustrations.

Thank you to our technical editor, Ioannis Atsonios, who has worked in academia, consulting, and industry in various positions including data product ideation, craft of proof of concepts, and actual productization, in addition to carrying out extensive research and development in machine learning, particularly in personalization systems.

We would like to give our kudos to all the reviewers: Aleksei Agarkov, Antonios Tsaltas, Arijit Dasgupta, Craig Henderson, Dinesh Ghanta, Flayol Frédéric, George Onofrei, Konstantin Kliakhandler, Lakshminarayanan A.S., Laura Uzcategui, Lucian M. Sasu, Maxim Volgin, Mikael Dautrey, Mike Wright, Mirerfan Gheibi, Nikos Kanakaris, Ninoslav Cerkez, Odysseas Pentakalso, Oliver Korten, Prashant Kowshik, Robert Diana, Sriram Macharla, Stephen John Warnett, Stipe Cuvalo, Vatsal Desai, Vishnu Ram Venkataraman, and William Jamir Silva; we thank you for your critiques and invaluable insights, which helped fine-tune numerous individual blocks of text and gave the book additional sharpness and focus.

Thanks also to the early access book readers and the students of our courses on ML system design, who challenged us with great questions and offered valuable suggestions.

We extend our heartfelt gratitude to our families and friends, whose patience and understanding allowed us the time and focus needed to bring this book to life. Your unwavering support made this journey possible, and for that, we are deeply thankful.

Finally, a huge thank you to the Manning team for providing us with the opportunity to publish this book and for their guidance in every step of the process.

about this book

Machine Learning System Design is a comprehensive step-by-step guide designed to help you work on your ML system at every stage of its creation—from gathering information and taking preliminary steps to implementation, release, and ongoing maintenance.

As the title suggests, the book is dedicated to ML system design, not focusing on a particular technology but rather providing a high-level framework on how to approach problems related to building, maintaining, and improving ML systems of various scales and levels of complexity.

As ML and AI are getting bigger and bigger these days, there are many books and courses on algorithms, domains, and other specific aspects. However, they don't provide an entire vision. This leads to the problem Arseny and Valerii have seen in multiple companies, where solid engineers successfully build scattered subcomponents that can't be combined into a fully functioning, reliable system. This book aims to, among other things, fill this gap.

This book is not beginner friendly. We expect our readers to be familiar with ML basics (you can understand an ML textbook for undergraduate students) and to be fluent in applied programming (you have faced real programming challenges outside the studying sandbox).

Who should read this book?

We hope this book will be helpful to

- Mid-career engineers: to hone their skills in building and maintaining solid ML systems and make sure they don't miss anything critical.

xvii

- Engineering managers and senior engineers: to fill the gaps in their knowledge and view ML system design from a broader perspective.
- Those starting their journey in applied ML: to have structured guidelines at hand before kicking off their first ML system.

How this book is organized: A roadmap

The book structure is designed as a checklist or manual, with an infusion of campfire stories from our own experience. It can be read all at once or used at any moment while working on a specific aspect of a ML system. At the same time, we try not to slip into sounding like a typical textbook or course on classic machine learning or deep learning.

We've split the book into four main parts so that its structure is in line with the life cycle of any system:

- Discovery
- Building a core
- Improvement
- Maintenance

Chapters 1–8 are based around the early stages of ML system design. Throughout chapters 1–4, we focus on overall awareness and understanding of the problem your system needs to solve and define the steps needed before system development has started. This phase rarely involves writing code and mostly focuses on small prototypes or proofs of concepts.

Chapters 5–8 delve into the technical details of the early-stage work. This stage requires a lot of reading and communicating, which is crucial for understanding a problem, defining a landscape for possible solutions, and aligning expectations with other project participants. If we compare an ML system to a human body, it's about forming a skeleton.

Chapters 9–12 are focused on intermediate steps. At this stage of the system life cycle, the schedule of responsible engineers is usually flipped, and there is way less research and communication and more hands-on work on implementing and improving the system. Here, we focus on such questions as how to make the system solid, accurate, and reliable. Continuing the human body metaphor, this is where the system grows its muscles.

The final part, featuring chapters 13–16, is dedicated to integration and growth. For an inexperienced observer, the system may seem ready to go, but this is a tricky impression. There are multiple (mostly engineering-related) aspects that need to be taken into account before the system goes live successfully. In the software world, a system failure is rarely a disaster like in civil engineering, but it's still an unwanted scenario. So at this stage you will learn how to make your system reliable, maintainable, and future-proof. If you're still not tired of human body metaphors, this is where the system gets its wisdom, because untamed strength can lead to nothing but trouble.

liveBook discussion forum

Purchase of *Machine Learning System Design* includes free access to liveBook, Manning's online reading platform. Using liveBook's exclusive discussion features, you can attach comments to the book globally or to specific sections or paragraphs. It's a snap to make notes for yourself, ask and answer technical questions, and receive help from the author and other users. To access the forum, go to https://livebook.manning.com/book/machine-learning-system-design/discussion. You can also learn more about Manning's forums and the rules of conduct at https://livebook.manning.com/discussion.

Manning's commitment to our readers is to provide a venue where a meaningful dialogue between individual readers and between readers and the authors can take place. It is not a commitment to any specific amount of participation on the part of the authors, whose contribution to the forum remains voluntary (and unpaid). We suggest you try asking them some challenging questions lest their interest stray! The forum and the archives of previous discussions will be accessible from the publisher's website for as long as the book is in print.

about the authors

ARSENY KRAVCHENKO is a seasoned ML engineer with a proven track record of building and optimizing reliable ML systems for various domains. Currently, he works as a Senior Staff Machine Learning Engineer at Instrumental. As a Kaggle Master, he is recognized for his expertise in competitive ML and has a passion for sharing his knowledge and experience as a public speaker on ML-related topics. Alongside his engineering experience, Arseny has served as an AI/ML advisor for VC teams and early-stage startups.

VALERII BABUSHKIN is an accomplished data science leader with extensive experience in the tech industry. He currently serves as Senior Principal at BP, where he is responsible for leading the company's data-driven initiatives. Prior to joining BP, Valerii held key roles at leading tech companies such as Facebook, Alibaba, and Blockchain.com. In addition to his professional achievements, Valerii is a Kaggle Grandmaster, formerly ranked in the top 30 globally, demonstrating his outstanding skills and expertise in the data science field.

about the cover illustration

The figure on the cover of *Machine Learning System Design*, titled "Les Pauvres," or "The Poor," is taken from a book by Louis Curmer published in 1841. Each illustration is finely drawn and colored by hand.

In those days, it was easy to identify where people lived and what their trade or station in life was just by their dress. Manning celebrates the inventiveness and initiative of the computer business with book covers based on the rich diversity of regional culture centuries ago, brought back to life by pictures from collections such as this one.

Part 1

Preparations

This part is fully dedicated to the early stages of machine learning system design. Chapter 1 introduces our vision of machine learning system (ML) design and highlights the areas where its principles can be useful. Chapter 2 thoroughly describes the problem space and solution space and the absolute priority the former has over the latter, as well as provides insights on defining the problem, risks, limitations, and costs of a mistake. Chapter 3 unveils the build-or-buy dilemma, looks at the problem as a source of inspiration, and suggests our view on problem decompositioning. Chapter 4 is dedicated to the design document as the essential building block of any ML system.

Essentials of machine learning system design

This chapter covers

- What machine learning (ML) system design is, why it is so difficult to define, and where you may first encounter it
- Who we believe will benefit most from reading this book, what information we're about to give you, and how it will be structured
- What principles of ML system design can be helpful and the best time to apply them

Machine learning (ML) system design is a relatively new term that often gets people from the industry puzzled. Many find it hard to compile a certain scope of responsibilities behind this term, not to mention trying to find a proper name for a respective role or position. The job may be done with various efficiency by ML engineers, software engineers, or even data scientists, depending on the scope of their role.

While all of the positions are valid, we believe that to become a seasoned expert in ML system design, you have to encapsulate expertise from each of the back grounds. Note that while some of the things we discuss in this book are specific to

ML systems, others will be familiar to those readers who have already built non-ML software systems (you will find this information in chapters 2, 13, and 16). This is because ML system design, although a new phenomenon, is still based on the classic fundamentals of software development.

But first we need to discover what ML system design is as a whole. In this opening chapter, we will suggest our take on the definition of ML system design and support it with examples from personal experience, both our own and those of our colleagues; we will describe the perfect persona for the position and share cases from our personal experience of why a coherent and consistent approach to designing an ML system will save you a lot of time in the long run and will help in delivering short-term business wins, which is crucial to gain the trust of colleagues in this new working method from the early stages.

1.1 *ML system design: What are you?*

ML system design might sound familiar if you have ever tried interviewing at deep tech/big tech companies (the first term commonly stands for startups or R&D units within large corporations that either work with or develop cutting-edge technology, and the second term refers to the largest and most dominant tech companies of the world that are often known for their high bar in talent acquisition and advanced engineering culture) for ML engineer/manager positions. Both of us have vast, deep tech experience, so while planning to write this book, we were convinced the definition was clear enough to everyone, and there was no reason to dwell on it.

However, after reaching out to a variety of people for their opinions on the outline, we saw that the term itself caused discord in opinions and interpretations. Perhaps this is due to the fact that the industry has long had a definite list of job titles, which gives candidates a relatively clear understanding of what set of functions and responsibilities they are applying for. The positions of software engineer, research engineer, ML engineer, and so on each entail a certain classic set of functions enshrined in textbooks and eloquently stated in job descriptions.

So, is there a job title associated directly with the term *ML system design*? Currently, there's no position completely tied to the scope we'll be describing in this book, but if you meet a person fulfilling this scope, their position will most certainly be data scientist.

In our attempts to understand the nature of this connection, we reached various people working in data scientist positions and eventually realized that the role implies a rather vast and vague list of responsibilities. Indeed, you can find 10 different people working in 10 different companies as a data scientist and ask them what they do—and you'll end up hearing about 10 completely different things:

- Create pivot tables in Excel.
- Set up a 10 PB distributed cluster.
- Build a real-time computer vision system.
- Deploy numerous chatbots.
- Visualize data in Tableau/Metabase/Looker/PowerBI.

- Write SQL scripts.
- Run A/B tests.
- Create recommender systems.
- Handle communication with stakeholders.
- Answer questions from top management.

As you can see, a short, crisp-sounding title carries a rather mottled set of functions, having grown into a unifying "jack-of-all-trades" term for anything that goes beyond the commonly accepted scope of work behind the roles of data engineer, ML engineer, and research engineer.

While contemplating this, we found that in the case of ML system design (or rather what later received such a name), the situation is quite the opposite: there is a phenomenon without a common name but with a clear set of functions and responsibilities, and what needs to be done is to organize them and bring them to a coherent structure of interrelated functions.

In the following chapters, we will be giving our own perspective on ML system design and even suggesting unconventional ideas and solutions, but before we dive in, we'd like to suggest our own definition:

Machine learning system design is a complex, multistep process of designing, implementing, and *maintaining* ML-based systems that involves a combination of techniques and skills from various fields and roles, including ML, software engineering, project management, product management, and leadership.

Figure 1.1 illustrates this definition.

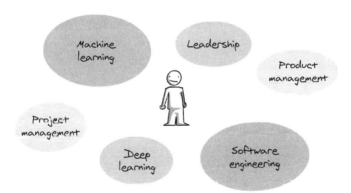

Figure 1.1 The variety of skills one should possess to succeed in ML system design

The reason we've highlighted *maintaining* in italics is that we believe that ML system design does not end at the release of an ML system. Apart from providing accurate predictions and ensuring efficient decision-making, your system must be scalable and flexible enough to be easily adjusted to changing business environments or any other factors, both internal and external. Thus, right after you go live, maintenance and fine-tuning your ML system will secure its efficiency in the long run, which can be crucial, especially when working under strict budget or capacity limitations.

But it is not only the term *machine learning system design* itself that has been questioned by those who have seen this book's synopsis or walked through the table of contents. We received a host of questions on various aspects of the book; the following are those we found the most notable:

- "Data scientist, machine learning engineer, and software engineer are different roles; why are you fusing them together?"
- "It confuses me a little that a book about ML systems covers things like data gathering and reporting, as this is exactly what separates classical machine learning from data science."
- "I was surprised there was no mention of MLOps in the outline, which is the common industry term for many of the components you're describing (reproducibility, testing, pipelines, etc.)."

For us, these questions became an additional indicator of the confusion between ML and data science, as well as between ML engineers and data scientists in the general public. We have our own perspective on that, but first, let us try to clarify our statements.

Coming from deep tech companies, we got used to calling people who do ML *machine learning engineers*, but the difference between ML engineer and software engineer is getting slimmer, especially since some prominent people call machine learning *software 2.0* (https://mng.bz/yoNe). At the same time, *data scientist* is a job title mostly tied to people who do product analytics and work with metrics, insights, etc. (Please note we are speaking about our experience in deep tech companies, but since these companies employ thousands of highly qualified pros and gradually set standards for the whole industry, we tend to take this approach as a benchmark.)

When people interview for an ML engineer position, they mostly walk through the software engineer hiring loop topped with additional sections, with ML system design being one of the most important. It is used to draw out signals about a candidate's expertise, maturity, and ability to overview complex systems and decompose them into blocks of interdependent tasks. This is not an easy exercise, as a candidate has only 40–45 minutes to present their design of a system randomly picked by the interviewer.

Eliezer Yudkowsky, a modern AI writer and philosopher, wrote, "The most dangerous habit of thought taught in schools is that even if you don't really understand something, you should parrot it back anyway" (https://mng.bz/r1Zy). It is very applicable to the tech interview flow in some companies: the interviewer provides a puzzle and expects a particular answer to be parroted back. After the interviewee is hired and becomes an interviewer of their own, the bad practice gets reinforced, and the company continues hiring people with perfectly memoized knowledge fragmentarily drawn from various fields. There is no guarantee these people understand the whole picture, and this is what we came across while conducting interviews ourselves.

We interviewed and hired ML engineers for various companies. Some were at the start of their career, some were seasoned experts, and some were solid software engineers switching to ML. However, there was a specific commonality among those who didn't get through the interview: while working on the ML system design section, they were concentrating too much on details, never getting to the bigger picture.

For us, these failures indicated an expectations mismatch; as young hiring managers, we were convinced that a person who knew all the algorithms, tools, and patterns would be a good fit for the role by default. But later we saw that sometimes people just couldn't combine their pieces of knowledge into an integrated vision.

In addition, building systems in a real environment is overwhelmingly different from discussing them during interviews. One can learn dozens of popular ML system design questions ("How would you design a job recommendation system for a LinkedIn-like website"?) and be puzzled when a similar problem occurs in real work.

But let's ignore the interview part for a while. ML experts get hired for a reason: companies need them to build, maintain, operate, and improve systems—and not just for the sake of writing some code or closing Jira tickets. Businesses need reliable ML systems to reach objectives and solve problems.

Building ML systems requires a wide scope of skills. To put it briefly, a person in charge must be able to answer three questions:

1 What are we building?
2 What is the purpose of the system?
3 How should it be built?

In practice, it requires a combination of skills from multiple roles: a bit of a product manager to understand the main goal and communicate it to peers and stakeholders, a fair share of ML researcher to empower the system, and, of course, a solid software engineering background to make the product usable, maintainable, and reliable. An ML system design expert should be able to think globally and dive deep enough locally if needed.

There are few people who can combine all these skills at the proper level. However, a lot of ML systems are being built these days, and someone has to design them. From our experience, it is common for an ML system to be designed by either a bright ML expert (because it's ML) or an experienced software engineer (because it's a system). They do the job but often struggle in the areas where they don't shine.

To sum it up, the confusion around ML system design is more typical for candidates with less expertise on the one hand and hiring managers or recruiters who are looking for that jack of all trades on the other. However, if we look at it from the point of view of an executive officer or an expert, a much broader picture appears. They know that you hire these specialists to build, maintain, and improve ML systems, and their end performance working on ML systems becomes the ultimate benchmark of their career growth.

We believe that it's the fusion of data scientist and software engineer with experience in academic ML that constitutes an expert in ML system design. People who end up designing ML systems may come from various backgrounds—software, practical ML, academic ML, data research—and we hope our hands-on experience aided by small bits of theory will help them close the gaps, systemize their knowledge in the areas they're familiar with, and feel more confident in the areas where they're lacking precious experience.

1.1.1 *Why ML system design is so important*

While you have MLOps as a set of tools to use for building and maintaining your ML system, you can consider ML system design a blueprint that you can rely on and refer to at any moment that will give you scalability and flexibility (a proper understanding of building blocks and their connections helps to identify bottlenecks and address other problems fluently). Most importantly, though, it provides a framework that will weld your whole system together.

Some projects are simple enough that they don't require that thorough of an approach. Let's take construction as an example. You could probably build a shed without an initial blueprint. But when your ambitions spread further to the level of a house or a skyscraper, you can't get away with not using a prearranged, detailed plan. ML system design is an architectural approach to engineering ML systems that incorporates the experiences of hundreds of experts who have worked in dozens of companies on a multitude of projects.

1.1.2 *Roots of ML system design*

Building complicated software systems has always been a challenge, and organizations had to crystallize the process somehow. People used a general principle for managing complexity through abstraction: build low-level blocks with complexity encapsulated into them, treat them as magic black boxes, use them to build higher-level blocks, and so on.

This process worked, but it had a weak spot: someone had to decide the structure of all these blocks (what are the highest-level components, what's their structure inside, and so on to the lowest level of implementation). The most responsible decisions were made by software architects—experienced engineers who worked with many systems.

This kind of approach is usually associated with the Waterfall methodology and Big Design Upfront paradigm. In other words, it assumes software projects start slowly and are deeply analyzed and documented before the first line of a real system code is written. This approach was and continues to be reliable but inertial and bureaucratic. In a world of rapid changes, the project could lose its initial sense before finishing.

Opponents of such slow but steady approaches are often enthusiasts of something called the agile software development paradigm. The authors of *Manifesto for Agile Software Development* (https://agilemanifesto.org/) stated four main values:

- Individuals and interactions over processes and tools
- Working software over comprehensive documentation
- Customer collaboration over contract negotiation
- Responding to change over following a plan

In other words, these people fairly state that many software systems can't be effective while trying to plan and document everything. Of course, sometimes such bureaucracy makes sense—e.g., for building software controlling medical devices or airplanes. But most software engineers work on other types of applications—office software, entertainment, websites, and mobile apps. That's how the software architect's role became associated with something slow and old school—the opposite of swift hackers changing the world rapidly without a software specification approved by the whole hierarchy of architects, managers, and other experts. This agile approach was popularized by the Silicon Valley hacker culture and thousands of successful startups. Even big companies like Meta try to keep such a culture—their internal motto is "Move fast and break things."

Let's summarize this little historical overview: at some point, industry faced a spectrum of software engineering processes, from a heavily regulated one led by software architects to the chaotic, anarchist "screw the hierarchy" hacker-style way of building things. And, as it often happens, things got mixed. More traditional companies tend to become more agile, and most anarchist startups mature, introducing processes and separate roles.

This mixture leads to a consensus that dominates tech companies these days: instead of delegating all the decisions to dedicated people like software architects, we will keep it the responsibility of regular software engineers; let them both design systems *and* write code for these systems. But this level of freedom didn't wipe out the initial need for decisions: someone still has to have a final word on how things are structured. Someone has to be responsible for the system design. Every engineer may be involved here and there, but seeing the whole picture is critical.

Skills in implementing low-level pieces of a designed system are not the same as skills in designing a proper system. That's why deep tech companies tend to have separate interview sections to check a candidate's skills in writing effective code (aka algorithms section) and designing systems: it's expected that engineers will wear both hats. The split between those two can be different: usually, junior engineers are silent readers of design documents, and senior engineers are authors or active contributors.

In a nutshell, there is a consensus: a solid software engineer should be able to operate on different levels of abstraction, from low-level implementation to high-level architecture decisions.

Everything we have said so far about the definition of system design is fair for any software—we didn't mention something ML related. However, not everyone who can successfully design a software system will succeed in designing an ML system—it's a very specific subset of systems. While designing an ML system, the person in charge should keep in mind many aspects that are not relevant to regular software. In this book, we'll focus on these aspects; readers interested in more general system design questions can look into other literature.

1.2   *How this book is structured*

There are several books covering system design, but literature on ML system design is scarce. We decided to contribute to this field and bridge the gap between supply and demand. Our goal is to share our knowledge and experience to help you convert the many things you know into a holistic system.

This book is structured as a comprehensive practical guideline on how to build complex, properly functioning ML systems in various domains, regardless of the size of the company you work for. This guideline includes

- The overall landscape with an overview of general structural principles and all the components that make up such systems, as well as the pitfalls you may get trapped in
- Low-level checklists of the tools that might come in handy at each step, with a brief reminder of why they are important

The book structure tends to resemble that of a checklist or manual, with an infusion of campfire stories from our own experience. It can be read at once or used at any moment while working on a specific aspect of an ML system.

Each chapter is a high-level checklist mandatory for every ML system. Note that while not all the items must be fulfilled, each of them must be remembered and considered.

In addition, each chapter answers the question regarding why and when the given item is important. It also includes a description of the landscape (what techniques and tools are suitable for the item). The description is systematized (not just a list of 100 buzzwords), although not necessarily exhaustive, as we believe that an experienced reader will be able to compare the example case with something from their background and draw their own conclusions. At the same time, we try not to slip into a typical textbook or course on classic ML or deep learning.

We come from quite different (and therefore, very intercomplementary) backgrounds: both of us have been involved in ML projects with over 20 years of combined "mileage" in a variety of roles, companies, and environments—from pre-seed startups to multibillion-dollar international corporations. Sometimes we worked long hours as individual contributors. Other times, our work primarily implied rapid team growth and coaching talented and aspiring young engineers. We have witnessed and have been part of successes and failures, big acquisitions, and massive job cuts. And, of course, we've discussed a lot of the successes and failures of ML projects with our friends.

But no matter how different our backgrounds are, there's one thing we strongly agree on: ML projects almost never fail because their participants can't use algorithms properly. There may be multiple reasons for a failure: a misdirected or completely unnecessary task, sloppy data handling, an unscalable solution with no growth potential—this list could go on and on.

There is a pattern so popular that we'll have to repeat some stories in different parts of the book: a deep expert in a narrow area focuses a lot on their area of expertise—maybe picks some similar areas but still doesn't get the big picture. As a result, some important nuances are missed, and it leads to project failure, missed deadlines, and violated budgets.

While books on ML usually provide the "right" answers, our main objective is quite the opposite. What we'd like to do is to teach you how to ask the right questions. These might be the questions you ask yourself, your teammates, users, stakeholders—you name it. Each one of us, as tech industry professionals, accumulates tons of valuable information but can't always connect the dots. This is where timely questions help structure all the knowledge around us.

We've split the book into four main parts so that its structure is in line with the life cycle of any system—research, creation, improvement, and maintenance.

The first two parts are based on the early stages of machine learning system design. Throughout part 1, we'll focus on the overall awareness and understanding of the problem your system needs to solve and define the steps needed before system development has started. This phase rarely involves writing code and mostly focuses on small prototypes or proofs of concepts. Part 2 delves into the technical details of the early-stage work. This stage requires a lot of reading and communicating, which is crucial for understanding a problem, defining a landscape for possible solutions, and aligning expectations with other project participants. If we compare an ML system to a human body, it's about forming a skeleton.

The third part is focused on intermediate steps. In this stage of a system life cycle, the schedule of responsible engineers is usually flipped. There is much less research and communication and more hands-on work implementing and improving the system. Here we focus on questions such as how to make the system powerful in multiple dimensions: solid, accurate, and reliable. Continuing our human body metaphor, the system grows its muscles.

The final part is all about integration and growth. For an inexperienced observer, the system may seem ready to go, but this impression is tricky. There are multiple (engineering, mostly) aspects that need to be taken into account before the system goes live successfully. In the software world, a system failure is rarely a disaster like in civil engineering, but it's still an unwanted scenario. So, at this stage, you will learn how to make your system reliable, maintainable, and future-proof. If you're not tired of human body metaphors, this is where the system gets a mind and gains wisdom because untamed strength can lead to nothing but trouble.

Overall, the opening chapters will contain more general information, which is nonetheless crucial for framing the problem and sets the core fundamentals for building a well-functioning ML system. The further you go into the book, though, the more complex and in-depth the material becomes, providing you with practical examples and exercises. Starting from the very next chapter, we will introduce two fictional cases, radically different from one another, that we will carry through the whole book. Both will require an ML system to solve their problems, and both will evolve as you continue exploring.

In every part of the book, we always prefer intuition over comprehensiveness. There are many aspects to building ML systems, and each one deserves a book of its own. However, we don't plan on writing a separate book on data gathering and preparation, another one on feature engineering, and another one on metrics. Instead, we describe the top of the iceberg and review the landscape structure while supporting our thoughts and points with links to noteworthy papers so readers can both familiarize themselves with top-level examples and add their own specific knowledge to the provided framework. We also do not aim to explain details related to particular libraries or engines. We will mention notable examples in certain chapters, but they are only for illustrative purposes in favor of higher-level abstractions.

Real systems are always more complicated than examples we see in blog posts, conference talks, and, of course, interviews. For all of these scenarios, people talk about high-level abstractions, but in reality, the devil is in the details. That's why we believe getting some intuition on problem-solving is so important: a successful ML system designer should be able not only to recognize some recipe from the cookbook and reproduce it but also to adapt themselves for company-specific details that can flip the table sometimes.

We hope this book will be useful for

- People preparing for an interview for an ML engineer/manager position
- Software engineers, engineering managers, and ML practitioners working with an existing complex system who want to either understand or improve it
- People who plan to design their own ML system or have designed one already and want to be sure they didn't forget anything critical

Due to the philosophy described here, the book is not beginner-friendly. We expect our readers to be familiar with ML basics (e.g., you can understand an ML textbook for undergraduate students) and fluent in applied programming (e.g., you've faced some real programming challenges outside the studying sandbox). Otherwise, this book is better read after studying basic material.

1.3   *When principles of ML system design can be helpful*

As we said earlier, applying these principles is critical to build a system complex enough to have multiple failure modes. Ignoring them leads to high chances of delivering something with feet of clay—a system that may work right now but is not sustainable enough to survive a challenge from the dynamic environment of reality. The challenge can be purely technical (what if we face 10 times more data?), product-related (how do we adapt for changed user scenarios?), business-driven (what if the system is to be included into a third-party software stack after an acquisition?), legal (what if the government puts forward a new regulation on personal data management?), or anything else. Recent years have only proved we can't foresee every possible risk.

Improving the system is even more important. As we'll describe in more detail in the upcoming chapters, building systems from scratch is a relatively rare event. People outside the industry may think software engineers spend most of their time writing code, while in reality, as we all know, way more time is dedicated to *reading* code. The same goes for systems: much more effort is usually spent improving and maintaining existing systems (which requires an in-depth understanding of system internals), not building them from scratch.

The difference between improving and maintaining is somewhat blurry. For the sake of clarity here, we define *improvements* as adding new functionality or changing existing functionality significantly and *maintenance* as keeping existing functionality working in a constantly changing environment (new customers, new datasets, infrastructure evolution, etc.).

Some principles included in the book are mostly focused on ML system improvement. They help identify weak spots and growth points of a system and even new applications sometimes.

Finally, some principles are more oriented toward ML system maintenance. The sad truth is that very often systems are maintained by teams who didn't participate in building them. So it's a double-edged sword: the building team should keep some principles in mind to simplify the lives of their followers, and the maintenance team should understand the principles to be able to understand the whole system logic in a timely manner and find proper workarounds to keep the system alive over a long period of time.

It is safe to say that close to 100% of ML projects that didn't have a well-written design document have failed, whereas a sweeping majority of those systems that were thoroughly planned found success. Although it should not necessarily be a complex, multipage piece of documentation, and it is often enough to have several pages of condensed information, the design document, in this case, plays two major roles. Not only does it set proper priorities within a project, but it also helps explain whether you actually need this project in the first place and drags your gaze away from the core idea (you might be too focused on the project itself) to see the whole picture. Please see chapter 4 for details.

After working for multiple businesses, we can firmly say that once there's structured documentation describing all aspects of your system functionality, any activity, from onboarding newly hired employees to applying core changes, is implemented many times faster. Instead of searching for the one and only loremaster who keeps all the knowledge to themselves (but still won't guarantee precision), you can address a certain document in the library.

Campfire story from Arseny

A long time ago, I worked for a ride-hailing company. One of its ambitious projects was to build a system for ride fare estimates. The regular pricing model was exactly like the one old-school cabs used for charging passengers: fare = X * time + Y * distance. The company needed to estimate the fare before the actual ride happened to inform both the driver and the passenger.

The project seemed clear and straightforward from the very start. All we needed to do was to fit a simple model that used geo features from the map service and wrap it as a microservice. It seemed so simple I didn't even think about writing a design document.

How the system initially looked in Arseny's imagination: a simple step-by-step algorithm

In reality, there were multiple pitfalls (we will cover most of them respectively in the following chapters):

- Geo features weren't enough for precise estimation, and more complicated features required advanced infrastructure (aka *feature store*, although back in the day, this was not a popular wording or pattern). This will be covered in chapter 11.
- As the model became more sophisticated, its predictions became less reliable (a certain number of results would turn out to be outliers—values that were either too big or too small).
- Errors were not uniformly distributed, so the model was biased. We touch on this topic in chapter 9.
- The executives wanted to override fare estimations sometimes with some promo activities or heuristics-based shortcuts. This subject is discussed in chapter 13.
- Too much time was spent building a model that didn't really solve the exact problem. We touch on this topic in chapter 2.
- The whole problem was prone to distribution drift and thus required smart monitoring. We cover more of the subject in chapter 14.
- The infrastructure was not ready for the scenario, which led to unacceptable latency in peak hours. This topic is covered in chapter 15.

- Some other teams were not aware that the system was being developed, and it led to API mismatches. This topic is discussed in chapter 16.

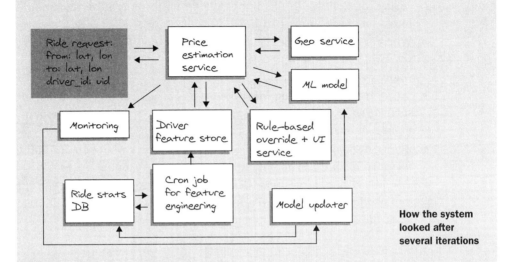

How the system looked after several iterations

The system was not deployed after all—before all the problems were fixed, the market situation changed significantly, and the need for the initial system faded. While the original idea for the system was great (some competitors used similar ideas), my colleagues and I failed to implement it in a proper way: some key aspects, both tech and product-related, were totally missed and were discovered only in the late stages of the project when the price of changes skyrocketed. At the same time, if some aspects had been taken into account at earlier stages, addressing them would have been trivial. If only I, my boss, or my teammates had read a book like this, we could have avoided this failure.

Still, for every few stories of failures, there's a story of success. The next story has less drama and might seem boring, but it's worth sharing for the sake of balance. Back in the day, Valeriy used to work at the Russian tech giant Yandex, when it acquired a startup providing real-time recommendations. When mergers like this happen, it takes time to fine-tune cooperation between the existing and new units, onboard new staff, sync business processes, etc. In this case, however, he was amazed at how smoothly and seamlessly a new business was integrated into a massive corporation. The reason behind it was a well-built design document that made this transition possible.

To summarize, we strongly believe that arranging a design document, preceded by asking your business the right guiding questions and setting up proper goals, is the key to success for your ML system—or a reason to cancel the project at the earliest stage, which is also a positive outcome, considering how much time, effort, and money you can save by dropping an unwanted activity. We'll dedicate at least three chapters to this stage of the project, as this is the most crucial part you'll have to deal with.

Summary

- While it's a relatively new term, *ML system design* is based on the classic fundamentals of software development, incorporating the existing knowledge from related disciplines. In this book, we will try to reorganize this knowledge base into a set of working algorithms.
- Whereas MLOps can be considered a set of tools for building and maintaining your ML system, think of ML system design as a framework that will weld the whole system together.
- To succeed in designing ML systems, it is crucial to be equally experienced in such disciplines as ML, software engineering, project management, product management, and leadership.
- Before designing an ML system, you should know what you are building, what the purpose of the system is, and how it should be built.
- The pillars of a successfully designed ML system are a consistent approach, a well-planned roadmap, and a list of preliminary actions that will organize your work and save time in the long term.

Is there a problem?

This chapter covers

- Problem space and solution space: which comes first?
- Defining a problem as the most important step
- Defining risks and limitations
- Costs of a mistake

To succeed in machine learning (ML) system design, you literally need to be an expert in multiple fields, including project management, ML and deep learning, leadership, product management, and software engineering. However, when stripped down to the bones, even the most complex and sophisticated solutions in ML system design will have the same framework and fundamentals as any other product.

The variety and amount of sheer knowledge gained in recent years gives you unprecedented freedom to choose exactly the approach you want toward your ML system, but no matter how refined the instruments of your choice are, they're no more than implementation mediums.

What are the business goals? How big is the budget? How flexible are the deadlines? Will the potential output cover and exceed overall costs? These are among the crucial questions that you need to ask yourself before scoping your ML project.

But before you start addressing these questions, there is a paramount action that will lay the foundation for successful ML system design, and it's *finding and articulating the problem your solution will solve (or help solve)*. This is a seemingly trivial point, especially for skilled engineers, but based on our own experience in the area, skipping this step in your preliminary work is deceptively dangerous. It goes even further when we realize that some problems cannot be solved on a proper level, due to either the current state of available technologies or the aleatoric uncertainty of the ill-posed problem. While in the first case, the problem can be a candidate for the future solution (e.g., today's level of text generation would seem totally unachievable for an ML engineer in the early 2010s), the second case means the problem should not be tackled at all (e.g., one cannot build an algorithm that can beat casino roulette).

In this chapter, we will cover the importance of knowing the problem before developing a solution; we will highlight risks and limitations you may face while defining a problem; and we will touch on what consequences can follow a mistakenly defined problem.

2.1 *Problem space vs. solution space*

> *I suppose it is tempting, if the only tool you have is a hammer, to treat everything as if it were a nail.*
>
> —Abraham Maslow, American psychologist

Imagine a boss coming to an engineer with an exciting new idea for a mind-blowing feature (we've all been there). For the sake of illustration, let's make the example more specific. Steve works as an ML engineer in a growing SaaS company. Steve's boss, Linda, just got back from a meeting with Jack, VP of sales, on a problem his team has been dealing with—too many customer leads with too few managers to handle them. Jack wonders if the ML team could come up with an AI solution that would automatically rank customer leads from best to worst based on potential profit for the company. This would help the sales team pick potential cash cows first and handle remaining leads residually. On paper, the feature looks stunning. It seems like a no-brainer!

Steve, a young but meticulous specialist, immediately has numerous questions regarding this project. What's the due date for delivery? How big is the dataset of existing leads to build an ML model around? What's the maximum time allowed to score a lead? What accuracy do we expect? What information do we have about each lead? How fast should the system be? What exactly does a "promising lead" imply? Which sales system do we integrate our solution with? After some back-and-forth Q&A, Steve knows the following:

- The dataset is currently fairly small (the company is a young startup).

- Jack wants the tool to integrate with the existing customer relationship management (CRM) so that the company doesn't spend money on new software and there's no need to retrain the team.
- Luckily, there are no hard limits on processing time, which means a reliable real-time API is not required.
- The due date is the usual "the sooner, the better."

Steve gets back to his desk and starts scoping the project. "Okay, this looks easy. We can frame it as a ranking or classification problem, craft some features, train a model, expose an API, integrate, and deploy—that should be it." However, two things still bother him:

- What's the best fitting method to handle classification problems of this kind?
- How should he integrate his Python code with the CRM used by Jack's team?

Three hours later, his browser is full of tabs with a few shot classification techniques and documentation on CRM API. He wants to suggest a precise time estimate on project delivery to his colleagues, but he'll have a hard time doing that because of one crucial mistake that may cost a lot at the early stage: while thinking and asking questions, he focused on the solution space, not the problem space.

To Steve's understanding, the information he received was more than enough to come up with a suitable solution, while in reality, it was just the tip of the iceberg. The remaining context could only be discovered by asking numerous specifying questions of multiple people involved in the project.

What are the problem space and solution space? These are two exploration paradigms that cover different perspectives of a problem. While both are crucial, the former should always precede the latter (figure 2.1).

Figure 2.1   An experienced engineer always handles the problem space first with specifying questions.

The problem space is often defined with "what?" and "why?" questions, often even with chains of such questions. There is even a popular technique named "Five Whys" that recommends stacking your "why?" questions on top of each other to dig to the very origin of the problem you're analyzing. Typical questions often look like this:

- Why do we need to build the solution?
- What problem does it solve?
- Why does the problem occur?
- What are the alternatives we know?
- Why do we want to make it work with given limitations (metrics, latency, number of training samples)?

After exploration, you are expected to have an understanding of what you should build and why.

The "what?" part, in its turn, is about understanding the customer and functional attributes (figure 2.2)—for example, "A tool that annotates customer leads with a score showing how likely it is that the deal will happen; it should assign the scores before sales managers plan their work at a Monday weekly meeting."

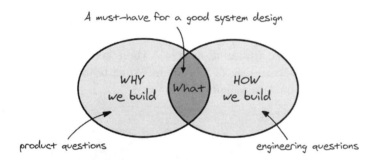

Figure 2.2   The questions you must ask before starting your project and the crucial difference between them

In some companies, asking these questions is a job done solely by product managers. However, it's not very productive for engineers to exclude themselves from problem space analysis, as a proper understanding of problems affects the final result immensely.

The solution space is somewhat the opposite. It's less about the problem and customer needs and more about the implementation. Here, we talk about frameworks and interfaces, discuss how things work under the hood, and consider technical risks. However, implementation should never be done before we reach a consistent understanding of a problem.

Reaching a solid understanding before thinking of a technical implementation allows you to consider various workarounds, some of which may significantly reduce the project scope. Maybe there is a third-party plugin for CRM that is designed to solve this problem. Maybe the cost of errors for the ML part of such a problem is not really that important despite Jack's first answer (stakeholders often start with the statement they need accuracy close to 100%!). Maybe the data shows that 95% of empty leads can be filtered out with simple rule-based heuristics. All of these assumptions lie outside the story, but if proven, each of them is an essential part of the overall context. It is unveiling this context that will give you insight into the problem.

There are two reasons why we began the chapter with Steve's story. First, it's common and will most probably resonate with you in one way or another. Second, it is applicable for any scenario, be it building a new system, modifying an existing solution, or passing an interview in a tech company.

Third, and most important, the scale and effect of consequences that derive from this kind of approach can be damaging to varying degrees:

- Steve will have to rewrite quite a big chunk of the end system.
- Linda will end up using a partial solution and compensating for the missing portion.
- The solution may be completely abandoned.

All these cases require understanding the problem first.

2.2 Finding the problem

Organizations which design systems (in the broad sense used here) are constrained to produce designs which are copies of the communication structures of these organizations.

—Melvin E. Conway

Some old-school enterprise companies still keep the culture that encourages ordinary engineers to focus on low-level implementation (just coding) and leave the design (including problem understanding and decomposition) to architects and system analysts. From our experience, due to increasing flexibility requirements, this culture is disappearing rapidly, giving way to more horizontal structures with more problem understanding delegated to individual contributors.

This means engineers don't have to be solid experts in the domain (it can be too complicated for a person without a proper background). The reason is simple: it's hard to learn the nuances of building a stock exchange or manufacturing quality control between meetings, code reviews, and training new state-of-the-art neural networks. But having a broad understanding is a must before starting an ML system design.

We encourage you to write down a problem statement using an inverted pyramid scheme with a high-level understanding in its basement and nuances at the top. It is a common and effective top-down approach that will help you gather as much general information as possible, determine what data is most valuable to your project, and then, using point by-point leading questions, delve into the specifics of a problem (figure 2.3).

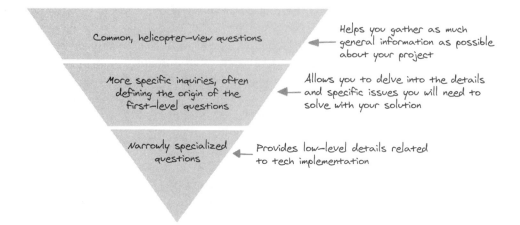

Figure 2.3   The inverted pyramid scheme is an approach we recommend for gathering data required for a successful project launch.

On the very top level, you can formulate the helicopter-view understanding of the problem. That's the level understandable to any C-level office of the organization where people don't care too much about ML algorithms or software architecture—for example:

- There are fraudsters in our mobile app who try to attack our legit users.
- Our pricing model demonstrated extremely low profit margins for some products while being absolutely uncompetitive in other categories.
- Customers complain that our software requires a lot of manual tuning before bringing value; it should be *automagic*.
- App users aren't engaged enough.

Having such a statement at the start gives many opportunities for the next exploration steps. Just try to question every word in a given sentence to make sure you can explain it to a 10-year-old child. Who are fraudsters? How do they attack? What report gave the initial insight about excessive prices? What bothers our customers the most? Where is the most time wasted? How do we measure user engagement? How are recommendations related to this metric? Ask yourself or your colleagues questions until you're ready to build the next, broader block of the pyramid that expands the initial one.

This next pyramid block requires more specific, well-thought-out questions. One of the successful techniques is looking for the origin of the previous-level answers. How do we decide this behavior was fraudulent? What kind of manual tuning do our customers have to perform? How are user engagement and recommendation engine performance currently correlated?

An even more powerful technique involves looking for inconsistencies in answers; people tend to group objects based on their similarity and distinguish objects based on their differences. There may be similar users; some are considered spammers and should be banned, while others are still legit, even if their behavior may overlap with that of a person outside of the problem domain. For an uninformed observer, the same added margin for similar goods may be acceptable or not, but what are the criteria? An engineer here doesn't have to find all the splitting criteria in a problem statement (they're not decision trees), but that's a good field to catch crucial signals and generate insights. This can be summarized by the following statement: trying to understand what people want is important; trying to understand what they need is critical.

Be sure to involve all the interested parties in the process. It's not only your boss or product manager who cares about the project; you're likely to have multiple stakeholders (it is crucial to understand which of the stakeholders is responsible for budgets and will be a point of approval for a given component of the system). Often, it is recommended to chat with experts at different levels to envelop both strategic and tactical perspectives. A high-level executive knows much about the goal of a given initiative. On the other hand, individual contributors who currently handle the absence of a designed system know tricks and details that may substantially affect the design.

Once you feel confident enough to explain the problem in simple terms, it's time to wrap it up. We recommend writing down your problem understanding. Usually, it's several paragraphs of text, but this text will eventually become the cornerstone of your design document. Don't polish it too much for now; it's just your first (although very important) step.

The importance of this step may vary, depending on the organization or environment. Sometimes the problem is easy to understand and, usually, very hard to solve—this is a common case in established competitive markets. Another side of the spectrum is startups that disrupt existing markets; here, the initial understanding of the disruption is rarely correct. One of the authors worked at a company where up to 50% of his time on a project was spent on defining goals and relevant context. After the context was clear, the ML engineering part of the project was smooth and straightforward.

Campfire story from Valerii

Back in 2019, I worked in a tech company that decided to expand its eCommerce department and "go offline." The new project named Super Bill was based on the following idea:

1. Customers could use the Super Bill app as a price comparison tool for grocery stores and could also upload their receipts to get cash back, as well as buy in-store using an app.
2. Brands could use the app to provide cash back for buying specific items, promoting their goods as substitution items or recommended items.

The problem was that a single item could have multiple names (as printed on a receipt) in various grocery chains. "Mars small," "M. bar small," "Mars bar small," etc., which could all be different spellings of the same stock-keeping unit (SKU), were to be mapped to the same item: Mars Candy Bar.

(continued)

The initial idea was to train a deep-structured semantic model and perform search engine matching, where the name from a receipt would play the role of Query, and SKU was the Document.

I didn't like that solution, as it was too complex and bulky for this kind of problem. It required gathering data, labeling it, training the model, assessing its quality, etc. So I decided to think it over. If I need to label data, I will do it only once per name in the receipt per grocery. Hence, I need no ML model for an already labeled sample, and this can occur quite often. Given that the item frequency follows Zipf's law, we needed to label the most popular name-SKU pairs, constituting a small fraction of all unique pairs but a larger fraction of all pairs to label (based on this empirical law, when a list of measured values is sorted in decreasing order, the value of the nth entry is approximately inversely proportional to n).

The remaining fraction can be labeled by employees with access to the whole SKU database, but we probably do not want to share this database with a crowdsourcing hand-labeling platform. At the maximum, we can provide a list of candidates from this database and check which one of them (if any) is a match.

So what can we do here? We can try to predict/extract the brand and predict the sample category in the receipts. Narrowing down the list of candidates is a relatively easy classification task or distance-based task, as we have a limited number of categories and brands and can use very simple techniques for postprocessing, such as Levenshtein distance. As soon as we have candidates, we can send them with a sample from the receipt to label through our crowdsourcing process. How often do we need to do that? The answer is only once for each SKU-grocery chain pair. This makes it a much easier and quicker solution compared to the initial idea. After all, we were not building search engines for billions of queries per day but rather a limited matching system.

We were able to put this solution into production in less than three weeks, which is astonishingly quick. All it took was understanding what problem we wanted to solve and gathering context.

P.S. Later, when we were preparing a similar system for another deep tech company with tens of millions of SKUs, we replaced the last layer of postprocessing with a deep semantic similarity model to produce a more intelligent system. That was a benefit of designing an easy-to-adjust decoupled system.

Once the problem statement is explicit enough, it's time to think about what we, as ML engineers, can do with it.

2.2.1   *How we can approximate a solution through an ML system*

Inexperienced or just hasty engineers often first try to drag the problem directly into a Procrustean bed of well-known ML algorithm families like supervised or unsupervised learning or a classification or regression problem. We don't think it's the best way to start.

For an external observer, an ML model is like a magic oracle: a universal machine that can answer any properly formulated question. Your job as an ML engineer would be to approximate its behavior—build this oracle using ML algorithms—but before mimicking it, we need to find the right question and teach users to ask it. In less metaphoric words, here we reframe a business problem into a software/ML problem.

Some questions may seem very straightforward:

- For the fraud problem, we want the oracle to label a user a fraudster as soon as possible—in a perfect world, even before they did anything. *This sounds like a sort of classification.*

- For the pricing model, we'd like to understand how much a customer is ready to pay for their goods without dropping the service in favor of a competitor (if we aim for a short-term problem only) or without thoughts like "This shop became too greedy; I should avoid them in the future" (if we care about long-term perspectives of the brand). *That's definitely similar to regression examples from textbooks.*

- For the recommendation system, we'd ask what we can suggest to the customer so they are happy with the service. *This very much resembles the ranking problem.*

Even with the metaphor of a magical oracle, we often had to leave multiple remarks that affected this potential answer. We'll pay attention to similar details and remarks here and there in the book, but the highlight here is the following: there may be no single simple answer for the problem, and your ML system design must be aware of it in advance.

In our pricing example, there may be a spectrum of goals, from maximizing profit right here right now to growing the company in the long run. A good ML system would be able to adapt to a specific point in this spectrum. In the following chapters, we will discuss the tech aspects of doing so.

Many ML practitioners, including the famous Andrew Ng, a renowned AI expert, professor at Stanford University, and founder of Landing AI, suggest using a heuristic of a human expert: let's build a system that answers in the same manner as the expert in the area would. It works for many domains (health care is a great example) and sets the bar of an early understanding of how solvable problems are with AI approaches. Unfortunately, it comes with disadvantages as well: there are problems where machines perform better than people. Such problems usually happen in domains when data is represented as a log of events (often a human behavior), not something carefully labeled. It's easy to find such cases in the ad tech and finance industries. So human-level performance may be a fair bar to reach, but it's not always the case.

And only after the question is clear does it make sense to dig into the way of algorithm approximation and draft a model capable of doing it. It doesn't have to be a single model: a pipeline of various models or algorithms is often a legit tradeoff. We will cover problem decompositioning as part of a preliminary search covered in the next chapter.

2.3   *Risks, limitations, and possible consequences*

Imagine you've built a fraud detection system: it scores user activity and prevents malicious events by suspending risky accounts. It's a precious thing—zero fraudsters have come through since its launch, and the customer success team is happy. But recently, the marketing team launched a big ad campaign, and your perfect fraud detector banned a fair share of new users based on their traffic source (it's unknown and therefore somewhat suspicious, according to your algorithms). Negative effects on marketing could have been way more significant than the efficiency in detecting fraud activity.

You may find this example obvious and not worth attention. However, the reality is ruthless: situations like this often happen in companies where teams are misaligned, and that was one of the risks you should have kept in mind while designing the system. You shouldn't think, "Our team is professional; a failure like that just can't happen here." So explicit thinking about risks is the way to go, as there's a high chance of potential risks spreading beyond the project team or a single department.

With great power comes great responsibility—this popular proverb is very applicable to ML software. ML is no doubt powerful. But besides the power, it has one more important and dangerous attribute, which is opaqueness for most observers, especially when the model under the hood is complicated. Thus, professional system designers should be aware of potential risks and existing limitations.

Software development classics suggest the idea of functional and nonfunctional requirements. In short, functional requirements are about the functionality of a new feature or system, its value, and its user flow, while nonfunctional requirements are about aspects like performance, security, portability, and so on. In other words, functional requirements determine what we should design, and nonfunctional requirements shape the understanding of how it should work under the hood. So when we talk about potential risks and limitations, we effectively gather nonfunctional requirements.

The cornerstone of any defensive strategy is a risk model. Simply put, it's an answer to the "What are we protecting from?" question. What are the worst scenarios possible, and what should we avoid? Answers like "incorrect model prediction" are not informative at all. A detailed understanding aligned with all possible stakeholders is absolutely required.

Campfire story from Valerii

Once I was building a dynamic pricing algorithm for another big tech company. It was a neat system able to optimize revenue, margin, or traffic, with constraints for the latter two. It could work on the user level, but as soon as you had user-level atomicity, it was possible to aggregate to any level you wanted. It could adapt to changes in user behavior very quickly and output prices for users in real time. It had a nice balance between exploration and exploitation, was able to take uncertainty into consideration, and was quick for training and inference. I even had a desire to write an article about it and came up with a name for it: "Double Bayesian Universal Contextual

Bandits for Dynamic Pricing." The figure outlines the algorithmic design of the system; isn't that nice?

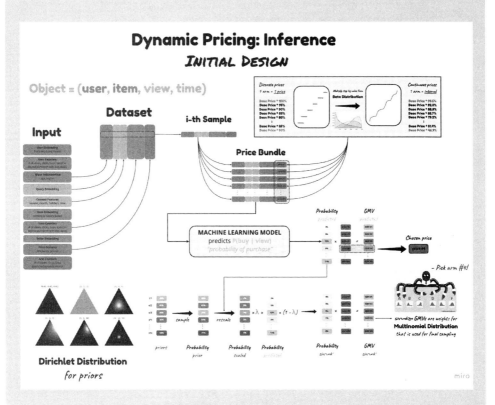

Initial design for the dynamic pricing system

However, possible risks, existing limitations, and undesired consequences have drastically changed the final design.

Risks: it turned out that you can't discriminate against people with different prices for the same item. You can discriminate between locations, of course, but if it is the same city and the same item and you sell online, the price must be the same. Technically, we still can discriminate, but that bears the risk of customers suing the company and, consequently, the company losing tons of money and reputation. Fortunately, we were more or less prepared for that, as we could aggregate on any level we wanted. Do you recall user-level atomicity?

Limitations: the second strike came from the backend side. It turned out we could change the price only as often as every 6 hours (at best!), and thus our ability to change the price in real time didn't matter that much. This was the final blow, forcing me to radically simplify the system, still with some ability to adapt, which will be covered in the next story.

(continued)

It's easy to see that limitations and risks shaped the final design, which I didn't mind, as I enjoyed the process of creating it and was ready to change it (see the next figure). But what if that was my opus magnum? How would I feel after that? The moral is simple—you need to find out any possible risks and limitations as soon as possible; otherwise, you can be forced to discard all your hard work.

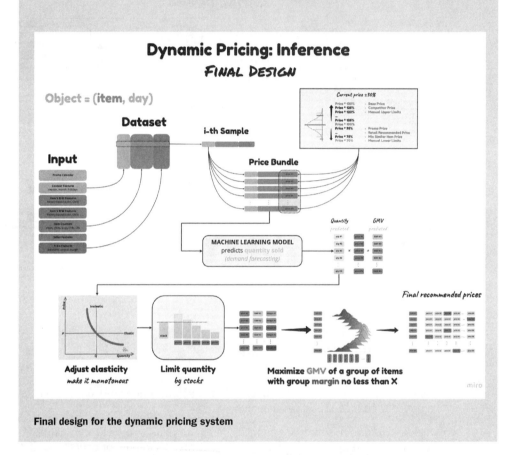

Final design for the dynamic pricing system

Understanding the risks and limitations will affect many future decisions, and we will cover this later in chapters dedicated to datasets, metrics, reporting, and fallback. Before we do, though, we'd like to give a couple of examples displaying how considering (or ignoring) valuable data can affect your goal setting.

2.4   Costs of a mistake

When talking about the costs of a mistake, we'd like to quote Steve McConnell, who precisely defines the difference between robustness and correctness in his book *Code Complete* (2nd ed., Microsoft Press, 2004) using examples of building an X-ray machine and a video game:

As the video game and X-ray examples show us, the style of error processing that is most appropriate depends on the kind of software the error occurs in. These examples also illustrate that error processing generally favors more correctness or more robustness. Developers tend to use these terms informally, but, strictly speaking, these terms are at opposite ends of the scale from each other. Correctness means never returning an inaccurate result; returning no result is better than returning an inaccurate result. Robustness means always trying to do something that will allow the software to keep operating, even if that leads to results that are inaccurate sometimes.

…

Safety-critical applications tend to favor correctness over robustness. It is better to return no result than to return a wrong result. The radiation machine is a good example of this principle. Consumer applications tend to favor robustness to correctness. Any result whatsoever is usually better than the software shutting down. The word processor I'm using occasionally displays a fraction of a line of text at the bottom of the screen. If it detects that condition, do I want the word processor to shut down?

This concept is even more applicable to ML systems, as they tend to be obscure for both developers and end users. A set of *if* and *while* statements is easier to keep in mind compared to enormous sequences of matrix multiplication in modern deep neural networks.

Imagine you're building an entertainment app like an AR mask for Snap or Tik-Tok. In the worst case, the added effect will look ugly for a frame—not a big risk, so robustness is a proper approach here. The opposite case is an ML solution for medical or transport needs. Would you prefer a self-driving car that just moves forward when it's not sure if there is a pedestrian nearby? Definitely not: that's why you want to opt for correctness here.

We'll talk more about this tradeoff and practical aspects of it in the third part of the book. At this point, we should only mention that understanding the costs of mistakes is one of the critical points in gathering predesign information. This is effectively a quantitative development of the risks concept: for risks, we define what can go wrong and what we want to avoid and later try to assign numerical attributes. A numerical aspect may vary greatly depending on a problem and doesn't have to be precise at this point, but it's essential for shaping the landscape.

From our experience, people often tend to think more about positive scenarios, while in reality, negative outcomes require more attention. The logic is simple: usually any system has one (or a few) positive scenarios, and many failure modes are considered negative scenarios. Of course, the probability of each failure mode is usually way less compared to the probability of a good outcome, but it's not always the case if we measure expected values. Imagine a trading system that makes a few cents in 99% of deals and loses the whole capital with the probability of 0.1% or, to be more dramatic, a medical diagnostic system that saves 3 minutes per patient for highly paid doctors but misses a serious but curable disease for every 1,000th patient.

Some mistakes, though, can be harmless or even positive. Back in 2018, Arseny worked in a company making an AR application—a virtual try-on for footwear. The app allowed the user to see how a pair of shoes looked on their feet before purchasing it. One of the first versions of the app contained an underfitted model responsible for foot detection and tracking. As a result, shoes were often rendered not only on human feet but also on top of pet paws and even toys. Many of the early users found it hilarious, so the cost of such a mistake was not significant. But, as the time went on, the effect disappeared after the model performance was improved for more conventional-user scenarios.

While estimating the cost of a mistake, you should also remember there may be second-order consequences. For example, your antifraud system might ban too many legitimate users today, and tomorrow they may spread this by word of mouth about your app ("Never use it; they banned me for nothing"), which may bury your growth potential. Your recommendation system provides unrelated suggestions, and later you end up training a new model based on logs of rare clicks on such a poor recommendation, thus falling into a negative feedback loop.

Another classic example of the cost of a mistake is credit risk scoring, a common task that can be found in almost any bank. Before being accepted or rejected, a borrower's application is usually processed by an ML-based system to output the risk score. This risk score can be either 1/0 (with a specified threshold) or vary and be continuous between 0 and 1.

Obviously, the cost of giving a loan to a potentially defaulting client and providing no loan of the same amount to a customer who would repay it successfully is not the same. How many people does the system need to repay the loan to the bank to outweigh one person who would go bankrupt? Shall we count people/credits given or the amount of money lent? Do we expect this ratio to be constant over time? Answering all of these questions and taking this information into account greatly increases the chance of a project being considered successful.

What does it mean for a person designing an ML system? Identifying the risk landscape helps us understand what kind of problems are to be avoided. Some errors are almost harmless, some can greatly affect business, and some can be life-threatening. A proper understanding of the costs of a mistake with regard to the system being designed is critical for the next steps, as it shapes requirements for reliability and data gathering, suggests better metrics, and may affect other aspects of design.

Summary

- The problem space always comes before the solution space. Doing otherwise will most probably cause backlash in the later stages of your project.
- When gathering background info from stakeholders and involved employees, start gathering wide context with the possibility of diving deeper when needed.
- When picking from a multitude of potential ML solutions, study their limitations and consider the risks these limitations may cause.
- Always evaluate the potential costs of a mistake. If there is one, examine the potential side effects it may cause: some may even lead to positive outcomes.

Preliminary research

This chapter covers

- Applying use cases from various domains to a given problem
- Facing and solving the "build-or-buy" dilemma in choosing a suitable solution
- Problem decompositioning
- Choosing the right degree of innovation

In chapter 2, we discovered that identifying a problem is the key element to developing a successful machine learning (ML) system. The better and more precisely you describe the problem, the higher the probability of building a product that will efficiently meet business goals.

Now we will delve into several key aspects that mark the next important stage of designing a comprehensive and efficient ML system—the solution space. This chapter will tell you more about finding solutions that helped solve similar problems in the past, the always tough choice between building our components and buying third-party products, a proper approach to decompositioning the problem, and picking the optimal degree of innovation, depending on the main objectives of our future system.

3.1   *What problems can inspire you?*

If I have seen further, it is by standing on the shoulders of Giants.

—Isaac Newton

Imagine you work for a taxi service like Uber or Lyft, and there is a worked-out fraud pattern: a legitimate driver starts working for the company, but later they pass their account to a person who can't be a driver (they even may have no active driver's license at all). Your goal is to do personal reidentification by taking a driver's photo in the document they uploaded when signing up, prompting the driver to take a selfie from their car, and verifying it's the same person as displayed on the driver's license. At the same time, there are very reasonable nonfunctional requirements: for the sake of privacy, you would prefer to avoid uploading a driver's photo from their device to your servers. One more aspect is the verification should be fast enough and resistant to various adversarial attacks (fraudsters can be so tricky!).

Let's summarize this case based on this information:

- The problem is based on face recognition. Thus, as a system designer, you need to familiarize yourself with the domain.
- The solution should be mobile-first. Thus, knowledge about ML on mobile devices is crucial.
- The solution should be resistant to fraud attempts (a dishonest driver can try to show a photo of a legitimate driver instead of their own face). Thus, experience in liveness detection will be useful.

All of these problems are commonly solved in the industry, but they are rarely dealt with in a single solution. The following are some examples. Big surveillance systems (like those used for airport security) do a lot of face recognition, but they are rarely limited in computing power, and their inference does not have to be squeezed into a phone. Many consumer entertainment apps, on the other hand, run inference on mobile phones, and their developers are very proficient in running models with limited resources. Finally, liveness detection is usually applied to biometric systems used for authentication (FaceID on the iPhone is the most common example).

Nothing beats experience, so if you're lucky enough to have successfully coped with all three problems, go right ahead. If not, we recommend you dedicate time to looking through use cases in various ML domains, because breadth of mind is your best friend here. You usually can't work with tens of production ML systems during a single year of your career, but studying this number of use cases is achievable and can compensate for the lack of experience.

While designing a system, it is useful to recall similar systems and use them as a reference. You're not obliged to copy certain patterns directly, but they can serve as an inspiration. We also advise that you not neglect failure stories, as they can become a hint of what to avoid in your case. This approach somewhat overlaps with the antigoals concept that we will touch on in chapter 4.

As often happens in the software world, there are at least two aspects of similarity: the domain aspect and the technical aspect (as shown in figure 3.1).

Aspects of similarity

Business/product aspect

Solutions with similar business problems and goals

Technical aspect

Solutions with matching technical requirements

Figure 3.1 Both aspects are equally important in looking for solutions that will help you build your system.

The former is about finding systems that are as close as possible in terms of a business problem; with the latter, we should recall systems with close technical requirements (e.g., platform, latency, data model, volume, etc.).

Campfire story from Arseny

I used to work on an image segmentation problem in a manufacturing optimization company. My job was to find specific components in images from the assembly line. The problem was about the accuracy I needed: it was subpixel. In other words, my system needed to give highly detailed outputs as it searched for extremely small objects.

Image segmentation for manufacturing data is not a common problem; you can't just Google it and grab the first recipe from the internet. But fine-grained segmentation is popular in other domains, such as medical image analysis and photo/video editing, where it's often referred to as image matting.

If you ever tried to change your background in the Zoom app, you must have noticed artifacts around your hair, and that's exactly because the related algorithm is far from perfect (most likely, it optimizes for computation efficiency, not fine-grained precision). Hair segmentation is a classic example of image matting: telling the hair from the background is complicated and requires specific tricks like avoiding image downsampling when possible and using "soft labels"—pixels labeled as both foreground and background with specific weights.

With this reasoning in mind, I learned more about the most advanced approaches to image matting and adapted them for my manufacturing data, which eventually reduced my test error significantly.

We also encourage you to ask yourself why certain decisions have been made in system designs and solutions you find relevant. Such exercises are valuable when developing and eventually applying your own intuition while designing a complicated ML system, including the ability to solve such dilemmas, such as whether to build from scratch or look for ready-to-go offers.

3.2   Build or buy: Open source-based or proprietary tech

Imagine you work for Slack, a team messenger with support for audio and video conversations. It has a feature: close to real-time speech recognition of audio conversations.

But Slack was initially designed as a text-first messenger, and probably the share of users who utilize it for voice conversations is considerably smaller. Text captions are used even less often, as this feature is not enabled by default, and its application is somewhat limited. At the same time, the requirements for speech recognition accuracy are high: such a feature will be useless or even harmful if the quality does not meet expectations.

The need for noncore functionality with proper quality may encourage your feature team to lurk through the market in search of ready-made solutions. We can't ignore Slack's scale: before the peak of the pandemic in 2019, it had 12 million daily average users. The currently claimed numbers have declined to 10 million, but it is still an impressive number. It means using a third-party tech provided by a vendor may cost too much, and kicking off the development of an internal, ideally tailored solution will be the optimal scenario. Which way will you choose?

3.2.1   Build or buy

There is a big dilemma related to complicated tech systems, including ML systems; it's often called "build or buy." When the problem is familiar, there is a good chance of finding a vendor already selling a solution as a service. Let's capture the main angles of how to look at this dilemma.

Is the problem related to the core part of the business? It is a common practice to focus on key competitive advantages and use third-party services for commodities like infrastructure. Fifteen years ago, most companies had dedicated system administrators who managed massive servers in data centers; these days, most companies rent virtual machines from a cloud server provider. That's an example of using a third-party service for a critical piece of infrastructure, which is, however, not crucial for winning over the market. Although there is an exception for companies where server infrastructure matters a lot (e.g., high-frequency trading, adtech, or cloud gaming), this area is subject to significant investments in R&D.

Many companies use third-party services for ML-related problems like machine translation, speech recognition, antifraud, and many more. Validating drivers' selfies with their license photos is a popular example of something to be delegated to a vendor.

Another aspect of the dilemma is economic. Say there is a vendor for this problem, and its service is good enough in terms of metrics, but the reasonable-price criteria are not met. Maybe your company is great at hiring talents in low-cost living areas (with a respective salary range), and thus building a system from scratch is cheaper compared to using a third-party solution. If a vendor provides reasonable pricing for a

California-based VC-backed startup, it doesn't mean the very same price is still reasonable for a company bootstrapped in Eastern Europe or Asia.

You can switch to an open source solution, but the choice between that and a purchased option may not be obvious. You can't say the cost of an open source solution is zero, as its maintenance is often associated with hidden costs related to infrastructural work and potential problem-solving. On the other hand, using a purchased solution allows the delegation of many of these problems to the vendor, which means you will need a preliminary estimate of potential spending before sticking to a certain option.

There is also an aspect that is often not disclosed publicly but is still very relevant to this dilemma: careerism. Not every decision is made in the interests of the business, and the bigger the company, the more common the pattern. Consequently, some employees may be interested in pushing the idea of building, not buying, to deliver a big-impact project and thus justify their way to promotion or add a fancy achievement to their resume. Of course, we do not support this way of solving the build-or-buy dilemma, but since these cases are not a rare thing in the business, we can't but mention them.

Overall, the build-or-buy dilemma boils down to several key factors that form the context in which you're working. Buying a ready-to-go solution means saving time on development (which may be a factor if you're a startup and release deadlines are tight and strict) and avoiding recruiting extra specialists who may be indispensable at the production stage but will be hard to find work for after the software is released. It also means that you get a tested, time-proven platform. However, you're tied to a vendor's schedule when it comes to patches or new releases. Building your own solution guarantees you're in control of the feature set, scalability, and release calendar and can fix critical bugs on the go without depending on the vendor. But having more control comes with a higher price in other aspects: you will need in-house support, and you will definitely require a solid team of experienced developers.

We recommend going for "buy" if

- You opt for a faster release.
- You don't have a dedicated team to develop/maintain the solution.
- There is high demand for this solution from many companies across various domains.

Be sure to look for a stable platform with a proven reputation in the market. We recommend going for "build" if

- You have enough time to spend on development.
- You prefer scalability and flexible on-demand updates over a scheduled release calendar.
- You can afford in-house support.
- You need not a good-enough but a cutting-edge solution.
- You have a vast legacy that requires smooth integration.

- You are dealing with highly sensitive data and cannot afford to rely on out-sourced information security or simply are restricted by legal regulations regarding sharing data with third parties.

There is also an extremely important budgetary component, which you can't neglect, but at the same time, it cannot be attributed to any of the previous lists. That's because the budget can affect your decision in either direction. You want to choose the buy option if developing your own solution may lead to overspending. On the other hand, the build option is your pick if none of the off-the-shelf solutions fit within your budget. Whatever your case is, budget is a crucial element that always needs to be considered.

Let's get back to the opening example with Slack. One of the ways to resolve the dilemma would be to start out with a vendor, make sure the functionality is appreciated by customers, highlight main usage scenarios, and kickstart an internal solution based on the gathered information.

Reminder: we have no idea how this feature was actually implemented. That's just how we would approach it.

The ratio of build versus buy decisions tends to shift over time. For example, at least 9 out of 10 natural language problems that would have required a very custom solution in the 2010s are solvable by a simple large language model (LLM) API call in the 2020s, making building such models from scratch far less attractive.

3.2.2   *Open source-based or proprietary tech*

Another dilemma may arise on the lower level of consideration, and that is open source tech versus enterprise-grade proprietary paid tech. At some point, you need to decide what database is used for storage or what inference server is preferable. It's important to have extensive knowledge of nonfunctional requirements (like required uptime, latency, load tolerance, etc.) to answer this question. For an initial approximation, the logic is as follows: when you're sure there is no need for urgent help from experts, the safe choice would be to use an open source solution. An opposite case would be when building a high-load, mission-critical system; it often makes sense to stand on the shoulders of a giant, such as a specific vendor. There are mixed scenarios as well—it is possible to buy enterprise-level support for open source solutions, and sometimes it can be a proper middle way.

It's worth noting that the principles listed here are not ML specific—in fact, almost the same reasoning is applicable when we're designing "regular" ML-free software.

3.3   *Problem decompositioning*

One of the most useful tools in a software engineer's toolbox is a "divide and conquer" approach, which is very applicable for ML, both on low-level algorithm implementation and the high-level system design level. That's the first thing you can apply when facing a complicated problem that seems unsolvable at its existing scale.

A canonical example of problem decomposition is a search engine design. A user can query any wild set of words, including those that were never queried before (around 15% of Google search queries are new), and get a relevant result in a few hundred milliseconds.

At a high level, a search engine effectively does one thing, which is to provide relevant results from a database quickly. Let's focus on two properties here: relevance and quickness. Would it be easier to fetch a somewhat relevant result quickly? We think so: just drop the sophisticated ranking algorithms and replace them with a simple "a document contains some of the queried words" heuristic. Scanning the whole database with such predicates is very doable. Would it be easier to find relevant results from a small subset of documents—thousands, not billions? Of course, on a small scale, we can apply sophisticated ML algorithms and big, although slow at inference, models.

We bet you've already guessed what we are leading to—it's time to combine those steps and make a two-stage system. The first stage is fast candidate filtering, and the second stage is a more sophisticated ranking across the identified candidates. Such an approach has been used in many search engines for decades.

This example can be developed further: instead of one iteration of candidate filtering, there may be a cascade of them. So, based on the query language and user location, documents in other languages can be filtered out even before the candidate filtering, reducing the number of documents that need to be processed downstream, as seen in figure 3.2.

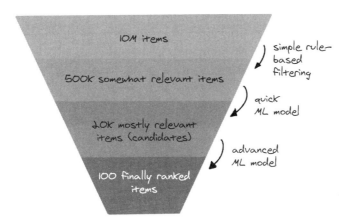

Figure 3.2   The process of problem decompositioning

Similar multistep pipelines are very popular in the computer vision domain: a deep learning model is applied first, with postprocessing responsible for the final answer. Another bucket of applications is related to texts and other semistructured data: one step extracts structured data, and these structs are processed downstream with more constrained models.

We know six reasons for decomposition:

- *Computation complexity*—Decomposition is applied to reduce the amount of required computation (just like in the search engine example earlier).

- *Algorithm imperfection*—A following step is used to adjust an error made in the previous step. Those readers who are strong in ML theory may recall some parallels to boosting algorithms families.
- *Using an algorithm's strengths while avoiding weaknesses*—For example, we need to count objects on an image. One of the approaches would be to train a convolutional neural network for a regression problem, but classic convolutional neural networks are not perfect for these needs by design (e.g., pooling layers tend to lose information of this kind; see figure 3.3). An alternative approach would use a model that would detect objects in the image and a classic computer vision algorithm on top of it to count contours from the previous step. The pure detector model can generalize better than the end-to-end regression model because of inductive bias, and the postprocessing step is deterministic and accurate.

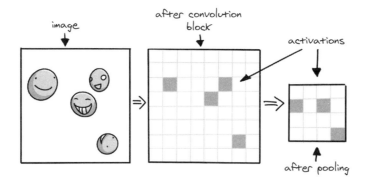

Figure 3.3   Two activation areas were merged together after the pooling layer, thus losing information critical for the object counting problem.

- *Data fusion needs*—ML solutions can't directly fetch data from other sources, so it is a popular pattern to run a model, fetch additional data based on the result, and process the fused data downstream. The recent interest in LLM applications is a good example here: many domain-specific LLM solutions follow the retrieval augmented generation pattern, which is essentially just pulling relevant data from a vector database and providing the LLM with this input as part of the prompt.
- *Handling corner cases*—ML solutions can fail, and decomposition helps address problems early. For example, a simple model (or just a bunch of conditional checks) can score input and raise an error if the input is likely to be invalid.
- *Applying different models or logic to different subsets of data*—There is a chance the model works well for a wide segment of users and is hard to generalize for the whole user base. It leads to a simple idea of routing users to different models or

system paths based on a simple heuristic (e.g., separate models for various geographies). We'll share more details on that in chapter 14.

We know this list may be incomplete, but these are the six most obvious reasons we've stumbled upon throughout our careers.

Sometimes pipelines are not designed in that sequential manner from the very beginning, and the idea of adding a step may appear later as part of further improvement. It may not be the best pattern, though: stacking up pieces one by one trying to cover the problems of a recently revealed previous step leads to a non-robust design, which is error-prone and hard to maintain because it doesn't follow a single idea. On the other hand, it is absolutely acceptable to leave dummy stubs in the initial design and even first implementations ("later there will be model-based candidate fetching, but for now we use random samples as proof of concept").

Campfire story from Arseny

I worked in an augmented reality company building virtual try-on solutions. One of the products was a shoe try-on, an app that detected feet in video streams and rendered chosen footwear. It required multiple algorithms combined to build, including an occlusion algorithm responsible for determining which part of a shoe should be visible and rendered and which part was hidden by objects in the frame.

This part of the solution brought many troubles before the initial release; the team had no good ideas on how to implement it in a proper, reliable way. At some point, the company's CTO took the lead and suggested an algorithm of his own that solved the problem for most cases. This algorithm had many disadvantages; it was not fast enough, not very generalizable, hard for the rest of the team to understand, and so on. But there was one big advantage that outweighed all of those—the algorithm worked in most cases!

Part of the shoe is not rendered because it's hidden by the leg.

The shoe itself is rendered.

Habanero Red/Vast Grey/Dune Red

Example of the ML-based solution rendering a shoe only in the areas where a real shoe could be captured by a camera

(continued)

The CTO's algorithm was part of the early design and implementation, and it became a valuable part of early product releases. Later, the team hacked together a completely different approach that mostly addressed the disadvantages of the old one, which, thanks to its proper design, didn't require significant changes. Just one step in the whole pipeline was replaced by one with a more advanced approach, which boosted overall experience for later versions.

The design principles of ML systems are being influenced by recent trends in the field. In the past, it was common to build pipelines featuring many small, sequential components. However, with the rise of deep learning models, the trend shifted toward an end-to-end single-model approach. It could potentially capture more complex relationships in the data, as they are not limited by assumptions and limitations of manual design, require less domain knowledge, and reduce the accumulation of errors between steps.

Speech processing is a good example of how an end-to-end approach changed the design. Before end-to-end, text-to-speech (TTS) models typically included two main components: one processed text input and converted it into linguistic atoms such as phonemes, stress marks, and intonation patterns, and another synthesized human speech with a predefined set of rules or a statistical model to map the linguistic information to the sound waves.

End-to-end TTS models, on the other hand, do not rely on explicit linguistic information as an intermediate representation. Instead, they directly map text input to an audio waveform using a single neural network model.

While end-to-end models were successful, they were not capable of containing knowledge on their own and often required the use of databases for many applications.

Recently, LLMs such as GPT-4 have achieved impressive zero-shot performance, meaning they can answer questions directly without any additional input or training. However, these LLMs are computationally expensive and are prone to hallucination (i.e., presenting false information as true; see "Survey of Hallucination in Natural Language Generation," https://arxiv.org/abs/2202.03629, for wider context), and their knowledge is implicit and not directly accessible for modification.

There is ongoing research in finding ways to combine the benefits of LLMs with the ability to use maintainable external sources of information. For example, the Bing AI and ChatGPT plugins (https://openai.com/blog/chatgpt-plugins) use additional online sources in a way similar to how people use search engines, and Galactica (https://galactica.org/) by Meta AI was among the first to introduce the concept of a working memory token, which allows the model to generate a snippet of Python code that can be executed by an interpreter to provide a precise answer. These ideas are developed even further in Toolformer (https://arxiv.org/abs/2302.04761v1), a model specifically trained to use various third-party APIs. Similar ideas are reflected in the quickly growing open source framework LangChain (https://python.langchain.com/api_reference). While these approaches are not yet widely used in production systems, they have the potential to change the way ML systems are decomposed.

Depending on their complexity and degree of novelty, ML systems may imply various levels of innovation. Some competitive areas require huge investments in research; in other domains, you can use a very basic ML solution. Let's find out how to define the level of innovation you need for your system.

3.4 *Choosing the right degree of innovation*

Ask any stakeholder of any ML system this straightforward question: how good (aka accurate) should the final product be? The most common answers are usually "perfect," "100%," and "as good as possible." But let's try to figure out what lies behind these straightforward yet ambiguous answers.

The answer "as good as possible" implicitly means "as soon as we meet other constraints." The most obvious constraints are time and budget. Would they want a perfect ML system in 10 years? Most likely not. Is the "acceptable good" system shipped by the end of next quarter better? Most likely, yes.

We will elaborate on the topic of precise understanding of the difference between "good enough" and "perfect" later, in chapter 5. But even in the earliest stage, when the design process has just started, the exact metric is not important yet. It's a rough understanding that is critical.

With the experience we've gained creating, maintaining, and improving ML systems with multiple scales and objectives, we've identified three different buckets of required perfection that all systems can be distributed between. Terms may vary, but to our mind, these are the most fitting:

- Minimum viable ML system
- Average human-level ML system
- Best-in-class ML system

A minimum viable system can be a very spartan solution with duct tape as the key bonding element. Aligned expectations from such a system would be "it mostly works," and an observer will be able to detect various failure modes. Such systems are considered baselines and prototypes; no innovation is expected.

Human-level performance adds a certain bar. Many successful existing ML systems don't even match human-level performance yet are valuable for companies. Thus, we can say that reaching this kind of performance requires a fair amount of research and innovation.

Finally, there is the best in class bucket. Some systems are hardly useful when they don't beat a significant share of competitors—this is often the case in super-competitive domains like trading or adtech or global products like search engines. A tiny shift in accuracy may cost millions in profits or losses, and in such cases, ML systems are designed with the idea of reaching the best result possible.

Why do we even talk about innovation here? The bridge between the problem space and the solution space strongly depends on the level of innovation we assume from the very beginning. With the "minimum viable system" bucket, we have exactly zero innovation—we just use the simplest and fastest solution we know and move forward. On the other side of the spectrum, we get endless innovation, where a system is never ready, and the team is always looking for new improvements to implement in the next release.

Distributing problems between these three buckets would be a very powerful technique, but there's one important factor we can't ignore: the level of required innovation is not static. In many cases—especially in startups—things are built as minimalistic as possible to be upgraded later. And it makes sense: the company first evaluates if the functionality is required by customers (or internal users) and then addresses customer feedback to improve the system. If a shipped feature is unique to the market, even its minimalistic implementation brings so much value that competitors immediately get on to improving their own products. It moves the initial system from the first bucket to the second bucket or even closer to the state-of-the-art league. Many startups face problems with such transition, and cases of designing a system that can evolve from prototype to a world-class gem (which is the art of engineering) are extremely rare. The lite version of such art is designing a system that can be rebuilt while keeping as many existing building blocks as possible, and that's a fairly high bar to aim for.

3.4.1 *What solutions can be useful?*

Knowing the level of innovation you need and some high-level structure of the system, you can look for implementation ideas on a lower level. When this chapter was being prepared, there were five popular sources of information to dive into.

arXiv

arXiv (https://arxiv.org/) is a website distributing academic papers mostly in science, technology, engineering, and mathematics disciplines. Math and computer science, including its subdisciplines, make up a solid share of over 2 million papers published there.

arXiv is a good place to get familiar with academic perspectives on your problem. Other than just reading everything related to your keywords, we encourage you to use the citations and links mechanism: once you find a relevant paper, it's likely you may be interested in getting familiar with older papers it mentions and newer papers citing it. arXiv is an ecosystem of its own kind—there are browser extensions and additional websites that can assist your search. A good start is to look for overview papers (often containing "survey" in their titles): usually they feature properly distilled wisdom on the topic.

arXiv on its own may seem a little too raw as a source of knowledge: it's barely possible to read all new papers, and its search mechanism is somewhat primitive from a modern perspective. There are multiple popular tools on top of arXiv that simplify exploration. Currently, we recommend https://arxivxplorer.com/, a modern search engine on top of paper abstracts, although it is very possible that there will be another fancy tool by the time the book is published (previously, the most popular add-on was https://arxiv-sanity-lite.com/).

PAPERS WITH CODE

As it is easy to guess, Papers with Code (https://paperswithcode.com/) is a compilation of academic ML-related papers that are accompanied by implementations in the code form. Papers are grouped by topics and ranked by performance when possible.

You can find the closest problem from the academic world and see the top N papers solving this problem, their metrics, some meta information (e.g., does this approach require additional data?), and—what's very important—links to public implementations. This website is a real game changer for those who prefer repositories to formal academic writing.

GITHUB

Once we've mentioned code implementations, we can't avoid GitHub (https://github.com). The most popular platform for open source software, GitHub has repositories for any occasion. The downside derives from its scale: if you're there to find something uncommon, you are effectively looking for a needle in a haystack.

GitHub is not specialized to the ML domain, but at the same time, most open-source ML projects are located there.

HUGGING FACE

The Hugging Face model hub (https://huggingface.co/models) is a major platform sharing numerous models and datasets. At the time of writing, the hub contained more than 560,000 publicly available ML models. Categorization and tags work quite precisely, with a huge portion of the models offering small interactive web-based demos to display their capabilities.

Hugging Face as a company started with a focus on natural language processing (NLP), and the hub has been the main platform for sharing NLP-oriented models. We recommend going there for research-related models if an ML problem you're solving includes text processing.

KAGGLE

Kaggle (https://kaggle.com) is the most popular platform for competitive ML. Organizations use the platform to host challenges and lure the world's best ML practitioners to fight for monetary prizes and, of course, glory. During competitions, participants share their ideas and code snippets related to a given challenge. At the end of a competition, winners and leaders usually reveal their secrets. Along with competitions, Kaggle serves as a hosting site for multiple datasets, so there is a good chance of finding a public dataset related to your problem.

Kaggle is the most exceptional piece on this list for several reasons. If a competition is organized poorly, the problem is somewhat ill-posed: instead of solving the real problem, competitors may try to look for shortcuts like data leakage. Also, final solutions are usually not applicable in practice: the models are gargantuan because latency limits can be off the table. Finally, the code snippets are rarely clean: contestants aim for rapid iterations, not for long-time maintenance.

Yet with all the mentioned disadvantages, Kaggle forums can be a source of great overviews for your problem, including both academic papers and hacker-style code that may become academic mainstream later. It's also worth mentioning that there are websites aggregating the best Kaggle solutions, such as https://farid.one/kaggle-solutions/.

We would like to highlight the fact that the current stage still doesn't require choosing solutions based on this research. It should give you more details on the landscape to make your decision-making process more reliable.

3.4.2   *Working on the solution space: Practical example*

Let's reiterate the points mentioned in the previous section using a single detailed example. Imagine you've joined a stock photo company. The business is effectively a marketplace: photographers join the platform and upload their shots, and customers who are looking for specific images for illustrative purposes (editors, designers, ad professionals) purchase rights for these photos. The marketplace makes money through commissions from sales. The company is highly interested in creating an effective search system on its website.

From one perspective, the photo stock is huge, featuring millions of images. When customers look for photos, they are often interested in something specific, which is hard to find with simple categorization or other naive taxonomy. So you've been hired to build a modern search tool that will be able to find the most relevant shots upon text queries from customers. How should you understand the landscape for the problem?

The build-or-buy question arises first. Let's assume you're guessing that companies of scale like yours usually design their own solutions, but that's not always the case. Some reconnaissance would be suitable. You can easily reveal the fact that many vendors—both huge enterprises and young startups—provide search engines as a service. When you try to prospect those, it's very likely that many solutions can turn irrelevant—your company needs a search engine for images based on text queries, which is not the most popular paradigm. There may be several tech providers suggesting something relevant, though, so let's keep them in mind.

First, let's consider the similar problems other companies solve:

- Of course, there are other photo banks, and some of them may have built nice search engines. There is little chance that they expose many details on how their engines are built (you could dig up some blog posts or conference talks), but it's not zero.
- There are generic-purpose search engines like Google and Bing. Obviously, the system you need is of a very different scale—you need to operate with millions of images while they do billions. Here, you might say, "How can I replicate such a juggernaut if my team is N times smaller?" Of course, it's unlikely anyone can compete with "the big guys" in terms of capacity, but you won't need to, as your main objective will be to find ideas that will meet the needs of your solution and not a line of code more.

- Very opposite of the previous point, you can find consumer-oriented projects that help categorize personal photo collections. They're not ready for millions but more like thousands of images. The good side is that of them are open source, so you can dive into the code directly to fetch ideas.
- Finally, there are some nonvirtual goods marketplaces—for example, selling clothes, furniture, and so on. Some of them are giants like Amazon, and some are niche-oriented and even smaller than your company. Their business is very much dependent on search quality, but their goods are not just images, and they usually have way more attributes (they may be text descriptions or seller information). Such search engines use more information about items, not only visual information; in the ML world, we call them multimodal.

Search engines are one of the most popular applications within the information retrieval discipline. Its practitioners were among the early adopters of many ML methods but didn't limit themselves to ML-only approaches. Familiarizing yourself with the discipline (or refreshing your memories) on a high level, starting from Wikipedia, can be suitable for those who don't feel confident in the domain. After learning more about information retrieval, you can dive deeper by reading more about image retrieval.

While reading documents on building search engines, you definitely see a pattern for decomposition: as in many search engines, not every document should be ranked in your scenario. From the very start, a user can specify requirements: for example, the photo should be provided as a raw file (as opposed to compressed JPEGs), be at least 5,000 pixels wide, and cost not more than $50. Such conditions can narrow the search candidates from millions to tens of thousands very quickly, while we didn't touch upon image and query semantics at all. This optimization would be very valuable and may become a cornerstone of your future design.

Another thing you could find is the fact that under the hood, most search engines effectively do one thing. They calculate a relevancy score for the pair of user queries and potentially related items (documents) and rank items based on this score (see figure 3.4):

```
relevancy = f(encode_text(query), encode_image(item))
```

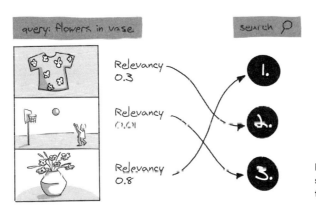

Figure 3.4 The breakdown of how a search engine ranks images based on their relevancy regarding a given query

In the case of our scenario, this brings up multiple open questions:

- What family of algorithms can the function f be?
- How do you encode a query (the text) and an item (the image)?
- How do you measure relevancy?
- How do you include user feedback in the system?

Each of these questions is wide and deserves a separate book (or at least multiple chapters), so, to be succinct, we only suggest that those questions should be kept in mind when you dive deeper into sources of information we mentioned before, from arXiv to Kaggle.

The next question is the degree of innovation you're looking for. There are several thoughts here:

- The company already has a very basic search tech. It's outdated and often yields irrelevant results, but it's still better than no search at all.
- The company's business can benefit from good search. Currently, many users can't find the shot they're looking for because of poor search results, and thus they leave the website and go to competitors. Proper search quality blocks other initiatives in the company: what's the point of launching a massive marketing campaign if new users will likely churn away, not being able to find what they need?
- The budgets are very limited. At the same time, after the first successful case of this project, there is a good chance that money will flow for new R&D initiatives.

The first point clearly shows that the very basic minimum viable product is not applicable here because you already have one. At the same time, limited budgets suggest you can't aim for a state-of-the-art solution at first. Thus, you need to design a solid system with a limited budget and the option to improve it further.

In this chapter, we have covered the most important elements of your preparation for writing a design document. You now know how to decompose the problem, what external and internal factors will influence your approach to the build-or-buy dilemma, what online sources are most helpful, and how to decide on the degree of innovativeness your solution should carry.

All this knowledge will be the basis not only for writing a design document for your system but also for using it to understand whether you need an ML system in the first place. The last point might sound intriguing and even controversial, so we will try to elaborate on it (as well as many others) in the next chapter.

Summary

- Look for solutions on the market that can fully or partially satisfy your needs. If those are found, ask yourself what parts of the system can use such solutions.
- Define the high-level view of the system. Try to draw it as three to five blocks that would be clear to a nontech executive.
- The build-or-buy dilemma can become a decisive factor in choosing between building your components and buying third-party products. To handle it

properly, consider various internal and external factors, including available time and the capacity of all the involved teams.

- Check the list of potential factors pointing to the necessity of decomposition-ing. If the problem you're solving meets any of them, it most probably needs to be decomposed, too.

- There might be a strong temptation to deliver a state-of-the-art product; still, you need to ask yourself how ready you are to invest in the system for the sake of innovation and whether the investment will pay off in the first place.

- Don't hesitate to lurk through popular online aggregators to find use cases you can utilize as references to your solution.

Design document 4

This chapter covers

- The most common myths around the design document
- Defining antigoals for an even sharper focus on core objectives
- Drafting a design document based on the information available
- Reviewing a design document
- The evolution of a design document

Once you have defined the problem your system should solve, as well as a list of stakeholders, and have a rough understanding of what technologies and solutions would be most appropriate for the product, as described in chapter 3, it is time to prepare a design document.

It is worth noting here that there is no set-in-stone order of actions at the early stage of creating a machine learning (ML) system. You can start preparing a design document as soon as you've identified the problem and goals (especially if you work in a startup, where the speed of delivery is often more important than following processes). But since this book is presented as a checklist, the list of actions is also displayed in a traditional sequence.

As one of the authors' managers once said, no fancy recommendation algorithm can beat a customer with a shopping list. These people have a goal and a plan for achieving it. Nothing can stop them.

If you think about it, writing code is just providing a specific set of instructions to achieve a particular goal. In a sense, a design document is a meta-algorithm set to accomplish a specific goal, with the involvement of many subalgorithms. Still, the design document is being regularly challenged by many as either one of the horsemen of bureaucratization or a rudiment used out of inertia.

In this chapter, we will examine the most common myths around the design document. We will introduce and define the concept of antigoals as additional guidelines that lead you toward the project's objectives, and we will start the practical part of this book, represented by two design documents based on close-to-real-life scenarios.

4.1   Common myths surrounding the design document

Over the years, the design document has seen a number of false assumptions and misinterpretations that may prevent you from putting together a well-organized paper appropriate for your project. Next we'll examine the most common misconceptions and explain why you shouldn't dwell on them.

4.1.1   Myth #1. Design documents work only for big companies but not startups

You could argue that dedicating part of your workload to preparing design documents would make only sense for big companies. There is a fair premise in this counterpoint: mature organizations need to invest more time and resources into writing design documents compared to a startup with a dozen employees. It doesn't mean, though, that small companies should prepare no design documents at all: as a well-known quote says, "Plan is nothing; planning is everything." The beauty of writing a design document lies in revealing blind spots in your vision, on both the product side and the technical side, which will save you a lot in the midterm, especially if you cut off irrelevant data. For the latter, we recommend applying the method we call "antigoals," which we will dedicate a separate section to later.

When the book was in early access, there was a common comment shared by our early readers: "Well, this is good, but that is not how it works in startups." While agreeing that startups' delivery cadence is different, we still stick to the idea that the design phase is necessary. It is true that cofounders and early engineers can find their consensus during a coffee break, whereas a massive corporation would waste 6 months on the same scope. We also agree that writing formal docs may be inefficient, but that is not what we advocate for. A simple note with a short description can be enough as soon as you are sure it gets all collaborators on the same page. Ignoring good practices of software and ML engineering is fine while you're hunting for a prize at a hackathon, but the hackathon style barely works at longer distances.

4.1.2 Myth #2. Design documents are efficient only for complex projects

There's a grain of truth to this statement if you look at a design document in its classic sense: a large, labor-intensive effort involving every detail of the final product, from general scope to risk validation upon deployment. After all, the compilation of such a document alone can take more time than the lifetime of the project itself!

Typically, such an argument can come either from a person with a lack of flexibility or from an ardent opponent of the design document who is eager to use any argument in their favor.

Practice shows that even for smaller projects, a well-structured design document ensures early identification of potential risks, serves as a reference for future enhancements if the project eventually expands, and, most importantly, helps prevent scope creep when every other stakeholder is tempted to add just one more feature.

Even simple initiatives can benefit from a design document with a proportional level of detail.

4.1.3 Myth #3. Every design document should be based on a template

Many companies, especially well-established enterprises, maintain their recommended templates with a strict, rigid structure, and it can be useful, considering the scale of their businesses. However, we recommend avoiding setting design docs templates in stone. Based on our experience, the template should never be a sacred dogma. Such templates may try to serve too many goals all at once, thus getting bloated and discouraging people from preparing and studying those documents. That is why we recommend keeping the core template minimalistic and extending parts here and there depending on system-specific requirements and context.

At first glance, the process of creating a design document may seem straightforward and simple. In reality, right from the start, you will encounter a whole load of factors that will interfere with the process and set you several steps back if ignored.

Remember: your task is not to create a draft document and convince everyone of its purity and correctness. Your task is to find as many weak points as possible (including motivating your stakeholders to find them) so that eventually, after a number of iterations, you have a document that allows you to start developing your ML system.

4.1.4 Myth #4. Every design document should lead to a deployed system

If you are an engineer and need to build a machine, you need to start with a blueprint. Other engineers will review it and provide feedback, which will probably lead to another iteration of blueprints—and another and another until your design is finally ready to be brought to life.

The same principle applies to designing ML systems. An ML system is a highly complex machine of interconnected domains that requires thorough preparation when your design document undergoes multiple iterations before implementation. Still, more often than not, a good design document leads to no ML project at all.

This might sound absurd, but let's imagine you're set to choose between two options:

- Spending 6 months working relentlessly on models, features, loss functions, and datasets, only to put your project on the shelf (where most ML projects end up finding themselves)
- Spending 2 to 4 weeks trying to describe
  - Why are we doing this project?
  - How do we do it?
  - Do we have everything we need?
  - Can we have a less efficient solution with less effort?
  - Is the desired result achievable?

Realizing that 90% of results can be derived from two IF statements can be frustrating, but it is still much better than the first of the two options.

4.2 Goals and antigoals

One of the goals of a design document is to reduce uncertainty about a problem by setting cornerstones and boundaries. Before the document is drafted, the level of understanding of both the problem and the solution is low and inconsistent among all involved parties. A technique that can help address such a problem is using antigoals—inverse statements that can help us narrow down both the problem space and the solution space.

Each part of a design document can be viewed as an answer to multiple questions: what are the goals of a potential system, what are the key success criteria, what tech aspects should we focus on, how do we solve a given subproblem, etc. A rookie mistake would be to miss tradeoffs and enumerate endless goals for the system: for example, it should do X, Y, and Z; have high performance; be precise; be easy to maintain and cheap to develop; and be intuitively understandable. Obviously, it's impossible to successfully fit all the good properties into one system, and you will require an approach to counterbalance this possible excessiveness.

Setting antigoals allows us to strike out the aspects we don't really care about that much and additionally highlight those we see as crucial. Let's say we're building a system that will be used internally, and the output artifacts are various reports to be read by the executive team and analysts. We can assume right off the bat that processing time won't be critical for such a system—it's only necessary to make it work fast enough that reports are ready by morning. Thus, "processing time" will be the first to join the list of antigoals so that we don't bother ourselves with this parameter. Or imagine building a recommendation engine for a boutique store: you sure won't need to support millions of items if the current number of goods contains only three digits (see figure 4.1), meaning excessive productivity is a no-go for the end solution.

Figure 4.1   A shop with <1,000 goods for sale and low traffic should not aim for scalability when building a recommendation system, as almost any tech solution can handle its load these days.

Antigoals like this help us focus only on important aspects and drop the ones that have no positive effect on reaching the main goal of the system.

The following example suggests what the lists of goals and antigoals would look like for a boutique store's recommendation engine:

- Goals:
    - Increased conversion from View to Add to Basket steps
    - Diverse recommendations for users
    - Low latency for users
- Antigoals:
    - Scalability in terms of the number of goods processed
    - Scalability in terms of concurrent users
    - Support for new goods categories

A similar logic is applicable to other blocks of a design document. If you formed an idea on implementation and later realized it had an intrinsic critical flaw, it would make sense to mention this issue in the document as a counterexample. Imagine you are designing a scalable system and considered using cloud infrastructure intensively until you learned that the biggest potential customer has strict limitations on using its own hardware for privacy reasons. In this case, a single sentence like "Cloud solution X could be a good option for data storage, but not applicable in this case because of Y's cloud privacy restrictions" can set important limitations and may spark ideas on alternative tech implementations: "If X is fine from the technical perspective, are there open source X alternatives that can be installed on our own servers?"

Antigoals should not be considered the main source of information in your design document but can become a spice that adds a missing flavor, growing into an essential part of the document's structure.

Questionable goals and their effect on the end result

We have two stories to highlight how unclear goal setting can affect the development of an ML system.

In 2016, Valerii worked in the collection department of a large bank. By that time, the bank's management had decided to introduce ML into its daily routine and lean on algorithmic support instead of operating with a set of rigid rules and gut feelings. One of Valerii's first tasks was to create a model picking the next user the bank must reach to maximize output—a user who can be activated by an incentive (a promise to pay, fee waiver, discount). The existing process involved a lot of manual work, yielding a conversion ratio of around 50%. The new process involving a pretty basic nonlinear model on a set of around 100 engineered features that provided astonishingly better results of 80% conversion was tested within the next 2 months, while the old process was still providing 50%.

The team was happy and excited to present the results to their senior vice president. The second after we finished the presentation, she said, "What's so special about these clients? I want to know their motivation." Addressing such a question in 2016 with a nonlinear model on 100 features was not an easy task, not to mention that *what people do* and *why they do it* are two completely different things. For example, from the very beginning, the goal of a senior vice president is to understand *why*, and the goal of the business is to understand *who*. As such, the team must design the system and model completely differently, aiming to answer both questions, even if it would be less efficient than answering just one. Thus, a bad (or improper) goal at the very beginning set the team 3 months back.

The second example covers the pricing algorithm we discussed in chapter 2. At the very beginning, our goal was to maximize gross merchandise volume based on turnover while keeping the margin at a given level.

At some point, the model found an ingenious way to achieve the goal. There was a boombox speaker in the product catalog, which the model started selling at a price lower than the purchase price. As a result, more speakers were sold in 24 hours than in the previous 90 days. To be fair, this was still within the margin limit because we didn't mind the margin being negative as part of the task.

However, you can imagine it was completely different from what we really wanted (the proper goal would be to increase the revenue while maintaining margin, affecting X% categories with Y% of SKUs in them with cannibalization no higher than Z). Sure, the revenue went up, and margins stayed within given limits, but in the end, everyone just ran to buy exactly that one model. No other speakers were bought.

Luckily, that was a test launch with a small number of items under dynamic pricing, showing that the initial goal was badly designed and we needed to develop a more thorough approach to goal setting. Fortunately, the overall design was decoupled and easy to adjust.

4.3   *Design document structure*

In this section, we could have focused on theoretical information about the contents and structure of the classic design document, but the truth is, a design document you prepare for an ML system will hardly rely on practices applied in traditional software development. On top of that, its structure may vary from company to company, so we do not think it makes sense to dwell on layout nuances. Instead, we recommend focusing more on what items need to be covered. Plus, our goal is to showcase the design document as an entity within ML system design. For that reason, starting with this section and for the rest of the book, at the end of each chapter there will be a large practical block representing a part of a design document that incorporates the main message from the given chapter. We see it as a crucial component of this book, which will go side by side with theory and campfire stories while offering an example of applying real-life solutions to problems.

In what follows, we will introduce you to two fictional cases, each with its own specifics, features, problems, and context. These two cases will form the basis of two different design documents, which will gradually grow and evolve from chapter to chapter, adding more depth and complexity. Eventually we will have two fully formed documents at our disposal.

In this section, we start to outline a design document for a project as it might have been written in real life. For this purpose, we introduce a fictional company, Supermegaretail, a retail company with a demand forecast project to launch.

In section 4.4, we give a very brief example of what the first chapter of a design document can look like. We will include only major topics; otherwise, it would not fit into a single book.

> **NOTE** Any text in the body of the design doc written in *italics* contains our supporting comments and is not part of the document itself.

DESIGN DOCUMENT: SUPERMEGARETAIL

PROBLEM DEFINITION

I. ORIGIN

Supermegaretail is a retail chain operating through a network of thousands of stores across different countries in various regions. The chain's customers buy various goods, primarily groceries, household essentials, personal care, sports supplements, and many more.

To sell these goods, Supermegaretail must purchase or produce them before delivering them to a store's location. The number of purchased goods is the key figure that needs to be defined, and there are different possible scenarios here.

For easier calculations, we assume that Supermegaretail bought 1,000 units of item A for the specific store:

1 Supermegaretail bought 1,000 units and sold 999 before the next delivery. This is an optimal situation. With only 0.1% left over, the retailer is close to the optimal revenue and margin.

2 Supermegaretail bought 1,000 units and sold 100 before the next delivery. This is usually an awful situation for an apparent reason. Supermegaretail wants to sell almost as many units as it purchased without going out of stock. The more significant the gap, the larger Supermegaretail's losses.

3 Supermegaretail bought 1,000 units and sold 1,000. This should be considered a terrible situation because we don't know how many units people would buy had they had the opportunity. It could be 1,001, 2,000, or 10,000. An out-of-stock situation like that obscures our understanding of the world. Even worse— it drives customers from Supermegaretail to its competitors, where they can buy the goods with no shortages.

An additional constraint is that we have a lot of perishable foods that can't stay on store shelves for long: they're either sold or wasted.

The project goal is to reduce the gap between delivered and sold items, making it as narrow as possible, while avoiding an out-of-stock situation with a specific service-level agreement to be specified further. To do that, we plan to forecast the demand for a specific item in a specific store during a particular period with the help of an ML system.

II. RELEVANCE AND REASONS

This section highlights the problem's relevance, backed by exploratory data analysis.

A. Existing flow analysis

What is the current way of ordering, delivering, and selling goods in Supermegaretail?

For Supermegaretail, the possible list might be as follows:

1 Planning horizon for making a deal with goods manufacturers:
   - It's a 1-year deal with the opportunity to adjust 90 days ahead within the first 9 months.

2 Additional discount with an increased volume:
   - It's an extra 2% off for every additional $20 million.

3 The number of distribution centers serving as logistics hubs between manufacturers and stores:
   - There are 47 distribution centers around the country, making them a point of presence and aggregated entity for the forecast.

4 Delivery cadence between distribution centers and stores:
   - Usually, every 2 days, there is a truck connecting the distribution center and the store.

5 Presence or absence of in-store warehouses:
   - There are no warehouses in most of the stores. However, the loading bay zone can be (and is) effectively used to store offloaded items for 2 to 3 days.

6 Who and at what stage decides what and where to deliver?
   There's a delivery plan coming down from the distribution center. A store's manager can override and adjust it.

7 Forecast horizon:
   – The primary forecast horizon is week-long and month-long. However, a 1-year horizon is needed when dealing with goods manufacturers.
8 Business owner of the process:
   – Logistics department
   – Procurement department
   – Operational department (store managers)

B. How much does Supermegaretail lose on the gap between forecasted and factual demand?

Although it is relatively easy to calculate the loss due to overstock and expired items, it is much harder to calculate the loss due to out-of-stock situations. The latter can be estimated through either a series of A/B tests or an expert opinion, which is usually much quicker and cheaper than running those tests.

The overall loss can be approximated by summing up the two, providing an estimate of the gain with an ideal and nonachievable solution.

The initial calculation showed the loss to be around $800 million during the last year.

Starting from the following section of the design document (but only for this chapter), we've sketched questions to avoid this being too voluminous. Answering these questions will help you decide on further actions, and the answers are revealed in the later chapters as we go through the different stages of the system.

C. Other reasons

- Can other teams use our solution, making development more appealing and reasonable?
- Perhaps we can sell demand forecast solutions to other retail companies (obviously not to direct competitors).

III. PREVIOUS WORK

This section covers whether this is an entirely new problem or something has been done before. Usually, it is a list of questions you ask to avoid doing double work or repeating previous mistakes.

- What if Supermegaretail was aware of this issue and had already implemented some demand forecast approach? It has various stores in different locations; its demand forecast is probably already pretty efficient. How does the company do it?
  - Rolling window?
  - Experts committee?
  - Rule of thumb + extra quick delivery?
  - Do we have some limitations to consider that we can't avoid, like minimum or maximum order size?
- Can we quickly improve the existing solution, or do we need an entirely new one?

- What if the Supermegaretail current forecasting is good enough for some categories and useless for others? In other words, can we use a hybrid approach here, at least in the very beginning, and start from the least successful categories, where the existing gap between predictions and actual sales is the widest?
- If our approach unintentionally breaks something, it is not that dangerous. We are testing it for categories where we always had problems while not touching categories where everything is good.
- In other words, we need to run an extensive and fresh exploratory data analysis of the existing solution.

IV. OTHER ISSUES AND RISKS

- Do we have a required infrastructure, or do we need to build it?
- If we pick something sophisticated, it can go crazy. What necessary checks and balances do we need to implement to avoid a disaster? Do we have a fallback in case something is broken?
- How sure are we that we can significantly improve the quality and reduce the manual load? Can we really solve this?
- What is the price of a mistake? Out-of-stock and overstock most likely have different costs of errors.
- If we deal with an out-of-stock situation, can we handle increased traffic?
- How often and on what granularity do we need to perform predictions?

As you can see, even a brief overview of the problem to solve and research using the previously gathered data can easily force us to write a 10-page doc. This draft will help us decide if we need to go further or if it is better to stop right now and avoid a complicated ML solution.

The next section of this chapter is no less important: it gives a practical example of how to review a design document. If you're new to ML system design, you probably haven't reached the stage of your career where you have enough experience and credibility to be involved in this kind of working routine. However, stepping up to review your first design doc is just a matter of time, so it's better to be prepared beforehand, and you will see some practical advice on the reviewing basics.

4.4   Reviewing a design document

> *Audi alteram partem [Let the other side be heard as well]*
>
> —Latin proverb

So far, we haven't seen a draft design doc written by a single person that would be complete enough to implement right from the start. However, we've come across some really decent drafts, which is more than enough after the first iteration.

This fact is essential and quite easily explained. Complex systems require input from many people with diverse expertise and backgrounds. As a design document author, part of your job is to make it more manageable for all the involved parties to navigate. Outlining your doc with chapters and subchapters will help domain experts see where to go from the beginning. Otherwise, the natural reaction for most people when they see a 10+ page doc is to close it and forget it.

Here come the first two critical points: the design doc must be accessible and visible to as many people as possible and easy to navigate for all participants.

As soon as people start reviewing any kind of content, they begin to criticize and offer alternatives. As an author, you want to encourage this type of behavior. After all, what are the chances you had the best and most appropriate design after the first iteration?

Try to derive an explanation for each proposition/fixture, as they could emerge from different conditions:

- Reviewers have used this tool before and think it is the best tool for everything.
- There are limitations in the current infrastructure. For example, we can't provide real-time support but can do batch jobs every 60 seconds. Does it affect the flow?
- We have people who can maintain technology A, but there's nobody to maintain technology B. Thus, it is better to move from technology B, mentioned in the design, to technology A.
- Reviewers want to boast about their knowledge of technologies and demonstrate this knowledge to a broader audience.
- Reviewers see another way to solve a given task and offer an alternative solution.

Try to understand the reasoning behind every input and solicit additional information until you fully understand the reasons. From our personal experience, the least helpful input (on the first iteration) would sound like "looks good to me." Try to find a part that looks the most questionable to you and ask the reviewer about it, expressing your concerns. A generally good practice would be to have a list of concerns, including things you are not sure of, to target reviewers' attention and facilitate requests.

A popular failure mode for design documents is writing too generically. That is a huge drawback for a design doc, and often it is caused by the fact that a single person may not have enough context to fill in all the gaps. As an initial author, you need to facilitate the others' inputs—for example, highlight some problematic areas with a lack of required information and encourage the reviewers to add missing parts of the puzzle.

We discussed how to create a design doc and what to expect from reviewers, but because the title of this section is "Reviewing a design document," let's try to reverse our suggestions and apply them from the reviewer's standpoint:

- Take a look at the design doc and try to navigate through the outline. Which chapters do where you feel most confident about?
- If the outline does not exist, check if there are open questions/things to consider at the end of the doc.
- Ask the design doc owner to provide those if they don't exist.
- When adding a comment, try to answer for yourself what value you are adding and what you want to achieve with it.

- If you're tempted to write "Looks good to me," think twice. Are you doing that because it indeed looks good to you or because you just want to save time or rely on others' opinions? If so, maybe it makes sense not to comment at all.

4.4.1 Design document review example

The case we've chosen for the our second example design document is the stock photo company we mentioned in chapter 3. Meet PhotoStock Inc., where we've been hired to build a modern search tool that will be able to find the most relevant shots upon customer text queries while providing excellent performance and displaying the most relevant images in stock.

The business is effectively a marketplace: photographers join the platform and upload their shots; customers who are looking for specific images for illustrative purposes (editors, designers, ad professionals) purchase rights for these photos. The marketplace makes money through commission from sales. The company is highly interested in making an effective search system on its website.

We provide part of a raw and poorly written design document based on what we discussed in the previous chapters and comment on it as if we were reviewing the document. This time, text highlighted in *italics* represents reviewers' comments.

DESIGN DOCUMENT: PHOTOSTOCK INC.

I. PROBLEM

Ninety percent of PhotoStock Inc. users find images via the search bar on our website. It makes the search bar a core component of the user experience.

Currently, the search engine is based on a fuzzy search algorithm powered by Elasticsearch, with its index updated automatically every Monday night. We assume it processes synonyms poorly. In addition, users can apply additional filters from presets that are manually created by the product team.

Many users are not happy with the search quality, which is proven by customer interviews and analysis based on clickstream. Only a small portion of search sessions leads to a purchase.

Reviewer: How many users exactly? Please add links to existing reports and dashboards for more context.

Reviewer: The search-to-purchase conversion is a function of many variables, and the relevancy of search results is just one of the factors. I suggest decomposing the problem further so we can estimate the missed revenue caused by poor search results more efficiently.

Reviewer: Please provide more information on the current search solution, as it's not clear how it works and interacts with other systems. What are the main failure modes?

Reviewer: How do we measure user happiness? Please add specific criteria.

II. GOALS

Increase the search-to-purchase conversion rate by 100%.

Reviewer: Why by 100%? Are there any reasons for this exact level of increase?

Reviewer: As mentioned before, the search-to-purchase funnel is not only determined by search quality. Let's narrow down the goals.

Reviewer: Are there any important nontechnical requirements like latency?

Reviewer: How do we currently measure conversion? How can we measure that it has been increased by this effort?

Reviewer: Have you defined antigoals to highlight the zones we don't need to focus on?

III. RISKS

We can lose many loyal existing customers as they can't follow their current behavior patterns.

If we release defective software, we can lose a significant source of revenue.

Reviewer: Interesting point on behavior patterns. Are there any examples of how users have to adapt to dysfunctions of the search engine?

Reviewer: With our infrastructure of blue-green deployment and A/B tests platform, we should be able to roll out the new system gradually; we should use it to mitigate such risks.

IV. REFERENCES

- [Link to YourPowerfulSearch, an enterprise-grade search system for market-places]
- [Link to an academic paper from the Bing Search Relevancy team]
- [Link to a Google Analytics dashboard showing various metrics related to a PhotoStock search]

Reviewer: Please add more internal search-related artifacts, such as PhotoStock BI dashboard and UX research.

Reviewer: I believe that YourPowerfulSearch is not the only relevant solution in the market; can we get a wider overview? The same applies to the paper from Bing.

Reviewer: How can we estimate the influence of search relevancy on our commercial metrics? This can affect a possible budget a lot.

You can see some patterns in the comments, such as

- Raising legitimate questions as early as possible
- Suggesting missing parts either as questions or statements

Early feedback at the design review stage can save a lot of time in the later stages. Questions should initiate and facilitate a healthy discussion and unlock better solutions and should never be aggressive or toxic.

4.5   *A design doc is a living thing*

This section was initially planned to be myth #5 in the list from the beginning of this chapter, but we believe this point is important enough to have its own spot as a separate section.

So why should there be no fear or hesitation in editing or criticizing a design doc at any stage? The answer is that a design doc is truly a living thing.

Usually, the evolution of design docs looks like this:

1 First iteration
2 Feedback from peers
3 Rewrite 60% of the doc
4 Feedback from peers
5 Rewrite 30% of the doc
6 Feedback from peers
7 Rewrite 10% of the doc
8 Start implementing the system
9 (Three months later) input from the real world
10 Rewrite 30% of the doc

With an evolution like that, you need to expect that the only time you could complete the design doc would be if you finished implementing the system, but even this is not guaranteed.

As soon as your system is implemented, life will expose its flaws, which you will have to address; or product managers decide they need new features, and the system has to be extended; or the government issues a new piece of legislation, which you have to consider; or there is an infrastructure migration or a new use case. You name it. To perform these changes, engineers need to understand the system and read design documents. By that time, a new pattern or technology could arise that perfectly fits the system.

If this is not the case, new features and refactoring need to be reflected in the design doc, bringing us to the design doc evolution mentioned earlier.

That is why a design document is never over. It is a living thing, as long as you have a service it describes. Even if you leave the company, others need to take the banner from you, if they don't want to end up with a completely unsupportable system.

Rewriting a solid share of the design doc may seem discouraging, but it is something you can benefit from in the long run. For complex systems, it even makes sense to practice the "design it twice" approach—admit that your first design is likely not the best one, and design it twice, taking two radically different approaches. As practice shows, this approach can reveal hidden problems and opportunities. Let us quote *A Philosophy of Software Design* (Yaknyam, 2018) by John Outerhout (a nice book we recommend to feel the spirit of a good design):

> *I have noticed that the design-it-twice principle is sometimes hard for really smart people to embrace. When they are growing up, smart people discover that their first quick idea about any problem is sufficient for a good grade; there is no need to consider a second or third possibility. This makes it easy to develop bad work habits. However, as these people get older, they get promoted into environments with harder and harder problems. Eventually, everyone reaches a point where your first ideas are no longer good enough; if you want to get really great results, you have to consider a second possibility, or perhaps a third, no matter how smart you are. The design of*

large software systems falls in this category: no-one is good enough to get it right with their first try.

A good design (and a good design doc, respectively) should reduce various complexity aspects of the system, be it understanding, building, modifying, or maintaining. And if the system promises to be complex from the very beginning, spending additional time to reduce this complexity in advance via multiple iterations is often a good investment.

People who prefer building over thinking may feel irritated by this point: "Come on, first you suggest writing docs instead of writing code, and now you suggest doing it over and over again?" Well, it makes little sense to run many iterations once you no longer receive new information, and sometimes you can't improve the design before some proof of concept is written. However, designing things twice is often a fair tradeoff between agility and preparedness.

Summary

- Just like correctly set goals are the benchmark for your system, antigoals represent areas to avoid. Make sure to keep them in mind and have them pointed out.
- A design document that is well put together will help you understand whether you need an ML system at all.
- Involve all your stakeholders in reviewing the draft design document.
- When you see a "looks good to me" answer, always contact your colleague once again for clearer, more precise feedback. Vagueness at the draft stage will very likely lead to change requests at later stages.
- If you're initiating a review for your design document, encourage people to criticize the current ideas and suggest alternatives.
- Consider inviting reviewers with various backgrounds and experiences to gather varied feedback.
- While reviewing a design document, ask specifying questions to point out weak or unneeded parts.
- Don't be afraid of multiple iterations, as no first draft will ever reach the final stage without edits.
- Remember, a design doc is a living thing and will be subject to edits even after the launch of your system.

Part 2

Early stage

In this part, we dive deeper into the technical details of the early-stage work. Chapter 5 covers the benefits of selecting proper metrics and losses for your ML system, defining and utilizing proxy metrics, and applying the hierarchy of metrics. Chapter 6 is dedicated to datasets, from choosing optimal data sources and processing raw data to defining properties of a healthy data pipeline and deciding how much data is enough for the best performance of the ML model. Chapter 7 reviews standard and nontrivial validation schemas, describes the split updating procedure, and overviews validation schemas as part of the design document. In chapter 8, you will learn more about various types of baselines, starting from constant baselines as the earliest, simplest yet highly efficient version of a model, to model baselines, feature baselines, and deep learning baselines.

Loss functions and metrics

In the previous chapter, we first touched on the topic of creating a design document for your machine learning (ML) system. We figured out why a design document is subject to constant edits and why all the changes you implement in it are not only inevitable but also necessary.

Unfortunately, an ML system can't directly solve a problem, but it can try to approximate it by optimizing a specific task. To do that efficiently, it must be adjusted, appropriately guided, and monitored.

To direct an ML system's effort, we use its algorithm's loss function to reward or punish if for reducing or increasing specific errors. However, the loss function is used to train the model and usually must be differentiable, meaning that there is a narrowed choice of available loss functions. Thus, to assess the model's performance, we use metrics; and while every loss function can be used as a metric (a good example would be root mean squared error [RMSE], which is quite often used as a metric, although we are not sure that is the best decision), not every metric can be used as a loss function.

In this chapter, we will discuss how to pick the best-fitting metrics and loss functions, focusing on how to do proper research and provide motivation for choice during the design process.

5.1   Losses

The *loss function*, also known as the *objective* or *cost function*, effectively defines how a model learns about the world and the connections between dependent and independent variables, what it pays the most attention to, what it tries to avoid, and what it considers acceptable. Thus, the choice of a loss function can drastically affect your model's overall performance, even if everything else—features, target, model architecture, dataset size—remains unchanged. Switching to a different loss function can completely reshape your whole system.

Picking the right loss function (i.e., choosing the way a model learns from its mistakes) is one of the most crucial decisions in designing an ML system. Recalling an evergreen anecdote, we can be pretty confident in optimizing for the mean while counting the average salary of bar visitors until Bill Gates walks in (https://mng.bz/M1w8).

Unfortunately, not every function can be used as a loss function. In general, a loss function feature two properties:

- It is globally continuous (changes in predictions lead to changes in losses).
- It is differentiable (its gradient can be calculated for optimization algorithms based on the gradient descent). There is one exclusion: in exotic cases, gradient-free optimization methods are applicable, although practitioners prefer to avoid them as gradient-based methods typically converge much better.

While these two points are relevant for any loss, it is important to select a loss function that will best match your particular case and will be closest to the final goal of your system.

This is where advanced loss functions come into play, providing tempting ways of improving your model. Unlike manipulations with features or the model itself, they don't usually affect the runtime aspect, meaning that all the code changes are only related to training pipelines, and isolating changes to a small part of a system is always a good property of design. But more often than not, we have witnessed ML engineers (especially recent graduates) sticking to a particular loss function just because they got used to applying it to similar problems. A notorious example is the regression problem with the mean squared error (MSE) or mean absolute error (MAE) loss function as the default choice and, many times, *the only choice* by many practitioners.

At the same time, while choosing a proper loss function (or a set of them) is a decision that may greatly improve your model's performance, it is still not a silver bullet. We have worked with a few ML engineers (often with respectable academic backgrounds and PhDs) who tried to solve all the problems they had with just one elegant loss function. This approach is on the opposite end of the spectrum from paying no attention to the loss function at all, but it is still far from ideal. A good ML system designer keeps many tools in mind, not overfitting for one. Overall, the heuristic is the following: the more research-heavy your system is, the more likely it is that you need to invest time in finding or designing a nontrivial loss function.

A couple of years ago, Valerii worked with an intern on building a model to predict the exchange volume of cryptocurrencies. As always, he asked the intern to prepare a design document before doing anything, and this was an insightful exercise. The intern thoughtlessly skipped the loss function chapter, listing some metrics he would use to assess the system performance without any reasoning behind them.

Why is this not acceptable? By using an example, we can review a simplified situation with a knowledge of loss functions for regression problems being narrowed down to the two most widely used loss functions: MSE and MAE.

Imagine that we have a vector of target values Y = [100, 100, 100, 100, 100, 100, 100, 100, 100, 1000] and a vector of independent variables X being equal for all samples.

If we train a model using MSE as a loss function, it will output a vector of predictions:

```
Y_hat = [190, 190, 190, 190, 190, 190, 190, 190, 190, 190]
```

If we train a model using MAE as a loss function, it will output a vector of predictions:

```
Y_hat = [100, 100, 100, 100, 100, 100, 100, 100, 100, 100]
```

> **NOTE** Please note that this is a thought experiment to highlight the idea and make it easier to comprehend. If we needed to, we could create synthetic data to reproduce the whole process—features, targets, and models—but for the sake of simplicity, we will use only the preceding numbers.

When we calculate MSE and MAE for a model with the RMSE loss function, it will result in the following numbers: MSE = 72,900, MAE = 162, with the mean of residuals equal to 0 and the median of residuals equal to –90 (figure 5.1).

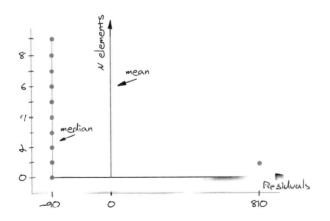

Figure 5.1 Residuals after optimizing the mean

When we calculate MSE and MAE for a model with the MAE loss function, the result will be MSE = 81,000, MAE = 90, with the mean of residuals equal to 90 and the median of residuals equal to 0 (figure 5.2).

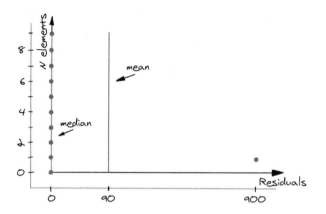

Figure 5.2   Residuals after optimizing the median

No wonder the model optimized for MSE yields better MSE, and as MSE tries to minimize the mean, the mean residuals are better. On the other hand, the model optimized for MAE delivers better MAE, and as MAE tries to optimize the median, the median residuals are better. But what does it mean for us? Which loss function is better? That depends on our application.

Let's say we are optimizing a navigation system for aircraft, and an error larger than 850 means that a plane will go off a landing field and crash. In this case, optimizing for MAE is not an ideal decision. Of course, we can say 9 out of 10 times that we have a perfect result, and only 1 out of 10 times a vehicle is destroyed, but this is not acceptable by any means. We have to avoid outliers at all costs or penalize them, thus using MSE or even some higher-degree modifications.

But suppose we are optimizing the amount of liquidity for a cryptocurrency exchange we need for every trading day. *Liquidity* refers to a cryptocurrency's capacity to be converted into cash or other cryptocurrencies without losing value, and it is essential for all cryptocurrency exchanges. High liquidity signifies a dynamic and stable market, allowing participants to trade quickly at reasonable prices. Excessive liquidity, however, means that allocated resources are not used. In this case, reserving more cash than required 9 times out of 10 is far from desired. We can review it from a different angle: the model optimized for MSE overallocated 810 units and underallocated 810 units, while the model optimized for MAE was on the spot 9 times out of 10 and underallocated 900 units, which seems like a better decision (if underallocation is less than 9 times worse than over allocation) to convey to the model what we need.

It's easy to see that even though we used MSE and MAE to train the models, we applied different criteria to assess them. For the aircraft navigation system, we counted the number of times when the difference between the actual and predicted value was greater than 850. For liquidity optimization, it was the number of times we were on the spot or under an overallocation weighted sum. This illustrates that training the model to optimize specific loss functions and assess this model's performance can represent two different tasks, which we will cover in section 5.2 on metrics. Before we proceed, we'd like to share some insights on the nuances and aspects of determining losses for deep learning models.

5.1.1 Loss tricks for deep learning models

In deep-learning-based systems, especially those processing text, image, or audio data, loss selection is even more crucial.

A properly chosen loss function can help with many problems related to model training, especially a sophisticated model and/or data domain. For example, a cross-entropy loss is a classical solution for the classification problem. One of the problems with it is related to class imbalance. If one class is heavily overrepresented, the model optimized by the entropy loss may face something called *mode collapse*—a situation when it outputs a constant (popular class) for any input. These problems have been solved in many ways (e.g., data undersampling/oversampling, custom weights for classes, etc.), but all of them required significant manual tuning and were not reliable. The problem was approached by researchers who tried to design a loss addressing it; the most notable result is probably by Lin et al. ("Focal Loss for Dense Object Detection," https://arxiv.org/abs1708.02002), and this loss is now taking its honorable place among tools helping to solve the data imbalance problem.

Focal loss (see figure 5.3) is a dynamically scaled cross-entropy loss where the scaling factor decays to zero as confidence in the correct class increases. Intuitively, this scaling factor can automatically down-weight the contribution of easy examples during training and rapidly focus the model on hard examples (more information can be found at https://paperswithcode.com/method/focal-loss).

Originally, this loss was introduced for the object detection problem specific to computer vision, and later, the approach expanded to many other domains, including

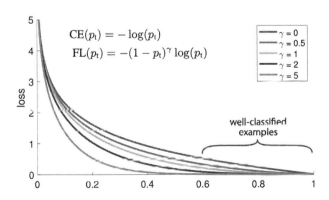

$$CE(p_t) = -\log(p_t)$$
$$FL(p_t) = -(1 - p_t)^\gamma \log(p_t)$$

- $\gamma = 0$
- $\gamma = 0.5$
- $\gamma = 1$
- $\gamma = 2$
- $\gamma = 5$

well-classified examples

Figure 5.3 The suggested focal loss function focuses more on misclassified examples while reducing the relative loss for well-classified examples (source: Lin et al.).

those unrelated to images, like audio or natural language processing. The most distant application of the focal loss we have found has been introduced in the paper "Can Natural Language Processing Help Differentiate Inflammatory Intestinal Diseases in China?" (Tong et al.; https://mng.bz/aV9X), which confirms how ideas spread across domains.

In some cases, a reasonable solution will be to combine multiple losses for a single model. The need for such an approach may arise with complex problems, often multimodal and often associated with multiple concurrent datasets. We will not provide many details on using combined loss functions here as it is research-heavy, but we would like to give some examples:

1 "Authentic Volumetric Avatars from a Phone Scan" (Cao et al.; https:// dl.acm.org/doi/abs/10.1145/3528223.3530143). The authors combined three families of losses (segmentation, reconstruction, perceptual). Generative computer vision models are often subject to considering combined losses.

2 "Highly Accurate Protein Structure Prediction with AlphaFold" (Jumper et al.; https://www.nature.com/articles/s41586-021-03819-2). The famous AlphaFold 2 model predicts 3D shapes of proteins from their genetic sequence with impressive accuracy. That's a huge thing for the biotech world, and it uses multiple auxiliary losses under the hood. For example, a masked language modeling objective, the one that is likely to be inspired by a loss function used in BERT-like architectures, is a popular family of natural language processing models.

3 "GrokNet: Unified Computer Vision Model Trunk and Embeddings for Commerce" (Bell et al.; https://mng.bz/Xxr6). This is a jewel among combined loss examples we can recall. The authors aim to build a single model to rule multiple problems, so they used 7 goods datasets and 83 (80 categorical and 3 embedding) losses!

In general, multiple losses are usually used either to help models' convergence or to solve multiple adjustment problems with a single model.

While loss functions help set up and fine-tune accuracy and efficiency and minimize errors for your system while training, metrics are used to evaluate its performance within a certain set of parameters.

5.2 Metrics

The loss function we optimize and the metric we use to assess our model's performance can be very different from each other. Recall that the end goal of the demand forecast system for Supermegaretail in chapter 4 was to reduce the gap between delivered and sold items, making it as narrow as possible while avoiding an out-of-stock situation. If we try to visualize the pipeline, it might look like figure 5.4.

We know that a proper loss function is essential, but what about metrics? Can't we pick some standard metrics, assess a variety of models, choose the best, deploy it, and estimate potential success through A/B tests?

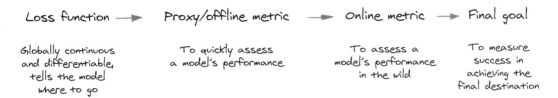

Figure 5.4   A general-purpose pipeline for a demand forecast system that perfectly fits the Supermegaretail case

Unfortunately, no. Choosing the right set of metrics has to follow just as carefully an elaboration as selecting loss functions. Even more, while the set of popular losses is finite, there is always an opportunity to tailor a custom metric for a specific business domain. Choosing the wrong metric, in its turn, can cause misguided optimization when we set our model to train for irrelevant values, which eventually leads to poor performance in real-world scenarios. As a result, we have to roll back several steps in model development, resulting in a significant waste of time and resources. But even choosing the right metric for your ML system will not guarantee the project's success.

> **Campfire story from Valerii**
>
> Some time ago, I was developing an ML system for a bank that regularly encountered the problem of nonpaying debtors. The system we were preparing had two main goals:
>
> - Reduce the number of delinquent payments
> - Make customers more responsive
>
> As a metric, we chose the conversion rate of clients from nonpayers to payers.
>
> The first thing we did was to implement a system of promised payments that worked as follows. Let's say Mr. Smith gets a call from the bank: "Mr. Smith, you haven't paid your loan on time. Can we expect you to pay the required amount within three days?" "Oh, of course, I will, I will," says Mr. Smith. The people at the bank hang up and check the "promised to pay" box. But then Mr. Smith would break the promise and not pay anything.
>
> The conversion rate by the time we started our work was 0.5, which means cases like that were occurring half the time. It's not that bad but definitely not brilliant.
>
> Given the attitude of people to such calls from banks and their desire to hang up as soon as possible, broken promises are a very common case. But the fact is, it's a stick with two ends. On the one hand, the client won't find it pleasant to talk to the bank, especially if they did not initiate the conversation. But the bank also isn't interested in futile communication, having to overspend on call centers and employees.
>
> As a solution, we built a system to predict the probability of clients agreeing to make their payment and fulfilling it. And we replaced human calls with text messages. This spared us from having to call our customers and talk them into making promises. The system was also supposed to predict customer behavior.

(continued)

At the validation stage, the system showed a conversion rate of 0.9—almost twice as high as manual work! Two weeks later and in combat conditions, however, the conversion plummeted to 0.35, and we had only a week until making a report to our vice president.

Something had obviously gone wrong, and we needed to figure out what it was. We examined how this metric worked before, and it was pretty simple: if the client had promised to pay the debt on a certain day of the month but did not do it within 3 days, they were marked as debtors. Why was it 3 days? The answer is that the gap between an actual operation and getting information about this operation in the bank's database was 3 days.

Let's say you are supposed to make your next loan payment by EOD March 1. At the end of the day, March 1, you go to the bank after work and pay the required amount. On March 2, a system checks the database and sees that the payment has not been made (no wonder, as the information will not reach it until March 4). "Looks like we have a delinquent," the system thinks and initiates a text message because, according to the data collected by the system, you have a high probability (90%!) of paying the required amount after receiving the message. Later on March 2, you get a text message from the bank asking you to pay the loan. "They must have got something wrong. I'll let them know I've already paid," you think and start filling out the form in the reply message. The problem is that the form does not allow you to enter a payment due date earlier than the current date. You can only specify that you will pay on March 2 or later. But you already paid on March 1. What do you do? You indicate that you paid on March 2 and submit the form. Three days later, the system checks the list of nonpayers, opens your profile, and sees that you promised to pay on March 2 but haven't done that within 3 days from this date.

When we reconfigured the system, the conversion rate almost reached the initial value, getting as high as 0.8, but the interim problems we faced show how reaching your metrics can be hindered by flaws in the overall system behavior.

On the surface, a framework for picking the right metric is very straightforward: choose the one that is closest to the final goal. However, as the next campfire story will show, it might be very tricky to do. You can try either finding that metric yourself or using some outside help. The following are some options we recommend considering:

- If you're lucky enough to have a hierarchy of metrics, which we will cover later on in this chapter, use it to navigate to the metric you need.
- Some companies have a dedicated department working on metrics; if that is the case, use their help.
- If neither of these two options is the case, you might use product managers and data scientists to develop the best metric.
- If the problem you're set to solve is similar to a problem solved before and the solution proved to be solid and efficient, it is natural to transfer metrics from one project to another with certain modifications, if necessary.

- If you have an A/B testing team, they also usually have enough knowledge to select or create a metric.

If you don't have the luxury of having the things mentioned here, you can do the following:

- Refer to the goals section in the design and align with it (it is essential to refresh what the end goals are, not how you remembered them). Knowing your goals will help you understand which metrics will help you achieve those goals or at least help you discard obviously inappropriate metrics.
- Try to decompose the end goal by writing a map similar to the hierarchy of metrics (see section 5.2.2). It will probably take more than one stage to achieve, but this kind of exercise will help you break down your big goal into several smaller components, each with its own metric. Having many small parts on hand will help assemble the greater whole.
- Find the best metrics describing the success of each stage.
- If something is hard to measure directly, replace it with proxy metrics (see section 5.2.2). Proxy metrics will allow you to gather necessary and very important information before your system goes into release.
- With this map, pick the metric that either represents the most critical stage or summarizes the map in the best possible way.

In the next campfire story, we will review the canonical binary classification problem.

Campfire story from Valerii

Recently, I had a conversation with a friend of mine regarding the evaluation of fraud models. Fraud models usually try to solve binary classification tasks where 0 is non-fraud and 1 is fraud.

No metric is ideal, and it always depends on the final goal. However, when we speak about fraud models, we usually want to maintain a ratio of fraud to legit transactions of some level. If we had 10 times more transactions, it would be okay to have 10 times more fraud, but not 20 or 30 times more. In other words, we want to have a probabilistic model.

Also, fraud usually belongs to the class imbalance problem, and that balance is not stable through time. One day the ratio can be 1:100 (outburst of fraudulent transactions), the next day, 1:1000 (an ordinary day), and the day after, 1:10,000 (fraudsters took a vacation).

The most popular set of metrics for this family of models is precision and recall, which may not be the best choice.

The problem with precision is that its calculations take both classes into account:

$$Precision = \frac{TP}{(TP + FP)}$$

(continued)

Imagine that we have a model that has a probability of 95% to predict that fraud is fraud (true positive [TP]) and 5% to predict that nonfraud is fraud (false positive [FP]).

Let's review three scenarios where P is the number of positive samples and N is the number of negative samples:

- $P = 10,000$, $N = 10,000$, $\text{Precision} = 0.95 \times \dfrac{10,000}{0.95 \times 10,000 + 0.05 \times 10,000)} = 0.95$

- $P = 100,000$, $N = 10,000$, $\text{Precision} = 0.95 \times \dfrac{100,000}{0.95 \times 100,000 + 0.05 \times 10,000)} = 0.99947$

- $P = 1000$, $N = 10,000$, $\text{Precision} = 0.95 \times \dfrac{1000}{0.95 \times 1000 + 0.05 \times 10,000} = 0.65$

As you can see, the class balance affected the metric significantly even when nothing else changed.

Now let's take a look at recall (Recall = TP/(TP+FN) = TP/P = True Positive Rate [TPR]) and examine the same three scenarios:

- $P = 10,000$, $N = 10,000$, $\text{Recall} = 0.95 \times \dfrac{10,000}{10,000} = 0.95$

- $P = 100,000$, $N = 10,000$, $\text{Recall} = 0.95 \times \dfrac{100,000}{100,000} = 0.95$

- $P = 1000$, $N = 10,000$, $\text{Recall} = 0.95 \times \dfrac{1000}{1000} = 0.95$

In this case, the class balance didn't affect the metric at all.

There is also a metric called specificity that can replace precision:

$$\text{Specificity} = \frac{TN}{N} = \text{True Negative Rate (TNR)} = 1 - \text{False Positive Rate (FPR)}$$

$$\text{FPR} = \frac{FP}{N} = \frac{FP}{FP + TN}$$

The same three examples show the following:

- $P = 10,000$, $N = 10,000$, $\text{Specificity} = 0.95 \times \dfrac{10,000}{10,000} = 0.95$

- $P = 100,000$, $N = 10,000$, $\text{Specificity} = 0.95 \times \dfrac{10,000}{10,000} = 0.95$

- $P = 1000$, $N = 10,000$, $\text{Specificity} = 0.95 \times \dfrac{10,000}{10,000} = 0.95$

Recall and specificity do not change because of class imbalance, as these metrics are class-balance insensitive.

Initially, my friend created a notebook (https://mng.bz/50v8) to prove me wrong. The following code demonstrates his train of thought:

```
import numpy as np

def gen_labels_preds(fraud, genuine, fraud_predicted,
    correct_fraud_predicted):
```

```
    labels = np.concatenate([np.repeat(True, fraud), np.repeat(False,
      genuine)])
  preds = np.concatenate([
    np.repeat(True, correct_fraud_predicted), # TP
    np.repeat(False, fraud - correct_fraud_predicted), # FP
    np.repeat(True, fraud_predicted - correct_fraud_predicted), # FN
    np.repeat(False, genuine - (fraud_predicted -
    correct_fraud_predicted)) # TN
    ])

  return labels, preds

def calculate_metrics(labels, preds):
  TP = (preds & labels).sum()
  FP = (preds & ~labels).sum()
  TN = (~preds & ~labels).sum()
  FN = (~preds & labels).sum()

  recall = TP / (TP + FN)
  precision = TP / (TP + FP)
  FPR = FP / (FP + TN)

  return recall, precision, FPR
```

He devised two models with the following metrics:

- A has 20 false positives, and 80% of the fraud is caught.
- B has 920 false positives, and 80% of the fraud is caught.

Then he tried his two models in three scenarios with different numbers of transactions and fraud cases. In scenario 1, the number of transactions was 100,000. Overall, there were 100 fraud cases, so the class balance was 1:1,000:

```
fraud = 100 # high imbalance
genuine = 100000
model_A_FP = 20
model_B_FP = 920


# Model A
a_total_fraud_predicted = model_A_FP + fraud*0.8
a_correct_fraud_predicted = fraud*0.8

a_labels, a_preds = gen_labels_preds(fraud, genuine,
a_total_fraud_predicted, a_correct_fraud_predicted)
a_recall, a_precision, a_FPR = calculate_metrics(a_labels, a_preds)

# Model B

b_total_fraud_predicted = model_B_FP + fraud*0.8
# Flags many more transactions
b_correct_fraud_predicted = fraud*0.8
```

(continued)

```
b_labels, b_preds = gen_labels_preds(fraud,
   genuine,b_total_fraud_predicted, b_correct_fraud_predicted)
b_recall, b_precision, b_FPR = calculate_metrics(b_labels, b_preds)

print("Model A Performance Metrics:")
print('TPR:', a_recall)
print("Precision:", a_precision)
print("FPR:", a_FPR)

print("\nModel B Performance Metrics:")
print('TPR:', b_recall)
print("Precision:", b_precision)
print("FPR:", b_FPR)

Model A Performance Metrics:
TPR: 0.8
Precision: 0.8
FPR: 0.0002

Model B Performance Metrics:
TPR: 0.8
Precision: 0.08
FPR: 0.0092
```

In scenario 2, he used the same metrics as in scenario 1. The number of transactions was 100,000. Overall, there were 10 fraud cases, so the class balance was 1:10,000:

```
fraud = 10 # high imbalance
genuine = 100000

# Model A
a_total_fraud_predicted = model_A_FP + fraud*0.8
a_correct_fraud_predicted = fraud*0.8

a_labels, a_preds = gen_labels_preds(fraud, genuine,
    a_total_fraud_predicted, a_correct_fraud_predicted)
a_recall, a_precision, a_FPR = calculate_metrics(a_labels, a_preds)

# Model B
b_total_fraud_predicted = model_B_FP + fraud*0.8 # Flags many more
    transactions
b_correct_fraud_predicted = fraud*0.8

b_labels, b_preds = gen_labels_preds(fraud, genuine,
    b_total_fraud_predicted, b_correct_fraud_predicted)
b_recall, b_precision, b_FPR = calculate_metrics(b_labels, b_preds)
print("Model A Performance Metrics:")
print('TPR:', a_recall)
```

```
print("Precision:", a_precision)
print("FPR:", a_FPR)

print("\nModel B Performance Metrics:")
print('TPR:', b_recall)
print("Precision:", b_precision)
print("FPR:", b_FPR)

Model A Performance Metrics:
TPR: 0.8
Precision: 0.2857142857142857
FPR: 0.0002

Model B Performance Metrics:
TPR: 0.8
Precision: 0.008620689655172414
FPR: 0.0092
```

In scenario 3, he again used the same metrics and 100,000 transactions. Overall, there were 1,000 fraud cases, so the class balance was 1:100:

```
fraud = 1000 # high imbalance
genuine = 100000

# Model A
a_total_fraud_predicted = model_A_FP + fraud*0.8
a_correct_fraud_predicted = fraud*0.8

a_labels, a_preds = gen_labels_preds(fraud, genuine,
    a_total_fraud_predicted, a_correct_fraud_predicted)
a_recall, a_precision, a_FPR = calculate_metrics(a_labels, a_preds)

# Model B
b_total_fraud_predicted = model_B_FP + fraud*0.8 # Flags many more
    transactions
b_correct_fraud_predicted = fraud*0.8

b_labels, b_preds = gen_labels_preds(fraud, genuine,
    b_total_fraud_predicted, b_correct_fraud_predicted)
b_recall, b_precision, b_FPR = calculate_metrics(b_labels, b_preds)

print("Model A Performance Metrics:")
print('TPR:', a_recall)
print("Precision:", a_precision)
print("FPR:", a_FPR)
print("\nModel B Performance Metrics:")
print('TPR:', b_recall)
print("Precision:", b_precision)
print("FPR:", b_FPR)
```

(continued)

```
Model A Performance Metrics:
TPR: 0.8
Precision: 0.975609756097561
FPR: 0.0002

Model B Performance Metrics:
TPR: 0.8
Precision: 0.46511627906976744
FPR: 0.0092
```

Model A is better according to both the receiver operating characteristic area under the curve (ROC AUC) and precision-recall AUC (PR AUC) metrics. Model B is a bad model but still gets a very good FPR (0.0092), even though, if it were put into production, the predictions would be rubbish (920 out of 1,000 fraud predictions would be incorrect). Precision allows us to see this. It's just 0.08 for model B, so we'd never even think about putting it close to production.

What is the fallacy here?

First, model B has an FPR of 0.0092, which is 46 times higher than model A, with its FPR of 0.0002. There is no good or bad FPR. It depends on your volume, and even a slight difference might turn out to be huge. For example, 0.99 has a 10 times higher case ratio than 0.999 (1:100 vs. 1:1000).

But even in the notebook example, while precision is only 10 times worse, the FPR of model B is 46 times worse; it's hard to call this a very good FPR.

As you can see from the previous calculations and the notebook, precision shows a very different number when there is a shift in class balance, even when the model's performance stays the same. In contrast, both TPR and FPR remain unchanged.

How do we combine this information and apply it to pick proper metrics?

In one of the companies we worked for, we had a goal to reduce spam and fraudulent behavior with more than 100,000,000,000 events per day. We set specificity to be at least 0.999999 (Specificity = TNR = 1 − FPR [in other words, we were okay to have one false positive per 1 million events]) and maximized recall (TPR) at that specificity rate. This proved to be more beneficial than using a standard recall-precision pair, given the volatile nature of underlying data.

Some cases, however, force you to improvise in order to find the metric that will be able to obtain a required behavior pattern from your system.

> **Campfire story from Arseny**
>
> I worked for a manufacturing optimization company and needed to improve a defect in its detection system, but in the midst of the process, another problem emerged: the metrics were not sensitive enough. The datasets required for running the planned scenario were too small—only 10 to 20 defective samples per customer product. And we couldn't get any more data because there were simply no more existing defective units. The defect ratio was just too low, thanks to the high engineering quality.
>
> Besides the dataset size, our customers weren't interested in intermediate results (e.g., how calibrated the defect probability of our model was). Their judgment was very straightforward. For the sake of simplicity, let me frame it like this:
>
> - There are 10 defective units and N regular units.
> - An ideal scenario is to have 0 errors.
> - 1 false positive or 1 false negative is good enough.
> - Otherwise, the system is unusable.
>
> Most of my attempts to improve the system as is were fruitless, until at some point I decided to design a custom continuous metric that utilized the internal metrics and had reasonable thresholds. The metric appeared very discrete:
>
> - "0" would mean "perfect system."
> - "1" would be "good enough."
> - "2" would stand for "garbage."
>
> With this metric in place, I was able to start improving the system gradually, step by step, while being confident that I was moving in the right direction.
>
> After a series of minor improvements, the cumulative effect transformed the system from "garbage" to "good enough" and from "good enough" to "perfect" for multiple customers.

One important factor in the success of your ML system will always be its consistency. To achieve this, there is a separate category of metrics, which we cover in the following section.

5.2.1 *Consistency metrics*

In applied ML, a model that has a consistent output when presented with slightly perturbed inputs is often desired. This property, known in different subfields as consistency, robustness, stability, or smoothness, can be formally defined as the requirement that the model be invariant under certain transformations, such that the difference between the model's output on the original input and the model's output on the perturbed input tends toward zero. In other words, we can express this property mathematically as

$$f(x) - f(x + eps) \to 0$$

where f represents the model, x represents the original input, and *eps* represents the perturbation applied to the input. Consistency metrics are not commonly discussed in academic ML but are an important consideration in practical applications where small changes to the input can have significant effects on the model's output from the product perspective.

Perturbations can be different. For example, for a solid computer vision model, a minor change of lighting usually should not change model outputs, or a sentiment analysis model should not be sensitive to changing words with synonyms. We will talk about such perturbations and invariants in more detail later, when discussing ML system testing in chapter 10.

There's another similar property: when the model is retrained (e.g., with the addition of new data or even with other seeds), we expect it to produce the same or close outputs, given that inputs remain unchanged. For an antifraud system, it is not acceptable if the same user is considered fraudulent today, legitimate tomorrow, and a fraudster again next week:

$$f_1 = \text{train(dataset\_version\_N)}$$
$$f_2 = \text{train(dataset\_version\_N+1)}$$
$$f_1(x) - f_2(x) \rightarrow 0$$

When the model outputs are different over time, the release of a new model (which should be a routine procedure for most ML systems) may affect the downstream system or end users of the system, disturbing their common usage scenarios. People rarely like unexpected changes in their tools and environment.

Such properties can be as important as default features we expect from a model (such as accurate predictions) because they shape expectations. As we discussed in earlier chapters, if a model can't be trusted, its utility is reduced. Thus, we need specific metrics to measure this kind of behavior.

Luckily, we formulated these properties strictly enough, so the biggest open question left is to estimate a proper type of noise or perturbation for the preceding formulas: what are the invariants, and how are the conditions expected to change over time?

With these estimations in place, you can attach your regular metrics to estimate consistency. For example, for the search engine example (Photostock Inc.), we don't want a document to change its rank for some query between releases of your system, and so the consistency metric could be a variance of ranks for the pair (query, document) over some time over corpora of documents and queries. Obviously, the less the variance is, the better it is for the system. Still, you can't forget about ill-posed situations—say, a dummy constant model tends to provide the lowest variance, but that's not the consistency ML engineers usually hunt for.

Consistency is often an important property of an ML system (see figure 5.5). If it's the case for your system, consider adding a metric reflecting how your system responds to the changes to input data, training data, or training procedure tweaks.

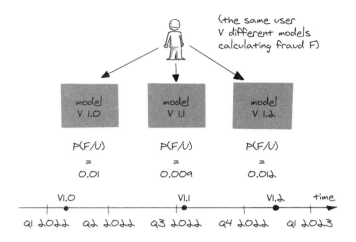

Figure 5.5 **New model releases are fairly consistent when estimating the probability (P) of the user (U) being fraudulent (F).**

Eventually, you will be able to form a single metrics system based on a clear hierarchy of offline and online metrics.

5.2.2 *Offline and online metrics, proxy metrics, and hierarchy of metrics*

Setting and improving appropriate metrics is an important step in building an efficient ML system. But even that is not our end goal, as we have to go one level deeper into the rabbit hole. When we had a plan to reduce spam and fraudulent behavior, the goal was not to have the highest recall at a given specificity. It was to improve the user experience by lowering the number of spam messages and making it safer by reducing the risk of fraudulent behavior.

In the Supermegaretail case, the goal was to reduce losses due to out-of-stock and overstock situations, which can be expressed in cash equivalent, but not mean absolute error (MAE), mean square error (MSE), weighted mean absolute percentage error (wMAPE), weighted absolute percentage error (WAPE), or any other metric.

In other words, the metric we used to assess the model during the training/testing/validation stages and the final metrics are rarely the same (see table 5.1).

The previously discussed set is also called *offline metrics* because we can apply and calculate them without deploying the model into production. In contrast, some metrics, usually our goal metrics, can be calculated only after implementing the system and using its output in the business. And although sometimes offline and online metrics might coincide, we still have to assess them differently. The most common way to evaluate online metrics (change/improvement) is through A/B testing.

We use offline metrics for a simple reason: we can use them before deploying the system. This method is quick and reproducible, and it doesn't require an expensive model deployment process. Offline metrics must have one quality: they must be a good predictor of online metrics. In other words, an increase or decrease in offline metrics has to be either strongly correlated or proportional to an increase/decrease in online metrics. Offline metrics play the role of proxy metrics for online metrics and can be used as efficient predictors of online metrics.

Table 5.1 Examples of offline and online metrics

Offline metrics	Online metrics
Recall at given specificity for spam message classification	Number of user complaints about spam messages
Quantiles of 1.5, 25, 50, 75, 95, and 99	Value of expired items, total sales
Mean reciprocal rank, normalized discounted cumulative gain	Click-through rate on search engine result page

But if we can find offline metrics that are strongly correlated with our online metrics with the improvement being transitive, we can do the same for offline metrics. Let's use an example to review this.

Imagine that we are building a recommender system for an eCommerce website. Our final goal is to increase gross merchandise value (GMV; this is a metric that measures the total value of sales over a given period). Unfortunately, as mentioned already, this is not something we can measure until we deploy our system into production and run A/B tests. We believe that increasing the number of items purchased will increase GMV. To achieve that, we want to increase the conversion rate by providing users with an offer that has a higher chance of being purchased (assuming this will increase the overall number of purchased items).

On average, 3% of offers end up being clicked, and 3% of those lead to a purchase: 3% times 3% means that if we show 10,000 offers, only 9 will lead to a purchase. This has two adverse, interconnected consequences:

- Low amount of class 1 data (purchase), huge class imbalance
- Increased A/B test duration

For example, for A/B tests with a 9/10,000 ratio of success to attempts, we would need 100 times more data than for the 90/10,000 ratio (quadratic dependency between a minimum detectable effect and a number of samples; please see the following for an example).

To mitigate that, we can use a proxy metric, click-through rate (CTR), with the following context in mind:

- No purchase can be made without a click. We can expect a positive correlation between the CTRs and conversion rates (CRs) and even calculate it.
- There are 33.3 times more clicks than purchases, meaning that we will have 33.3 times more training data for class 1 of the system, and A/B tests will become 1,111 (33.(3)^2) times faster. (To be precise, we can expect that variance will change as well, as var $= p \times (1 - p)$, so with $p = \frac{9}{10000}$, var $= 0.000899$ and with $p = \frac{3}{100}$, var $= 0.0291$, meaning that overall we will increase the speed of convergence by $\frac{1111}{\frac{0.0291}{0.000899}} \sim 33.33$ times.)

Using CTR instead of CR helps us iterate faster and with higher sensitivity, both offline (estimating metrics and loss is easier with more data for the class of interest) and online (at least partly through A/B testing).

We can represent this in the following relation:

- CTR → CR → (overall number of purchased items) → GMV

We can further generalize this by building a hierarchy of metrics:

1. The global, company-wide metric is revenue.
2. Global revenue (GMV) is composed of the revenue from different products, including the product we are responsible for.
3. Our product revenue is affected by
   - Average purchase price
   - Purchase frequency
   - Number of users (they are interconnected and have mutual influence, thus dotted lines)
4. Purchase frequency is affected by CR.
5. The conversion rate is affected by CTR.

A hierarchy of metrics (see figure 5.6) facilitates finding proper proxy metrics. Even though creating it lies outside the scope of designing an ML system, it will be handy to have one in place and refer to it during the design process. Using a common ground helps prove the choice and reduces the risk of failure.

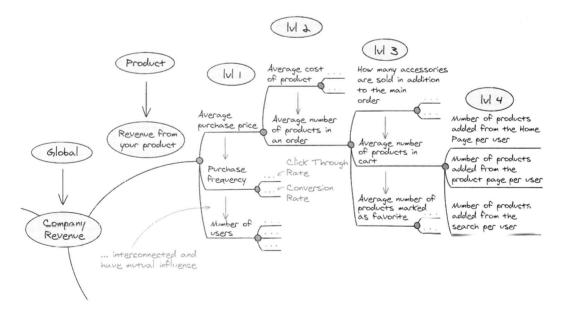

Figure 5.6 Hierarchy of metrics

A hierarchy of metrics is especially important when the system gets mature enough so that some metrics can be contradictory. A friend of ours once told us a short anecdote about building a recommendation system: a variant that demonstrated higher engagement by internal users (they preferred new recommendations over previous versions) appeared to be way less profitable on a wider audience.

A hierarchy of metrics and proxy metrics concepts are connected to the multicomponent losses we discussed earlier. For example, when building this recommender engine for Supermegaretail, we can tailor a specific loss function that will consider multiple levels of user activity (clicks, purchases, total amount of purchased items) and balance our interest between metrics.

Campfire story from Arseny

Once I worked on a brand-new product feature based on computer vision. The proposed solution was broken down into components, with each component and subcomponent carefully annotated with metrics. Due to the innovative nature of the feature, the metrics were custom—mostly ratios between various possible outcomes. We designed the metrics hierarchy in collaboration with a product executive. After several experiments aimed at moving the needle for one of the metrics, I developed a gut feeling that it was imbalanced. To test this, I ran an adversarial experiment by replacing the model predictions with random noise generated with specific parameters. Surprisingly, the random model scored perfectly! The metric was originally designed to favor recall over precision, but such an extreme imbalance was clearly not desirable, so we had to redesign it as soon as possible.

5.3 *Design document: Adding losses and metrics*

Starting in chapter 4, we began to introduce design documents for two fictional cases: Supermegaretail and PhotoStock Inc. Here we continue to elaborate on the development of ML solutions for each case and cover the selection of loss functions and losses. We start with Supermegaretail followed by PhotoStock Inc.

5.3.1 *Metrics and loss functions for Supermegaretail*

Let's refresh our memory on the Supermegaretail case. There, we were to reduce the gap between delivered and sold items, making it as narrow as possible while avoiding an out-of-stock situation with a specific service-level agreement (SLA) to be specified further.

DESIGN DOCUMENT: SUPERMEGARETAIL

II. METRICS AND LOSSES

I. METRICS

Before picking up a metric on our own, it makes sense to do some preliminary research. Fortunately, there are many papers related to this problem, but the one that stands out is "Evaluating Predictive Count Data Distributions in Retail Sales Forecasting" by Stephen Kolassa (https://mng.bz/eVl9).

Let's recall the project goal, which is to reduce the gap between delivered and sold items, making it as narrow as possible while avoiding an out-of-stock situation with a specific SLA to be specified further. To do that, we plan to forecast the demand for a specific item in a specific store during a particular period using an ML system.

In this case, this paper's abstract looks like an almost perfect fit:

> *Massive increases in computing power and new database architectures allow data to be stored and processed at increasingly finer granularities, yielding count data time series with lower and lower counts. These series can no longer be dealt with using approximative methods appropriate for continuous probability distributions. In addition, it is not sufficient to calculate point forecasts alone: we need to forecast the entire (discrete) predictive distributions, particularly for supply chain forecasting and inventory control, but also for other planning processes.*

(Count data is an integer-valued time series. It is essential for the supply chain forecasting we are facing, where most products are sold in units.) With that in mind, we can briefly review this paper (within the following lettered list) and pick the metrics that are most appropriate for our end goal.

A. Measures based on absolute errors

MAE optimizes the median; the weighted mean absolute percentage error (wMAPE) is MAE divided by the mean of the out-of-sample realizations, and the mean absolute scaled error is obtained by dividing the MAE by the in-sample MAE of the random walk forecast.

Optimizing for the median does not differ much from optimizing for the mean in a symmetric predictive distribution. However, the predictive distributions appropriate for low-volume count data are usually far from symmetric, and this distinction makes a difference in such cases and yields biased forecasts.

B. Percentage errors

The mean absolute percentage error (MAPE) is undefined if any future realization is zero, so it is singularly unsuitable for count data.

The symmetric MAPE is a "symmetrized" version of the MAPE, which is defined if the point forecasts and actuals are not both zero at all future time points. However, in any period with a zero actual, its contribution is 2, regardless of the point forecast, making it unsuitable for count data.

C. Measures based on squared errors

Minimizing the squared error leads naturally to an unbiased point forecast. However, the MSE is unsuitable for intermittent-demand items because it is sensitive to very high forecast errors. The same argument stands for nonintermittent count data.

D. Relative errors

Prominent variations are the median relative absolute error and the geometric mean relative absolute error.

In the specific context of forecasting count data, these suffer from two main weaknesses:

- Relative errors commonly compare absolute errors. As such, they are subject to the same criticism as MAE-based errors, as detailed earlier.
- On a period-by-period basis, simple benchmarks such as the naive random walk may forecast without errors, and thus, this period's relative error would be undefined because of a division by zero.

E. Rate-based errors

Kourentzes (2014) recently suggested two new error measures for the intermittent demand: MSR and MAR, which aim to assess whether an intermittent demand point forecast captures the average demand correctly over an increasing period of time. This is an interesting suggestion, but one property of these measures is that they implicitly weigh the short-term future more heavily than the mid- to long-term future. One could argue that this is exactly what we want to do while forecasting, but even then, a case could be made that such weighting should be explicit—by using an appropriate weighting scheme when averaging over future time periods.

F. Scaled errors

Petropoulos and Kourentzes (2015) suggest a scaled version of the MSE, the sMSE, which is the mean over squared errors that have been scaled by the squared average actuals over the forecast horizon. The sMSE is well-defined unless all actuals are zero, is minimized by the expectation of f, and, due to the scaling, can be compared between different time series. In addition (again because of the scaling), it is not quite as sensitive to high-forecast errors as the MSE. Specifically, it is more robust to dramatic underforecasts, although it is still sensitive to large overforecasts.

G. Functionals and loss functions

An alternative way of looking at forecasts concentrates on point forecasts that are functionals of the predictive distribution. One could argue that a retailer aims at a certain level of service (say 95%) and that therefore they are only interested in the corresponding quantile of the predictive distribution. This would then be elicited with appropriate loss functions or scoring rules. This approach is closely related to the idea of considering forecasts as part of a stock control system. From this perspective, quantile forecasts are used as inputs to standard stock control strategies, and the quality of the forecasts is assessed by valuing the total stock position over time and weighing it against out-of-stocks.

Though the authors did not see this as the best solution and proposed an alternative, the last paragraph of the paper is quite promising. Not only does it make sense from a business perspective to predict different quantiles to uphold SLA, but it is desirable from the point of view of having the loss function equal to the metric. Thus, quantile metrics for quantiles of 1.5, 25, 50, 75, 95, and 99 look like a proper choice. Moreover, suppose we need to pay more attention to a specific SKU, item group, or cluster. In that case, quantile metrics support the calculation of object/group weights (for example, item price).

I.II. METRICS TO PICK

Quantile metrics for quantiles of 1.5, 25, 50, 75, 95, and 99 both as is and with weights equal to SKU price and an additional penalty for underforecasting or overforecasting if deemed necessary are calculated as point estimates with 95% confidence intervals (using bootstrap or cross-validation). In addition, we can further transform this metric, representing it not as an absolute value but as an absolute percentage error at a given quantile. All consideration from the Petropoulos and Kourentzes article regarding percentage errors have to be taken into account. Ultimately, a set of experiments will help to decide a final form. We will probably have both, as it makes sense to check both absolute values in money/pcs and percentage error.

Online metrics of interest during A/B test are

- Revenue—expected to increase
- Level of stock—expected to decrease or maintain the same
- Margin—expected to increase

$$\frac{\sum_{i=1}^{N}(\alpha - I(t_i \leq a_i))(t_i - a_i)w_i}{\sum_{i=1}^{N} w_i}$$

- Alpha—coefficient used in quantile-based losses
- W—Weights
- I—Indicator function
- A—Model output
- T—Label

II. LOSS FUNCTIONS

With metrics equal to our loss functions, it is straightforward to pick the latter. We will train six models using a quantile loss of 1.5, 25, 50, 75, 95, and 99, resulting in six different models, providing us with various guarantees for the corresponding quantile of the predictive distribution.

As a second line of experimentation, we will additionally review the Tweedie loss function. Tweedie distributions are a family of probability distributions, including the purely continuous normal, gamma, and inverse Gaussian distributions; the purely discrete scaled Poisson distribution; and the class of compound Poisson–gamma distributions that have positive mass at zero but are otherwise continuous. These qualities make it an attractive candidate for our count data.

5.3.2 *Metrics and loss functions for PhotoStock Inc.*

Next up is the PhotoStock Inc. design document, where a whole different set of losses and metrics should be applied based on the nature of the business case and the problem to be solved. In the case of PhotoStock Inc., we were hired to build a modern search tool that can find the most relevant shots based on customers' text queries while providing excellent performance and displaying the most relevant images in stock.

DESIGN DOCUMENT: PHOTOSTOCK INC.

II. METRICS AND LOSS FUNCTIONS

I. METRICS

When choosing metrics for a new PhotoStock search engine, we should keep in mind the expected behavior of the system, which includes the following:

- Users click on links in search results, with higher results getting more clicks. This behavior can be reflected in the CTR metric, which evaluates how many users click on search results.
- Users purchase images they find via search. This behavior can be reflected in the CR metric, which evaluates how many clicks lead to purchase.
- Users see diverse suggestions on the search engine result page (SERP). There are no ready-to-go solutions here because we don't have a solid definition of diversity. Let's discuss it later with the UX team. As a baseline, we can use the number of different categories of images represented on SERP as a measure of diversity. In the future, we should research other companies' experiences— Airbnb's paper "Learning to Rank Diversely at Airbnb" (https://arxiv.org/abs/ 2210.07774).
- Search results look reasonable from the human perspective. This behavior can be reflected in the metric of human evaluation, which displays how many users think that search results are reasonable.

CTR and CR are online metrics, which means that they can only be measured when the system is live. Diversity is an unsupervised offline metric, which means that it doesn't require any additional data and can be measured on a regular basis at no cost. Human evaluation, on the other hand, is a supervised offline metric, which means that it requires additional data (human evaluation) and thus takes time and effort to collect.

To introduce offline proxy metrics for CTR and CR, we can use classic metrics for ranking problems, such as mean reciprocal rank (MRR) and normalized discounted cumulative gain (NDCG). MRR is a metric that calculates the average of the reciprocal ranks for a given set of results, which is a measure of the mean of the inverse of the rank for the first relevant result. NDCG is a metric that calculates the average of discounted cumulative gains (DCGs) for a given set of results, which is a measure of the sum of relevance scores taken from the first N results divided by the ideal DCG. In its turn, DCG is the sum of relevance scores among the first N results in the order of decreasing relevance.

Both MRR and NDCG require a list of relevant results for each query to calculate the metrics. We can use the same list of relevant results for both MRR and NDCG, but we need to create this list using crowdsourcing to ensure that it is representative of the results that users are likely to see. While MRR may be appropriate as an offline metric for CTR, it may not be a good proxy for CR because a crowdsourced list of relevant results is not representative of the real purchase data. Therefore, to accurately measure CR, we should consider using real purchase data. However, for the first version of the system, we may only be able to monitor CR online using A/B tests and a gradual rollout.

To summarize, here's how we can divide metrics:

- Fast offline metrics: MRR, NDCG, diversity
- Slow offline metrics: human evaluation
- Online metrics: CTR, CR

II. LOSSES

To use loss functions for training a search engine, it is important to consider available data and desired outcomes. In this case, the three main aspects we would like to optimize for are clicks, purchases, and diversity.

For the clicks and purchases aspect, we can use binary cross-entropy loss as a measure of success. However, it's important to note that the data for clicks and purchases may be imbalanced, meaning that there may be more examples of one class than the other. In such cases, it may be beneficial to use a loss function that is more robust to class imbalance, such as focal loss or other loss functions designed for this purpose.

Focal loss is a loss function that was introduced in the paper "Focal Loss for Dense Object Detection" (https://arxiv.org/abs/1708.02002v2). It is a generalization of a binary cross-entropy loss commonly used in classification tasks. The key difference between a focal loss and a binary cross-entropy loss is that focal loss down-weights easy examples, which are those examples that are classified correctly with high confidence. This is useful in cases where the data is imbalanced, as it helps the model to focus on the hard examples, which are typically more important for improving the overall performance of the model, so it seems relevant for the PhotoStock search engine.

As for the diversity aspect, we can add a term to the loss function that penalizes the similarity in results. One potential way to do this is to use the entropy of the category distribution of the results as a measure of diversity. However, this approach may not always be feasible, so the diversity loss should be considered optional.

Overall, the final loss function can be written as

$$L = \alpha \times L_{\text{click}} + \beta \times L_{\text{purchase}} + \gamma \times L_{\text{diversity}}$$

Here, alpha, beta, and gamma are represented as hyperparameters that control the relative importance of the three components. These hyperparameters can be tuned to find the optimal balance between the three aspects.

5.3.3 *Wrap up*

The examples from these two design documents show how important it is to choose the right metrics and loss functions. Just like any other key element in building an ML system, metrics and loss functions should coincide with the goals of your project. And if you feel there's more time needed to define the appropriate parameters, please find a few days in your schedule to do it so you don't have to roll back a few miles in a month or more.

The next chapter covers data gathering, datasets, the difference between data and metadata, and how to achieve a healthy data pipeline.

Summary

- Don't fall into the temptation of using time-tested loss functions just because they worked on your previous project(s).
- A loss function must be globally continuous and differentiable.
- Loss selection is an important step, but it is even more crucial with deep learning-based systems.
- Consider applying consistency metrics when small changes to the inputs can have significant effects on the output of your model from the product perspective.
- Offline metrics can be applied before putting your project into production and play the role of proxy metrics for online metrics.
- Make sure to have the hierarchy of metrics at hand, as it will be useful while working on the design of your system.

Gathering datasets 6

In the preceding chapters, we've covered the inherent steps in the preparation for building a machine learning (ML) system, including the problem space and solution space, identifying risks, and finding the right loss functions and metrics. Now we will talk about an aspect your ML project simply won't take off without—datasets. We will compare them with vital elements of our lives. Just like you'll need fuel to start your car or a nutritious breakfast to get a charge before a busy day at work, an ML system needs a dataset to function properly.

There is an old popular quote about real estate; the three most important things about it are location, location, and location. Similarly, if we were to choose only three things to focus on while building an ML system, those would be data, data, and data. Another classic quote from the computer science world says "garbage in, garbage out," and we can't doubt its correctness.

Here we'll break down the essence of working with datasets, from finding and processing data sources to properly cooking your dataset and building data pipelines. As a culmination of the whole chapter, we will look at datasets as a part of design documents, using the examples of Supermegaretail and PhotoStock Inc.

6.1   *Data sources*

You can use absolutely any source to find data for your dataset. The availability and quality of these sources will depend on your work environment, your company's legacy, and many other factors. Which should be addressed in the first place will depend mostly on the goals of your ML system. Here we list the most popular data sources or their categories while accompanying them with real-world examples:

- *Global activities*—This is a huge category of data sources that includes any activity in a single entity that is regularly recorded and stored on an ongoing basis. As an example, in the stock trading business, traders around the globe act on the stock market, and the result of their actions (trades and prices) later becomes available for other parties.
- *Physical processes*—These are global changes happening on the planet as we speak. They can be environmental shifts monitored on various levels, from satellite images to microsensors on farming lands.
- *External databases*—Certain third-party companies thrive on collecting domain-specific data using their proprietary methods and know-how. You will want to address them, if their data meets your requirements and needs.
- *Local business processes*—Here we are going from global to local. The business itself can generate a huge amount of data as it operates and grows. If you work in eCommerce, purchase history can be your primary source of data.
- *Labeling by a dedicated team*—Your company can hire a team of experts to generate labels for a specific problem.
- *Labeling by end system users*—This is a similar approach, where the company may provide a user interface for end users. There, they will specify the inputs for your ML system.
- *Artificially generated datasets*—This is where data is created by scientific simulators, rendered environments, or other synthetic sources. Items created with generative AI (e.g., image generators or large language models) can be attributed to this category as well.

Some data sources are unique, and having access to them may be a significant competitive advantage. Many big tech companies like Google and Meta are successful mainly because of their valuable user behavior data used for ad targeting. On the other hand, other datasets are easy to acquire; the information is either free to download or can be created for a nonrestrictive price (many datasets sold by data providers are relatively cheap). This doesn't mean that cheap equals low quality, as it all depends on what kind of data you need. It might turn out that this particular free-of-charge source fits your ML system perfectly. There are also intermediate points on this spectrum, though, and not in terms of price. Access to data can be limited in some regions or be in a "gray zone" legality-wise. Mature companies tend to follow the law (and we recommend you do so as well!), while young startups with the YOLO mentality sometimes consider minor violations.

Some datasets become valuable when enriched or annotated/labeled. *Annotation* means combining a raw dataset with proper labels or, in other words, creating a closely tied dataset and connecting it with a new one. It is a popular pattern of mixing a unique proprietary dataset with a public data source and getting a much more valuable dataset as a result.

Ad tech companies, mentioned earlier, may benefit from joining datasets as well. Let's take a look at a classic example. A company operates a free-to-play game, which means it has a lot of players, and only some of them pay money. The number and list of paying customers is kept secret and available only to the game's publisher. At the same time, its partnering ad network has millions of detailed user profiles derived from behavior. When these datasets are combined (see figure 6.1), it opens a great marketing opportunity: the company can target its new ad to potential customers who are similar to its paying players. Data exchanges like this increase the efficiency of online marketing and thus are one of the powers driving the modern web.

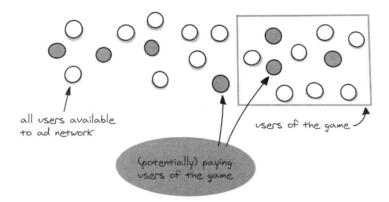

Figure 6.1   Combining data sources of two completely different businesses can eventually benefit both.

When we're talking about joining datasets, it's not always the case of a straightforward connection between similar datasets (like a SQL join between two tables). An important concept here is multimodality, which is an intersection of various modalities in a dataset. In simple words, modality is a kind of information we receive; it is common to describe the world as multimodal for humans (we hear sounds, see colors, feel motions, etc.). In ML-related literature, multimodal datasets are those that combine various kinds of data to describe one problem. Think of images of an item being sold and its text description. Combining datasets of different origins and modalities is a powerful technique.

Speaking about combining data sources, Arseny once helped kickstart a startup as an advisor. The company worked in the agri-tech area, helping farmers and related companies to increase their operating efficiency, and its secret sauce was based on datasets. The way it worked was as follows. One data source was public, using satellite images of the planet available thanks to several space initiatives like Landsat by NASA and Copernicus by ESA (where you can fetch countless images of agricultural lands). But having those images alone could not bolster the efficiency of the startup, as it lacked information describing these agricultural lands. The main problem is most agricultural companies are far from innovative, and there is no single solid source of data on what crops were grown, the yield results, and more. Such data is poorly digitized but is really valuable for multiple business needs: it can be used to reduce the amount of fertilizer used, to estimate future prices for food commodities, and so on. Eventually, the team implemented smart ways of gathering such data and merging it with the huge photo database. An ML system built on these joint datasets helped the company to grow rapidly.

Defining data sources and the way they interconnect is the first cornerstone of solving the data problem for the system. But raw data is often almost useless until we make it available for the system and ML model, filter it, and preprocess it in other ways.

6.2 *Cooking the dataset*

Experienced engineers who work with data know that in the vast majority of cases, the data in its raw form is too raw to work effectively. Hence the name *raw data*, meaning a chaotically compiled, unorganized giant clump of information. Thus, initial raw datasets are rarely in good enough shape to use them as is. You need to cook the dataset to apply it to your ML system in the most efficient way possible.

We've gathered a list of techniques you can use to properly cook your dataset, with each technique presented in a separate subsection. This list is not strictly ordered, and the order of actions may vary depending on your domain, so there is no single universal answer. In some cases, you can't filter data before labeling, while sometimes filtering happens multiple times throughout the cooking process. Let's briefly touch on these techniques.

6.2.1 *ETL*

ETL, which stands for "extract, transform, load," is a data preparation phase, such as fetching information from an external data source and tailoring its structure to your needs. As a simplified example, you can fetch JSON files from a third-party API and store them in local storage as CSV or Parquet files.

NOTE The high-level goal of ETL is to solve the data availability problem.

Data availability at this point implies two things:

- Data can be fetched easily and effectively for a training process (e.g., if the target dataset is a product of multiple interactions from multiple sources, it is useful to understand how to make it fetchable with a single click, command, or call).
- Data will be available for training and runtime phases. We don't care if fetching data is effective for inference at this point (we will discuss it later, in chapter 11), but we need to guarantee the same data sources are available for inference.

NOTE Designing an effective ETL process is an art of its own, as it requires a good understanding of various data storages and data processing tools. We only scratch the surface of this topic in our book and recommend consulting other sources for a more in-depth understanding.

The important question here is: "Should I care about data storage and structure at this point?" The answer to this question lies in the following spectrum:

- Sometimes datasets are small enough, and the chances of a sudden growth by multiple orders of magnitude are minuscule. It means you can choose almost any storage (e.g., the one that is already actively used in your organization or the one you're most familiar with). You would be surprised how often inexperienced ML engineers tend to overengineer things here, like designing a distributed multicluster storage for a static tabular dataset with thousands of rows and tens of columns.
- Sometimes it's clear from the very beginning that your dataset will be huge and will grow rapidly, so you should pay close attention as you design the data model. We don't consider ourselves world-class experts in data engineering of this kind and recommend checking out other books if this is the case for your system. Our favorite work on the subject is *Designing Data-Intensive Applications* by Martin Kleppmann.

6.2.2 *Filtering*

No data source is absolutely perfect. By *perfect*, we mean clean, consistent, and relevant to your problem. In the short story at the beginning of this chapter, we mentioned APIs that provide satellite images, but the company only needed those that weren't too cloudy and were related to agricultural regions; otherwise, storing irrelevant data would significantly increase the costs. It meant that a good chunk of preliminary work of selecting appropriate satellite photos had to be done as the very first step.

Data filtering is a very domain-specific operation. In some cases, it can be done fully automatically based on a set of rules or statistics; in others, it requires human attention at scale. Experience shows that the end approach normally lies somewhere between those two extremes. A combination of the human eye and automated heuristics is what works best, with the following algorithm being a popular approach: look through a subset of data (either randomly or based on some initial insight or feedback), find patterns, reflect them in the code to extend coverage, and then look through a narrower subset.

While the absence of data filtering leads to extensive noise in the dataset and thus worse performance of the whole system, overly aggressive filtering may have a negative effect as well: in some cases, it may distort data distribution and lead to a worse performance on real data.

6.2.3 Feature engineering

Feature engineering means transforming the data view in a manner so it's most valuable for an ML algorithm. We'll cover the topic in more detail later in the book when it's time to discuss intermediate steps, as it's rarely detailed during the early stages of ML system design. At this stage, we tend to focus on the question of how to get initial data to make a baseline model, which requires some level of abstraction at the current stage.

Sometimes features are not engineered manually but created by a more complicated model; unlike "regular" features, they can be non-human-readable vectors. In these cases, it's more precise to use the term *representations*, although at some level of abstraction, they're the same thing: inputs to the ML model itself.

For example, in a big ML-heavy organization, there may be a core team building a model that generates the best possible representations of users, goods, or other items at scale. Their model doesn't solve business problems directly, but applied teams can use it to generate representations for their specific needs. That is a popular pattern when we're talking about such data as images, videos, texts, or audio.

6.2.4 Labeling

In many scenarios, a dataset itself is not too valuable, but adding extra annotations, often known in the ML world as *labels*, is a game changer. Deciding what kind of labels should be used is extremely important, as it dictates many other choices down the road.

Let's imagine you're building a medical assistance product, a system that helps radiologists analyze patients' images. It is one of the most popular ML applications in medicine that is still very complicated to design properly. A use case may seem simple: a doctor looks at an image and judges if there is a malignancy, so you want doctors to label the dataset.

There are numerous ways to label it (see figure 6.2), including

- *Binary classification style*—Is there a malignancy in the image?
- *Multiclass classification style*—What kind of malignancy is in the image, if any?
- *Detection style*—What region of the image contains a malignancy, if any?
- *Segmentation style*—Exactly which pixels of the image represent malignancy, if any?

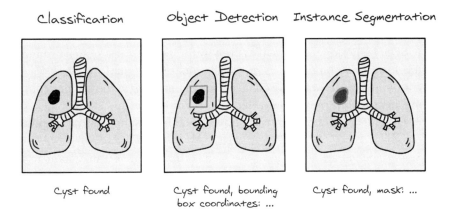

Figure 6.2 Various approaches to data labeling

These ways of labeling data require different labeling tools and different expertise from the labeling team. They also vary in terms of time required. The method affects what kind of model you can use for the problem, and, most importantly, it limits the product. Making the right decision in this case is impossible unless you follow the steps from chapter 2 and gather enough information about product goals and needs.

In some situations, labeling data with the proper level of detail is nearly impossible. For example, it could take too much time, there may not be enough experts to cover enough data, or the toolset is not ready. In these cases, it is worth considering using weakly supervised approaches that allow the use of inaccurate or partial labels. If you're not familiar with this branch of ML tricks, we recommend "A Brief Introduction to Weakly Supervised Learning" (https://mng.bz/75My) for an overview; more links for further reading are at Awesome-Weak- Supervision (https://mng.bz/mRp2).

Efficient data labeling requires a choice of a labeling platform, proper decomposition of tasks, task instructions that are easy to read and follow, easy-to-use task interfaces, quality control techniques, an overview of aggregation methods, and pricing. Additionally, best practices should be followed when designing instructions and interfaces, setting up different types of templates, training and examining performers, and constructing pipelines for evaluating the labeling process.

When datasets need to be labeled manually, there are two main ways to go: an in-house labeling team or third-party crowdsourcing services. In a nutshell, the former provides a more controlled and consistent labeling process, while the latter can scale up the annotation process quickly, possibly at a lower cost. The simplest heuristic of choosing one over another is based on the labeling complexity: once it requires specific knowledge or skills, it makes sense to develop an in-house team of curated experts; otherwise, using an external service is a good option.

There are dozens of crowdsourcing platforms available; the most popular is probably Amazon Mechanical Turk. As we opt for width over depth in this book, we will not focus on features of different platforms. Instead, we focus on generic properties of labeling with crowdsourcing:

- Labelers tend to make mistakes even in the simplest tasks, such as binary classification of common objects. Most labelers on the platform work for multiple customers, so there is little chance they will memorize the nuances of the labeling instructions you've provided. As a result, labelers should be considered interchangeable, and the instruction should be as simple and nonambiguous as possible.

- Some labelers are more attentive than others, and you may want to motivate them to dedicate more time to your tasks, not other gigs. Other labelers can be less attentive or adversarial; for example, they may try to use bots generating unverified labels instead of their own judgment. It is crucial to be able to distinguish the former from the latter. The most popular way of doing so is by including tests in the labeling process. Pick a share of a dataset with a label you're confident in, and use it for labeling tasks so you can measure accuracy and other metrics of each particular labeler. You can also log some details of the labeling process for a clearer picture. If labels are generated very fast, it may be a strong signal of a bot or other illegal automation tool.

- The labeling task should be designed in a way that reduces the variance caused by crowdsource workers. Consider the following scenario: a company is developing a chatbot and employs labelers to evaluate responses (questions and several possible answers). The most straightforward evaluation method here would be to ask labelers to rate each answer with a single number (e.g., 1 to 5). However, such labels might be inconsistent. A basic improvement in this case would be to introduce multiple evaluation criteria so that each answer is assessed separately based on factual correctness, tone of voice, and so on. These labels would be more consistent but still far from perfect. Another improvement would be asking for a pairwise comparison. Instead of assigning a number to each answer, labelers would perform a ternary comparison based on the criteria (version A is better / version B is better / A and B are equal). These labels are easier to collect, and the expected variance between labelers' outputs is lower.

In the 18th century, the French mathematician and philosopher Marquis de Condorcet stated a theorem applicable to political science. De Condorcet revealed the following idea: if a group needs to make a binary decision based on a majority vote and each group member is correct with a probability $p > 0.5$, the probability of a correct decision by the group grows with the number of group members asymptotically. This could be a formal reason for collective decision-making in the early days of the French Revolution, and now the very same flawless logic is applicable to ML systems!

Let's imagine we have three labelers annotating the same object for a binary classification. The problem is tricky, so each one is only right in 70% of cases. So we can expect a majority vote of three labelers to be correct in $0.7 * 0.7 * 0.7 + 0.3 * 0.7 * 0.7 + 0.7 * 0.3 * 0.7 + 0.7 * 0.7 * 0.3 = 78.4\%$. That's a nice boost!

These numbers should be interpreted with a grain of salt. Condorcet's jury theorem implies assumptions that are not exactly met here: labelers are not completely independent, and their origin of error is correlated (this may be the case when data samples are noisy and hard to read). But still, an ensemble of labelers is more accurate compared to a single labeler, and this technique can be used to improve labeling results.

This idea can be modified to decrease costs. One algorithm modification we have faced is the following:

- Label the object with two labelers.
- If they agree, the label is accepted.
- If not, add three more votes and use the majority vote as a label.

With this modification, more votes are used for complicated samples that lack consistency, while fewer votes are required for simple cases.

The heuristic described here is a simple though powerful baseline. However, if data labeling is a key ingredient for your problem and you see the need to invest some effort, there is a lot of research dedicated to better design. Some of the materials we recommend are "A Survey on Task Assignment in Crowdsourcing" (https://arxiv.org/abs/2111.08501) and a tutorial by crowdsourcing vendor Toloka.ai (https://toloka.ai/events/tutorial-wsdm/).

Labelers' consistency and mutual agreement may and should be measured. While ML practitioners often tend to use regular ML metrics to estimate it, those who have a statistical background may recall a concept called *interrater reliability* and its separate set of metrics (Cohen's kappa, Scott's pi, and Krippendorff's alpha, to name a few). These metrics help keep the labeling team's work reliable, filter out unscrupulous labels (thus greatly improving the overall system performance), and, in some scenarios, give a solid upper bound for the performance of your model (recall the human-level performance we mentioned earlier in chapter 3).

Labeling teams require proper tooling, which may boost efficiency and improve the quality of created labels. If you go with third-party tooling, it's very likely it will have a toolset for the most popular problems; for your own team, you need to set up or create your own. Aspects of choosing an existing solution or building a brand-new one are very domain specific, although the general approach is: the more popular the ML formulation of your problem, the more chances you have to find a modern quality toolset for the labeler team. As an example, there are multiple software solutions to create labels for image detection at scale, but once you need to annotate videos with 3D polygon meshes, you're very likely to require something custom made.

Recent advances in large foundation models have become a game changer in the labeling process as well: they often can be used to gather initial labels in a few-shot setup with the accuracy higher than nonexpert human labelers. One of many examples of a tool used for large language model labeling is Refuel Docs (https://docs.refuel.ai/), notable for being focused on text data; however, using foundation models is also possible in other domains (e.g., addressing universal segmentation models like Segment Anything [https://segment-anything.com/] or multimodal solutions like LLaVA [https://llava-vl.github.io/]).

There are various algorithmic tricks that may help simplify/reduce the efforts required for the data labeling aspect of building a system, but we will not go into an in-depth review of those in this book, as they are too subject-specific. What we would like to additionally highlight is that very often efforts invested in the data labeling process and tools can be a driver for the success of your ML system.

6.3   *Data and metadata*

While datasets are used for the ML system we're building, there is a layer of information on top of it—let's use the word *metadata* for it. Metadata is information that describes certain properties of your datasets. Here are some examples:

- *Time-related attributes*—These include when the event happened and when it was processed and stored.
- *Source attributes*—Source attributes tell whether or not data is gathered from multiple sources.
- *User attributes*—If a user is somehow involved in dataset generation, which is not a rare situation, their metadata becomes important metadata of related data samples.
- *Versions*—If the data is processed, it can be useful to understand which version of software has been involved in processing.

Metadata is crucial for data flows and guarantees their consistency. Let's get back to the previous scenario with a medical application. Imagine that a company hired 10 medical professionals to label data for your system. After working for over a year, they have finally labeled a big dataset. Suddenly, you get an email: one of the labelers turns out to be a fraud, his diploma is fake, and his license has been suspended. This is an unacceptable situation because a tangible part of the data can be considered unreliable, which jeopardizes the entire dataset. So you enact the only adequate solution, which is to stop using his labels in the model ASAP. While this example is somewhat exaggerated, tens of less significant problems will occur in your system over time. Problems with data sources, regulatory interventions, and attempts to interpret model errors will make you refer to metadata on a regular basis.

As we discussed earlier, while recipes for datasets may vary, most likely, your dataset will be cooked properly. It's okay to reveal new aspects of the problem, thus adjusting the dataset structure over time, and reflect them accordingly in how the dataset was processed. All these differences should be reflected in metadata.

Another source of changes is testing and bug fixing. Imagine that you work for a ridesharing company and are to solve a problem of estimating how long it will take to reach point A from point B. You start with historical data your company generated, and there is a preprocessing job that extracts the information from logs and stores it in your favorite database, so you end up with a table like `latitude_from`, `longitude_from`, `datetime_start`, `datetime_finish`, `distance`, `data_source`.

At some point, the company makes a big acquisition of a competitor, and you decide to add its data to your ETL process. A new engineer on the team starts coding, new sources are attached, new data points are added to your dataset with the same schema, and suddenly your model performance drops. What happened?

Fast forward: your company stored distance in kilometers, while the acquired team stored distance in miles. An engineer who handled the integration knew it and implemented the support of miles for the new source but accidentally enabled it for the old one as well. So new data samples are correct for the new data source but not for the old one. If you had a metadata field like `preprocessing_function_version`, you could easily find affected samples. Without it, you need to gather the dataset from scratch after the code defect is discovered.

Defects like this are not the only scenario where you may need to reveal the date of data sample origin. Some ML systems may affect data sources, creating a phenomenon called a *feedback loop*. A very common example of a feedback loop is recommender systems: let's say a marketplace sells many items, and there is a block on the website titled "You may also be interested in these goods." As a naive baseline, the company could put in the items that are most popular overall. But when this baseline is replaced with an ML system, new items appear, and old leaders lose their popularity in favor of new recommended items. With the poor design of such a system, there is a chance for an item that may not be that good to gain its place among popular ones and dominate for a long time. Storing the information when the sample was generated and what versions of related systems were live at the moment is crucial (not enough, though!) to avoid feedback loops.

Another important scenario related to metadata is *stratification*, a process of data sampling that shapes the distribution of various subgroups. For example, say a company started its operation in country X, gathering a lot of data related to customers from X. Later the company reached a new market, Y, and has a goal of providing the same level of service, including accuracy of ML models, for customers in both countries. It will require representing customers from X and Y in training and test datasets with proper balance.

Stratification is crucial for validation design and resisting the algorithmic bias, and both topics will be covered in future chapters.

6.4 How much data is enough?

After everything we've mentioned on the importance of datasets, inexperienced ML practitioners may think that building a data pipeline that will stream numerous samples is enough to build a good system. Well, that's where we can't say confidently yes or no.

First, not all data samples are equally useful. Growing the dataset size is only useful if new objects help the model learn something new and related to the problem.

Adding samples very similar to existing ones is pointless; the same goes for extremely noisy data. That's why there is a popular research avenue dedicated to finding the most samples for dataset extension called *active learning*. The simplest intuition is to enrich the dataset with samples where the model was incorrect (this signal is often fetched using humans in the loop processed) or demonstrated the lowest confidence. The academic community has developed tens of methods related to active learning; see a recent survey (e.g., "A Comparative Survey of Deep Active Learning" by Xueying Zhan et al., https://arxiv.org/abs/2203.13450) for more information.

One more aspect related to dataset size is *sampling*. While in most cases the question we ask ourselves is "How do we get more data?" sometimes it is "What part of data should I use to increase efficiency?" It usually happens when a dataset needs no manual labeling and is generated by a defined process—for example, the clickstream in popular B2C web services (search engines, marketplaces).

Sampling is effective when a dataset is not only huge but also tends to be imbalanced and/or may contain a lot of duplicates. Different strategies can be applicable here, and the most common of them are based on stratification, where you split data into groups (based on key features or algorithmically defined clusters) and limit the amount of data used for each group. The amounts don't have to be equal—for example, if the temporal component is relevant to your problem, it's very likely you will want to prioritize fresh data over old groups.

Another point is about *data noisiness*. A while ago there was a strong consensus in the ML community that a few clean samples are better than multiple noisy samples. Things have changed recently, however; the progress with large models like GPT-3 and CLIP demonstrated that at a certain scale, manual filtering is almost impossible (processing a dataset of 500 billion text tokens or tens of millions of images would cost a fortune), but using a huge amount of weakly or self-supervised (automatically, using heuristics) data works, so for some tasks massive imperfect datasets are more suitable than smaller hand-picked ones.

> **NOTE** While some amount of noise is safe to have in the training data, it's way less acceptable for validation/test datasets. We'll cover it more in chapter 7.

You could be expecting the model's performance to be improved as a square root of dataset size asymptotically, no matter what metric is being used. This estimation is very rough and does not have to fit your problem exactly, but it may give you some intuition (see figure 6.3).

Not every model can be improved by adding new data because of the uncertainty of origin. Uncertainty primarily comes from two central origins:

- Lack of knowledge or information (known as *epistemic uncertainty*)
- Uncertainty found in the given data itself (also called *aleatoric uncertainly*)

Aleatoric uncertainty emerges primarily due to the existing complexity in the data, like overlapping classes or additive noise. A critical characteristic of data uncertainty is that no matter how much additional training data gets collated, it does not reduce.

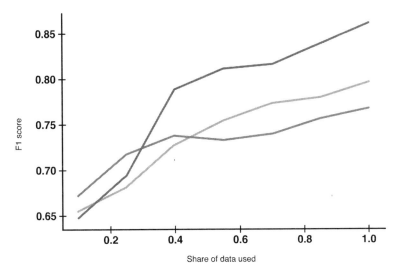

Figure 6.3 A plot showcasing model metric improvements over dataset size for a real project. Each line demonstrates the dynamics of the target metric for a single task once the dataset size is growing.

On the other hand, epistemic uncertainty occurs when the model encounters an input located in a region that is either thinly covered by the training data or falls outside the scope of the training data (see figure 6.4).

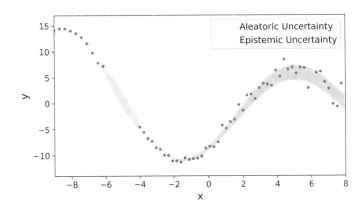

Figure 6.4 A schematic view of the main differences between aleatoric and epistemic uncertainties (source: "Explainable Uncertainty Quantifications for Deep Learning-Based Molecular Property Prediction" by Chul Yang and YiPei Li, https://mng.bz/n0ZV)

Once you have gathered some data and formed a training pipeline (see chapter 10 for details), it unlocks an option of making an informed decision on how much more data you need and estimating the economic efficiency of new data. It is especially reasonable when working with expensive data (e.g., labeled by highly skilled professionals). A high-level algorithm is the following:

- Split the dataset into buckets so that the bucket size is close to uniform and similarity between samples of different buckets is maximized. This way, each sample for a user goes to the same bucket determined by a user ID (this brings us back to the stratification aspect mentioned earlier).
- Fix the computational budget if applicable. No matter what the dataset size is, you train the model for N batches.
- Train the model on data subsets in a range from a tiny share of the dataset to the whole thing, ensuring the subset used is cumulative (e.g., if sample X was used when training on a 10% subset, it must be used on 20%, 30%, etc.).
- Calculate key metrics for each trained model and make a plot using a horizontal axis for dataset size and a vertical axis for the metric itself.
- With some imagination enabled, extrapolate how much more data is required to squeeze another 1% of metric change.

The precision of this metric is low, and it doesn't take systematic aspects into account (e.g., concept drifts that we'll discuss in chapter 14), although even this precision is often crucial to making an important decision on how much we should invest in the data labeling pipeline.

6.5 *Chicken-or-egg problem*

One of the hardest problems you may face with regard to datasets is a problem of a cold start (aka chicken-or-egg problem): when you need data to build a system but the data is not available until the system is launched. What a terrible loop to get stuck in!

It is often a problem for startups or companies trying to launch products in new markets or verticals. And, as often happens in the ML world, the go-to solution is approximation. Since we don't have data perfectly matching our problem, we need to find something as close as possible. What data will be close depends on the problem, so let's look at some examples.

For this example, let's imagine a company focused on employee safety that builds products monitoring how workers follow safety rules in various environments. The new product should check if hard hats were worn on factory grounds. When the product is available, there will be a lot of data coming from customers who agree to share it, but before that, customers' cameras are not available for the company.

So how do we approach the problem?

- *Approach 1*—Let's use the computer graphics world. We take a stack of 3D human models and render them on the factory backgrounds, both wearing hats and not.
- *Approach 2*—Let's use public sources. We look for relevant images in public sources (from Google images to photo banks) and scrape or buy them.
- *Approach 2.5 (hybrid)*—Let's do a crossover: we take some images of people from the factory and draw/render hats on some of them.

- *Approach 3*—Let's try acting! Your team buys hard hats, goes to an abandoned factory, and runs a photo session with hats on.
- *Approach 4*—Let's get lazy. We find a public dataset with people wearing very similar hats but outdoors, on a construction site—not too close but still something.
- *Approach 5*—Let's build a very naive baseline with no actual ML under the hood and suggest it to the customer to break the loop. An example of such a baseline could be finding human heads using an existing face detector and then cropping those faces and adding a simple heuristic trying to localize a hat (e.g., a bright enclosed blob).
- *Approach 6*—Instead of using a naive baseline, we integrate a solution provided by a large vendor if it is available. This option works better if vendors' labels can be reused from the legal perspective. However, proxying a vendor's output can provide you with initial unlabeled data that has its own value.

These examples may not always be reasonable and applicable, but they represent several ways of solving this problem:

- Generating synthetic data
- Using available data from similar situations
- Creating data manually
- Taking data from a similar problem and trying to adjust it
- Use a dummy baseline model or third party to bootstrap

We should mention that not every scenario is applicable to every problem. You obviously won't build a medical system for lung cancer detection using images of brain scans, and a naive baseline as a medical advisor is no good at all. But training on scans from other hospitals using the same equipment may be a good idea to consider; while every scanner will be calibrated slightly differently, together they can provide some generalization (a model trained on data from hospitals A, B, and C is likely to be useful for hospital D). Scraping other websites is rarely greenlighted in a respectful public company, although it is a popular technique among small startups. Synthetic images obtained by a straightforward rendering pipeline are usually not the way to go because they're not realistic enough (imperfect lighting, shadows, etc.). But with some secret sauce, you can make them realistic. In the paper "MobilePose: Real-Time Pose Estimation for Unseen Objects with Weak Shape Supervision" (Hou et al., 2020, https://arxiv.org/abs/2003.03522), researchers rendered objects on top of augmented reality recordings (with accurately estimated lights) to make images way more realistic and thus valuable for a model.

In every scenario, we need to keep in mind that data is not a representative sample of the real distribution we're going to work with when the system goes live. This means validation results should be taken with a grain of salt, and replacing such proxy datasets with more realistic ones is a top priority. Let's talk about it when discussing the properties of a healthy data pipeline.

6.6   *Properties of a healthy data pipeline*

Data gathering and preprocessing need to have three important properties:

- Reproducibility
- Consistency
- Availability

Let's review the properties one by one.

Reproducibility means you should be able to create a dataset from scratch if needed. There should be no golden data file in your storage that is crafted by a wise engineer with a bit of dark magic. But there must be a software solution (a simple script, more advanced pipeline, or big system) that allows you to create such files again using the same origin as used before. This solution needs to be documented and tested well enough so every project collaborator is able to run it when needed.

The reasoning behind reproducibility is similar to the infrastructure-as-code paradigm popular in the DevOps community. Yes, it may seem easier to create an initial dataset manually in the first place, but it's not scalable in the long run and is very error-prone. Next time—when a new batch of data is going to be added—you may forget to run a preprocessing step, thus causing implicit data inconsistency, a hard-to-detect problem that will affect the whole system's performance.

Consistency itself is the key. ML problems often have situations when labels are partially ill-defined, and defining a strict separating plane is impossible. In such cases, experts who do labeling tend to disagree with each other.

A very demonstrative example from our background is related to the credit card transactions classification problem. Customers are expected to give each transaction a label describing the purpose of the expense. The initial label taxonomy contains "food and drink," "bars and wineries," and "coffee houses." A rhetorical question arises: What label is more suitable for payment for a coffee and a sandwich ordered in a wine bar? A partial solution for this example would be to have some kind of protocol on how ties are to be broken and how blurry boundaries are resolved (e.g., "when a merchant type and purchased item type are conflicting, the first to be opened takes precedence")—it greatly simplifies model training and especially validation.

Consistency is not only about labels. All aspects of data should be consistent: what the data origin is, how data is preprocessed, what filtering is applied, etc. It is relatively easy when the system is being built within a small company and way more challenging for an international corporation, and some formal definitions can be helpful. Once you feel there is a chance of misreading a core term used in the data pipeline, it may be useful to add it to the design doc to make sure the whole team is on the same page.

One more aspect of consistency is how data is gathered at the system-building stage and what the system inputs are during system usage. It is a common problem, and in ML terms, it leads to distribution mismatch, a problem affecting model performance and fairness that is not easy to detect before the system goes live.

We recently mentioned the feedback loop phenomena—the model affects data origin and thus violates the consistency assumption. We also described situations when data is not available until the system launch, and this also may lead to a mismatch. Problems like this are still among the most challenging aspects of applied ML, and you can never ignore them while designing a system.

Data consistency is always an open question, so you should care about it at every stage of ML system development, from initial drafts to long-term maintenance. We will get back to this aspect in chapter 14 when discussing monitoring and drift detection (there will even will be a short but rather cool campfire story from one of our friends).

Last but not least is availability. This property is actually an umbrella for two ideas: availability for a system and availability for engineers. The first can also be named *reliability*; a system designer should be very critical of nonreliable data sources. Here is a good situation for a negative example—one where things can ultimately go wrong. Imagine a system that depends on a third-party API enriching your data stream, and everything was good until it wasn't—a small company powering the API lost its key site reliability engineer and thus the ability to handle the infrastructure. If your system's dependency on this data source is critical, their problems become your problems.

Of course, it doesn't mean using third-party APIs is not an option. As we mentioned earlier, using external solutions is often a good practice—and not only provided by giants like Amazon, Google, and Microsoft. But data availability is important, and these risks should be taken into account seriously. There are some services provided by vendors that can be less reliable (we can't imagine a top-priority problem caused by the outage of an experimental visualization tool), but data sources are not one of them.

The same philosophy goes for internal systems (e.g., those controlled by your peers from other teams). There are different control gears for external and internal systems: for the former, service-level agreements are used to estimate risks, while internal systems exist only in mature organizations. At the same time, in smaller companies, it is easier to be aligned with a team maintaining the system and effectively reducing related risks.

It is also worth mentioning that problems related to data availability are not strictly software related. Even if all related systems are built and maintained properly, there may be problems of more sophisticated origins—for example, caused by information security and privacy rights (such as new legal regulations that affect using personal data or your key customer CEO's decision that their data should not leave their infrastructure anymore).

Availability for engineers can be overestimated: you can hear something like "Come on, our engineers can fetch the data even if it's not a simple operation—they are professionals and will handle the tech difficulties, if any." Most likely it is true—we assume our readers and their colleagues are outstanding professionals, but you can't ignore time constraints. Imagine that an engineer went for lunch with their buddy from another team; they chatted about work-related stuff, and after a cup of coffee, a new hypothesis related to the system of current interest popped up.

If data is attainable easily, you can make an informative decision relatively quickly by pulling the dataset, aggregating some statistics, and maybe even running basic experiments. If the idea gets confirmed in the first naive approach, it can be prioritized higher, meaning more resources should be allocated. Who knows, maybe it is going to be a significant improvement in the future.

Otherwise, if pulling data and making data-driven decisions is time-consuming, the hypothesis is likely to be ignored ("Well, it might be interesting, but I have so many things to do and finding the data will take so long!"). To avoid these cases, we recommend dedicating a share of engineering efforts to building tools that will make datasets more available to people who should work with data. While it is somewhat applicable to any engineering productivity tools, return on investment is especially high when the tools improve data availability. As we said in the very beginning, it's hard to overestimate the importance of quality data for ML systems, and thus smoothing interactions with the datasets is a good investment in the long run.

This is sufficient depth in the information on consistency and availability at this point in the book. We will return to these two properties of the pipeline in greater detail later in chapter 10. Meanwhile, it's time to move on to the practical part of the chapter: the design document.

6.7 Design document: Dataset

As we describe steps for the data problem, it organically leads us to additional questions to be answered in the design document. The following is a checklist of questions we suggest asking yourself at this point.

- ETL:
  - What are the data sources?
  - How should we represent and store the data for our system?
- Filtering:
  - What are the criteria for good and bad data samples?
  - What corner cases can we expect? How do we handle them?
  - Do we filter data automatically or set up a process for manual verification?
- Feature engineering:
  - How are the features computed?
  - How are representations generated?
- Labeling:
  - What labels do we need?
  - What's the label's source?

As often happens, answering these questions can spawn even more questions. Give yourself the freedom to think about those. Time dedicated to answering data-related questions always has an outstanding return on investment in ML systems design.

6.7.1 Dataset for Supermegaretail

Now let's go back to preparing the design document. This time we are preparing a section devoted to datasets for our imaginary companies. As usual, we'll start with Supermegaretail.

DESIGN DOCUMENT: SUPERMEGARETAIL

III. DATASET

The atomic object of the dataset is a bundle of (date, product, store), and the target variable we aim to predict is the number of units sold.

I. DATA SOURCES

There are multiple sources of data we can utilize for our objective.

INNER SOURCES

- *Historical data on purchases (i.e., transaction history)* is collected from the chain of Supermegaretail stores and saved to a centralized database. It will be our *primary source* of truth: the number of sales, the amount of money spent, the discounts applied, transaction ID, and so on.
- *Stock history* is the second most important source of truth for our problem since it directly determines how many units of each product can be sold in each store. This source can help estimate how many products are available for sale at the beginning of each day and how many were expired and withdrawn from sale.
- Metadata of *each product, store, and transaction.*
- Calendar of planned *promo activities.* This is a significant factor affecting future sales that definitely needs to be taken into account.

OUTER SOURCES: MANUALLY GATHERED DATA

- *Price monitoring.* Prices and other product info collected from our competitors. They are manually gathered daily from a subset of stores of different competitors. It could be done either by our in-house team or by a third party (outsourced). A hybrid approach also can take place. Each product should also contain a global product identifier (barcode) so we can easily match collected data with our product. Knowing aggregated competitors' prices and their dynamics helps us understand what is happening in the market.

OUTER SOURCES: PURCHASED DATA

- *Weather history and forecast* we buy from the meteorological service. Weather is an important factor directly affecting consumer behavior.
- *Customer traffic* estimation near our stores (from telecom providers).
- *Global market indicators.*

MOBILE APP AND WEBSITE DATA (OPTIONAL)

- Supermegaretail has a *delivery service* (even if it generates less than 5% of revenue). We will collect *additional data* about specific sales in a specific location. Sometimes this information can be a valuable predictor.
- Also, mobile and web services collect implicit feedback about user activity, including views, clicks, or adding to the cart, which also can predict sales in physical stores.

II. DATA LABELING

Since we are dealing with a demand forecasting problem, we don't need extra data labeling derived directly from the transaction history.

III. AVAILABLE METADATA

We forecast demand based on the SKU per store level with three key elements: products, stores, and transactions.

PRODUCTS

- Product ID and barcode.
- Category codes of different levels (1, 2, 3). We can use a hierarchy of categories for a rule-based measurement of similarity between products. Also, other categorical info like brand, manufacturer, or pricing group.
- Shelf life, which determines how bad it is to overpredict sales for this product.
- Date when the product was added to the assortment matrix of the chain.
- Dimensions and weight of the product.

STORES

- Store ID.
- Location (coordinates), with the support of third-party sources—we can use it to add information about the weather, flow of people, and distance to critical points, as well as other related things like city, region, and associated logistics center.
- The nearest competitors' stores (with their IDs and distances).
- The size of the store and its format. They determine which products and how many unique products will be in the assortment at this store.
- The dates when the store is open and closed.

TRANSACTIONS

- *Timestamp.* This allows us to enrich the dataset with things like holidays.
- *Customer ID* (if a loyalty card is applied). Despite the fact that the final unit of the dataset is (product, store), a bundle of (customer, product) can be used in a separate data pipeline for calculating product embeddings via aggregating transactions to a user-item matrix and its factorization. The embeddings will contain patterns of purchasing behavior.
- *Store ID* and *product ID*.

IV. AVAILABLE HISTORY

Demand forecast is nothing new for Supermegaretail. Critical ETL processes are already in place. Supermegaretail has been collecting data for more than 3 years.

This history is essential for our forecasting model to learn patterns, catching the seasonality of sales, estimating trends, etc. The same is applicable for products and stores metadata. Weather data (which we take from external sources) has been available for a period in the past as long as we need.

Stocks history and promo activities have been gathered as well.

Price monitoring data of competitors has been collected for the last 2 years.

V. DATA QUALITY ISSUES

Transactions, stock, and promo data may contain missing or duplicated values, so additional filtering or preprocessing is required before aggregation.

The external data we bought has already been cleaned and passed some quality control before coming to us. However, necessary checks need to be implemented.

The competitors' prices cover about 25% of SKU and have gaps.

VI. FINAL ETL PIPELINE

The top-level scheme is as follows:

1 The transactions data is aggregated daily.

2 Newly aggregated partition is added to the table of transaction aggregates.

3 (Optional) We rewrite not only the last day but the previous 2 to 3 days to fix possible corruptions in the data (duplicates, incomplete data, duplicated data, and so on).

4 We join other sources of internal/external data based on data, product ID, or store ID.

5 Finally, we calculate features based on the joined dataset.

Optionally, we can add a data pipeline for product embeddings, as described in section III, if needed.

6.7.2 Dataset for PhotoStock Inc.

Let's now switch to the PhotoStock Inc. design document.

DESIGN DOCUMENT: PHOTOSTOCK INC.

III. DATASET

I. DATASET AND SOURCES

One potential data source that can be used to gather information for the PhotoStock Inc. search engine is the data associated with each photo in the stock library. This data may include information such as tags, labels, and descriptions associated with the photos, which can provide valuable context about the content of the photos. This dataset should also contain URLs of actual photos and URLs of thumbnails we used. We suggest naming this dataset "description dataset."

Another potential data source is the search queries that users have submitted to the PhotoStock Inc. platform. These queries can provide insight into the types of photos that users are looking for and can be used to help guide the development of the ML models. When combined with user clicks, they provide a strong signal of relevancy and user interest. An extension of this dataset may contain further information about sessions related to these clicks: how much time did a user spend on the photo page, and did they purchase it afterward? We suggest naming this dataset "clicks dataset."

Additionally, we can hire labelers to manually assign relevancy scores to pairs of queries and images. The labelers will be given a set of search queries and a selection of images from the PhotoStock Inc. library and will be asked to assign a relevancy score to each query–image pair based on how closely the image matches the content of the query. Initially, query–image pairs should be selected randomly from the pool of past user queries and available photos in the stock library; however, it could be improved later to involve some active learning approaches and getting signals for the pairs where the model is less confident or tends to have more errors. We suggest naming this dataset "labels dataset."

We could have considered some public text/image datasets (e.g., COCO—Microsoft Common Objects in Context) for model bootstrapping. However, given that there is a solid history of user interactions, it should be fine to use our own data, while the public datasets will be only used indirectly—we can start with models pretrained on such datasets earlier.

Description and clicks datasets are generated organically by the main flow of the PhotoStock Inc. business. So it doesn't require too much attention from us right now, except for building proper ETL process and storage. The labels dataset needs to have its own budget given that it requires hiring a labelers team or using a third-party service.

II. METADATA, FILTERING, AND SUBSAMPLING

The description dataset is expected to be clean enough given that photo descriptions are moderated by the content quality team, as their quality is already a core part of our product. The clicks dataset is expected to be noisy because of different patterns in user behavior and the existence of scraping bots; we need to suggest heuristics to handle these problems. The extended version, with data on purchases, can be less noisy but also way smaller considering the conversion rate from click to purchase. Given these aspects, we expect the click+purchase and labels datasets to be more valuable for validation, while description and clicks without purchases are potentially more noisy and thus more suitable for training.

To address the quality problems with filtering, we should take care of metadata. The description dataset should be annotated with seller information and change dates; the clicks dataset should be annotated with user information, clicked item seller information, and additional search session information. At this point, there is no need to aggregate all the information about user and seller information. It may be part of further feature engineering steps, but at the very least we need to be sure to store `relevant user_id`, `seller_id`, `session_id`, and `purchase_id` to keep the ability to join this data for later use.

Given the volume of searches and purchases at PhotoStock Inc., it's not likely we need additional subsampling for purely engineering needs; full datasets can be processed. However, we may need to run subsampling to adjust class balances: there are way more items clicked than purchased, shown at the search engine result page than clicked, etc.

III. ETL AND DATA PREPARATION

Training data should be fetched on a regular (daily for now) basis in a batch manner. We suggest using the Flyte framework to orchestrate the jobs because it's already a framework of choice for other batch jobs in PhotoStock Inc.

No fancy stuff is required here—just gathering the data from production databases and storing it separately in the form of Parquet files for a simpler read should be enough. We don't expect any need for sophisticated preprocessing for now.

IV. LABELING

It's not clear what platform we should prefer for human labeling; it's also an open question whether we should use an in-house team (e.g., our customer support and moderators teams) or hire a third-party service. This question needs to be addressed together with these team managers. Also, we should get cost estimates from some third-party services to compare the costs of internal labeling with them.

We need to label pairs (query, image) and divide them among three classes:

- Relevant
- Irrelevant
- Can't answer

We should be ready to split "Relevant" into "Very relevant" and "Somewhat relevant" for higher granularity; the same goes for "Irrelevant." As for "Can't answer," we need to require labelers to type a reason why they can't label it—first iterations of labeling can provide us with newer insights on the dataset.

Summary

- Don't limit yourself to just one data source. Determine if you have enough internal sources or if you need to look outside the ecosystem of your business and expand your search range.
- Access to unique datasets can give you a significant competitive advantage. In their turn, datasets that are easier to acquire can bring great value if "cooked" properly.
- When working on datasets, don't neglect metadata, which is crucial for data flows and guarantees its consistency.
- Keep in mind that there is no strict sequence of techniques when preparing a dataset. The final order of operations will depend on the business goals of your system, the domain in which you operate, and other factors.
- Avoid situations where a dataset is populated with samples similar to those already present. Instead, fill the dataset with samples where the model did not work correctly.
- Make sure you have data that you can feed to the system before running it.
- Remember that the data pipeline must meet three criteria: reproducibility, consistency, and availability.

Validation schemas 7

This chapter covers

- Ensuring reliable evaluation
- Standard validation schemas
- Nontrivial validation schemas
- Split updating procedure
- Validation schemas as part of the design document

Building a robust evaluation process is essential for a machine learning (ML) system, and in this chapter, we will cover the process of building a proper validation schema to achieve confident estimates of system performance. We will touch upon typical validation schemas, as well as how to select the right validation based on the specifics of a given problem and what factors to consider when designing the evaluation process in the wild.

A proper validation procedure aims to imitate what knowledge we are supposed to have and what knowledge can be dropped while operating in a real-life environment. This is somewhat connected to the overfitting problem or generalization, which we'll cover in detail in chapter 9.

It also provides a reliable and robust estimation of a system's performance, ideally with some theoretical guarantees. As an example, we guarantee that a real value will be in the range between the lower confidence bound and upper confidence bound 95 times out of 100 (this case will be covered in a campfire story from Valerii later in the chapter). It also helps detect and prevent data leaks, overfitting, and divergence between offline and online performance.

Performance estimation is the primary goal of validation. We use validation to estimate the model's predictive power on unseen data, and the preferred schema is usually the one with the highest reliability and robustness (i.e., low bias/low variance).

As long as we have a reliable and robust performance estimation, we can use it for various things, like hyperparameter optimization, architecture, algorithm, and feature selection. To some extent, there is a similarity to A/B testing where schema yielding lower variance provides higher sensitivity, which we will cover later in the chapter.

7.1   Reliable evaluation

When validating anything, it is almost always a good idea to build a stable and reliable pipeline that produces repeatable results (see figure 7.1). Standard advice that you most probably can find in the literature comes down to the following three classic conditions: all you need to do is to split the data into training, validation, and test datasets. A training set is used for model training, a validation set is designed to evaluate performance during training, and a test set is used to calculate final metrics. This three-set approach is well known to those familiar with competitive ML (e.g., challenges hosted by Kaggle) or academia. At the same time, there are subtle but important distinctions within applied ML that we will discuss further in this chapter.

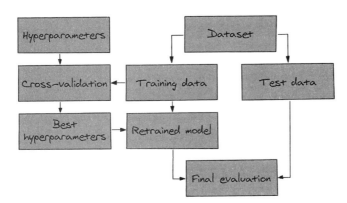

Figure 7.1   Basic high-level model development cycle

There are some points to pay attention to:

- A simple train-validation-test split assumes that all three datasets come from the same distribution and that this will hold in the future. This is a strong assumption that has to be validated by itself. If this assumption doesn't hold, there is no guarantee of future performance.

- There must be a repeatable use of the validation set to estimate model performance. Overestimating the model's performance based on the validation set leads to a bias and overfit toward this set. Stop and think: when we talk about things like hyperparameter optimization, feature selection, or model selection from a high-level perspective, it is basically a part of the learning process as well. By induction, the test set can be abused in the same manner.

That is why using the same validation split over and over again for evaluation and searching for optimal hyperparameters or anything else will lead to biased/overfitted and nonrobust results. For this reason, instead of viewing validation as the thing done once at the very beginning, we view it as a continuous process to be done repeatedly once the context of the system changes (e.g., there are new sources of data, new features, potential feedback loops caused by model usage, etc.).

We are never 100% sure what the world will bring next; that's why we must expect the unexpected.

7.2   Standard schemas

As practice shows, you won't need to reinvent the wheel when picking a validation schema for your ML system. Most of the standard schemas are time-tested and well-performing solutions that mostly require you to pick one that fits the requirements of your project. We will briefly cover these schemas in several subsections.

Classic validation schemas are well implemented in the evergreen Python ML library scikit-learn, and all the relevant documentation is worth reading if you have doubts about your knowledge of the material. The information is available at https://mng.bz/aV6B.

7.2.1   Holdout sets

We'll start by splitting the dataset into two or more chunks. Probably the golden classic mentioned in almost any book on ML is the training/validation/test split we discussed earlier.

With this approach, we partition data into three sets (it might be random or based on a specific criterion or strata) with different ratios—for example, 60/20/20 (see figure 7.2). The percentage may vary depending on the number of samples and metrics (the amount of data, metric variance, sensitivity, robustness, and reliability requirements). Empirically, the bigger the full dataset, the smaller the share that's dedicated to validation and testing, so the training set is growing faster. The test set (i.e., outer validation) is used for the final model evaluation and should never be used for any other purpose. Meanwhile, we can use the validation set (i.e., inner validation) primarily for model comparison or tuning hyperparameters.

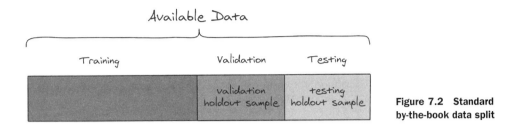

Figure 7.2 Standard by-the-book data split

7.2.2 Cross-validation

The holdout validation is a good choice for computationally expensive models, such as deep learning models. It is easy to implement and doesn't add much time to the learning loop.

But let's remember that we take a single random subsample from all the data. We are not reusing all available data that might lead to biased evaluation or underutilization of available data. What's the worst part? We get a single number that does not allow us to understand the distribution of the estimates.

The silver bullet for resolving such a problem in statistics is a bootstrap procedure. In the validation case, it would look like randomly sampling train validation splits many times, training and evaluating the model each iteration. Training a model is time-consuming, and we want to iterate quickly for general parameter tweaking and experimentation. So how can we do it?

We can use a similar but simplified sampling procedure called *cross-validation*. We can split data into K folds (usually five), exclude each of them one by one, fit the model to the K − 1 folds of data, and measure performance on the excluded fold. Hence, we get K estimates and can calculate their mean and standard deviation. As a result, we get five numbers instead of one, which is more representative (see figure 7.3).

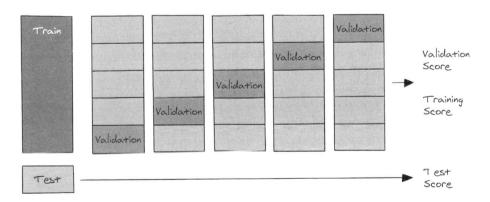

Figure 7.3 K-fold split: each sample is assigned to a fold, and each fold provides validation once and trains once in the rest of the training rounds.

There are several variations of cross-validation, including:

- *Stratified cross-validation* (we need to maintain the balance of classes).
- *Repeated cross-validation* (we split into K folds N times, so that each object participates in the evaluation N times).
- *Grouped cross-validation* (when objects are similar within groups, we may want to avoid a leak; the entire group must be fully included either in the training sample or in the validation sample).

Suppose we predict the flow rate of oil at hundreds of wells. Wells are grouped based on their location: neighboring wells extract oil from the same oil field, so their production affects each other. For this case, a grouped K-fold is a reasonable choice. Finding a proper criterion for grouping samples while assigning them to folds is one of the key decisions for validation overall, and mistakes here greatly affect the result.

7.2.3   *The choice of K*

The only question left is what number of folds to choose. The choice of K is dictated by three variables: bias, variance, and computation time. The rule of thumb is to use K = 5, which provides a good balance between bias and variance.

An extreme case for K is a leave-one-out cross-validation when each fold contains a single sample of data; thus K is equal to the overall number of samples in the dataset. This schema is the worst in terms of computation time and variance, but it's the best in terms of bias.

There is a classic paper by Ron Kohavi from 1995 titled "A Study of Cross-Validation and Bootstrap for Accuracy Estimation and Model Selection" (https://mng.bz/4pn5) that provides the following guidelines:

- Increasing the number of folds reduces bias and improves performance estimation.
- At the same time, variance increases along with the number of folds due to a lower number of samples in each validation fold (the estimates become too noisy). With an assumption of consistent bias, the sensitivity of the validation schema is determined by variance.
- Using repeated cross-validation for model comparison goals with K = 2 or K = 3 repeated 10 to 20 times is a good idea. However, for the bias optimization, repeated K-fold isn't helpful since estimates between different repeats already share consistent bias.
- The number of required folds naturally decreases with the growth of the dataset size. The more data you have in each fold, the more representative it is.
- For simpler models (which is the case when dealing with baseline solutions) and well-behaved datasets, you expect both bias and variance to decrease with the number of folds.

It is important to remember that the validation schema's high sensitivity (i.e., low variance) only matters when the changes we try to catch in the model's performance are small.

7.2.4 *Time-series validation*

When dealing with time-sensitive data, we can't sample data randomly. Sales of products on neighboring days share some information with each other. Similarly, recent user actions provide a hint on some aspects of their later actions. But we can't predict the past based on data from the future. In time series, the distribution of patterns is not uniform along the dataset, and we must figure out other kinds of validation schemas. How do we evaluate the model in this case?

Validation schemas used in time-series data are similar to the holdout set and cross-validation but with nonrandom splitting by timestamp. The recommendations for choosing the number of folds and their size in rolling cross-validation are similar to the ordinal K-fold.

Time-series validation adds several extra degrees of freedom that need to be considered. A great paper, "Evaluating Time Series Forecasting Models" by Cerqueira et al. (https://arxiv.org/pdf/1905.11744.pdf), elaborates on the following points:

- *Window size*—The size of the testing set should reflect how far we make the forecast and how long the model will stay in production before retraining.
- *Training size*—There are two options in regard to the amount of data used for training: we either use all available history or limit the training size to one or two previous periods (those can be weeks, months, or years, depending on a given seasonality) and discard all previous history as irrelevant.
- *Seasonality*—There are patterns in data that depend on cycles of days, weeks, months, quarters, or years. We should select sizes of testing and training sets accordingly to capture these patterns. For example, to capture yearly patterns, the training data should include at least 2 years of history. Another example is a weekly seasonality in a testing set: to minimize variance between folds, each should contain the same days of the week (so we take whole weeks in each fold).
- *Gap*—There can be a gap between training and testing data, which pursues two goals. First, it prepares us for a lag in receiving new data (which leads to a lag in features), and second, it makes training and testing data less correlated, thus minimizing the risk of a leak. For instance, we may skip 2 to 3 days between training and testing sets in both cases.

While time-series validation is one of the most defect-sensitive validation methods, relying solely on the simple "don't look at future data while training" rule would be far too shortsighted. Following this rule can save you from 95% of typical mistakes; still, there are cases where you may need to break it. For example, ML applied to financial data (such as stock market time series) is known for its high bar in precise validation requirements. At the same time, some experts in the area highlight that trivial time-series validation, as shown in figure 7.4, can lead to overfitting caused by limited data subsets (for more details, see "Backtesting Through Cross-Validation," chapter 12 of Marcos Lopez de Prado's *Advances in Financial Machine Learning*, Wiley). A similar reason to violate this rule may be rooted in your need to estimate how the model performs in anomaly scenarios. To get this signal, you can train the model on data from 2017 to 2019 and

2021 to 2023 and later test it on data from the COVID period of 2020. Such a split barely works as the default validation schema but still can be useful as auxiliary information.

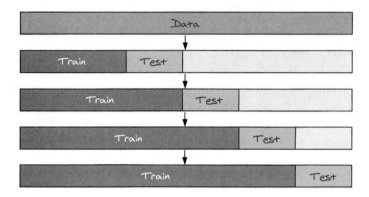

Figure 7.4   Standard time-based split. The test dataset always follows the train one, so train samples are "past" and test is "future."

Sometimes you need to use a combination of different schemas. In the earlier example of flow rate prediction, we might combine grouped K-fold validation with time-series validation:

```
import numpy as np
from sklearn.model_selection import GroupKFold

import numpy as np
from sklearn.model_selection import GroupKFold
from sklearn.exceptions import NotFittedError

def grouped_time_series_kfold(model, X, y, groups, n_folds=5,
n_repeats=10, seed=0):
    scores = []
    np.random.seed(seed)
    unique_groups = np.unique(groups)

    for i in range(n_repeats):
        gkf = GroupKFold(n_splits=n_folds)
        shuffled_groups = np.random.permutation(unique_groups)

        for train_group_idx, test_group_idx in gkf.split(X, y,
        groups=shuffled_groups):
            train_groups = shuffled_groups[train_group_idx]
            test_groups = shuffled_groups[test_group_idx]

            # Find the earliest and latest indices for train and test groups
            train_indices = np.where(np.isin(groups, train_groups))[0]
            test_indices = np.where(np.isin(groups, test_groups))[0]
            train_end = np.min(test_indices)
```

```
# Ensure temporal order
train_mask = np.isin(groups, train_groups) &
(np.arange(len(groups)) < train_end)
test_mask = np.isin(groups, test_groups)

model.fit(X[train_mask], y[train_mask])
score = model.score(X[test_mask], y[test_mask])
scores.append(score)

return np.array(scores)
```

Campfire story from Valerii

When I was working in the dynamic pricing service of a large online retailer, we were set to build a sales forecast model that would predict sales volumes 1 week ahead, along with postprocessing the predictions to determine optimal prices.

Initially, we took the previous week for validation. As new daily data became available, the validation week was shifted 1 day forward. However, it was observed that the performance metrics on the validation set showed significant fluctuations from day to day. This made it difficult to determine how the model's quality was changing in the context of periodic feature additions and adjustments, as well as changes to prediction postprocessing.

We wanted to understand the fluctuations in the metrics, and after thoroughly investigating the issue, we discovered that the variety of products changed by 15% week to week and by 40% month to month. Additionally, the sales dynamics of individual products were found to be highly heterogeneous (e.g., 10 units sold today but 0 units sold in the next 2 days). As a result, we relied on changes in the metric, which were caused by the daily updates to the validation set, rather than on actual changes in the model's quality.

To address this issue, we implemented a "delayed shift" validation approach. Instead of updating the validation set daily, we updated it once a month while still using a 1-week validation period. This ensured that the data used for calculating metrics remained relatively fresh (no older than 1 month) while keeping the validation set fixed for an entire month. Consequently, the comparison between the two models became more meaningful, and the performance metrics became far less noisy.

7.3   Nontrivial schemas

We've reviewed standard validation schemas that cover most ML applications. Sometimes they are not enough to reflect the actual difference between seen and unseen data, even if you use a combination of them (e.g., time-based validation with group K-fold). As you know, inadequate validation leads to data leakage and, consequently, too optimistic model performance estimation (if not random!).

Such situations require you to look for unorthodox processes. Let's review some of them.

7.3.1   *Nested validation*

Nested validation is an approach used when we want to run hyperparameter optimization (or any other model selection procedure) as part of the learning process. We can't just use an excluded fold or holdout set, which we will need for the final evaluation to estimate how good a given set of parameters is. Access to the score on the testing data while fitting any parameters is a direct way to overfitting.

Instead, we use a fold-in-fold schema. We add an "inner" split of training data in each "outer" split to tune the parameters first. Then we fit the model on all available training folds with selected hyperparameters and make a prediction for the data that was not seen during hyperparameter tuning. Thus, we get two layers of validation, each of which can have its specific properties (e.g., we may prefer the inner layer to have lower variance and the outer layer to have a lower bias). We can apply nesting not only to cross-validation but also to time-series validation and ordinal holdout split (or mixed schemas of different natures) (see figures 7.5 and 7.6).

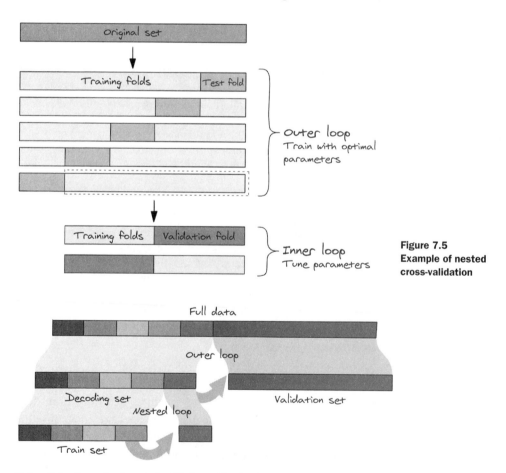

Figure 7.5
Example of nested cross-validation

Figure 7.6   Example of nested validation with mixed schemas: holdout split for the outer loop and K-fold for the inner loop

7.3.2 Adversarial validation

Instead of using a random subsample of data like in a standard holdout set, you may prefer to choose a different path. There is a technique called adversarial validation, a popular approach on ML competition platforms such as Kaggle. It applies an ML model for better validation of another ML model.

Adversarial validation numerically estimates whether two given datasets differ (those two may be sets of labeled and unlabeled data). And, if so, it can even quantify it on the sample level, making it possible to construct an arbitrary number of datasets, representative of each other, providing a perfect tool for estimation. An additional bonus is that it does not require data to be labeled.

The algorithm is simple:

1 We combine datasets of interest (cutting off the target variable, if present), labeling the anchor dataset (the one we want to represent) as 1 and marking the rest as 0.

2 We fit an auxiliary model on this concatenated dataset to solve the binary classification task (thus 0 and 1 marks).

3 If datasets are representative of each other and come from the same distribution, we could expect receiver operating characteristic area under the curve (ROC AUC) to be near 0.5. If they are separable (e.g., ROC AUC is greater than 0.6), then we can use the output from the model as a measure of proximity.

Note that while this trick was used in ML competitions for a long time (the first mention we found has been there since 2016, http://fastml.com/adversarial-validation-part-one/), it was not part of more formal research until 2020 when it appeared in the paper "Adversarial Validation Approach to Concept Drift Problem in User Targeting Automation Systems at Uber" by Pan et al. (https://arxiv.org/abs/2004.03045).

We can use this kind of splitting in many cases. When we're checking the similarity of labeled and unlabeled datasets, there are questions we should keep in mind. How different are their distributions? What features are the best predictors of this difference? Analyzing the model created by adversarial validation may answer these questions. We will also reuse this technique for a similar matter in chapter 9.

7.3.3 Quantifying dataset leakage exploitation

We find an interesting validation technique in a paper by DeepMind titled "Improving Language Models by Retrieving from Trillions of Tokens (2021; https://arxiv.org/abs/2112.04426), which proposes a generative model trained on the next-word-prediction task.

The paper's authors enhance the language model by conditioning it on a context retrieved from a large corpus based on local similarity with preceding tokens. This system memorizes the entire dataset and performs the nearest-neighbors search to find chunks of text in the history that are relevant to the recent sentences. But what if the sentences we try to continue are almost identical to those the model has seen in the training set? It looks like there is a high probability of encountering dataset leakage.

The authors discussed this problem in advance and proposed a noteworthy evaluation procedure. They developed a specific measure to quantify leakage exploitation.

The general idea is the following:

1   Partition the dataset into training and validation sets as in the usual holdout validation.

2   Split both into chunks of fixed length.

3   For each chunk in the validation set, retrieve N nearest neighbors from the training set based on chunk embeddings (here we will omit how chunks are transformed into embedding space, but you can find the details in the paper).

4   Calculate the ratio of tokens that are common in the two chunks (they use a score similar to the Jaccard Index); this gives us a score ranging from 0 (a chunk is totally different) to 1 (a chunk is a duplicate).

5   If this score exceeds a certain threshold, filter out this chunk from the training set.

This approach forces the model to retrieve useful information from similar texts and paraphrase it instead of copy-pasting it. You can use this procedure with any modern language model. It is a good example of an exotic technique that allows for minimizing data leakage and increasing the representativity of your dataset. A clear understanding of how the model will be applied will help you develop your own nontrivial validation schema if standard approaches are unsuitable.

7.4   *Split updating procedure*

> *We spend as much time on the test data as on the training data.*
>
> — Andrej Karpathy

Regardless of which schema we use, we will probably apply it to a dynamically changing dataset. Periodically we get new data that may differ in distribution and include new patterns. How often should we update the test set to make sure our evaluation is always relevant?

There are at least two goals we may want to reach while designing a split update procedure for new data. First, we want our test set to be representative of these new patterns. From this point of view, the evaluation process should be adaptive.

Second, we want to see an evaluation dynamic: how has the model been changing through time with all updates in the architecture or features? For that, the estimates must be robust.

Some of the most common options are as follows (see figure 7.7):

- *Fixed shift*—When dealing with data that has a strong dependence on time and novelty, we are not interested in evaluating the model's performance on data

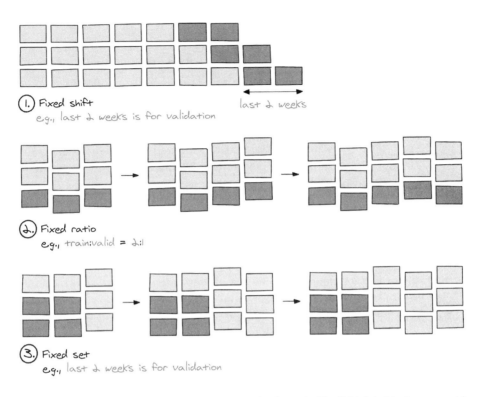

Figure 7.7 Common options for updating train/validation sets. The light data blocks are used for training, while the dark ones are used for validation.

from a year ago or older due to the drastic change in target distribution. Instead, we would like to use only recent data for validation.

For instance, we take the last 2 weeks as a validation set (starting from the last finished day) and update this set daily while retraining the model used for evaluation each time.

- *Fixed ratio*—When dealing with images or text, we don't gather new labels for data regularly. In contrast to the first case, we may have no strong dependence on data recency, meaning that newly added data may not be more important than the old data. Typically we expand the set of available data after receiving an extra portion of labels.

  If we include newly labeled data only in the training set, we increase metrics due to more data available for the model. If we include this data only in the validation set, the model may miss some unseen patterns. The optimal solution is to keep the ratio between training and validation dataset sizes unchanged so that newly added data will be split accordingly.

- *Fixed set*—Sometimes, instead of a balanced subset of all currently available data, we would like to evaluate our model's quality on an unchanged "golden set" used as a benchmark. This approach guarantees that the two models are still comparable in terms of any metric, even if there is a long modeling period between them.

  This fixed set can be sampled from the dataset before modeling or cherry-picked manually to contain a diverse range of hard cases and reference responses. It is not supposed to be updated by design to ensure consistent model comparison. If we extend this golden set in the future, we will treat it as a completely new benchmark.

Remember: we should perform validation on the whole pipeline, including the dataset; inference on the test set should be the same as in production. If we want to compare models side by side accurately, we should somehow save previous versions of both datasets and models. Tools for data version control and model version control (such as DVC, Git LFS, or Deep Lake) may be of help.

Once there are clues that the options here do not cover your particular use case, you may want to dive deeper into the literature dedicated to dynamic (nonstationary) data streams and concept drifts to get a holistic overview of related theory (e.g., "Scarcity of Labels in Non-Stationary Data Streams: A Survey" [https://mng.bz/gAXE]). We will also touch on the surface of the concept drift problem in chapter 11 as one of the underlying reasons why setting up a reliable validation schema is not easy.

Campfire story from Valerii

When I was working in a big tech company, we would train a number of ML models on a local ML platform to catch spammers, scammers, scrapers, and other malevolent agents. However, the platform only produced point estimates when assessing model performance on the validation set. This turned out to be a problem, as offline estimation often was significantly different from online performance, creating either a considerable number of falsely banned users or wrong expectations.

To illustrate the point estimate problem, let's take a coin toss example.

If we flip a fair coin 100 times, we can calculate the number of times it lands heads. That is our point estimate. If we do it again, we will end up with another number. If, instead, we say that 95 out of 100 times, we expect this number to be within the range of 40 to 60, this is a confidence interval. The lower confidence bound will be 40, meaning that we expect this number to be at least 40 in 95% of cases.

The point estimate lacks robustness, as it does not consider an ever-present uncertainty, which is easy to illustrate graphically. The plots in the following figures demonstrate the variance of the two metrics, precision and recall, using the same threshold, ML classifier, and validation data generated by the same distribution on offline data.

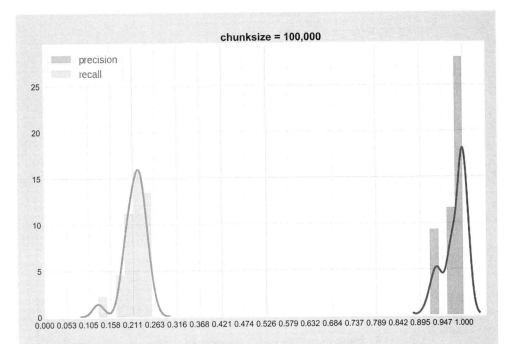

Distribution of precision and recall with sample size equal to 100,000; every point is an independent dataset.

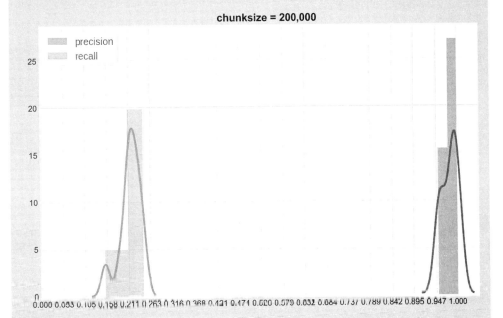

Distribution of precision and recall with sample size equal to 200,000; every point is an independent dataset.

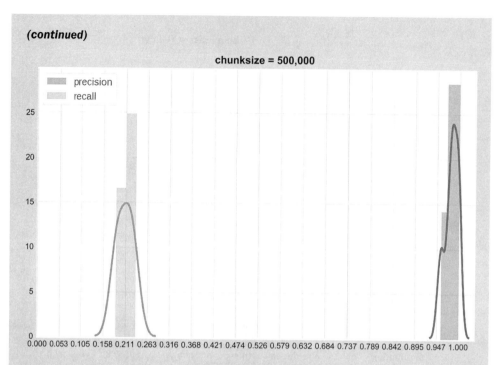

Distribution of precision and recall with sample size equal to 500,000; every point is an independent dataset

It was no surprise that when we compared offline point estimates and online performance, they were almost always far apart. Even within offline evaluation, the variance was huge even when the validation data size was 500,000. This situation lacks robustness and creates fragility in the whole system.

With chunks of test data, it is easy to show uncertainty for precision, recall, or other metrics. Still, there are better ways to do this. The gold standard would be random sampling with replacement or, in other words, bootstrap. Unfortunately, bootstrap is very computationally expensive. For each bootstrap iteration (between 10,000 and 100,000), we have to sample the multinomial distribution of length N (with the sample size reaching thousands or millions) and do this N times.

This proved to be a problem. On the one hand, I couldn't use the existing estimation solution provided by the platform, as it needed to be more reliable and robust. On the other hand, integrating bootstrap into every validation step was also impossible, as it would make even a single training loop run too long.

The solution came from math. Suppose we review each sample independently and run bootstrap in parallel. In that case, we can switch from multinomial sampling to binomial(n,1/n) and independently sample each observation for each bootstrap iteration. With N >> 100, sampling a Poisson with lambda parameter = 1 becomes a close approximation of binomial(n,1/n)—in other words, binomial(n,1/n) ~ Poisson(1) with N >>100. (You can find more details at https://mng.bz/0myR.)

No N exists in Poisson(1), making it completely independent of the data size and easy to parallel. This significantly increased speed (circa 100–1,000 times in my case with some additional tricks).

We can pick a confidence bound to hold once we have distribution for the metric of interest. In the following figure, we can see a 99% lower confidence bound. On average, 99 times out of 100, recall will not be lower than 0.071.

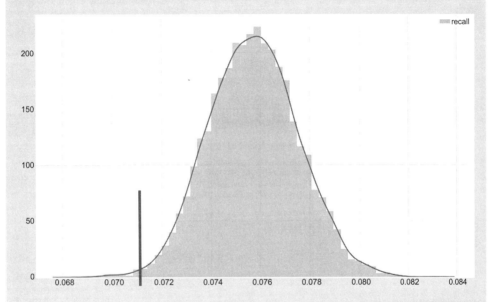

Distribution recall with every point being a bootstrapped original dataset; the red line is a 99% lower confidence bound.

There is one more thing to take into consideration here. Some metrics, including precision and recall, depend on the threshold we pick to calculate them. The following figures demonstrate the distributions of precision and recall with and without some minor noise (normally distributed with mean = 0 and standard deviation −0.0125) applied to the samples.

It is easy to see that the results with and without applied noise differ significantly, with increased recall and decreased precision in the latter. In a sense, these plots prove that in this case, the decision boundary margin is narrow and not robust. Adding some noise as a hyperparameter helps to estimate the distribution confidence intervals with increased trust in decision boundary robustness.

(continued)

Distribution without noise

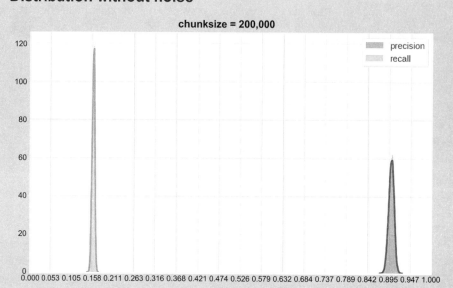

Distribution of precision and recall with sample size of 200;000; every point is a bootstrapped original dataset, no noise added.

Distribution with noise

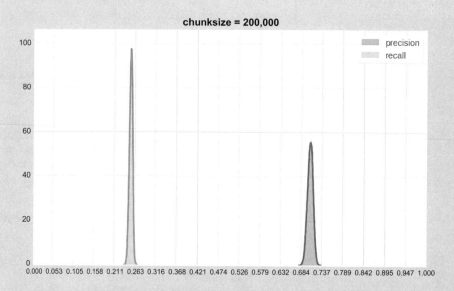

Distribution of precision and recall with a sample size of 200,000; every point is a bootstrapped original dataset, noise added.

Estimating recall at a given precision/specificity is nothing new, but combined with Poisson bootstrap and noise addition, it created new metrics: bootstrapped lower confidence bound of recall at a given precision and bootstrapped lower confidence bound of recall at a given specificity. These metrics provided guaranteed (within a specific confidence level), reliable, and robust estimation of ML model performance.

Metrics embedded into a native ML platform

7.5   Design document: Choosing validation schemas

Time for another block of the design document, and this time we will fill in the information about preferred validation schemas for both Supermegaretail and PhotoStock Inc.

7.5.1   Validation schemas for Supermegaretail

We start with Supermegaretail.

DESIGN DOCUMENT: SUPERMEGARETAIL

IV. VALIDATION SCHEMA

I. REQUIREMENTS

What are the assumptions that we need to pay attention to when figuring out the evaluation process?

- New data is coming daily.
- Data can arrive with a delay of up to 48 hours.
- New labels (number of units sold) come with the new data.
- Recent data is most probably more relevant for the prediction task.
- The assortment matrix changes by 15% every month.
- There's seasonality present in the data (weekly/annual cycles).

Despite the fact that the data is naturally divided into categories, it is irrelevant to the choice of validation schema.

II. INFERENCE

After fixing a model (within the hyperparameter optimization procedure), we train it on the last 2 years of data and predict future demand for the next 4 weeks. This process is fully reproduced in both inner and outer validation.

It is important to note that there should be a gap of 3 days between training and validation sets to be prepared for the fact that data may arrive with a delay. Subsequently, this will affect which features we can and cannot calculate when building a model.

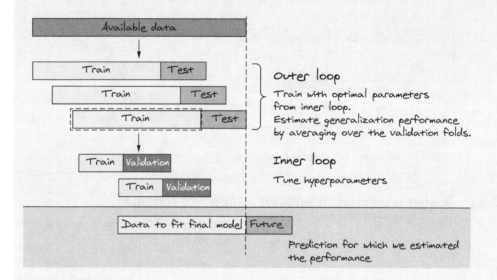

III. INNER AND OUTER LOOPS

We use two layers of validation. The outer loop is used for the final estimation of the model's performance, while the inner loop is used for hyperparameter optimization.

First, for the outer loop, given that we are working with time series, rolling cross-validation is an obvious choice. We set K = 5 to train five models with optimal parameters. Since we are predicting 4 weeks ahead, the validation window size also consists of 28 days in all splits. There is a gap of 3 days between sets, and the step size is 7 days.

The following is an example of the outer loop:

- First outer fold:
  - Data for the testing is from 2022-10-10 to 2022-11-06 (4 weeks).
  - Data for the training is from 2020-10-07 to 2022-10-06 (2 years).
- Second outer fold:
  - Data for the testing is from 2022-10-03 to 2022-10-30.
  - Data for the training is from 2020-09-29 to 2022-09-28.
- Fifth outer fold:
  - Data for the testing is from 2022-09-12 to 2022-10-09.

– Data for the training is from 2020-09-09 to 2022-09-08.

Second, for the inner loop, inside each "train set" of the outer validation, we perform additional rolling cross-validation with a three-fold split. Each inner loop training sample consists of a 2-year history as well to capture both annual and weekly seasonality. We use the inner loop to tune hyperparameters or for feature selection.

The following is an example of the inner loop:

- Second fold of the outer loop:
  – Training data for the second outer fold is from 2020-10-03 to 2022-10-02.
- First inner fold:
  – Data for the testing is from 2022-09-05 to 2022-10-02 (4 weeks).
  – Data for the training is from 2020-09-02 to 2022-09-01 (2 years).
- Second inner fold:
  – Data for the testing is from 2022-08-29 to 2022-9-25.
  – Data for the training is from 2020-08-26 to 2022-08-25.
- Third inner fold:
  – Data for the testing is from 2022-08-22 to 2022-09-18.
  – Data for the training is from 2020-08-19 to 2022-08-18.

If the model does not require model tuning yet, we can skip the inner loop.

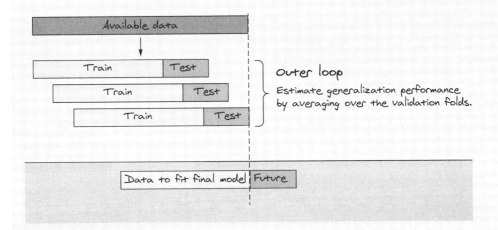

IV. UPDATE FREQUENCY

We update the split weekly along with new data and labels (so that each validation set always consists of a whole week). This will help us catch local changes and trends in model performance.

Additionally, we have a separate holdout set as a benchmark (a "golden set"). We update it every 3 months. It helps us track long-term improvements in our system.

7.5.2   *Validation schemas for PhotoStock Inc.*

We will now add the information on validation schemas for PhotoStock Inc.

DESIGN DOCUMENT: PHOTOSTOCK INC.

IV. VALIDATION SCHEMA

Search query is the main object of validation. There are four main caveats to keep in mind when planning a validation strategy for the PhotoStock Inc. search engine:

- Validation and test sets should be representative of the production data; in other words, they should represent real user queries.
- Validation and test sets should be diverse; in other words, they should cover as wide a range of topics and contexts as possible.
- Queries by the same user should only appear in either the training, validation, or test sets but not in multiple sets, so we avoid data leakage.
- Duplicate queries should be removed from the dataset to avoid data leakage.

Thus, we suggest using the following splitting strategy:

1 Group queries by user; each query is assigned to a user once. If another user has the same query, it's ignored.
2 Random-split users into training, validation, and test sets with a fixed ratio (to be determined; we don't know what ratio is the best, but we can start with 90/5/5).
3 Assign new users to their split once and never change it.

Random split assignment should address potential distribution skewness in the data. For example, we may guess there is a seasonality effect in searches (weekend users are amateurs, while weekday users are professionals) and there is some distribution drift over time (new topics emerge; old topics fade away). The random split should address those issues, although additional analysis is required to confirm that.

To assign splits to users, we suggest using a deterministic bucketing approach: we split users into buckets based on their user_id hash and then assign each bucket to a split. This approach is universal because it allows the split ratio to change in the future. For example, if we want to increase the size of the validation set, we can just assign more buckets to the validation set from the training set.

The following is an example of the bucketing approach:

```
def assign_bucket(user_id):
    _hash = sha1(user_id.encode()).hexdigest()
    return int(_hash, 16) % n_buckets

def assign_split(user_id):
    bucket = assign_bucket(user_id)
    if bucket < n_buckets * train_ratio:
        return 'train'
    elif bucket < n_buckets * (train_ratio + val_ratio):
        return 'val'
```

```
    else:
        return 'test'
```

For the initial project phase, we don't plan to add more subsets (e.g., "the golden set"), although we can't exclude this possibility in the future.

Summary

- Use validation schemas as a way to measure your model's predictive power accurately.
- Try to avoid using the same validation split repeatedly for evaluation and searching for optimal hyperparameters, as it may lead to biased/overfitted and nonrobust results.
- Try to design a validation schema to reflect how the model is applied in practice.
- When looking for a needed number of K folds, base your choice on the following three variables: bias, variance, and computation time.
- To do this, consider how the data differs between seen and unseen data (whether there are groups, classes, time, or other essential properties you should take into account).
- Design a nonstandard schema to fit a particular problem if necessary.
- Remember that different schemas for different goals can work together nicely.

Baseline solution 8

Everything should be made as simple as possible, but not simpler.

— Albert Einstein

When we start to think about the building blocks of our future machine learning (ML) system, the essential part of it, or core component of it, seems to be a model built using ML techniques. In some sense, this is so true that we may even think that "this is it: this is the primary point where I should spend most of my time, energy, and creative power."

But in reality, this may turn out to be a trap that the majority of ML projects fall into and get bogged down in without ever reaching production. An ML model is not necessarily the most important thing in the context of an ML system and its

136

design document. Although the temptation is great, you should always keep in mind that it is extremely easy to spend a lot of time, team effort, and, more importantly, money on building a cool, modern, and sophisticated AI model that doesn't ever bring any value to users and your company. A mediocre model in production is usually better than a great model on paper.

One of the first versions of this book's title was *Machine Learning System Design That Works*, and it corresponds to the primary goal of any ML project, which is to build a system that will work; only then, when it brings profit, will we start to iteratively improve it while gradually increasing its complexity (if needed). In this chapter, we will discuss the baseline solution, the first step in bringing our system to life. We will cover why baselines are needed, as well as the purpose of building them. We will go all the way from constant baselines to sophisticated specialized models and also through various feature baselines.

8.1 Baseline: What are you?

A baseline is the simplest possible (but working!) version of a model, feature set, or anything else in your system. It's the minimum viable product (MVP) in the world of ML systems that brings value from the start without yet diving into complexity. Let's elaborate a bit more on the MVP analogy by outlining key goals that may equally apply to both:

- *Reduce the maximum risk with the lowest amount of time, cost, and effort invested in a product.* At the beginning of the product's life, it is still unclear whether the market needs it, what use cases the product will have, whether the economy will converge, and so on. To a large extent, these risks are peculiar to ML products, too. In a way, a baseline (or MVP) is the easiest way to test a hypothesis that lies at the heart of your product.
- *Get early feedback.* This is the fail-fast principle cut down to the product scale. If the whole idea of your ML system is wrong, you can see it at an early stage, rethink the entire plan, rewrite the design document with new knowledge, and start anew.
- *Bring user value as soon as possible.* Each company aims to generate revenue by making its customers happy. If we can bring value to customers early with a baseline and then update it stage by stage while generating a predictable amount of money, why not do this? It will leave everyone in the equation satisfied.

These three points form the grand basis of similarities between a baseline and an MVP. However, there are three more purely baseline-specific goals:

- *A placeholder to check that components work properly*—Baselines are like smoke tests. As Cem Kaner, James Bach, and Brett Pettichord once said in their *Lessons Learned in Software Testing*, the phrase "smoke test" comes from electronic hardware testing. You plug in a new board and turn on the power. If you see smoke coming from the board, turn off the power. You don't have to do any more testing.

First you want to check whether the system works and, second, whether it works correctly. To "compile" the whole system, you don't need a powerful ML model. You need something that predicts something with the required format, optionally, based on something. Why not choose the easiest possible alternative?

- *A thing to compare with*—Shall we go further and think about how much our investment in the model could pay in the future? The baseline is a "base line." It is the origin of the coordinate plane—something we compare new models with in terms of some metrics.

  When working in the industry, the model's performance is not the only metric by which we compare models. Others require effort, interpretability, maintainability, and so on. We'll cover them in section 8.5.

- *A fallback answer*—Unlike MVP, when we move on to its second and subsequent versions, we don't throw out the baseline completely. It is good practice when it lives in parallel with the sophisticated model. The system switches to the baseline response when this primary model goes south while making a prediction.

So what are the advantages of a well-chosen baseline? Simplicity automatically brings a lot of pros with it: it is robust, not prone to unexpected behavior and overfitting (due to fewer degrees of freedom), easy to build and maintain, and not too pressing on computing resources. Consequently, baselines are easy to scale. As an additional bonus, from non-ML colleagues' perspective, simple models are easier to interpret and make it less difficult to understand what is going on under the hood. It can help increase trust in our ML product, which can be critical when the stakes are high. However, simplicity is not a goal by itself but a valuable property.

If we think of our ML system as a Lego model, a baseline is an opportunity to assemble all the other blocks as fast as possible. Still, we encourage you to make your system as modular (i.e., "orthogonal") as possible by design. This will make later updates easier, including the transition to more complex models and features (initial design doesn't dictate how fast you can update a system in the future). The initial system should be simple and agile, not trivial or restricted, with a baseline.

Still, despite all the advantages baselines provide without requiring a lot, they are not used as often as they deserve. The bitter truth is that, unfortunately, complexity sells better. There is a brilliant article from Eugene Yan that we strongly recommend reading. It's called "Simplicity Is an Advantage But Sadly Complexity Sells Better" (https://eugeneyan.com/writing/simplicity/), highlighting the main reasons why many choose complexity over simplicity, which are:

- Complexity signals effort.
- Complexity signals mastery.
- Complexity signals innovation.

- Complexity signals more features.

This leads to complexity bias, where we give undue credit to and favor complex ideas and systems over simpler solutions.

Of course, baselines are not a silver bullet, and there are reasonable cases when baselines are not necessary or are even irrelevant:

- *Accuracy is crucial.* In many cases, an error of a couple of percentage points will not even be noticed. But if we can't afford decreased quality—for example, in some medical applications like cancer detection or when dealing with autonomous cars—a baseline will be a bad life-saving rope. In this case, explicit switching to manual control would be a better idea.
- *There is a high degree of certainty.* We clearly understand what the user wants (for example, based on a competitor's experience), or we have our own experience of implementing identical systems. In this case, we don't need to reinvent the wheel and waste our time on gradual iterations if we have a plan already proven in battle and can just copy-paste the system.
- *We are rebuilding an already-working system.* Suppose we already have a working search engine based on the deep semantic similarity model (DSSM) architecture. The whole pipeline is already implemented and tested. So when it consistently brings value to users, it is a good time for optimization in terms of speed and accuracy—for example, by switching to a Transformer-based model. It is not the right place to think about baselines because the old version is effectively a baseline.

Still, we believe that even if complexity at an early stage can be justified in certain cases, it can't be the go-to solution by default because it incentivizes people to make things unnecessarily complicated; it encourages the "not invented here" mindset, where people prefer to build from scratch and avoid reusing existing components even though it saves time and effort, and it wastes time and resources while often leading to poorer outcomes.

That is why we believe a baseline solution is the first thing to do, with incremental improvements where and when needed.

8.2 Constant baselines

A good metaphor for a baseline is building a bridge: sometimes you don't need a team of bridge construction engineers, huge budgets, plans, or years to build it. Sometimes you just need a stably fixed log. A baseline is the very log that allows you to connect components and solve a given task at a minimal scale—in the case of a baseline, a temporary, primitive, easy-to-build solution (see figure 8.1).

The idea we want to convey before going into detail is simple: build a lean, operable ML system first, and improve it later. Think of the complexity of possible solutions as a continuum. Choose an appropriate initial point in this range based on the effort–accuracy tradeoff, and move ahead. Don't spend too much time on modeling unless it's necessary.

Figure 8.1   Before building a complicated model, start with a primitive baseline, which may well be the most appropriate foundation for your future ML system.

Keeping in mind that analogy, let's start the discussion with the most spartan solutions that look like a log bridge. When we initiate a search for a suitable baseline, we often ask ourselves, "What is the most straightforward ML model that could solve the problem?" or "What is the right ML model to start from?" but frequently these questions turn out to be the wrong ones to ask. We believe the right one could sound like, "Do we need ML at all to solve this problem?"

Sometimes we either don't even need ML for the problem or at least should not reinvent the wheel on our own and can instead use a third-party vendor. We already discussed this alternative in chapter 3 (section 3.2).

But let's say we decided to build our own model. Good modeling starts with no model at all: with trying to hack a defined metric by picking the most trivial and lazy solution from the solution space. It will be the very first approximation of our problem. You can argue that a constant baseline represents a model by itself. With a constant baseline, we approximate all dependencies and interactions by a constant.

To immediately give an idea of what we are talking about, here are a couple of examples that you already know:

- For regression tasks, constant baselines are average or median predictions (in time-series forecasting, you can take both by last day/week/month/year) by the last available value (e.g., for the corresponding user or item). Also, this could be some user-defined constant that maximizes the metric.

- For classification tasks, it will be prediction by the major class (let's say, in the antifraud problem, we can assume that there is no fraud at all) or the constant prediction of the probability of a positive class.
- For ranking, this could be either a random order of documents or sorting based on an irrelevant numerical property like document ID or a simple heuristic like "number of queried keywords contained in an item description."

In a way, a constant baseline is like the first term in the Taylor Series or the mean predictor as the first base estimator in gradient boosting (see figure 8.2). Neither even depends on variable x; they already do (although roughly) something related to our problem—no more, no less.

$$\boxed{f(x) = f(c)} + f'(c)(x - c) + \frac{f''(c)}{2!}(x - c)^2 + \dots$$

Figure 8.2   A constant baseline is like the first term of the Taylor Series—the simplest approximation that sets the foundation for more complex models.

8.2.1   Why do we need constant baselines?

There are two goals for building such a baseline.

The first one is benchmarking. It is helpful to get a baseline value of a selected metric for a random prediction. A simple sanity check compares your model against simple rules of thumb. Indeed, it would be sad to do 2 weeks of hardcore ML modeling and then finally implement the most straightforward possible baseline in 5 minutes that beats your model. It sounds ridiculous, but the situation is quite common in real life.

There's a cool story from Valerii about this case. He was lucky enough to work with an engineer who is a wonderful person and a great specialist. Once, she won an ML competition with the goal of predicting some factory time series with just a constant baseline—or, as she likes to correct him, a stepwise constant. Conducting ML competitions is usually a very straightforward process. Participants have a labeled dataset and an unlabeled dataset. Their goal is to build a model using the labeled dataset that will output predictions to the unlabeled dataset that are the closest to the actual ones (available to the organizers only). Now imagine the frustration of other participants who have been engineering dozens of features for months and tuning parameters of their gradient-boosting models.

This case inspired us to look for and start with the simplest models, and this is something we'd like to encourage everyone to do. Don't limit yourself to them, though. It will give you a much more adequate understanding of your metric and target values from the beginning so you can get a vision of what can be done with given data and what cannot.

The second goal of constant baselines is to provide a bulletproof fallback. If your real ML model could not make a prediction during runtime, due to some raised error, because of running into response-time constraints, or because there is no history for calculating features (aka the cold start problem with new users and new items)—or it simply goes crazy (which sometimes happens)—your ML service should return at least something. So, in this case, a constant baseline is all you need.

At the same time, we can easily imagine situations where a constant baseline is too primitive and brings no value at all. So the simplest usable baseline should be more complicated, represented as a set of heuristics/regular expressions or as a shallow model. Constant baselines tend to work fine for simple regression/classification problems on tabular or small text data; however, it is impossible to build a chatbot or voice recognition system with a constant baseline.

8.3   *Model baselines and feature baselines*

If we move further along the complexity scale, our next stop is rule-based models, although it is not always possible to draw a clear line between constant baselines and rule-based ones, as in most cases we can define the last one as a constant on top of some grouping. But there is also another well-known and illustrative example of rule-based baselines: to start solving natural language processing problems with just regular expressions.

A couple of years ago, Arseny worked for a taxi aggregator company, where he was involved in developing a service that would predict the time it would take for the nearest car to get to a client. The problem was apparent: if we overpredicted, the client could decide not to wait and would look for another service; if we underpredicted, the client would wait longer than we promised, which would mean we disappointed them.

Arseny's colleague, who was a senior engineer at the time, treated it like a standard regression task and started with models like "always predict 5 minutes" or "if borough == 'manhattan': return 4." Long story short: these types of baselines were hard to beat with hardcore ML alchemy, and ironically, the latter was even in production for a while as a fallback.

The "if district == X: return Y" model is an excellent example of a rule-based baseline. We can generate similar models by taking the mean/median/mode of some category or several categories—in our example, the median by location.

The further we go down the progression, the more complex our model gets and the more connections between objects' properties and the labels it can find.

A typical sequence of baselines in an ML problem would begin with the following: constant baseline, rule-based baseline, and linear model (see figure 8.3). We need something more sophisticated and specialized only if these baselines are insufficient for our task.

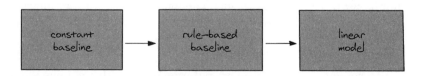

Figure 8.3   A typical sequence of baselines at the early stage of designing your model

For example, when building a recommender system, we start with some constant retrieval, then try collaborative filtering (e.g., alternate least squares), factorization machines, and, finally, deep learning (e.g., deep structured semantic model) if needed.

Whatever problem you face, be aware of simple approaches in this field. They don't necessarily perform worse than more sophisticated ones.

A vivid example of that can be found in the paper called "Are We Really Making Much Progress? A Worrying Analysis of Recent Neural Recommendation Approaches" by Maurizio Ferrari Dacrema et al. (https://arxiv.org/abs/1907.06902) that took RecSys' Best Paper Award in 2019 (https://recsys.acm.org/best-papers/). The paper is notable for unveiling strikingly impressive stats. The research group examined 18 algorithms that had been presented at top-level research conferences in the preceding years. After studying these algorithms, only seven of them could be reproduced with reasonable effort. Things got even more interesting when it turned out that six out of seven algorithms could often be outperformed using relatively simple heuristic methods (e.g., those based on nearest-neighbor or graph-based techniques). The only remaining algorithm clearly outclassed baselines; however, it could not consistently outperform a well-tuned nonneural linear ranking method.

A nonexhaustive list of examples from the already-mentioned Eugene Yan article includes the following:

- Tree-based models (random forest, gradient boosting) in most cases beat deep neural networks on tabular data, especially on small/medium datasets (say, < 1 million) (https://arxiv.org/abs/2207.08815).
- Greedy algorithms outperform graph neural networks on combinatorial graph problems (https://arxiv.org/abs/2206.13211).
- Simple averaging is often not worse than complex optimizers on multitask learning problems (https://arxiv.org/abs/2201.04122).
- A dot product of embeddings outperforms neural collaborative filtering in item recommendation and retrieval (https://arxiv.org/abs/2005.09683).

Up to now, we have been talking about baselines focusing on models. But what about features? Features are effectively a part of the model and sometimes are even the most important part of it. In classic ML, we have to engineer features manually, and choosing features for a baseline is based on the same principles; we start with a small group of essential features (most likely, those that are easier to calculate). There are two ways of adding new features:

- Engineering new features, which is challenging and time consuming and requires building new ETL pipelines
- Generating features that derive from ones that already exist

The sequence of baseline features we need to try should look like this: the original minimum set of features, all sorts of interactions and counters, then embeddings, and then something more complicated (see figure 8.4).

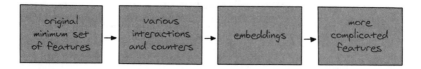

Figure 8.4 A sequence of baseline features you need to try: from the simplest to the more complicated

What are the properties of a good bunch of features to start from? The answer is exactly the same as for the models, and we'll discuss it further.

For a typical problem usually solved with deep learning methods, there can be a simple baseline built with shallow models. As we recall, deep learning is a part of representation learning, which means that instead of handcrafting features, we delegate this work to a neural network. However, for some problems like image or text classification, you can apply naive approaches (rule-based or linear model-based). For example, naive Bayes was a very strong baseline in a natural language processing world before BERT-like architectures emerged. For computer vision, some problems can be solved by using a histogram of pixel color (or even just mean/median value!) as features for a linear model. Having said that, for most scenarios, starting with a simple deep learning model—either foundational in a few-shot setup or a trained one—can be a better choice because these models have already proven themselves in a wide variety of tasks.

Arseny once designed a take-home exercise for candidates, where they were provided with a script solving anomaly detection problems on a simple image dataset. The script contained two baselines—one with a neural network and one with a color histogram—and candidates were instructed to improve either of them to beat some metric. Both baselines already performed on a similar level, and both were implemented specifically poorly, so the candidates had room for improvement. The majority of candidates preferred working on a more complicated deep learning solution, and only the most experienced of them noticed that it was possible to reach the required result with a single line of code changed for a histogram-based baseline.

8.4 *Variety of deep learning baselines*

When a problem is not trivial and suggests the use of deep learning because of the data structure (which can be applicable to most computer vision or language processing problems), the variety of baselines is slightly different. The most common are reusing pretrained models and training/fine-tuning the simplest models.

Reusing pretrained models is a common practice if a problem is not unique and there is a model that has been trained on a similar task. For example, if we want to train a model that can recognize breeds of pets, we can reuse a model that was trained on an ImageNet dataset. ImageNet is a dataset that contains images of 1,000 classes, and more than 100 of them are dog breeds. So, once your goal is to recognize cats and dogs, you can reuse a model that was trained on ImageNet dataset without retraining it. This is a common practice for many generic problems like speech recognition, object detection, text classification, sentiment analysis, end so on.

A slightly more advanced version of this approach is reusing features (also known as *embeddings* or *representations*) from a pretrained model to train a simple shallow model. For example, you can take a pretrained model that was trained on an Image-Net dataset and use its representations from the last backbone layer (before the final classification layer) to train a simple linear model that will classify images into a custom set of classes. This approach is especially useful when the dataset is small and the final task is more or less trivial (e.g., classification), so training large models from scratch is not likely to work. This approach is also known as a specific case of transfer learning. We have seen cases where such a baseline was literally unbeatable, and no fancy models were able to outperform it.

An even more specific version of using pretraining models is using pretrained models or third-party APIs capable of zero-shot or few-shot performance (meaning they require no or a few training samples to provide a result). A glorified example of such an API is the GPT family, but there are many APIs available for different tasks—for example, all major cloud vendors have a long list of AI solutions, such as Amazon Rekognition or Google Cloud Vision AI in the computer vision niche; detailed information about them is out of the scope of this book.

Using a third-party API by a major vendor as a baseline has a nice side effect: it is a bargaining chip in negotiations, such as selling a software product to a big enterprise or proving a startup tech is solid to potential investors. Potential customers may not know what a good metric is for a given problem (recall chapter 5), but comparing your tech to an AWS solution frames the problem in a proper way. Arseny knows at least three startups that have used this approach, bragging about how they beat alternatives such as Amazon, Google, and OpenAI. In all three cases, the companies' claims were legit, and that's expected, as major vendors aim to tailor one-size-fits-all solutions, while startups can offer more niche ML systems doing one thing just great.

Finally, if none of these options work, you can try to train a simple model from scratch. However, it is recommended to avoid recent state-of-the-art models and use something simpler and time proven. Recent models are often more "capricious" during training, while some older "stars" are already more researched, and recipes for stable training are well-known. A popular example of such models is the ResNet family for vision and the BERT family for natural language processing. Our personal heuristic is to start with models that are at least 2 years old, but it is not a strict rule. It depends on the level of innovation required for the system as discussed in chapter 3.

It's worth noting that there are multiple shades of fine-tuning between "training a shallow model on top of a pretrained model" and "training a model from scratch." Choosing the right degree of fine-tuning is very case-specific and may require some experiments. For example, when training a text classification model based on BERT, you can gradually complicate the scope of training:

- Train only the last layer.
- Train some blocks using adapter methods such as low-rank adaptation (https://arxiv.org/abs/2106.09685).
- Train some encoder blocks.
- Train normalization layers.
- Train embedding layer.
- Train full model.
- Train full model + tokenizer.

This variety leads to the question, "How do we choose a proper baseline?"

8.5   *Baseline comparison*

Let's examined various features and model baselines, starting with the trivial ones. We can answer the central question, which is how to decide when to stop adding complexity and how to determine a suitable baseline for our system. There are multiple factors we should consider simultaneously; some of them are

- Accuracy
- Effort (mostly, time of development)
- Interpretability
- Computation time

The most fundamental is the tradeoff between a model's accuracy (or other ML metric) and the effort it requires. The first component in the equation is accuracy. When you move from a constant baseline to a rule-based baseline, from a rule-based one to a linear model, or from original features to their aggregations and ratios, you already start to get a feeling for what increase in metrics these small changes give. Is it responsive or not? How difficult is it to significantly surpass your constant baseline? Is it reasonable to invest more time attempting to gain more accuracy?

In some sense, as an ML engineer, you do backpropagation by getting "feedback" from your training loop and updating your understanding of the problem with its data and accuracy distribution across the solution space.

The second component is effort. By "effort," we mostly mean time and computing resources. No ML project has an infinite budget and, hence, an infinite amount of time. We consider the time required to implement a new model (or feature), train it, debug it, and test it. You should also pay attention to all the attendant complications and pitfalls that may arise on the way, especially infrastructural ones.

Let's examine a constant baseline. It takes almost no time to implement, and it provides us with the lowest accuracy. So we will map it into the (0, 0)-point in time-accuracy coordinates (as shown in figure 8.5).

Let's take a look at the linear model. It requires more effort but also most likely provides us with better accuracy. We will probably find the corresponding point to the right and higher than the previous one, and so on. On the other hand, it is important

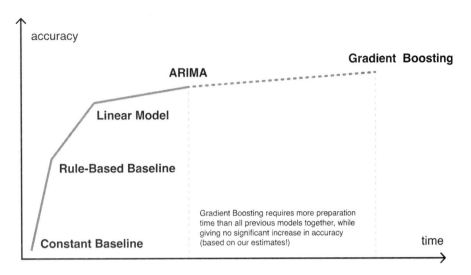

Figure 8.5 Simple baselines are easy to build but sacrifice final system metrics (example for a time-series prediction).

to understand that as the model improves and evolves (and therefore gains in complexity), the cost–accuracy ratio begins to decrease. A striking example of such a drop in efficiency is gradient boosting, which we mentioned earlier. Based on our estimates and experience, gradient boosting requires more input than all the simpler models you would use at the earlier stages put together while giving no significant increase in accuracy.

We should estimate how long it would take to try a more complex model each time and how much additional accuracy it could provide. Once we understand that the next step requires too much effort for almost no significant score improvement, we should stop. This "early stopping threshold" differs depending on the concrete domain and problem.

But what if something goes wrong or some additional change in the model is required? What model would be easier to debug or update?

- On the left of the spectrum, we have linear regression with an exact form solution.
- A deep neural network with sophisticated training and inference pipelines is on the right.

Which one would you prefer to face?

Maintenance, which we will touch upon in more detail in chapter 16, includes the amount of additional work that is necessary for debugging implemented features or a model. We could count maintenance as a part of the extra effort the more complex baseline requires.

Another essential property of a baseline is computation time. How does the computation time of our model and its features affect the response time? Does our baseline meet the service-level agreement? Is it the natural limit for solution space, especially when dealing with real-time systems? But even with no real-time requirements, computation time also determines how fast we will iterate during more thorough experimentation in the future.

Finally, we have interpretability. This parameter matters when we deal with the very first iteration of any ML system, especially for other teammates. When we deal, for example, with sensitive or medical data, it becomes a safety problem, too, not just a question of trust in the predictions of our model only. The general pattern is trivial: the simpler the baseline, the easier it is to explain how it works.

We'll discuss this topic in detail later in chapter 11.

8.6 *Design document: Baselines*

As long as baselines can be part of your design document, we are going to fill this gap for our fictional companies, Supermegaretail and PhotoStock, Inc.

8.6.1 *Baselines for Supermegaretail*

Let's start with the forecast system. Here, seasonality will be a huge factor when choosing a prediction model, so we can't but consider it in our design document.

DESIGN DOCUMENT: SUPERMEGARETAIL

V. BASELINE SOLUTION

I. CONSTANT BASELINE
As a constant baseline for Supermegaretail's demand forecasting system, we plan to use the actual value of the previous day per SKU per grocery. Knowing that data sometimes could appear with delay and that grocery sales experience strong weekly seasonality, we will go 1 full week back instead of going 1 day back. As a result, our prediction for a specific item on September 8, 2022, will be the actual sales value for this item on September 1, 2022.

II. ADVANCED CONSTANT BASELINE
Chapter 5 mentioned quantile losses of 1.5th, 25th, 50th, 75th, 95th, and 99th percentiles. We can calculate the same with our baseline using a yearly window.

III. LINEAR MODEL BASELINE
We will use a basic set of features to use linear regression with quantile loss; for a start, we can only use target variables but with multiple lags and aggregations like sum/min/max/avg/median or corresponding quantiles for the last 7/14/30/60/90/180 days or different rolling windows of different sizes. The same magic could be done with other dynamic data beyond sales date, like price, revenue, average check, or number of unique customers.

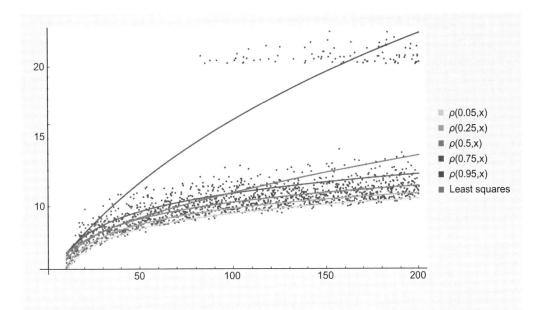

IV. TIME-SERIES-SPECIFIC BASELINE

Autoregressive integrated moving average (ARIMA) and seasonal ARIMA (SARIMA) are both autoregressive algorithms for forecasting; the second one considers any seasonality patterns.

Both require fine-tuning multiple hyperparameters to provide satisfying accuracy. To avoid this, we may prefer a state-of-the-art forecasting procedure that works great out-of-the-box and is called Prophet (https://github.com/facebook/prophet). The nice advantage of Prophet is that it's robust and doesn't require a lot of preprocessing: outliers, missing values, shifts, and trends are handled automatically.

V. FEATURE BASELINES

What additional information can some baselines and possible future models benefit from?

We will include extra static info about products (brand, category), shops (geo features), and context (time-based features, seasonality, day of the week)—all of them with preprocessing and encoding appropriate for a chosen model.

Features that are also suitable for the baseline are counters and interactions. Examples include

- The difference between current and average price (absolute and relative)
- Penetration: the ratio of product sales to sales of a category (of levels 1, 2, 3) for rolling windows of different sizes
- Number of days since the last purchase
- Number of unique customers

8.6.2   *Baselines for PhotoStock Inc.*

Now we switch to the PhotoStock Inc. case, where we are building an advanced search engine set to provide better, more accurate results and eventually increase sales.

DESIGN DOCUMENT: PHOTOSTOCK INC

V. BASELINE SOLUTION

We suggest three approaches to our baseline model for the PhotoStock Inc. search engine problem.

I. NON-ML SOLUTION AS A BASELINE

Currently, PhotoStock Inc. uses a simple non-ML solution for its search engine. It is a keyword-based search engine with the ElasticSearch database capable of fuzzy search. It doesn't require any training, and it is already deployed to production, so it is a solid candidate for a baseline model.

It has two drawbacks, though: it doesn't use images in the search, only metadata (e.g., tags, descriptions, etc.), and it's not too easy to embed it into a new ML pipeline for comparison. However, it's still very useful to have it as a baseline model because it will allow us to compare the performance of an ML model with the performance of a non-ML solution.

II. SIMPLE ML SOLUTION AS A BASELINE

Following the previous example, we can use a simple ML model as a baseline. It will not use images but only metadata. Such a model can use queries and metadata as raw input, transform them into features using a naive term frequency—inverse document frequency (TF-IDF) vectorizer, and then use a simple linear model to predict a relevance score. On top of that, it will be easy to implement and train, and its outstanding simplicity can help with early-stage debugging and understanding of the problem.

III. PRETRAINED MODEL AS A BASELINE

Finally, we can use a pretrained model as a baseline. Given the problem's origin, we need a solution capable of unifying visual and text domains, and the most famous one is CLIP (https://openai.com/research/clip). CLIP was released in 2021 and proved to be useful across various tasks. There are also several CLIP successors available, so they can be reviewed for future iterations if needed.

CLIP, in a nutshell, is an image encoder and a text encoder trained to predict which images were paired with proper text descriptions. It was trained on a huge dataset and thus demonstrates reasonable performance on a variety of tasks. CLIP is open source and is distributed under the MIT license, so it can be used for commercial purposes.

To make it work for our use case, we can start by using its output for a pair of queries (images) as a relevancy score. This approach doesn't use metadata and text descriptions, so it can be either combined with a previous approach or developed further to use a two-component score—for example:

relevancy_score = distance(query, image) + distance(query, description)

Both distances can be computed using CLIP—one using both text and image encoders and the other using only a text encoder.

As a first step, we may avoid any training at all. As for the next steps, we can start fine-tuning the model or its components on our dataset.

Summary

- Consider baselines an integral point of ML system design, as they effectively solve technical, ML, and product-related problems (interconnecting components, setting up a metric to compare with, and understanding product UX with a weak model inside).
- Even though baselines are perceived as something as easy as ABC, the skill of recognizing where to start, both in terms of features and models, is underestimated.
- As you dive deeper into your project, your common progression will lean toward the following progression: constant baseline, then rule-based baseline, then linear model, then something more complicated.
- While building a complex model from the start may seem tempting, always consider kicking off with a constant baseline; this will save you resources and time and point to whether you're moving in the right direction with minimum expenses.
- When a problem implies the use of deep learning, the most common practice is reusing pretrained models, training/fine-tuning the simplest models, or training a simple model from scratch if neither of the first two approaches works.
- When choosing between various baseline options, consider accuracy, effort (mostly time of development), interpretability, and computation time as key factors, with the accuracy–effort tradeoff being especially important.
- As your model evolves and gains in complexity, the cost accuracy inevitably decreases. This is especially the case with switching to gradient boosting, which, as practice shows, requires more input than all previous models put together while giving no significant increase in accuracy.

Part 3

Intermediate steps

P art 3 is focused on intermediate steps. Chapter 9 overviews the learning curve analysis, provides a closer look at the residual analysis, and helps in finding commonalities in residuals. Chapter 10 is dedicated to training pipelines, covers tools and platforms we can use to build and maintain training pipelines, and presents such topics as scalability and configurability of training pipelines. Chapter 11 addresses features and feature engineering, analyzes features, gives hints on selecting appropriate features for the ML model, and lists pros and cons of feature stores. In chapter 12, we give an overview on measuring and reporting results and discuss the benefits of conducting A/B tests.

Error analysis

9

Once we've assembled the initial building blocks, which include gathering the first dataset, picking the metrics, defining the evaluation procedure, and training the baseline, we are ready to start the iterative adjustments process. Just as backpropagation in neural networks calculates the direction of the fastest loss reduction and passes it backward from layer to layer, error analysis finds the fastest improvement for the whole system.

Error analysis steps up as the compass that guides the iterative updates of your system. It helps you understand the error dynamics during the training phase (learning curve analysis) and the distribution of errors after the prediction phase (residual analysis). By analyzing these errors, you can identify commonalities, trends, and patterns that inform improvements to your machine learning (ML) system. In this chapter, we will examine its crucial stages and types and provide examples that we hope will give you a better understanding of the subject.

155

Error analysis is often skipped when ML systems are designed for a reason that seems somewhat legit at first glance—this step is not part of *building the system* per se. However, time spent on error analysis is always a good investment as it reveals weak spots and suggests ways of improving the system. Leaving this step out of this book would be a huge mistake from our side.

9.1   *Learning curve analysis*

Learning curve analysis evaluates the learning process by plotting and analyzing the learning curve, showing the relationship between the model's training performance and the amount of training data used. Learning curve analysis is designed to answer two vital questions:

- Does the model converge?
- If so, have we avoided underfitting or overfitting issues?

If both questions lead to negative answers, there is no need for the rest of the analysis.

Before we get into details, what is a learning curve? The term was coined in behavioral psychology, where it is used to display the learning progress of a person or animal observed over time (see figure 9.1). For instance, we may analyze the number of mistakes made by a subject in every new test iteration or study how much time it takes for a mouse to find a path through the labyrinth compared to the trial number.

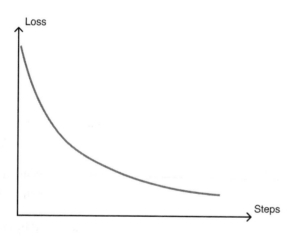

Figure 9.1   **Basic representation of a learning curve**

In ML, a learning curve is essentially a graphical representation that shows the dependency of a chosen metric on a specific numerical property, such as the number of iterations, dataset size, or model complexity. Let's do a brief breakdown of all three properties:

- *Number of iterations*—This kind of curve depicts an evolution of the loss or metric during training and helps examine the model's convergence. In some sources, it is referred to as a loss curve or a convergence curve. A good example of iterations is the number of training epochs in neural networks.

- *Model complexity*—This type of learning curve shows how performance varies based on changes in the complexity of your model. As its complexity increases, the model tends to fit the training data better but may start to generalize poorly on the unseen data. Examples of parameters for model complexity are the tree depth, the number of features, and the number of layers in a neural network.

- *Dataset size*—This learning curve reveals how the number of samples in the training dataset affects the model's performance. It is helpful in determining whether the model would benefit from more data.

These properties reveal the three most common types of learning curves. Before diving into each, we should recall "the quest for the grail of machine learning," the overfitting and underfitting problem, sometimes referred to as the bias–variance tradeoff (see figure 9.2).

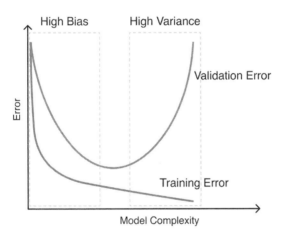

Figure 9.2 **With an increasing number of model parameters, training error tends to become lower and lower while minimizing bias. At the same time, the model variance increases, providing us with a U-shaped validation error.**

9.1.1 *Overfitting and underfitting*

Overfitting happens when a model conveys a great performance on training data and a bad performance on unseen data. Usually, this happens when it learns the training data so well that it becomes too specialized and fails to generalize, focusing too much on insignificant details and patterns that are not present in the new data.

On the other hand, underfitting occurs when the model is too simple and misses some important relationships between features and the target variable, resulting in poor performance on both the training data and new data.

Both are strongly related to the bias-variance tradeoff, which is the balance between the model's complexity and the amount of input data. The greater the model's capacity to capture useful signals from data, the lower the bias and the higher the risk of overfitting. On the other hand, reducing a variance requires decreasing complexity, thus leading to a more biased model.

Bias is an error caused by the low capacity of the model to capture useful signals in the data. In other words, the model is biased toward its simplified assumptions about the data. When the model is biased, we call it *underfitting*.

Variance is an error caused by the model's high sensitivity to small fluctuations in the training set. The model is poorly generalized on new data, which, in terms of the model's parameters, is highly varied from what it has seen in the training set. Often, high variance is a primary reason behind *overfitting* (assuming nothing is broken in other parts of the system).

A good learning algorithm is expected to minimize both bias and variance simultaneously. The bias–variance tradeoff, however, vividly demonstrates that reducing variance often involves increasing bias and vice versa. The quest here is to find the right balance between the two. This is when learning-curve analysis can guide us.

Keep in mind that the model's redundant complexity (i.e., high variance) is not the only reason behind overfitting. Some other possible scenarios include

- *Data leakage* (using information that is not supposed to be known during inference)
- *Noisy or highly granular features* that force the model to capture irrelevant patterns
- *Existence of outliers* that have a large impact on the loss function
- Overall *poor ability* of the model to extrapolate
- Training sets and validation sets simply belonging to *different distributions*

Regardless of a given case, learning curves are an effective tool to detect underfitting and overfitting. Armed with the knowledge about overfitting and underfitting, we are ready to go through different types of curves and the hints they give us in this quest.

9.1.2   *Loss curve*

A loss curve (also referred to as a convergence curve or learning curve) based on learning iterations is the first thing that comes to mind for ML engineers when they hear the term "learning curve." It shows how much the algorithm is improving as it puts more and more learning effort into the task.

The curve plots the loss (or metric) on the vertical axis and the number of training iterations (or epochs) on the horizontal axis. As the model trains, the loss should decrease, ideally forming a downward slope toward the bottom of the curve.

In contrast to learning curves where axis X is the dataset size or the model complexity (which we will talk about soon), the iteration-wise curve requires only one training run, which makes its tracking practical even for large datasets when a single training run takes hours or even days. The loss curve helps keep your finger on the pulse all the way until the end of training. If you've run just 10 training epochs out of 200, you can already get insights on whether the loss value is progressing as expected or if there are issues that make further training pointless.

Be sure you track loss curves, collect them for all conducted experiments, and make them available for future analysis. Incorporating loss-curve monitoring into the training pipeline in the early stages of its building is a valuable one-time effort because you will need these insights for all future experiments, and it is helpful for the overall pipeline's reproducibility (we'll have an in-depth look into this subject in chapter 10).

9.1.3 Interpreting loss curves

There are several main patterns in the behavior of loss curves that deviate from what is expected by design. Let's conduct a brief analysis of each pattern and see how we can interpret different patterns we may encounter while debugging the system (what conclusions can be made and what steps should be taken to debug detected issues).

PATTERN 1

Pattern 1 shows that the loss curve diverges (not converging to the desired loss value and oscillating instead; see figure 9.3). How can we try to make the training process more stable? Consider the following:

- Check if features and targets are correlated in any way—or if samples and labels are passed to the model in the right order.
- Reduce the learning rate to prevent the model from bouncing around in the parameter space.
- Reduce the dataset size to a single batch (or 10–100 samples) and check if the model is able to overfit them.
- Start with a simpler model and add complexity incrementally. Each time, check whether it outperforms the constant baseline or rule-based baseline.

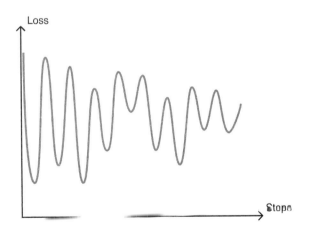

Figure 9.3 Loss is oscillating, which demonstrates a lack of convergence.

PATTERN 2

Pattern 2 shows a loss explosion or trending toward NaN (not a number) (see figure 9.4). This behavior indicates computational problems when either the gradient is exploded (in which case solutions like gradient clipping, lower learning rate, or differ-ent weights initialization techniques may help) or some mathematical problems emerge (e.g., division by zero, the logarithm of zero or negative numbers, or NaNs in data—thus, it usually indicates an error in implementation or lack of data preprocessing).

Figure 9.4   **A model was converging until something went wrong.**

PATTERN 3

Pattern 3 shows that the loss decreases, but the metric is contradictory (see figure 9.5). If the model continues improving based on the loss but the metric is stuck, it may sig-nal that the chosen metric is inadequate for the problem or poorly implemented. Typ-ically, it happens in classification and other related tasks where we use metrics that include a certain threshold.

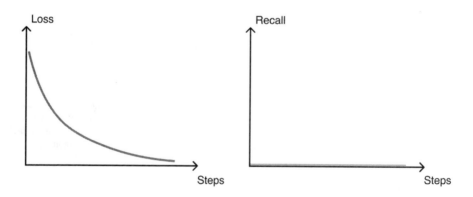

Figure 9.5   **Loss decreases while the metric stays constantly low.**

Campfire story from Valerii

When I was working at a company providing messaging services, one of the tasks we had was the improvement of existing antispam and antifraud systems. The main challenge we faced was that the model, which had been trained on a given dataset, showed promising metrics during offline testing but didn't perform as expected after deployment.

After digging into possible causes, we found three main problems:

- We didn't use proper metrics for offline testing. For example, such metrics as precision at defined recall are not that useful for fraud detection as they are class sensitive (precision), while specificity at a defined recall yielded better results (see chapter 5). However, recall is somewhat of Schrödinger's cat itself, as we never had its full picture for fraud (there were fraud cases we missed, and we didn't know how many of them); thus, our recall could be calculated only on a subset of known fraud cases.

- The second problem was hiding in performance evaluation. We conducted it on a point estimate basis, but reality has a tendency to deviate from point estimates, and given the scale of 100 billion events per day, even a 0.1% deviation would translate to a significant number (100 million) of events being misclassified compared to what we expected.

- The third problem lay in the fact that we evaluated the system through a spam/nonspam binary classification, using log loss as the loss function. What we really needed was to keep users happy and reduce spam to the appropriate levels (there is always spam, but sometimes it's not a big deal, and other times it is a problem), excluding such cases as receiving 100,000 messages from a single number within 1 second.

While the first two problems were challenging but somewhat manageable, the third problem was extremely complex, demanding a proper hierarchy of metrics, a custom loss function, and continuous experimentation.

That is the essence of ML: we train a model using specific loss, we measure its performance using different sets of metrics in the hope of achieving something different from the first and second, and sooner or later, we will face a plateau where the first or even second element improves but the third does not react.

The most important lesson we learned from this case was that while you can adjust your error analysis until it reaches perfection, it will not save you from a fiasco if you incorrectly pick metrics in the first place.

Pattern 4

Pattern 4 shows the converging training curve with unexpected loss values. While the curvature of the training curve appears promising, the observed values are perplexing. To identify such anomalies in advance, it is advisable to do a sanity check by running a simple unit on a single batch that asserts if the loss falls within the expected range. Often, the reason behind such an issue lies in scaling transformations (e.g., normalization of an image or a mask in segmentation).

PATTERN 5

Pattern 5 shows that the training loss decreases while the validation loss increases (see figure 9.6). This is a classic textbook example of overfitting due to high variance. In these cases, you should restrict the model's capacity, either by reducing its complexity directly or by increasing regularization.

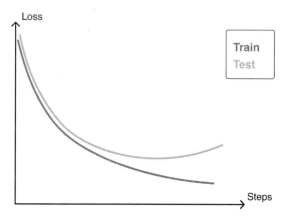

9.1.4 *Model-wise learning curve*

After we ensure the model converges and the training loss reaches the plateau with no dras-

Figure 9.6 Loss is decreasing for training but not validation, reflecting potential overfit.

tic overfitting or underfitting, we can wrap up our learning-curve analysis and move on. This is especially relevant at the stage of initial deployment.

However, if we face overfitting/underfitting issues or there is enough time to experiment with the optimal model size, that is when the second type of learning curve comes into play (see figure 9.7):

1 First, we pick a hyperparameter that represents a varying model complexity. Again, it may be the tree depth in gradient boosting, a regularization strength, a number of features, or a number of layers in a deep neural network.

2 We define a grid for this hyperparameter (e.g., 2, 3, 4, …, 16 for the tree depth; 10^{-2}, 10^{-1}, 1, 10, 10^2, 10^3 for regularization term).

3 We train each model until convergence and capture the final loss/metric values.

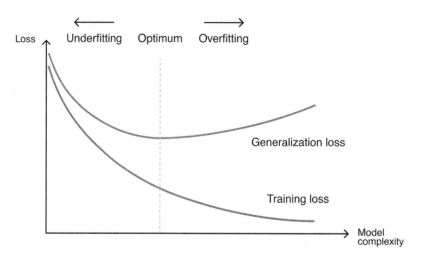

Figure 9.7 Finding the optimal model complexity based on learning curves

Now we map these values on the vertical axis and corresponding hyperparameter values on the horizontal axis. This learning curve helps us easily see what range of model complexity (determined by this hyperparameter) is optimal for the given data.

9.1.5 Sample-wise learning curve

Finally, let's vary the dataset size. We discussed this technique in detail in chapter 6, section 6.4. In short, we keep the validation set unchanged and probe different numbers of samples in the training set: 100, 1,000, 10,000, and so on. As in the model-wise learning curve, we train the model until it reaches convergence and plot training and validation learning curves.

If we extrapolate the validation metric, we can estimate how much new data we need to increase the metric by 1% and vice versa. If we expect to gather N more samples of data, we can forecast what metric gain it'll give.

Besides this extrapolation, the sample-wise learning curve also serves the purpose of revealing overfitting and underfitting. Specifically, what insights do we get by analyzing training and validation curves?

- If the curves almost converge (there is a small or no gap between curves at the maximum number of samples), the model generalizes well, and there's no need to add more samples to the dataset, as it will not increase the model's performance.

- Specifically, if the training and validation curves almost converge but the loss level remains high in both, it reports a high bias problem (underfitting). In this scenario, increasing the dataset size will not help either. What can be fruitful is using a more complicated model.

- If there is a large gap between the curves, it signals either a high variance problem or simply a difference between the training set and validation set. In the first case, we should reduce model complexity or gather more data to combat this problem. In the second case, we need to examine the data-splitting procedure and ensure it fairly represents real-world scenarios the model will encounter.

A sample-wise learning curve indicates whether the current bottleneck in the system is the amount of data or not. Understanding the metric dependency on dataset size guides our next steps in improving the system, which could include a combination of gathering more data and investing effort in feature engineering and model hyperparameter tuning.

9.1.6 Double descent

The bias–variance tradeoff runs like clockwork for classical ML models and deep neural networks of moderate size. However, for modern overparametrized deep neural networks, things get more perplexing.

There is a phenomenon called *double descent* where the test error first grows better, then worse, and then better again. Surprisingly, researchers found different regimes of double descent corresponding to all three learning curves: epoch-wise, model-wise, and sample-wise.

It is still an open question what the mechanism behind the double descent is, why it occurs, and whether it means that overfitting for large deep neural networks is not an issue. The common hypothesis behind the double descent is the following:

- If the model's capacity (the number of parameters) is lower than the dataset size, it tries to approximate the data, leading to the classical regime where the bias–variance tradeoff takes place. We call this model *underparametrized*.
- At the interpolation threshold, the model has sufficient ability to fit the training data perfectly and reach zero bias. There is effectively only one such model in this parameter space. Forcing this model to fit even slightly noisy labels will destroy its global structure.
- However, in an *overparametrized* regime, there are many models of this kind. Some of them not only interpolate the train set but also perform well on the test set. It turns out that stochastic gradient descent leads to such "good models" for reasons we don't yet understand.

For further details, we recommend reading "Deep Double Descent" by OpenAI (https://openai.com/research/deep-double-descent).

The modern scaling laws of large neural networks redefine our modeling strategies. The double-descent phenomenon may surprise those who are only familiar with the classical bias–variance tradeoff, and it is crucial to consider it when selecting a model for the system (especially when working with large convolutional networks and transformers), as well as when determining training and debugging procedures.

We only mention this here to highlight that most of the heuristics described previously are not solid laws set in stone. As with many things in ML design, they reveal signals—often useful ones—but may not be an exact fit for a particular problem.

9.2   *Residual analysis*

Certainly, coming up with new ideas is important, but even more important, to understand the results.

— Ilya Sutskever

Once we've ensured that a ML model has converged and is not plagued by underfitting or overfitting, the next step in model debugging is to perform residual analysis. This involves studying individual predictions made by the model compared to their corresponding true labels. Residual analysis involves calculating the differences between the predicted and actual values, known as *residuals* (see figure 9.8):

$$residual_i = y\_pred_i - y\_true_i$$

First, what exactly are residuals? In the narrow sense, residuals are simply the differences between predicted and true values in regression. In a wider sense, residuals can be any sample-wise differences or errors between model predictions and ground truth.

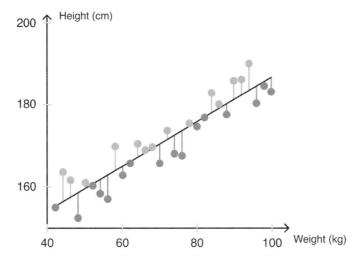

Figure 9.8   Basic case: single regressor x. Each vertical line represents a residual error (e) or, simply, residual. Lines above the regressor have negative signs (the actual value is higher than the predicted value), and lines below the regressor have positive signs.

Thus, to align residuals to a specific loss, you may prefer using a single term of the loss sum as a pseudo-residual instead of raw differences, which are a squared error for mean squared error, a logarithmic error for root mean squared logarithmic error, or a class label multiplied by the predicted probability of this class for LogLoss.

Often, residuals are associated only with regression and classification tasks. But what about residuals outside of regression and classification tasks? Looking more broadly, we will find equivalent tools in almost any ML-related task.

For instance, in the search engine context, true labels are often mappings from a search query to the top N most relevant documents or products. To calculate residuals in this context, we can measure the difference between the rank predicted by the model and the true rank of each item in the top N list (see figure 9.9).

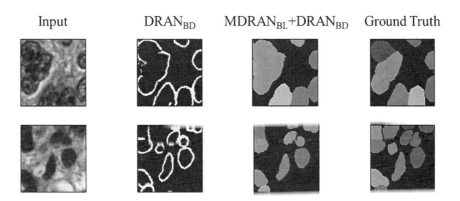

Figure 9.9   Example of residuals for the image segmentation problem (image source: https://arxiv.org/abs/1810.13230)

In image segmentation, we can compute the differences between predicted and ground truth masks for each image, which yields 2D residuals that highlight which parts of an object are not covered by the mask or are covered incorrectly.

9.2.1   *Goals of residual analysis*

Residual analysis helps identify patterns in the errors made by the model so that we can detect clear directions for improving the system. Whereas the overall error of a model is usually represented by a single number, such as a loss or metric, the residual analysis does the opposite. It examines the raw differences between predictions and true labels, providing a more fine-grained diagnostic of the model's performance.

Along with that, there are other main purposes of residual analysis:

- *Verify model assumptions.* First, it challenges our basic assumptions about the model. Do residuals follow a normal distribution? Are the model's predictions biased or not? If we identify any significant discrepancies, we may need to reevaluate our approach or choose a different model.
- *Detect sources of metric change.* The overall performance may increase or may remain unchanged. Either way, capturing a significant change in the metric distribution is possible. Which data samples show varying residual patterns with different models? In which data subset do we have the greatest number of wrong answers? What samples affect the final score the most?
- *Ensure fairness of residuals.* Residual analysis enables us to evaluate if the model treats every sample fairly and has the same distribution across different cohorts. If we identify any significant skewness or disparities, we can make respective adjustments to ensure that the model is unbiased and treats all samples equally.
- *Perform worst-case and best-case analysis.* Is there a commonality between the top N samples with the biggest residuals? What should we change so that our model performs better in these cases? What about a top N list with the smallest residuals?
- *Examine corner cases.* How does our model perform on users with the shortest or longest history or on shortest/longest audio records, texts, and sessions, depending on the problem we solve? How does it deal with items with the lowest/highest price, zero stocks, or highest revenue? We must be familiar with business cases and the nature of data to evaluate all possible pitfalls.

These questions are the essence of the residual analysis, and finding answers to them closes the feedback loop of offline evaluation. The earlier we start capturing hard samples (and loss curves) for conducted experiments, the better. It is a good practice to collect 10 to 20 objects with the largest residuals after training as attendant artifacts. It is difficult to overestimate the value of thinking through such steps in a training pipeline in a design document.

In the project's later phases, we transform it into a part of automatic reports for every trained model, along with model drift monitoring and data quality reports. Let's say the metric increased in most cases but dropped a bit in a crucial segment. Depending on our policy, we may either reject this version or simply pay extra attention to this change in forthcoming iterations.

9.2.2 *Model assumptions*

Whichever model we train, we have prior assumptions about its predictions, biases, and residual distribution. The assumption check helps us ensure that we picked the right model, collected enough data, and engineered the right features. If the assumptions reveal an unexpected pattern, it may prompt the exploration of alternative solutions.

Again, from the design perspective, we need to figure out in advance what we assume to be true about the model's predictions or, specifically, residuals and express it via corresponding unit tests. It will prevent unexpected model behavior after the next deployment. In the following chapter, we will dive into a more holistic overview of tests and their role in the training pipeline. Let's explore two different examples to see how assumptions can be applied.

EXAMPLE 1. LINEAR REGRESSION ASSUMPTIONS

Suppose we solve the demand forecasting problem using a simple linear regression. What are the key assumptions we make here?

- *Linearity*—The relationship between predictors (x) and target (y) is linear.
- *Strict exogeneity*—Residuals should be zero-centered.
- *Normality*—Residuals are assumed to be normally distributed.
- *Homoscedasticity*—The variance of the residual is the same for any value of X.
- *Independence*—Residual error terms should be independent.

After fitting our model, we check whether these assumptions hold true. Potential problems include

- *Nonlinearity* in X-Y relationships
- *Bias* in residuals
- *Heteroscedasticity:* nonconstant variance of error terms
- Presence of data points with *extremely high influence:* outliers in predicted values (y) or in regressors (x)

To check regression assumptions, we'll examine the distribution of residuals. For this purpose, we plot residuals in four different ways and build so-called *diagnostic plots* (see figures 9.10 and 9.11):

- *Residuals vs. fitted*—Utilized to evaluate the assumptions of a linear relationship. A horizontal line that lacks distinct patterns suggests a linear relationship, which is favorable. No difference between the solid and dashed lines means strong linear dependence.
- *Normal quantile-quantile (Q-Q) plot*—Used to examine whether the residuals are normally distributed. We plot quantiles of the standard normal distribution as x-coordinates and quantiles of standardized residuals (residuals after subtracting the mean and dividing by standard deviation) as y-coordinates. If the resulting points are close to the straight line (dotted line on the plot), residuals follow a normal distribution.
- *Scale-location*—Used to assess the homogeneity of variance among the residuals. A horizontal line with evenly dispersed points is a strong sign of homoscedasticity.

This is not the case in our example, where we have a heteroscedasticity problem (higher fitted values have higher variance).

- *Residuals vs. leverage*—Used to identify influential cases, meaning extreme values that could affect the regression results when included or excluded from the analysis. *Leverage* refers to the extent to which the coefficients in the regression model would change if we removed a particular observation from the dataset. There is a commonly used measurement for influential data points called Cook's Distance.

Case 1: Assumptions are met

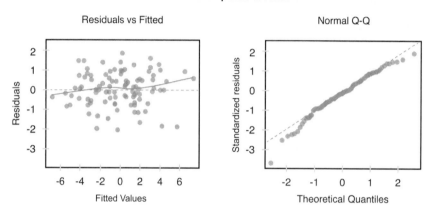

Figure 9.10   Four diagnostic plots for linear regression's residual analysis in both cases (Case 1: Assumptions are met)

Case 2: Assumptions are not met

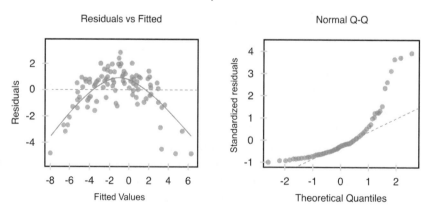

Figure 9.11   Four diagnostic plots for linear regression's residual analysis in both cases (Case 2: Assumptions are not met)

Sometimes it is beneficial to force the model to follow our assumptions more strictly by incorporating our prior knowledge directly into the model.

EXAMPLE 2. ATTENTION PLOT

Imagine you're the product owner of a banking application, and your next big update is to add a voice assistant. After looking into your "inner circle" of specialists, you hire Stacy, a world-class master in text-to-speech (TTS) systems. After several weeks of work, Stacy builds a first version of a voice synthesis system.

In the realm of TTS tasks, there exists a fundamental assumption: the order of characters in a text should progress linearly over time in the corresponding audio segments. When we read a text, it's natural to assume that the text's position aligns closely with the audio we hear. This stands in contrast to other sequence-to-sequence tasks, like machine translation, where an attention module is necessary to resolve word alignment between languages with different syntax or token ordering, such as English and Chinese.

To assess the validity of this assumption, Stacy employs an *attention plot*—a visual representation that depicts the activation map between audio frames (x-axis) and characters (y-axis). By observing this plot at regular intervals during training, Stacy aims to evaluate how closely it resembles a nearly diagonal matrix.

To force the attention matrix to exhibit a near-diagonal pattern, Stacy employs a technique known as *guided attention*. Whenever the attention matrix deviates significantly from the diagonal, it is penalized using an auxiliary loss. This heuristic not only accelerates the training process but also steers the model toward meaningful solutions that align with the underlying assumption from the start (see figure 9.12).

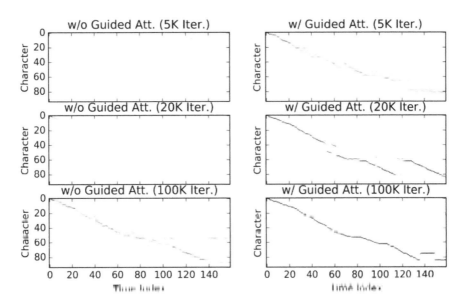

Figure 9.12 Attention plot evolution through training without (left) and with (right) guided attention loss

The deviation of the attention plot from the diagonal matrix is nothing but residuals. Residuals of moderate size are appropriate: some characters people speak more quickly than others; therefore, the plot will not represent a straight line. However, large residuals reveal the specific sounds or character combinations that the model can't learn well.

Armed with this knowledge, Stacy could shape a forthcoming data-gathering strategy to address the model's difficulties and improve its performance.

To learn more about the architecture of a typical TTS network, including details on the construction of the attention module in this case, we recommend studying the paper "Efficiently Trainable Text-to-Speech System Based on Deep Convolutional Networks with Guided Attention" (https://arxiv.org/abs/1710.08969).

9.2.3   *Residual distribution*

If none of the model's assumptions are met, it is a sign to adjust the training pipeline, collect more data, engineer new features, or explore alternative models and losses. But how do we determine the necessary improvement steps? The guess-and-check approach may seem tempting, but we don't recommend it for exploring the solution space.

Let's, for example, violate the normality assumption for the same linear regression (figures 9.13–9.15).

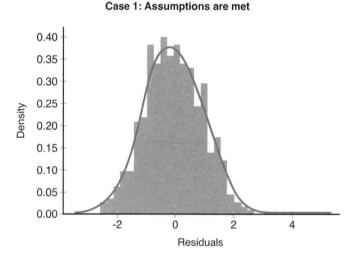

Figure 9.13   In Case 1, we observe a normal residual distribution when linearity assumptions are met.

Case 2: Assumptions are not met

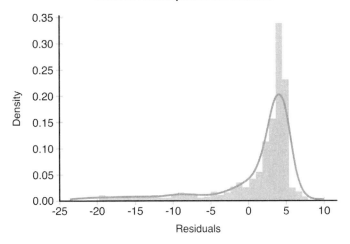

Figure 9.14 Case 2 displays nonnormal residual distribution when linearity assumptions are not met due to the log-normal distribution of the target (there is a clear skewness in the distribution).

Case 3: Assumptions are not met

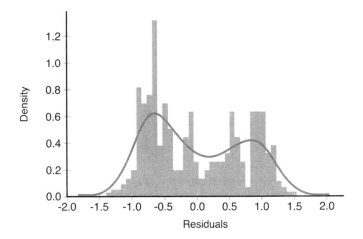

Figure 9.15 In Case 3, there's a nonnormal residual distribution for linear regression when linearity assumptions are not met due to the nonmonotonic dependence of the target from the regressors.

In this example, we are lucky and instantly see what's wrong with the model:

- *Case 2*—It seems we don't consider the distribution of the target variable. Entities like revenue, sales, and prices follow a log-normal distribution, whereas the mean squared error or mean absolute error that the regression models minimize is not suitable (at least not directly). To overcome this issue, applying logarithm transform to the target often helps.

- *Case 3*—Residuals form multiple clusters. In this case, transforming the target will not be of any use. The target variable dependence on features is not monotonic. What can help in this case is either trying a model that can catch nonmonotonic dependencies or engineering new features that will help the linear model to reduce nonmonotonic dependencies to monotonic and even linear ones.

9.2.4   *Fairness of residuals*

In ML, fairness is an indicator of inequality among data. How do individual samples contribute to a loss or metric? By what cost do we increase the metric? Does the new model add inequality among residuals or reduce it? Basically, *fairness* is another term for defining the skewness of the residual distribution.

Not every metric change is meant to be equal. Some improvements are distributed uniformly among all samples, while others add significant growth in one stratum and provoke a decrease in the rest. The concept of "fairness" in residual analysis pushes us toward a more holistic model evaluation procedure, far beyond estimating single-valued metrics.

To get a better understanding of what fairness is, consider figure 9.16.

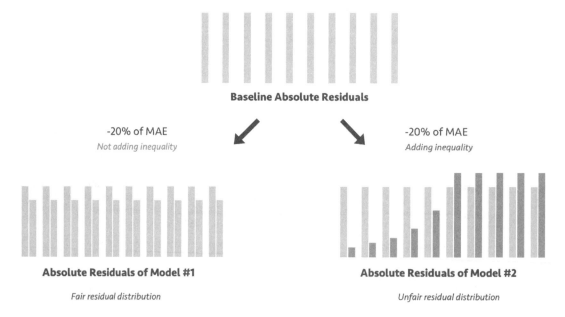

Figure 9.16   Fair vs. unfair residual distribution

In this simplified example, we have two models. Both decrease the mean absolute error (MAE) by 20%. However, we prefer to deploy the first model because it reduces absolute residuals uniformly among all 10 samples. In contrast, the second model drastically improves metrics on one half and reduces them on the other half. In this case, we add inequality to the residual distribution, so we call this distribution unfair.

One way to assess fairness quantitatively, instead of relying purely on visualizations, is to use the Gini index from economics (see figure 9.17). To compute it, the residuals should be sorted based on their absolute values, and then the cumulative proportion of the absolute values should be divided by the cumulative proportion of the number of residuals.

For total fairness (Gini = 0.0), almost all residuals have the same contribution to the total error. For total inequity (Gini = 1.0), a single residual is stealing the covers. Those are two extremes that you will rarely face in real life, while the common values are always somewhere in between.

There are two main reasons to care about fairness. First, we want the

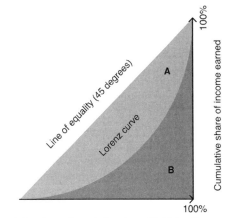

Figure 9.17 **Graphical representation of the Gini coefficient: the graph shows that the Gini coefficient equals the area marked A divided by the sum of the areas marked A and B—that is, Gini = A/(A + B). It is also equal to 2A and to 1 • 2B because A + B = 0.5 (since the axes scale from 0 to 1).**

model to have high performance among all users, items, or other entities it will be deployed on, not just a fraction of them. This also includes reducing overall inequality in residuals step by step in each iteration of the system.

Second, we want to not only improve the overall error numbers but also reduce each residual. If we increase the search engine quality by 5%, it reduces prediction quality on some segments of users by 20%, which damages the users' experience. The gains we get by improving the average quality may be easily neutralized by the increase in the churn of these users.

In the long term, we chase close-to-equal growth among all strata. There are exceptions to every rule, and fairness is not that critical for every single project and every metric. We should pay attention to the error cost produced by residual distribution tails. This should define our tradeoff between average and sample-wise improvements.

9.2.5 *Underprediction and overprediction*

In regression tasks, we often split residuals by sign—positive residuals indicate overprediction (predicted values are greater than true values), while negative residuals indicate underprediction.

Depending on the problem we are set to solve, one or another bias of the model is preferred. For instance, if we are building a demand forecasting system, missed profit is a less desirable outcome than moderate overstocks. On the other hand, if we predict a client's creditworthiness for a bank, we are better off underestimating it than overestimating it.

Therefore, the cost of an error is often asymmetric, and it should tell us residuals of which sign and size we should pay attention to the most.

9.2.6 *Elasticity curves*

One of the demand-specific error analysis tools is the elasticity plot. It is not a universal tool applicable for any ML system, but because it is crucial for pricing-related applications, it is worth our attention. Although we discussed most of the curve-shaped ways of analysis earlier, this example belongs here as it can be seen as a special case of residual analysis.

One of the core model assumptions behind demand forecasting is price–demand dependency—the higher the price, the lower the demand, and vice versa. This is true for almost all kinds of products (except some special cases like Veblen and Giffen goods, if you recall Microeconomics 101).

An elasticity plot is a special case for a more generic concept called a *partial dependence plot*, in which we vary some features and analyze how the predicted outcome changes. It is used for model interpretability (which we will cover in chapter 11).

There are two ways to plot the elasticity curve for our model:

- Using training data (with real prices known):
  - Taking the sales history of a particular SKU
  - Predicting sales for each data point (Y)
  - Taking the historical price for each data point (X)
  - Plotting X-Y (price → predicted sales) dependency

- Using a mixture of synthetic and real data:
  - Taking the last price for a particular SKU
  - Multiplying this price by different coefficients (–20%, –19%, –18%, …, +19%, +20%)
  - Recalculating all price-based features and predicting sales (Y) for each new row
  - Plotting X-Y (price → predicted sales) dependency

As we mentioned before, in a perfect case, the plot demonstrates an inverse dependency: the higher the price, the lower the sales. However, if this plot demonstrates the opposite, is noisy (partly or fully nonmonotonic), or has any other controversial patterns, it will signal one of the following:

- We don't have enough price variability for this SKU to capture its elasticity (e.g., a short history of sales).
- The sales for this SKU are way too stochastic. For instance, this SKU is often affected by promo campaigns, seasonality, or other external factors).
- The model can't capture it for whatever reason ("a hard case").

The "better" the plot (more monotonous in the negative direction), the more we can rely on the model's predictions for these SKUs. If the elasticity is "bad," it signals that forecasting is not reliable and should be further investigated rather than deployed for these "hard" SKUs (see figures 9.18 and 9.19).

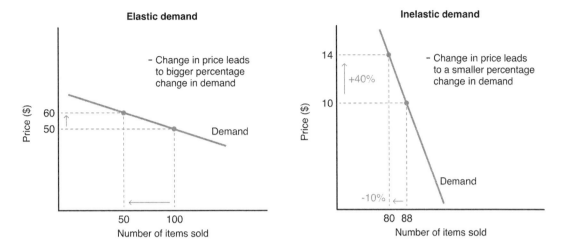

Figure 9.18   Theoretical example of elastic demand   **Figure 9.19   Theoretical example of inelastic demand**

Plotting elasticity not only for predicted sales but for actual sales as well is helpful. It is also helpful to understand whether this particular SKU reveals distinct elasticity. If it doesn't, we should not expect it for the predicted demand.

If you feel like you need more context on the price elasticity concept, we recommend the article "Forecasting with Price Elasticity of Demand" (https://mng.bz/GN5v).

A friend of ours recently told his own campfire story about using an elasticity curves application. He had been working on a pricing problem, and their solution was effectively a glorified elasticity plot. They built a gradient-boosting model that predicted the number of sold items using various features, including price-based ones and estimated sales for different possible prices. Their first model revealed a surprising pattern: instead of having a smooth look, the plot had a visible "ladder" of steps. After deeper analysis, they realized that the origin of the steps was related to the features they used; continuous variables were split into buckets with low cardinality (e.g., only 256 buckets for all possible prices across all the items on the marketplace), and it limited the model's sensitivity. After the number of buckets was increased, the model was able to capture more detailed patterns, and the elasticity curve became smooth, improving the overall system performance.

9.3   Finding commonalities in residuals

Now that we've examined residual distribution as a whole, it's time to investigate the patterns and trends in residual subgroups. To do that, we approach the problem from both ends (see figure 9.20):

- We group samples by their residuals and analyze features in each group.
- We group samples by their features and analyze residuals in each group.

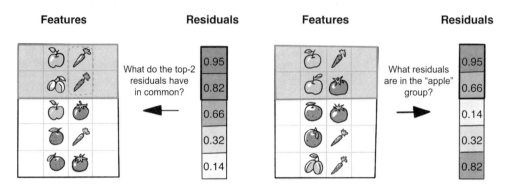

Figure 9.20   Two approaches to finding commonalities in residuals: picking subsets by residuals rank or by sample attributes

Grouping residuals by their values includes best-case and worst-case analysis; it also covers overprediction and underprediction problems. Grouping residuals by their properties produces group analysis and corner case analysis.

9.3.1   *Worst/best-case analysis*

The goal of worst/best-case analysis is to define typical cases where the model works fine and where we should avoid making decisions based on this model. What do residuals have in common in these extreme cases?

> #### Campfire story from Valerii
> Getting back to a case mentioned in previous chapters, once we deployed a dynamic pricing system in a large marketplace that set a price for an item based on predicted demand. We started to encounter moments when it failed to forecast sales accurately. We decided to focus on the top 200 products by their residual size. Soon we realized the most distinguishable clusters of problems:
>
> - The first cluster revolved around *new products* that had recently been added to the marketplace's assortment matrix. This issue is known as the *cold start* problem. These items posed a challenge as the lack of historical data hindered accurate predictions. It became clear that relying solely on our ML model would not suffice in such cases. Instead, we needed to develop heuristics that would use the warming up of sales for products within the same category to establish a solid foundation for forecasting.
> - Another cluster emerged from the *electronic devices category*, revealing a different predicament. These products exhibited sparse sales over time, making it

difficult to depend on our model's predictions. Recognizing this, we made a crucial decision to exclude these items from our pilot and explore alternative ways of improving the prediction quality. We contemplated the idea of splitting the model into larger categories, believing it would capture the specific dynamics within each group more effectively.

- However, the most significant bias was influenced by *marketing activities*—big sales, promotional codes, and discounts. The model struggled to account for these factors, resulting in noticeable underpredictions represented by large negative residuals. To rectify this bias, we incorporated a promo calendar into our feature set. By doing so, we could empower the model to make corresponding corrections, thus enhancing the accuracy of predictions.

In addition to identifying the areas where our model fell short, we also investigated residuals that were close to zero to determine the boundaries of our model's applicability. This analysis helped us understand where we could have confidence in the model's predictions, where the quality might be satisfactory but within acceptable limits, and where it became risky to rely on the model's forecasts.

By examining these residual patterns, we gained a comprehensive understanding of the strengths and limitations of our dynamic pricing system, enabling us to make informed decisions about its rollout and ensure its appropriate usage.

9.3.2   *Adversarial validation*

If the manual worst-case analysis won't provide new insights, a "machine learning model for analyzing machine learning models" could help. In chapter 7, we discussed a concept called adversarial validation. It was derived from ML competitions and is used to check whether the distribution of the two datasets differs. Often we concatenate, train, and test datasets with labels 0 and 1.

Adversarial validation can be easily transferred to the rails of residual analysis: we set 0 for "good" samples of data and 1 for "bad" samples (e.g., taking the top-N% biggest residuals in the second case). We should try different thresholds for our particular set.

The rest of the algorithm is similar: we fit a simple classifier (e.g., logistic regression) on these labels and calculate the receiver operating characteristic area under the curve (ROC AUC). If two classes are separable (area under the curve is significantly greater than 0.5), then we analyze the model's weights, and this gives us a hint of which exact features best distinguish our "worst" cases from others.

Sometimes we find no easily defined patterns during worst-case analysis. This is fine. It means that we have already captured the most low-hanging fruits in the model improvement space.

9.3.3   *Variety of group analysis*

Group analysis enables the identification of distinct patterns and trends within the residuals of various groups, segments, classes, colors, or clusters. For instance, in both binary and multiclass classification scenarios, one effective approach involves splitting the residuals by classes (i.e., by target variable), allowing for separate analysis of the residuals in each group.

Many typical applications processing tabular data, such as fraud detection systems, rely on grouping samples based on specific characteristics, such as geography or traffic source. By analyzing the residuals within each segment, it becomes possible to uncover common biases present in the model's predictions. These insights can then guide further model refinement by incorporating more relevant features or adjusting the weights of existing features.

When dealing with the data in the form of text, images, or videos, there may be no distinct cohorts or groups by default. In such cases, an alternative method involves manually classifying a set of N residuals and assigning labels to each issue encountered (e.g., identifying images that are too dark or blurry or flagging texts with specific wording or style). This process allows for the discovery of specific problematic clusters where the model underperforms. Consequently, it provides guidance on what type of data should be collected next to improve the system.

9.3.4 *Corner-case analysis*

Corner-case analysis aims to test the model in rare circumstances. Typically, we would like to have a benchmark, a fixed set of already-captured corner cases, to quickly examine the behavior of each new model.

Here are some ideas for what we can check during corner-case analysis:

- *Forecasting models*—Users/items with short or no history, users/items with extremely large numbers of actions/sales, highest and lowest values in feature X, users/items with rare actions/sales
- *Image segmentation*—Bad-quality images, low-resolution images, high-resolution images, occlusions and reflections, abnormal lighting conditions, multiple objects in one image, no objects in the image
- *Language models*—Shortest and longest texts, jokes, offensive topics, simple arithmetic, text with typos, text with N different languages, extensive usage of emojis
- *Voice recognition*—Shortest or longest audio, bad-quality audio, audio with no voice, music instead of audio, samples with pronunciation that are too fast or too slow, loud environment, silent voice, samples with multiple speakers (aka "cocktail party")

While the best/worst-case analyses ask which data our model digests excellently or badly, the corner-case analysis and cohort analysis ask about the model's performance on predefined subsets of data.

Campfire story from Arseny

When I was working for the augmented-reality company, one important piece of the system was a key-point detector based on a deep learning model. The task was to identify several key points that were later used to understand the object coordinates. The training pipeline was written with proper diagnostic tools from the very beginning, so we identified at an early stage that certain samples with high loss demonstrated one common pattern—some images contained mirrors or other reflecting surfaces (even a puddle on a rainy day!), and the model could pick not the key point versus its reflection. It meant we needed additional properties from the system: choose the "real" object, remember it between frames, and ignore key points that belong to mirrored objects. Early understanding of this problem helped us tinker with a solution that could mitigate the reflected key points situation.

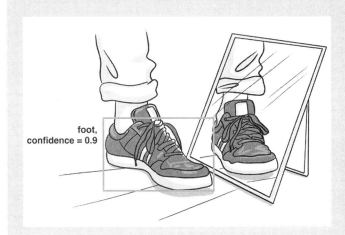

foot,
confidence = 0.9

**Model detects the real
foot, not the reflection**

9.4 Design document: Error analysis

Because we're convinced that error analysis should be among the essential elements of ML system design, we will include this phase in both our design documents.

9.4.1 Error analysis for Supermegaretail

We start off with Supermegaretail, where we will suggest the approach that will help the company achieve its main goal—to reduce the gap between delivered and sold items, making it as narrow as possible while avoiding out-of-stock situations.

DESIGN DOCUMENT: SUPERMEGARETAIL

VI. ERROR ANALYSIS

Remember that we have six quantile losses for 1.5th, 25th, 50th, 75th, 95th, and 99th quantiles of the target and corresponding six models for each. The constant baseline estimates these quantiles for each product based on the last N days of its sales. These baselines already have some residual distribution with some specific bias that is helpful to consider.

Comparing more complex models (linear models and gradient boosting) with these dummy baselines will give us an understanding of whether we are moving in the right direction in modeling and feature engineering.

I. LEARNING-CURVE ANALYSIS

i. Convergence analysis

A step-wise learning curve based on the number of iterations comes into play only when we start experimenting with the gradient-boosting algorithm. The key questions we should answer when examining the loss curve are

- Does the model converge at all?
- Does the model beat baseline metrics (quantile loss, mean absolute percent error, etc.)?
- Are issues like underfitting/overfitting presented or not?

Once we ensure the model converges, we can pick a sufficient number of trees on a rough grid (500-1,000-2,000-3,000-5,000) and fixate for future experiments. For simpler baselines, convergence analysis is not needed.

ii. Model complexity

We will use a model-wise learning curve to decide an optimal number of features and overall model complexity.

Let's say we fixate all hyperparameters except the number of lags we use: the more we take, the more complicated patterns and seasonalities our model can capture—and the easier it will be to overfit training data. Should it be $N - 1$, $N - 2$, $N - 3$ days? or $N - 1$, $N - 2$, ..., $N - 30$ days? The optimal number can be determined by the "model size vs. error size" plot.

Similarly, we can optimize window sizes. For instance, windows "7/14/21/..." are more granular than "30/60/90/..." ones. The appropriate level of granularity can be chosen, again, by using a model-wise learning curve.

In the same fashion, we tweak other key hyperparameters of the model during the initial adjustments—for instance, regularization term size.

iii. Dataset size

Do we need to use all the available data to train the model? How many last months are enough and relevant? Do we need to utilize all (day, store, item) data points, or can we downsample 20%/10%/5% of them without noticeable downgrading in metrics?

Here comes the rescue: the sample-wise learning curve analysis that determines how many samples are necessary for the error on the validation set to reach a plateau.

We should make an important design decision of whether to use (day, store, item) as an object of the dataset or move to less granular (week, store, item). The last option reduces the number of required computations by a factor of 7, while model performance can either be left unchanged or even be increased.

This design decision affects not only the demand forecasting service speed and performance but also the overall product (a stock management system), drastically reshaping the landscape of its possible use cases. Therefore, despite the possible advantages, this decision should be agreed upon with our product managers, users (category managers), and stakeholders.

II. RESIDUAL ANALYSIS

Remember that we have an asymmetric cost function: overstock is far less harmful than out-of-stock problems. We have either expired goods or missed profit. The uncovered demand problem is a much worse scenario, and in the long run, it is expressed in customers' dissatisfaction and an increased risk that they will pass to competitors.

i. Residual distribution

The mentioned peculiarity of the demand should guide us throughout the residual analysis of our forecasting model: positive residuals (overprediction) are more preferred than negative ones (underpredictions). However, too much overprediction is bad as well.

Therefore, we plot the distribution of the residuals along with their bias (a simple average among raw residuals). We expect this to be true in one of the following possible scenarios:

- A small positive bias reveals slight overprediction, which is the desirable outcome. If, in addition, residuals are not widely spread (low variance), we get a perfect scenario.
- Equally spread residuals in both negative and positive directions would be okay but is less preferred than the previous scenario. We should force the model to produce more optimistic forecasts to ensure we minimize missed profit.
- The worst scenario is when we have a skew in favor of negative residuals. It means our model tends to increase customers' dissatisfaction. This would definitely be a red flag for the current model version deployment.
- If we have a skew but favor positive residuals, this is unambiguously a good case for Supermegaretail as well and, hence, is less preferred than the first case.

These scenarios are applicable when we try to estimate unbiased demand (we use median prediction for that). But as mentioned, we also have several other models for other quantiles (1.5%, 25%, 75%, 95%, 99%).

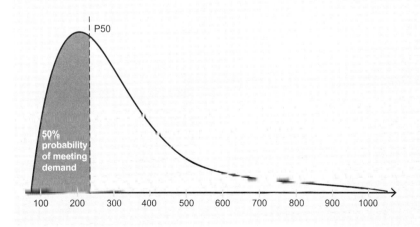

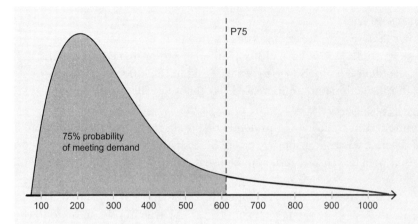

For each of them, we analyze the basic assumption behind each model—for example:

- Is it true that 95% of residuals are positive for a model that predicts a 95% quantile?
- Is it true that 75% of residuals are negative for a model that predicts a 25% quantile?

ii. Elasticity

We should validate the elasticity assumptions using elasticity curves. There is no solid understanding of whether all the goods are expected to demonstrate elasticity, and this needs to be confirmed with stakeholders.

If we face problems related to elasticity, we have two options to improve the elasticity capturing:

- *Postprocessing* (fast, simple, ad hoc solution)—We can apply an additional model (e.g., isotonic regression) for prediction postprocessing to calibrate forecasts.
- *Improving the model* (slow, hard, generic solution)—This requires additional modeling, feature engineering, data preprocessing, etc. There is no predefined set of actions that will solve the problem for sure.

iii. Best-case vs. worst-case vs. corner-case

Each time we roll out a new version of the model, we automatically report its performance in best/worst/corner cases and save the top-N% cases as artifacts of the training pipeline. The following is a draft of a checklist of questions for which we should find answers in this report:

- What's the model's prediction error when the sales history of an item is short? Are the residuals mostly positive or mostly negative?
- What about items with a high price or with a low price?
- How does prediction error depend on weekends/holidays/promotion days?
- What are the commonalities among the items with almost zero residuals? Is a long sales history necessarily required for them? How long should the sales

history be to get acceptable performance? Does the model require other conditions that can help us to distinguish those cases where we are certain about the quality of the forecast?

- What are the commonalities among the items with the largest negative residuals? We would 100% prefer to exclude these cases or whole categories from A/B-testing groups or pilots. We should also focus on these items when we start to improve the model.
- What do the items with the largest positive residuals have in common?

9.4.2   Error analysis for PhotoStock Inc.

Now we get back to PhotoStock Inc., which requires a modern search tool able to find the most relevant shots based on customers' text queries while providing excellent performance and displaying the most relevant images in stock.

DESIGN DOCUMENT: PHOTOSTOCK INC.

VI. ERROR ANALYSIS

To enable early diagnostics of potential problems, we should include tools for error analysis from the very beginning. In this section of the document, we want to plan in advance some parts we want to focus on.

i. Learning curve analysis

- Loss curves should be enabled for sanity checks and further tuning of vital hyperparameters like early stopping threshold, learning rate, and many others.
- Given our loss is composite (contains multiple components; see the previous Metrics and Losses section), we need to be able to see the loss curves per component to adapt its weights.
- It should be possible to train the model on subsamples of data to draw sample-size learning curves later and estimate how new data improves the overall performance.
- In parallel with loss curves, there should be metric curves to ensure they're fairly correlated.
- Given the dataset may be shared, we need to be able to see the curves per shard as well.

ii. Residual analysis

- For each training epoch, we should report the most interesting samples, such as samples with the highest/lowest loss overall and per component.
- For each displayed sample, metadata should be available, so we report not only the search query and relevant images but also category, tags, query geo, query lang, and other attributes that may arise later.

After training each candidate model (the model that is considered to be good enough to be used for the real system), we suggest the following procedure:

- Sample 100 results with high loss/metric.
- For each one, suggest a short hypothesis about how this sample is outstanding (e.g., the suggested image is blurry, the image description is overoptimized, the query is too short, etc.) and group the results by these resolutions. Further analysis should be performed every time new steps of system improvement are planned, as it is a significant source of the signal.

In the future, we can consider applying interpretability techniques here as well because, at some point, questions like "Why image X is semantically close to image Y" will arise. However, from the current perspective, it can be postponed.

Summary

- Don't hesitate to apply error analysis while designing your ML system, as it will help you reveal its weak spots and suggest ways of improving it.
- Learning curve analysis is a vital first step for defining the efficiency of your model. If the model does not converge and there are overfitting and/or underfitting issues, there is no need for the rest of the analysis.
- The presence of either overfitting or underfitting is an indicator of a possible imbalance between the model's complexity and the amount of input data.
- Depending on the type of loss curve you're observing during error analysis, there is a certain list of actions you need to take to debug detected issues.
- Designed to calculate the differences between the predicted and actual values, residual analysis is essential for verifying model assumptions, detecting sources of metric changes, ensuring the fairness of residuals, performing worst-case and best-case analysis, and examining corner cases.

Training pipelines

10

This chapter covers

- The essence of training pipelines
- Tools and platforms you can use to build and maintain training pipelines
- Scalability and configurability of training pipelines
- Methods of testing pipelines

There's an empirical heuristic to distinguish experienced machine learning (ML) engineers from newcomers: ask them to describe a working system's training procedure in one sentence. Newcomers tend to focus on models, while somewhat experienced individuals include data processing. Mature engineers often describe the pipeline—a list of stages required to produce a trained ML model in the end. In this chapter, we will walk in ML engineers' shoes to analyze these steps and discuss how to interconnect and orchestrate them.

10.1 Training pipeline: What are you?

Imagine a small pizza chain company. Its business has been a success in the local market, but the owners who understand that software is eating the world (a phrase

taken from Marc Anderssen's article, https://a16z.com/why-software-is-eating-the
-world/) and everything is going digital know there's more pie to grab. So it makes
this digitalization bet before the COVID pandemic and hires several engineers to
build mobile apps, a simple customer relationship management plan, and multiple
internal software systems. In other words, the company doesn't have the scale or appe-
tite of a tech giant, but it follows major trends and knows how to invest in software
now to make significant profits later. Suffice it to mention that its app helped the company survive the pandemic in 2020.

Now, with the company following trends and the AI hype train full steam ahead, it's
no surprise that it hires Jane, a young and promising ML engineer whose interest in ML
is undeniable. After onboarding, the CTO delegates her first problem to solve: build an
AI-powered assistant that will help Pizzaiolos perform basic visual assessments like listing and calculating the number of components on the pizza base for each order.

The software development lifecycle in this pizza company hasn't included ML systems so far. Thus, engineering manager Alex asks Jane to prepare a model and a small
code snippet showing how to run it; the internal systems team will handle the rest.

Fast-forward several months later: Jane gathered a small dataset and trained a
model, and it all looked fine during the initial testing, so Alex's team managed to
wrap it in a service. But right before deployment, the product manager brought multiple new recipes that were added to the menu and said the model should be able to
support those too. This was nothing complicated and involved just adding some more
data, changing the labels map, and retraining the model—sounds like something that
shouldn't affect the deployment schedule much. However, after a discussion, Jane and
Alex realized it would take several more months, even assuming the new dataset is
readily available. What went wrong here? Jane performed all the required steps to
train a model—manually validating datasets, applying numerous data processing and
cleaning steps in the Jupyter Notebook environment, training the model with multiple interruptions, validating the result with the chef and customer happiness team on
an ad hoc basis, uploading the trained model to the company's shared storage, and
sending the link back to Alex.

> **NOTE** She did all the right things but followed an ad hoc approach, with no
> proper effort to make those steps reproducible in a single, transparent workflow.

With this example, we want to show that ML is not just about training a model but also
about building a pipeline that allows for the preparation of the model and other artifacts in a reproducible way. In this chapter, we will discuss the steps in the pipeline,
how to orchestrate them, and how to make them reproducible.

10.1.1 Training pipeline vs. inference pipeline

In the ML world, the term "pipeline" is used in many different contexts. Usually, people refer to a pipeline as a series of ordered steps and processes. Each step is a pro-
gram that takes some input, performs some actions, and produces some output. The

output of one step is the input for the next step. Speaking more formally, we can usually describe the pipeline as a directed acyclic graph (DAG) of steps.

To make things more complicated, the model itself is usually a pipeline of another kind. For example, a simple logistic regression classifier is often enhanced with a feature scaling step, resulting in a pipeline of at least two steps. Usually, there's also basic feature engineering (e.g., one-hot encoding for categorical variables), so even the simplest model has the properties of a pipeline. Other modalities like images, text, audio, etc., require additional preprocessing steps. For instance, a typical image classification model is a pipeline of image reading, normalization, resizing, and the model itself. If we switch to natural language processing, the pipeline almost always starts with text tokenization, etc. All in all, there's a lot of space for ambiguity and confusion surrounding the term "pipeline" itself. To make things clearer, we will use the following terminology.

Training pipeline refers to a pipeline used to train a model. It's a DAG of steps that takes the full dataset and, optionally, additional metadata as input and produces a trained model as output. It is a higher-level abstraction than the model itself (see figure 10.1).

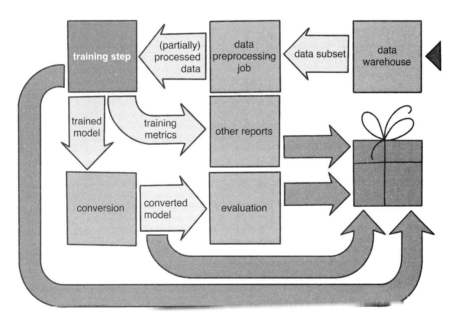

Figure 10.1   A DAG scheme representing a training pipeline

Inference pipeline refers to a pipeline used to run a model in production or as part of a training pipeline (e.g., training a neural network with gradient descent requires numerous inference steps, each of which is a pipeline). It's a DAG of steps that takes raw data as input and produces predictions as output. It is a lower-level abstraction than the training pipeline (see figure 10.2).

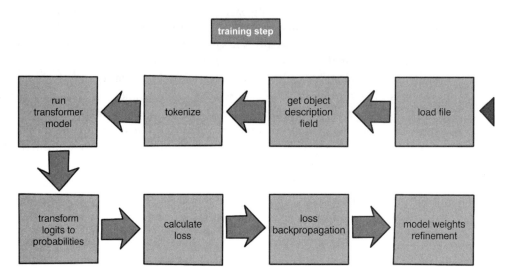

Figure 10.2   A scheme representing a training step in a pipeline

In this chapter, we will focus on the training pipeline, while the inference pipeline will be discussed in chapter 15. At the highest level, a typical training pipeline includes the following steps:

1 Data fetching
2 Preprocessing
3 Model training
4 Model evaluation and testing
5 Postprocessing
6 Report generation
7 Artifact packaging

Let's briefly break down each of the steps.

Data fetching is the first step in the pipeline. It is responsible for downloading the data from the sources and making it available for the subsequent steps. As mentioned in chapter 6, we do not consider ourselves data engineering experts, so we will not discuss data fetching and storage in detail.

Preprocessing is usually the second step in the pipeline. It is a very generic term that can have a different meaning for a respective task. In general, preprocessing is a set of actions performed to prepare the data for model training. While we separate the training and inference pipelines for the sake of the book's structure, the distinction can be somewhat blurry in practice. For example, you can fully preprocess the raw dataset before training the model or, alternatively, make it part of a single model inference. In this context, we are discussing training-specific preprocessing. Feature selection is one example of such preprocessing: we only do it before training and freeze the selected features for the subsequent steps. *Model training* is the core of the training pipeline. It is a step that takes preprocessed data and produces a trained model; it is usually the longest and most complex (especially in deep learning-based systems) step in the pipeline.

After the model has been trained, it can be *evaluated and tested*. These are different aspects aiming to answer the same question: how good is the model? Evaluation is a step of computing metrics, while tests are a set of checks performed to ensure that the model is working as expected.

Postprocessing is a step that is performed after evaluation and testing. It is a set of actions performed to prepare the model for deployment. Here, we can convert the model to a format supported by the target platforms, apply posttraining quantization or other optimizations if applicable, prepare tasks for human evaluation, and so on. It is worth noting that postprocessing and evaluation can be swapped. For example, we can evaluate the model before converting it to the target format, or alternatively, we can convert the model to the target format and then evaluate it using the deployment format.

Artifact packaging is the last step in the pipeline. It is responsible for packaging the model and other artifacts (e.g., config files with preprocessor parameters) into a format that can be easily deployed to production. The goal here is to simplify further deployment and separate the training and deployment pipelines. Ideally, the output should be as agnostic as possible to the training pipeline. For example, the model is exported to a universal format like ONNX for backend serving or CoreML for iOS serving, all config files are exported to a universal format like JSON, and any changes in the training pipeline should affect deployment as little as possible. Otherwise, the deployment pipeline will be tightly coupled with the training pipeline and will require many changes after each training pipeline update, becoming an obstacle for rapid model development and related experiments.

Reports are a special case of artifacts. It is a generic term that can be related to many things, including a basic table containing validation/test metrics, various types of error analysis (recall chapter 9), additional visualizations, and other auxiliary information. While these artifacts are not directly used for deployment, they're crucial to consider the training successful; no responsible engineer can release a newly trained model without having at least a short look at proper reports. The only exception we have seen is a variation of an AutoML scenario when many new models are trained automatically per user requests. In this case, manual validation is not always possible; thus, engineers can only review suspicious outliers. We will touch on the topic of the release cycle in chapter 13.

Some of these artifacts are related to experiment tracking and reproducibility, and those are crucial for projects with multiple contributors or involved parties. When a researcher works alone on their own problem, they can track all their ideas and experiments using a simple notebook or a text file. However, when a team of researchers works on the same problem, they need a more structured way to track, compare, and reproduce their experiments. A centralized repository for all experiments is one tool that can help achieve this.

10.2   *Tools and platforms*

Tools and practices related to the training pipeline, along with the inference pipelines, deployment pipelines, and monitoring services in the context of the ML system design, are often attributed to ML operations (MLOps). Given that MLOps is a relatively new field, there are no well-established standards for platforms and tools. Some of them are relatively recognizable (MLflow, Kubeflow, BentoML, AWS Sagemaker, Google Vertex AI, Azure ML), some are gaining traction right now, and some are still in the early stages of development.

In this book, we don't want to highlight any specific platform or tool, so we will not discuss them in detail. Given the pace of changes in the MLOps landscape, it's very likely that our current understanding of the tools and platforms will be outdated by the time the book is published. Instead, we will focus on the principles and practices that are common to all platforms and tools. In the simplest case, you can implement a full training pipeline using generic non-ML tools—by creating a series of Python scripts connected with shell scripts, for example. However, this is rarely the case in practice: usually, there are some ML-specific tools that introduce abstractions and simplify the pipeline implementation. Most MLOps tools are "opinionated," which means that using them strongly suggests a particular way of structuring your code. In the long run, this improves the training pipeline's code consistency and makes it easier to maintain in the future (see chapter 16). Typical features required from the training pipeline platform are

- *Resolving dependencies*—As the pipeline is a DAG of steps, it's important to resolve dependencies between steps and run them in the right order.
- *Reproducibility*—Given a set of parameters and pipeline version (e.g., specified by git commit), the pipeline should produce the same result every time.
- *Integration with computational resources (such as cloud providers or Kubernetes installations)*—For example, users should be able to run the job on a specific compute instance (e.g., a virtual machine with X CPU cores and N GPUs) or on a cluster of instances.
- *Artifacts storage*—Once the training pipeline has been run, its artifacts should be available. Experiment tracking can be viewed as a subset of this feature.
- *Caching intermediate results*—As long as many steps in the pipeline are computationally expensive, it's important to cache intermediate results to save resources and time.

Besides features, it is important to mention some nonfunctional requirements that practitioners need from platforms, including cost-effectiveness and data privacy (especially in such sensitive areas as healthcare or legal).

It's important to emphasize here that features don't have to be covered by the same platform. For example, you can use a generic platform for running the pipeline and a custom tool for experiment tracking because market solutions don't satisfy custom requirements. Sometimes it's just a matter of cost optimization. Arseny worked in a company that used a hybrid of two tools just because one provided many useful features and an overall nice developer experience, while the other was integrated with a cloud provider with the cheapest GPUs for training. In this situation, it was reasonable to spend some time on integration and save a lot of money on training costs.

Choosing proper tools is determined by the problem scale and the infrastructure of the company. FAANG-level companies usually have their own ML platforms and tools that can operate on a proper scale, while smaller companies typically prefer a set of open-source tools and cloud services. Every tool has its own adoption cost, so it's important to choose the proper tool for the right problem. To the best of our knowledge, there is no one-size-fits-all solution, unlike with many other more mature software engineering problems (see figure 10.3).

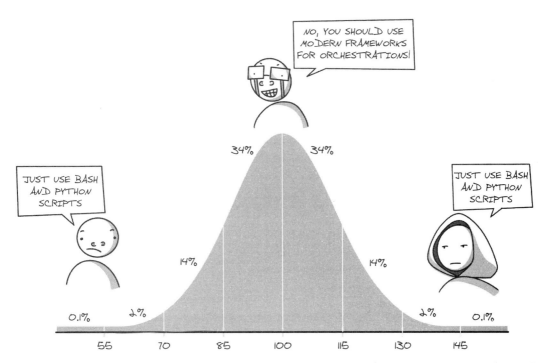

Figure 10.3   Using proper frameworks for a training pipeline is usually a good practice, although sometimes it is enough to keep things simple.

10.3   Scalability

Scalability can be a crucial property of the training pipeline for certain problems. If we're dealing with a dataset of thousands of samples of almost any kind, it's not a significant concern, as even a single machine can likely handle it. However, when it comes to huge datasets, the situation changes. What constitutes a huge dataset? It depends on the problem and type of data (1 million tabular records are nothing compared to 1 million video clips), but what if we have to choose a criterion "for a dataset that doesn't fit into the RAM of a single machine"?

The current size of a dataset should not be confused with the size of a dataset expected to be used in the future. We may face a cold-start problem (see chapter 6), and having even thousands of samples may be a significant advantage for the initial phase of system development. However, in the future, it can grow by several orders of magnitude, and if you want to use all the data, you need to be able to handle it.

While there is no silver bullet for training models on huge datasets, there are two classic software engineering approaches to scaling. Those are vertical and horizontal scaling (see figure 10.4).

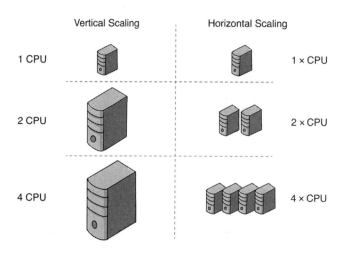

Figure 10.4   Vertical scaling vs. horizontal scaling

Vertical scaling means upgrading your hardware or replacing the training machine with a more powerful node. The biggest advantage of this approach lies in its simplicity; adding more resources (especially if using cloud compute resources, which is often the case) is very easy. The drawback, however, is how limited vertical scaling is. Let's say you doubled or even quadrupled machine RAM and upgraded the GPU to the latest generation. If that's not enough, there isn't much you can do within the vertical scaling approach.

Horizontal scaling involves splitting the load between multiple machines. The first level of horizontal scaling is using multiple GPU machines; in this case, an ML engineer often needs to introduce small changes to the pipeline code, as most of the heavy lifting is already done by the training framework. However, this isn't true horizontal scaling, as we're still talking about a single machine. Genuine horizontal scaling involves using multiple machines and distributing the load among them. Nowadays, this type of scaling is often provided by frameworks as well, but it is more complex and usually requires more engineering effort during implementation. DeepSpeed by Microsoft, Accelerate by Hugging Face, and Horovod, originated in Uber, are some examples of such frameworks.

One ML-specific way of scaling is subsampling: if your dataset is overly huge, it could be reasonable to subsample it and reduce the required compute resources. The most straightforward way of subsampling is applicable to most problems and involves removing duplicated samples. However, there are more aggressive methods: downsampling near-duplicates (samples that are very similar based on a simple distance function; e.g., Levenshtein distance for strings) and downsampling based on an internal ID (e.g., not more than X samples per user) or an artificial ID (e.g., clusterizing the full dataset with a simple method and keeping not more than X samples per cluster).

In ML pipelines, scaling often requires changing other pipeline parameters: for example, batch size is limited by GPU memory, larger batches lead to faster convergence, and the learning rate schedule depends on both batch size and expected convergence schedule. So the ability to alter the parameters is important.

10.4 Configurability

When ML engineers design the configurability of a training pipeline, there is a spectrum with two bad practices on each side: underconfiguration and overconfiguration.

Underconfiguration means that the pipeline is not configurable enough, making it difficult to change the model's architecture, dataset, preprocessing steps, etc. Things are hardcoded here and there in a convoluted way, and it's hard to understand how the pipeline works or alter even the simplest aspects. This is a typical problem in the early stages of ML development. When the pipeline is small and simple, it's easy to understand and change. Therefore, researchers without a software engineering background may find it unnecessary to introduce proper software abstractions, leading to the addition of more and more code without proper structure. This antipattern often occurs among such researchers.

Overconfiguration is not ideal either. A typical ML pipeline has many hyperparameters related to dataset processing, model architecture, feature engineering, and the training process. In reality, it's hard to predict all the possible use cases and parameters that can be changed, and inexperienced developers may try to cover all the possible cases and introduce as many abstractions as possible. At some point, these additional abstraction layers only increase complexity. Note that in this section, we use "parameters of the training pipeline" and "hyperparameters of the model" interchangeably. Just as a reminder, hyperparameters are those parameters of the model that are not learned during the training process but are set by the user.

In the example of overconfigured code in the following listing, we see how a multi-level hierarchy of subconfigs may complicate things.

Listing 10.1   Multilevel hierarchy of subcodings

```
def train():
    ...
    batch_size = 32
    ...
    learning_rate = 3e-4
    ...
    model.train(data, batch_size, loss_fn)
    ...

^ example of underconfigured code: things are too rigid


class Config(BaseConfig):
    def __init__(self):
        self.data_config = DataConfig()
        self.model_config = ModelConfig()
        self.training_config = TrainingConfig()
        self.inference_config = InferenceConfig()
        self.environment_config = EnvironmentConfig()


class DataConfig(BaseConfig):
    def __init__(self):
        self.train_data_config = TrainDataConfig()
        self.validation_data_config = ValidationDataConfig()
        self.test_data_config = TestDataConfig()


config = Config(
    data_config=DataConfig(
        train_data_config=TrainDataConfig(
            ...
        ),
        validation_data_config=ValidationDataConfig(
            ...
        ),
        test_data_config=TestDataConfig(
            ...
        ),
    ),
    ...
)
```

To find a good balance between the two extremes, you should estimate the probability of various parameters being changed. For example, it's practically 100% certain that datasets will be updated, and it's not very likely that activation functions inside the model will be changed. So it's reasonable to make datasets configurable while ignoring activation functions. Changeable parameters differ for various pipelines, so the only way to find a good balance is to consider what potential experiments you would deem low-hanging fruits in the next few months. One helpful guide we recommend for deep learning-based pipelines is provided by the Google team: https://github.com/google-research/tuning_playbook.

After preliminarily deciding which hyperparameters are tunable, it's important to determine the tuning strategy. When computational resources are limited, hand-crafted experiments are preferable. When resources are abundant, it makes sense to apply an automated hyperparameter tuning method, such as a straightforward random search or a more advanced Bayesian optimization. Tools for hyperparameter tuning (e.g., Hyperopt, Optuna, and scikit-optimize) can be part of the ML platform and may dictate how the configuration files should look.

From our experience, extensive hyperparameter tuning is more applicable for small datasets, where it's possible to run numerous experiments in a reasonable time. When a single experiment takes weeks, it's more practical to rely on the intuition of the ML engineer and run a few experiments manually. It is worth noting that experiments with smaller datasets may help build this intuition, although not every conclusion may generalize to a large training run.

It is important to find a proper way to config the training pipeline (see figure 10.5).

Figure 10.5   A pipeline requires proper config for optimal performance

The most typical approach would be dedicating a single file (often written in a specific language like YAML or TOML) that contains all the changeable values. Another popular way to go is using libraries like Hydra (https://hydra.cc/). One antipattern we have seen is having the config spread between the training pipeline files with the same parameter specified in multiple files that have various priority levels (e.g., batch size can be read from file X, but if not specified there, try fetching from file Y). It could be error-prone at the experimentation stage, especially if experiments are performed by less experienced engineers who are not familiar with this particular pipeline.

10.5   *Testing*

One common problem we often see in ML pipelines is the lack of tests. It's not surprising, as testing ML pipelines is not an easy task. When building a regular software system, we can test it by running it with some input and checking the output. However, running a training pipeline may take days, and obviously we can't run it again after every change we implement. Another problem, as mentioned earlier, is that ML pipelines are often not configurable enough, making them difficult to test in isolation. Finally, given the number of possible hyperparameters, it's nearly impossible to test all the possible combinations in a reasonable time. Simply put, introducing tests to ML pipelines is a challenging task. But it's worth doing!

Proper tests serve three purposes:

- Avoiding regression bugs while introducing changes
- Increasing iteration speed by catching defects earlier
- Improving pipeline design overall, as it forces an engineer to find the proper balance of configurability

Our suggestion for testing ML pipelines is to use a combination of high-level smoke tests for the whole pipeline and low-level unit tests for at least its most important individual components.

A smoke test should be as fast as possible so you can run it on a small subset of the dataset, a small number of epochs, and maybe with a reduced version of the model. It should check that the pipeline runs without errors and produces reasonable output—for example, it ensures that the loss is decreasing on this toy dataset. The following listing shows a simplified example of a smoke test for a training pipeline.

> **Listing 10.2   What a smoke test for a training pipeline might look like**

```
from unittest.mock import patch, Mock
import torch
from training_pipeline import train, get_config


class DummyResnet(torch.nn.Module):
    def __init__(self):
        super().__init__()
        self.model = torch.nn.Sequential(torch.nn.AdaptiveAvgPool2d(1),
                                         torch.nn.Conv2d(3, 2048, 1))

    def forward(self, x):
        return self.model(x).squeeze(-1).squeeze(-1)


def test_train_pipeline():
    config = get_config()
    config["dataset_path"] = "/path/to/fixture"
    config["num_epochs"] = 1
```

```
mock = Mock(wraps=DummyResnet)
with patch('training_pipeline.models.Resnet', mock):
    result = train(config)
    assert mock.call_count == 1
    assert result['train_loss'] < .5
    assert result['val_loss'] < 1
```

Smoke tests like this significantly increase iteration speed, thus simplifying experimentation and debugging. However, there is a downside. Like any integration tests, they require a lot of maintenance efforts on their own. This is because almost any significant pipeline change may affect the code. Lower-level unit tests should cover individual components of the pipeline. It's not uncommon to have a few of them or even none at all—and there's no reason to be ashamed if you don't have them. However, we recommend covering at least the most sensitive components. An example of such a sensitive component could be the final model conversion—imagine the model is trained with Pytorch and later is supposed to be deployed to iOS (and run with CoreML) and the backend (and run with ONNX). It's important to make sure that the model is converted properly and the conversion process doesn't introduce any changes, which means results by the converted models should be the same as by the original model.

10.5.1 *Property-based testing*

Another group of tests is applicable to the trained model, inspired by the property-based testing approach. Property-based testing is a software testing approach that involves generating random inputs for a function or a system and then verifying that certain properties or invariants hold true for all the inputs. Instead of writing specific test cases with predetermined inputs and expected outputs, property-based testing focuses on defining the general properties that the system should satisfy and then automatically generates test cases to validate those properties.

In the context of an ML project, property-based testing can be used to ensure that the final trained model behaves as expected and satisfies certain properties. The following are some examples of properties that can be tested in an ML project:

- *Consistency*—Given the same input data, the model should produce the same output or prediction consistently, regardless of the number of times it is executed:

$$f(x) = f(x)$$

- *Monotonicity*—In simple ML models, the output should be monotonically increasing or decreasing with respect to certain input features. Property-based testing can be used to verify that the model's output follows the expected monotonic behavior:

$$f(x) < f(y) \text{ if } x_i < y_i$$

Monotonicity is often expected in various price prediction models. For example, the price of a house should increase with its square footage if the rest of the features are fixed.

- *Invariance under transformations*—Some ML models should be invariant under specific transformations of the input data, such as scaling or rotation. Property-based testing can be used to check that the model's output remains unchanged when the input data is transformed in a specific way:

$$f(x) = f(g(x))$$

where g is an expected transformation. This could be a rotation or scaling for images, changing an entity to its synonym for natural language processing, altering the volume of a sound for audio, and so on.

- *Robustness*—The model should be robust to small perturbations in the input data. Property-based testing can be used to verify that the model's output does not change significantly when the input data is perturbed by a small amount:

$$f(x) \approx f(x + \epsilon)$$

- *Negation*—The model should provide the opposite prediction when the input data is flipped. Property-based testing can be used to verify that the model's output is the opposite of the expected output when the input data is negated. The simplest example is the sentiment analysis, where the model usually should predict a negative sentiment if the word "love" is replaced with "hate":

$$f(x) = -f(-x)$$

We already covered a very similar concept in section 5.2.1. The difference is that in one case, we expect some variation in the results (and we want to measure it), while in the other case, we expect strict consistency (and thus we want to assert it). Using some data samples as fixtures and writing property-based tests for them is a good way to ensure that the model behaves as expected and maintains its reliability.

An exact list of tests is not usually included in the design document; however, we recommend thinking about it in advance and mentioning it in the document. The design document is often used as a reference for implementation, so it's useful to mention the tests in it.

> **NOTE**   If you're interested in ML testing, we recommend Arseny's slides with a deeper review of the topic: https://arseny.info/reliable_ML.

10.6   *Design document: Training pipelines*

As we continue our work on two separate design documents for our imaginary businesses, it's time to cover training pipelines for Supermegaretail and PhotoStock Inc.

10.6.1 Training pipeline for Supermegaretail

Let's see how a potential pipeline could look for Supermegaretail.

DESIGN DOCUMENT: SUPERMEGARETAIL

VII. TRAINING PIPELINE

I. OVERVIEW

The demand forecasting model for Supermegaretail aims to predict the demand for specific items in specific stores during a particular period. To achieve this, we need a training pipeline that can preprocess data, train the model, and evaluate its performance. We assume the pipeline should be scalable and easy to maintain and allow for experimentation with various model architectures, feature engineering techniques, and hyperparameters.

II. TOOLSET

The suggested tools for the pipeline are

- Python as the primary programming language for its versatility and rich ecosystem for data processing and ML
- Spark for parallel and distributed computing
- PyTorch for deep learning models
- MLflow for tracking experiments and managing the machine learning lifecycle
- Docker for containerization and reproducibility
- AWS Sagemaker or Google Cloud AI Platform for cloud-based training and deployment

III. DATA PREPROCESSING

The data preprocessing stage should include

- *Data cleaning*—Handling missing values, removing duplicates, and correcting erroneous data points
- *Feature engineering*—Creating new features from existing ones, such as aggregating sales data, extracting temporal features (day of the week, month, etc.), and incorporating external data (e.g., holidays, weather, and promotions)
- *Data normalization*—Scaling numeric features to a standard range
- *Train–test split*—Splitting the dataset into training and validation sets, ensuring that they do not overlap in time to prevent data leakage

IV. MODEL TRAINING

The model training stage should accommodate various model architectures and configurations, including

- *Baseline models*—Simple forecasting methods like moving average, exponential smoothing, and autoregressive integral moving average
- *ML models*—Decision trees, random forests, gradient boosting machines, and support vector machines

- *Deep learning models*—Recurrent neural networks, long short-term memory networks, and transformers (if needed!)

We should also implement a mechanism for hyperparameter tuning, such as grid search or Bayesian optimization, to find the best model configurations.

V. MODEL EVALUATION

Model performance should be evaluated using metrics we derived prior to that, such as quantile metrics for quantiles of 1.5, 25, 50, 75, 95, and 99, both as is and with weights equal to SKU price. It is calculated as point estimates with 95% confidence intervals (using bootstrap or cross-validation) plus standard metrics such as mean absolute error (MAE), mean squared error (MSE), or root mean squared error (RMSE). We should also include custom metrics specific to Supermegaretail's business requirements, such as the cost of overstock and out-of-stock situations. (See *Validation* chapter.)

VI. EXPERIMENT TRACKING AND MODEL MANAGEMENT

Using a tool like MLflow, we should track and manage experiments, including

- Model parameters and hyperparameters
- Input data and feature engineering techniques
- Evaluation metrics and performance
- Model artifacts, such as trained model weights and serialized models

VII. CONTINUOUS INTEGRATION AND DEPLOYMENT

The training pipeline should be integrated into Supermegaretail's existing CI/CD infrastructure. This includes setting up automated training and evaluation on a regular basis, ensuring that the latest data is used to update the model, and deploying the updated model to production with minimal manual intervention.

VIII. MONITORING AND MAINTENANCE

We should monitor the model's performance in production and set up alerts for significant deviations from expected performance. This will enable us to catch problems early and trigger retraining or model updates when necessary (see chapter 14).

IX. FUTURE WORK AND EXPERIMENTATION

The training pipeline should be flexible enough to accommodate future experimentation, such as incorporating additional data sources, trying new model architectures, and adjusting loss functions to optimize for specific business objectives.

10.6.2 *Training pipeline for PhotoStock Inc.*

Now we go back to PhotoStock Inc., where we are required to build a smart in-house search engine to boost correct result output.

DESIGN DOCUMENT: PHOTOSTOCK INC.

VII. TRAINING PIPELINE

The multimodal ranking model is a core component of the PhotoStock Inc. search engine, and we need a training pipeline to train this model. As discussed earlier, we have a solid baseline based on the pretrained CLIP model. However, we need to finetune it on our own dataset, which is a combination of images and text descriptions. While the dataset is not going to be large in the beginning, it can grow down the stretch, so we need to make the pipeline somewhat scalable. We assume we can start with training it on a single top-class GPU, but we want to be able to scale it to multiple GPUs on a single machine in the future. We don't aim for fully distributed training at the moment.

We suggest the following toolset for the pipeline:

- *PyTorch*—The default deep learning framework, as it's the most popular one worldwide and has a lot of community support
- *PyTorch Lightning*—A high-level framework to simplify the training loop and make it more reproducible
- *Flyte*—A workflow management tool because it's already used in the company for data engineering jobs, and we can reuse some of the existing code
- *AWS Sagemaker*—A training platform because AWS is already used in the company, and it's easy to integrate with Flyte
- *Tensorboard*—A simple visualization tool for training metrics
- *Docker*—A containerization tool to make the pipeline more portable and reproducible

The pipeline's output should be two models: a text encoder and an image encoder. Both should be converted to static graph representation (ONNX) and saved to S3. Additionally, we should output the list of training parameters that will be used for inference (prompt generation, image preprocessing, distance function). Finally, every run should produce a report with training metrics. All the artifacts should be saved to S3 after the run.

We expect active experimentation in the following areas:

- *What to finetune*—Some components, the full model, or a combination of both with a custom scheduler.
- *Augmentation techniques*—We can use different augmentation techniques for images and text.
- *Various loss functions*—With different weights for different components.
- *Various backbones for the CLIP model family*—For example, convolutional-based or transformer-based encoder for images; there is no strong intuition about which one is better, so we need to experiment with both.
- *Ways to generate text prompts for the text encoder*—It must be a composition of image description, tags, etc.
- *Ways to preprocess image inputs*—For example, resize, crop, pad parameters.

Summary

- Remember that ML is not just about training a model. One of its pillars is building a pipeline that allows for the preparation of the model and other artifacts in a reproducible way.

- While the difference between training pipelines and inference pipelines may seem somewhat vague and hard to distinguish, we suggest the following definition for each: a training pipeline is used to train a model itself, while an inference pipeline is used to run a model in production or as part of a training pipeline.

- The life cycle of a typical training pipeline includes seven sequential steps, from data fetching, preprocessing, training, evaluating, and testing the model to postprocessing, artifact packaging, and report generating.

- At this point, there are no well-established standards for platforms and tools to use when working with pipelines. However, there are time-proven solutions in general ML that you can find fitting for the type of system you're designing.

- At some point, you will face a choice between the two scaling methods for your pipeline—vertical scaling or horizontal scaling. The former is simpler and easy to achieve yet is limited by the potential maximum performance of your machine. The latter, however, allows much bigger opportunities for enhancing the performance of your hardware.

- Try to find a way to make your pipeline well-balanced in terms of its configurability. If you fall into either of the extremes (underconfiguration or overconfiguration), your pipeline will be either too rigid and resistant to change or overly complex for a given set of objectives.

- Don't neglect testing your pipeline! It will help you avoid regression bugs while introducing changes, increase iteration speed by catching defects earlier, and improve the overall design, as it will force you to find the proper balance of configurability.

Features and feature engineering

- The iterative process of feature engineering
- Analyzing feature importance
- Selecting appropriate features for your model
- Pros and cons of feature stores

It is often said that a mediocre model with great features will outperform a great model with poor features. From our experience, this statement couldn't be more true. Features are the critical inputs for your system; they drive your algorithms, provide essential patterns for the model, and feed the data it needs to learn and make predictions. Without good features, the model is blind, deaf, and dumb.

While the role of feature engineering is not crucial for a system designed with a deep learning core in mind, no machine learning (ML) practitioner can ignore their role. In a sense, framing some fancy multimodal data into a deep learning model or even making a prompt for a large language model is a specific way of feature engineering, and that's why classic feature-related techniques like feature importance analysis are still very relevant.

This chapter explores the art and science of creating effective features. We will cover tools that help determine the most valuable features for the system, the engineering challenges we can face, the factors and tradeoffs we should consider while selecting the right subset of features, and how we can ensure that the selected features are reliable and robust.

11.1 *Feature engineering: What are you?*

Feature engineering is an iterative process that involves creating and testing new features or transforming existing features to improve the model's performance. This process requires domain expertise, creativity, and data engineering skills to build new data pipelines for the system. Given its time-consuming and iterative nature, feature engineering often devours a significant portion of resources allocated to modeling.

To secure a fruitful and streamlined modeling process, you should always make sure you assemble an effective feature engineering strategy while designing a system. This plan will become a compass to guide the team through identifying and engineering the most impactful features while minimizing the risk of wasted efforts. By prioritizing iterations in the proper order and charting the course, we can avoid potential pitfalls and ensure our actions add value to the end goal.

Feature engineering in ML is similar to crafting prompt structures in generative models, such as large language models and text-to-image generators. Both features and prompts serve as enhanced inputs that guide the model's "attention focus" (literally or figuratively) toward the most relevant data aspects.

> **NOTE** By developing proper features and prompts, we inject a specific perspective, context, or "inductive bias" into the model, leading it to favor specific outcomes. Despite their different nature, features and prompts share a single goal, which is to contextualize the model with our domain knowledge and direct it toward the outcomes we aim for.

Speaking of powerful deep learning models, in certain domains, such as audio and image processing, feature engineering used to be a complicated problem. Then the deep learning revolution happened, and its practitioners were delighted because instead of engineering endless, barely reliable features, they could now delegate to a deep learning model trained end-to-end. There are even ML practitioners who never engineered features outside of study projects! This trend may be interpreted as a signal that this chapter can be safely skipped. However, we believe that even deep learning-based pipelines may benefit from feature engineering and related techniques. A great example of that comes from Arseny's experience.

Campfire story from Arseny

I was once working on an ML system with a deep learning model under the hood. The system would take an image, process it with a deep learning model, and apply ML-free postprocessing to output a certain number. However, there were inaccuracies within the first step that greatly affected the final result, and the system was not considered production-ready due to poor performance. Improving the first component was hard because of severe data limitations (the system had to work in a few-shot setup—a formal way to say the model should be functional using only a few labeled samples per class). But the trick that eventually saved the day was a simple regression model that refined the final output. Thanks to utilizing handcrafted features, the model was not that data hungry. As a result, a combination of deep learning for the heavy lifting job and a simple feature-based model for inductive bias was powerful enough to make the system production-ready and eventually actively used.

11.1.1 Criteria of good and bad features

Let's break down some of the feature characteristics as well as the tradeoffs we should keep in mind:

- *Model's performance*—Features should align with the business problem and capture relevant aspects of the data to provide meaningful dependencies with the target variable. Working with domain experts helps develop the right set of features, as well as generate new ones. When it comes down to feature importance analysis, it helps to precisely evaluate the contribution of a given feature and get insights into which features bring us closer to the project's goal.

- *Amount of historical data*—Limited historical data can result in missing values, reducing the overall quality of the dataset. Re-creating missing data through a one-time data engineering effort retrospectively seems like a good solution, but it is not always feasible. On the other hand, the lack of a sufficient amount of historical data can prevent forecasting models from capturing trends and seasonality in feature value.

- *Tradeoffs between the quantity and the quality of features*—While having more features improves the predictive power of an ML model, too many irrelevant or redundant features will lead to overfitting and eventually to decreased performance. We always prefer the model to focus on a small set of strong and diverse features rather than spreading its focus on many generated and correlated ones.

- *Interpretability and explainability*—These are the crucial factors to consider when designing features. While complex features may improve the model's performance, they can also reduce interpretability and make it difficult to explain the reasoning behind predictions. On the other hand, simple features may be more interpretable, but they can only capture a part of the nuances in the data. Striking a balance between interpretability and performance is essential and may vary depending on a specific system and domain.

- *Development complexity of features*—Complex features may require more time to develop. They either depend on other features and sophisticated data pipelines or rely on new data sources, which makes them more challenging to implement and maintain. They require more data engineering efforts to create and maintain data pipelines. Therefore, it's important to carefully consider the cost and benefits of each feature and decide whether additional complexity is worth the investment.

- *Feature cost and service-level agreement (SLA)*—In addition to considering the computational complexity of individual features, you must also consider the overall time required to compute all the features, as well as the required RAM to support the constantly growing load. This includes the time required to compute each feature and any dependencies between them. Feature interactions dictate the order of feature calculations and the possibility of their parallelization. For example, for real-time applications, features that require much time to compute may not be feasible due to SLAs. Moreover, it is important to consider data availability for training and inference pipelines. If we cannot get all the necessary data during serving, the model will end up with inaccurate or incomplete predictions.
- *Risks of poorly designed features*—Fragile features lead to the fragility of the whole system. They can be sensitive to data or model changes, causing unstable or unpredictable behavior. Features that rely on external data sources or APIs may be subject to changes or disruptions, affecting the model's reliability. To prevent it, we should carefully test and validate features before integrating them into the model and monitor their performance over time to ensure they continue to provide business value.

Feature engineering is aimed to be continuous, as business goals and data distributions change over time. We must constantly evaluate and update our feature set to ensure it remains relevant and effective in solving business problems. When developing features, it is important to keep track of the changes made to each feature, including their versioning and mutual dependencies. It makes the system reproducible and maintainable.

11.1.2 *Feature generation 101*

With the mentioned criteria and limitations serving as our compass, we are ready to discover common ways of generating new features.

The most obvious way to fetch a new feature is to add a new data source to your data pipeline or use a column that previously was not incorporated into the dataset. This data source can be either internal (e.g., an existing table in the database) or external (e.g., buying data from a third-party provider). On the one hand, these new features are low-hanging fruit with a valuable contribution to the model's performance. On the other hand, they require most of the data engineering efforts, take a lot of time to manage, and may cause infrastructural problems, as greater complexity always requires more effort for maintenance.

If new sources are not used, there are two alternatives—to transform the existing features or to generate new features based on a combination of two or more of the existing ones.

Transforming numeric features includes scaling, normalization, and mathematical functions (e.g., using logarithms to improve distribution skewness). The type of model dictates the appropriateness of transformation. For instance, a common thing will be finding no increase in gradient boosting metrics after applying monotonic transformations to its features because the core element of the algorithm—a decision tree—is invariant under monotonic transformations of inputs.

When dealing with time-series data, it's common to utilize transformations such as lags (shifting the feature's values backward in time to create new features), aggregates (calculating measures like mean, max, or min over a specific time window), or generating statistical features from past data, such as the standard deviation or variance over different time periods.

Quantile bucketing (or *quantization*) is a specific case of transformation. It converts continuous features into categorical features by grouping them into discrete buckets based on their values. For example, Uber applies this approach in its DeepETA network (https://mng.bz/zn6B; see figure 11.1).

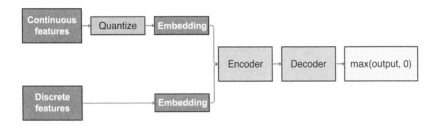

Figure 11.1   An overview of the DeepETA model pipeline: example of combining base feature engineering and a deep learning model (source: https://mng.bz/0MoN)

This network employs the transformer architecture to predict the estimated time of arrival, processing a diverse array of tabular data. The data, which includes continuous, categorical, and geospatial features, is all transformed into discrete tokens and subsequently into learnable embeddings suitable for the transformers. You can read more about DeepETA in the paper "DeeprETA: An ETA Post-Processing System at Scale" by Xinyu Hu et al. (https://arxiv.org/pdf/2206.02127.pdf).

Categorical features often necessitate transformations, which can be accomplished through methods like one-hot encoding, mean target encoding, ordinal encoding (this method ranks categories based on some inherent order), or the hashing trick, which allows handling large-scale categorical data. It is important to note that while being powerful, mean target encoding can easily lead to data leakage if not properly implemented, as it uses information from the target variable to create new features.

For sequential data like text, we can use techniques such as bag-of-words, term frequency-inverse document frequency (TF-IDF), and BM25 to transform the data into a form that can be processed by ML algorithms. It is worth noting that these methods lose information about word order; this disadvantage can be partially addressed by using longer N-grams instead of single words (unigrams). We can also use pretrained language models such as BERT to represent input data in a low-dimensional embedding space, which we can feed to the final model.

Remember that we can represent almost any sequential data as tokens, not texts. For example, in industries like online retail and media streaming services, we can interpret a user session as a sequence of visited product pages or watched videos. Each visited page will have its learnable representation (an embedding). Afterward, we can use these embeddings in our recommendation system as a prompt in the "next page prediction task" to get an idea of what product/video the user is looking for.

If we want to use product embeddings in the tabular dataset, one of the common options is to utilize the distances between products. Examples of features here would be

- How close are the top five neighbors to product X?
- What is the average/minimum price of the top five closest products for product X?
- What is the absolute/relative difference between the prices of product X and product Y?

Although these sophisticated features do add to the complexity of the training and inference pipelines, the signals they provide may lead to a major advancement in the model's performance.

What about merging signals from multiple features into one? When we have multiple features in our dataset, we can combine them to create a feature that is more informative or meaningful for our model. For example, instead of having separate features for the number of clicks and the number of purchases a user has made on an eCommerce site, we can combine them to create a new feature such as "purchase-to-click ratio," which might be a better indicator of the user's buying intent.

In the case of a taxi aggregator company, instead of having separate features for the "number of rides" and "total distance traveled," we could combine them to create a new feature like "average distance per ride," which might provide more valuable insights into drivers' and passengers' behavior.

We should also consider the relationship between the existing features. For example, absolute product sales for a certain period may provide little information. However, comparing them to sales of other products in the same category or sales in previous periods may reveal valuable patterns or trends. Combining signals from multiple features can create new features that capture more complex relationships in the data and improve the model's performance.

The technique of combining multiple features is usually referred to as *feature interactions* or *feature cross*. This technique is especially important for linear models because such features may unlock the linear separability of data points.

11.1.3 *Model predictions as a feature*

As we discussed earlier, if a feature depends on another feature, any changes or updates to the latter may require corresponding changes or updates to the former. It creates maintenance/debugging challenges and increases the system's complexity over time.

Model predictions can be thought of as a specific case of a feature where the output of the model is used as an input to another model or system. This approach is sometimes called *model stacking*. While using model predictions as features can be powerful and effective, it poses some engineering challenges and risks.

The simplest example of using model predictions as a feature is target encoding (https://maxhalford.github.io/blog/target-encoding/). In this approach, the categorical feature is encoded by the mean target value (with a certain degree of regularization) and is used as a feature in the model. However, there is a risk of data leakage where the encoding is based on information from the training data that is not available during inference. This can result in overfitting and poor performance on the new data if we don't use advanced validation techniques like nested cross-validation (see chapter 7).

Another example is using third-party models (e.g., weather forecasts as a feature in a demand prediction model). While weather data can be highly informative, there is a risk that forecasts may need to have the necessary historicity. In such cases, forecasts with the necessary historicity are preferable to forecasts with higher precision. Besides, relying on external data sources can introduce additional dependencies and risks beyond the ML team's control.

Finally, using third-party or open source models as feature extractors in deep learning systems can pose risks, too. While the generated embeddings can absorb useful patterns in the data, there is a danger of model drift or instability if the external model is updated without proper versioning and vice versa—with no updates, the model may lose its value due to a drift in your data. This can result in unexpected behavior and drastically drop the performance of your ML system.

To mitigate these risks and challenges, it is important to design the feature engineering pipeline carefully and have robust testing and monitoring procedures in place (the former is described in chapters 10 and 13; the latter can be found in chapter 14). This can include using cross-validation and other techniques to prevent leakage, validating external data sources and models, and having processes in place for monitoring and updating features over time.

11.2 Feature importance analysis

Once the initial set of baseline features has been selected for the model, understanding which features affect the model's predictions the most can provide valuable insights into how the model makes decisions and where further improvements can be made.

ML models can often be seen as black boxes that provide no insight on how they arrive at their predictions. This lack of transparency can be problematic for engineers, stakeholders, or end users who must understand the rationale behind decisions provided by a given model.

In pursuing model transparency, we employ two key concepts: interpretability and explainability. Both are aimed at demystifying the workings of an ML model:

- *Interpretability* revolves around comprehending the internal mechanics of a model, shedding light on how and why it generates its predictions.

- *Explainability,* however, is about articulating the model's behavior in terms that are comprehensible to humans, even when the internal mechanics of the model are complex or opaque (https://mng.bz/KDvj).

Feature importance analysis serves as a tool for achieving both interpretability and explainability, as it helps pinpoint the features that greatly contribute to the model's predictions. The results of feature importance analysis are collected as part of the training pipeline artifacts and may play a role in the model verification procedure, which delivers the "to deploy, or not to deploy" verdict to a freshly trained version of the model (you can find more details in chapter 13). A good example here is a system that determines the cost of a trip in a taxi aggregator application, as shown in figure 11.2.

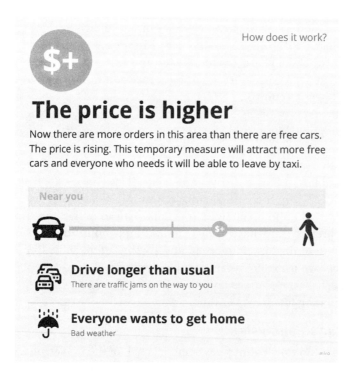

Figure 11.2   An example of a taxi aggregator app's UI that clarifies why its dynamic pricing algorithm chooses this particular price in this area and during this time of the day

Under the hood, the app works with all the crucial features and analyzes the current live data like traffic density, weather conditions, and so on, when determining the end price. What it also does, however, is provide the rationale behind the suggested price in a convenient and user-friendly form. With this delivery, the user understands why a typically cheap ride they take on a regular basis suddenly goes up in price.

In addition, feature importance analysis can increase trust in our ML system. This is particularly important in high-stakes domains such as medicine and financial fields. While the General Data Protection Regulation (https://gdpr.eu) does not strictly enforce explainability, it does suggest a level of transparency in automated decision-making, which could be beneficial or even essential in many ML applications (https://mng.bz/9oX7).

Identifying the most important features explains the variables driving the model's predictions and the reasons behind them. This information can help optimize those features to boost the model's performance and remove irrelevant or redundant features to improve efficiency. Additionally, it can guide us through debugging by, for example, detecting overfitting or evaluating the usefulness of newly added features.

11.2.1 Classification of methods

Let's explore methods of feature importance analysis and how they can be applied to improve the transparency and performance of an ML system.

Navigating the terrain of feature importance analysis can be daunting, but having a map of available methods can show us the right direction. These methods can be broadly classified based on their properties, such as type of model, level of model interpretability, and type of utilized features.

CLASSICAL ML VS. DEEP LEARNING

The methods applied for feature importance analysis can differ substantially between classical ML and deep learning models. For classical ML models, where features are often manually selected based on domain knowledge or statistical analysis, determining feature importance is straightforward—we can either directly inspect model weights and decision rules or exclude/modify a separate feature to investigate its contribution to the model's prediction.

On the other hand, deep learning models, which automatically learn feature representations from data, present unique challenges for importance analysis. Given the complex, nonlinear transformations and the high level of abstraction, there is more involved than simply looking at the model's parameters to understand feature importance. Instead, we rely on advanced techniques like saliency maps, activation maximization (read more in "Visualizing Deep Convolutional Neural Networks Using Natural Pre-Images" by Aravindh Mahendran et al., https://arxiv.org/abs/1512.02017) or layer-wise relevance propagation (read more in "Layer-wise Relevance Propagation for Neural Networks with Local Renormalization Layers" by Alexander Binder et al., https://arxiv.org/abs/1604.00825) and its successors to make sense of what is happening inside neural networks. Please bear in mind that the list of examples is not exhaustive, and none of them is truly universal, as the problem of explainable deep learning is not solved in general and remains in an active research stage.

MODEL SPECIFIC VS. MODEL AGNOSTIC

Model-specific methods use the structure and parameters of the model to estimate feature importance. For example, in tree-based models, we can count how many times we split particular features during training time or the total gain it gives among all splits. Similarly, we can look at the magnitude and sign of the coefficients assigned to each feature for linear models.

In their turn, model-agnostic methods treat a model as a black box. They often involve perturbing the input data and observing the effect on the model's output. Examples of model-agnostic methods include

- *Permutation feature importance*—Measures the importance of each feature by randomly permuting its values in the dataset and observing the resulting decrease in model performance
- *SHapley Additive exPlanations (SHAP) values*—Estimate the contribution of each feature to a specific prediction by averaging over all possible combinations of features

INDIVIDUAL PREDICTION VS. ENTIRE MODEL INTERPRETATION

Another important distinction is whether the methods are designed for individual predictions or for interpreting the entire model (see figure 11.3). Methods that focus on individual predictions estimate the importance of features for a particular input, delving into why the model has made a particular decision. On the other hand, methods that interpret the entire model estimate the importance of features in a more general sense, elaborating on the overall behavior of the model.

Some examples of methods that focus on individual predictions include local interpretable model-agnostic explanations (LIME); see the paper "Why Should I Trust You?" by Marco Tulio Ribeiro et al. (https://arxiv.org/abs/1602.04938), which approximates the decision boundary around a particular input using a simpler, more interpretable model (e.g., linear regression), and anchor explanations (learn more in the paper "Anchors: High-Precision Model-Agnostic Explanations" by Marco Tulio Ribeiro et al. (https://mng.bz/j0vr), which identify a rule that sufficiently "anchors" a decision, making it interpretable by humans.

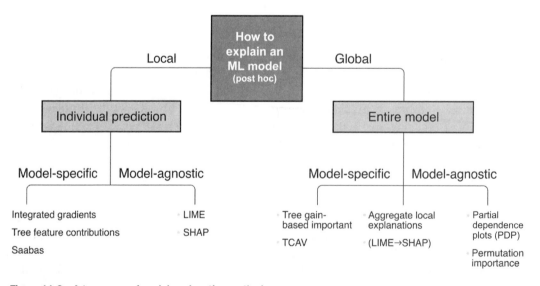

Figure 11.3   A taxonomy of model explanation methods

Often we use a combination of methods to mitigate the limitations of individual approaches and gain a more complete understanding of the model. Keep in mind, though, that no one-size-fits-all method can provide a definitive answer to all feature importance questions, and the choice of methods should be tailored to the specific problem and context.

11.2.2 Accuracy–interpretability tradeoff

Highly interpretable models may sacrifice accuracy in favor of transparency, and vice versa—models that achieve high accuracy often do so at the cost of interpretability (see figure 11.4). Modern large language models based on transformers, such as GPT, provide a vivid example. They have revolutionized the field of ML by achieving state-of-the-art performance in a wide range of natural language processing tasks. However, they are also often highly complex, with billions of parameters, making it difficult to understand how they arrive at their decisions.

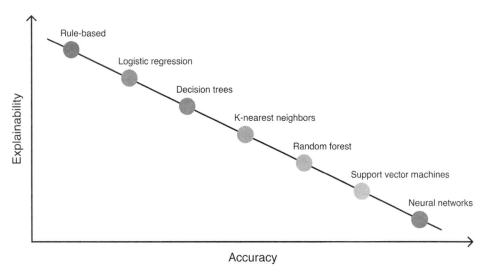

Figure 11.4   The more sophisticated the model we use (and therefore, usually the more accurate), the less explainable it becomes.

The accuracy–interpretability tradeoff remains a challenging problem as new unexplored architectures arrive. The choice of a method should be tailored to the specific problem and context, considering factors such as the importance of interpretability, the complexity of the model, and the desired level of accuracy.

11.2.3 Feature importance in deep learning

Feature importance analysis for models that work with tabular data is a comprehensible problem with a clear solution; we have easily separable features and well-known tools to measure how each of them influences the model, target variable, or final metric.

However, in the context of deep learning, especially with data types such as images, audio, or text, feature importance can become less clear and more challenging. Deep learning models, by nature, automatically learn hierarchical representations from the data, often in a highly abstract and nonlinear manner. In these cases, a "feature" can refer to anything from a single pixel in an image to a single word or character in a text or a specific frequency in an audio signal to complex attributes, like the location of an object in an image, the sentiment of a sentence in a text, or a specific sound pattern in a voice record.

Despite that, it is still possible to gain insights into what the model considers important in raw input data and which patterns it pays attention to. Let's explore a few techniques for feature importance analysis in deep learning:

- *SHAP values*—Similar to classical features, SHAP values estimate the contribution of each token or pixel in the model's outcome, providing a model-agnostic explanation of which individual parts of input affect the model the most.

- *Saliency maps*—Saliency maps are a form of local explanation highlighting the regions in the input image sensitive to the model's output. Essentially, they compute the gradient of the output for the input, resulting in a heatmap where each pixel indicates how much changing that pixel would affect the output. Among examples of saliency map methods are GT, SalNet, SALICON, and Sal-ClassNet. Figure 11.5 is taken from the paper "Top-Down Saliency Detection

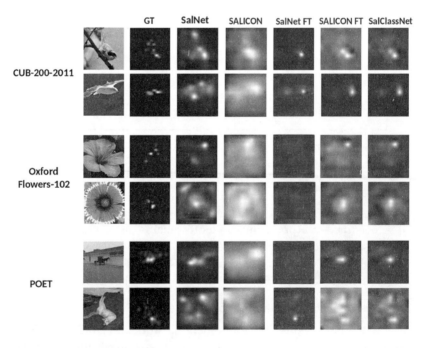

Figure 11.5 Examples of output saliency maps generated by different methods (source: https://arxiv.org/abs/1709.05307)

Driven by Visual Classification" by Francesca Murabito et al. (https://arxiv.org/abs/1709.05307), which can provide basic intuition on how saliency maps work.

- *Perturbation-based techniques*—These methods determine the importance of a feature by observing the effect on the model's output when the feature is altered or removed. A good example of a perturbation-based technique is occlusion, which is applied primarily in vision models where portions of an image are systematically occluded (covered up), and the subsequent changes in the output are tracked. The idea of occlusion first appeared a while ago in a work by Matthiew D. Zeller et al., "Visualizing and Understanding Convolutional Networks" (https://arxiv.org/abs/1311.2901) and was actively used in newer developments like "RISE: Randomized Input Sampling for Explanation of Black-Box Models" by Vitali Petsiuk et al. (https://arxiv.org/abs/1806.07421). This helps visualize which parts of an image are considered the most relevant by the model for its predictions.

- *Attention in transformers*—In transformers, an attention mechanism is a natural form of feature importance. Attention scores indicate the weight the model gives each token in the sequence for making a prediction. These attention weights can be visualized and interpreted as the model's focus, emphasizing how the model (specifically, a particular attention head) "reads" and understands the input text (see figure 11.6).

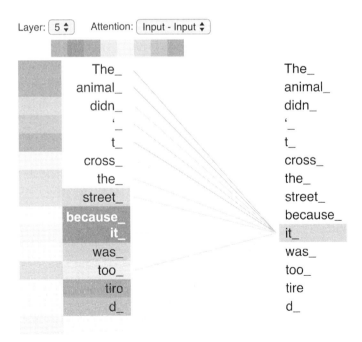

Figure 11.6   Visualization of an attention head in the Encoder-Decoder Transformer

As you can see, we start to observe the parallels with classical ML. Although deep learning models present unique challenges in feature importance analysis, there are still methods that can provide insights into how the model makes decisions and which patterns are the essential predictors for the target variable.

11.3 Feature selection

> *Perfection is finally attained not when there is no longer anything to add, but when there is no longer anything to take away.*
>
> — Antoine de Saint-Exupéry

In the previous sections, we've learned about the art of feature engineering and how to transform raw data into meaningful features. However, not all features are equally useful; some may be irrelevant, redundant, or too complex for our model to handle effectively.

This is where feature selection comes in. By carefully selecting the most informative features, we can improve our system's performance and interpretability while reducing its complexity and training time. We will explore the techniques, best practices, and potential pitfalls of feature selection and learn how to choose the right features for our specific ML problem.

11.3.1 Feature generation vs. feature selection

The feature generation and feature selection processes in ML can be compared to gardening. Similar to gardeners who plant various seeds in the soil, we generate a range of features, explore new data sources, experiment with different feature transformations, and brainstorm new ideas that might improve the model's performance.

However, just as not all plants in the garden will thrive, not all features will benefit the model, and at some point, we will have to prune away dead or unproductive plants (in our case, discard irrelevant or redundant features) to sustain healthy growth. This cycle of nurturing and pruning, of adding and reducing, is a constant in the life of ML systems as we continually refine and improve our feature sets.

The ancient Greek philosopher Heraclitus once said, "Opposition brings concord. Out of discord comes the fairest harmony." This also holds true in ML, where we achieve optimal performance by keeping the balance between generating new features and carefully selecting the most informative ones.

11.3.2 Goals and possible drawbacks

You may ask, "Okay, but why care so much about feature selection in the first place?" There are certain benefits to it:

- *Greater accuracy and less overfitting*—Picking the most informative features helps the model focus on the most important signals. Removing irrelevant or redundant features reduces the risk of overfitting when the model becomes too complex and fits noise in the training data rather than the underlying patterns.

- *Easier to explain*—A decision made by 10 meaningful features is easier to interpret and understand than one produced by 100, even if the model's performance is higher in the latter case.
- *Easier to build and debug*—If, during the feature selection stage, we gathered the insight that three out of five data sources we tried are now redundant, we can save a lot of time and computing resources by removing them from the training and serving pipelines. A simpler data pipeline takes less effort to maintain and troubleshoot.
- *Faster training and serving time*—As we reduce the number of features, the model's complexity decreases, leading to shorter training times and lower computational costs.

For convenience, we have gathered all the benefits of feature selection into a single scheme in figure 11.7.

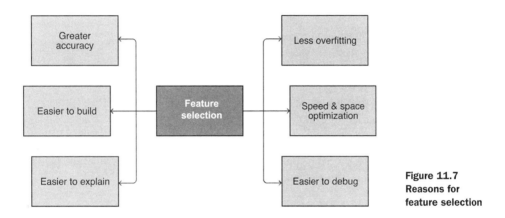

Figure 11.7 Reasons for feature selection

In real-time applications, the need for speed often takes precedence, even if it means compromising the model's accuracy to fulfill SLAs. For instance, in speech recognition systems like those used in virtual assistants, users expect instant and accurate transcription of their spoken words into text. Even the most minor delays could disrupt user experience and make the system appear less efficient.

Perfect personalization becomes worthless if it slows prediction by 300 ms, causing negative perception. Therefore, lightweight personalization with moderate quality is more appropriate than a model that accumulates all possible inputs from a user but makes them wait.

Case study

Amazon conducted a series of A/B tests to formulate this tradeoff in pure numbers: every 100 ms delay costs 1% of sales. For a business with a $500 billion annual revenue, a 1% drop equals $5 billion—not a loss it can afford (https://mng.bz/WVga).

There are also potential risks and drawbacks of feature selection besides the balancing between computational time and accuracy:

- *Loss of potentially valuable signals*—Removing features may lead to losing important information that can improve the model in the future. We may overlook some reasonable preprocessing or aggregation and hastily conclude that the feature has no useful signal.

- *Unforeseen interactions*—Removing certain features can create unforeseen interactions between features, leading to unexpected behavior and reduced model performance. It is essential to consider the relationships between features and the potential interactions that may arise when selecting them.

- *Bias*—Certain features may be more heavily weighted than others, leading feature selection to biased predictions. Imagine if we only select highly correlated features with the target variable. In this case, we might introduce bias into the model and fail to capture important information that is not highly correlated but can still be relevant to the prediction task.

- *Risk of overfitting*—Similar to hyperparameter optimization, feature selection is a learning procedure. And any learning procedure that ingests a target variable requires a proper validation schema (see chapter 7 for details). Suppose we use the same data to select features and evaluate the model's performance. In that case, there is a high risk of overfitting the test data, leading to overly optimistic performance estimates.

Besides these problems, if done regularly, feature selection adds a computationally intensive stage to the training pipeline that we should also consider, especially when greedy wrapper methods are used.

11.3.3 *Feature selection method overview*

There are various methods available for feature selection, each with its pros and cons (see figure 11.8). The most common approaches are filter, wrapper, and embedded methods. Let's take a closer look at each of the three.

Filter methods work by filtering features independently from the model, using simple ranking rules based on the statistical properties of a single feature (univariate methods) or the correlation with other features (multivariate methods). These methods are easily scalable (even for high-dimensional data) and perform quick feature selection before the primary task.

The order in which characteristics are ranked in univariate filter methods is determined by the intrinsic properties, such as feature variance, granularity, consistency, correlation with the target, etc. Afterward, we leave top-N features as our subset and either fit the model or apply more advanced, computationally intensive feature selection methods as the second feature selection layer.

In multivariate methods, we analyze features in comparison with each other (e.g., by estimating their rank correlation or mutual information). If a pair of features represent similar information, one of them can be omitted without affecting the model's

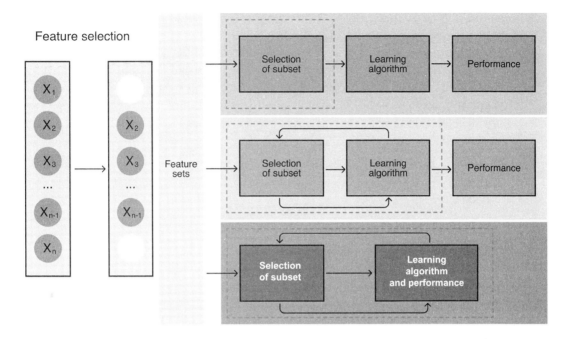

Figure 11.8   **Families of feature selection methods**

performance. For example, the feature interaction score (regardless of the way it is measured) can be incorporated into an automatic report. When the score is high, it triggers a warning for potential reduction in the model's performance before the training begins.

Wrapper methods focus on feature subsets that will help improve the quality of the model's results used for selecting based on a chosen metric. We call them this because the learning algorithm is literally "wrapped" by these methods. They also require designing the right validation schema nested into outer validation (to choose the right validation schema, please see chapter 7).

Wrapper algorithms include sequential algorithms and evolutionary algorithms. Examples of sequential algorithms are the sequential forward selection, where features are included one by one starting from the empty set; SBE (sequential backward elimination), where features are excluded one by one; and their hybrids—floating versions when we allow inclusion of an excluded feature, and vice versa. In evolutionary algorithms, we stochastically sample subsets of features for consideration, effectively "jumping" through the feature space. A common example of an evolutionary algorithm is to run a variation of differential evolution in a binary feature mask space where "1" indicates an included feature and "0" denotes an excluded one.

The main disadvantage of these methods is that all of them are computationally intensive and often tend to converge to local optima. Despite that, they provide the most accurate evaluation of how the subset affects the target metric. Use them carefully, especially if your hardware specs are limited.

With *embedded methods*, we use an additional "embedded" model (which may or may not be of the same class as our primary model) and make decisions based on its feature importance. A good example is the Lasso regression, due to the ability of the L1-regularization to turn the coefficients to zero if they are not relevant to the target variable, as shown in figure 11.9.

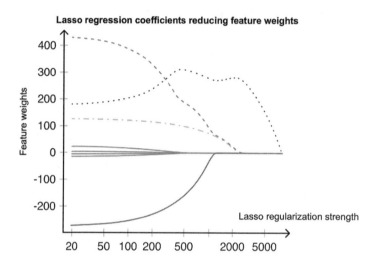

Lasso regression coefficients reducing feature weights

Figure 11.9 Lasso regression eliminates features one by one by reducing their coefficients to zero as L1 regularization term grows.

Another widely used feature selection algorithm is recursive feature elimination (RFE), which consists of training and removing the worst K features on each step based on the embedded model's feature importances.

Embedded methods lie somewhere between filter methods and wrapper methods as far as the required computation and selection quality are concerned.

When it comes down to choosing the methods to start with, we prefer rough cut-offs for the initial reduction of the number of features rather than using Lasso selector or RFE, depending on which one outputs more meaningful subsets. Computationally expensive methods may have better performance, but faster methods tend to be good enough for initial feature pruning, especially if you suspect that some features are total garbage.

There are plenty of dummy and still-useful methods that also serve reasonable feature selection baselines. For example, we can take a feature, shuffle its values, concatenate it to the initial dataset, and train a new model. If the importance of a given feature is less than the importance of this random feature (often called a *shadow feature*), it is likely to be irrelevant to the problem. We can label this algorithm as a trivial instance of the wrapper methods.

Campfire story from Valerii

One of Valeri's previous projects, which was related to dynamic pricing, used a model that needed to be improved. The reason was simple—the model didn't perform as precisely as desired, and after doing basic error analysis, he realized that the majority of errors were caused by SKUs with large numbers of items sold. Further investigation revealed that while some features, specifically those based on price history, were critical, other features were barely significant, and filtering them out using Lasso regression simplified the model. When the number of features was reduced, it made using simple feature interactions (polynomial combinations of the survived features) much more feasible due to the reduced number of overall features (10^2 is 100, while 20^2 is 400). It didn't help at first due to specific preprocessing, but once the preprocessing was changed, it provided a noticeable positive effect; input data was normalized to (0..1), and some interactions could turn into zeros because one component is equal to zero, regardless of the second component, so $0*0$ and $1*0$ produce the same output, but actually they are very different. So by adapting the scaling range to (1..10) to address the multiply-by-zero problem, converting numbers to float16 for smaller RAM consumption, applying polynomial feature interactions (much easier to do on numbers in the range 1–10 from a memory perspective), and then scaling it again to 1–10 and training a simple Ridge regression on top of new features, I was able to reduce the error by 30%. It is worth noting that previous attempts at model improvement had been focused on using more complicated models like gradient boosting and neural nets, but investing in feature engineering appeared to be a shorter path, beating more sophisticated approaches.

Campfire story from Arseny

Arseny was once working on a system that was effectively a text classification: given the transaction description (a cryptic half-truncated string full of acronyms) and its additional attributes (e.g., amount of money transferred), the system needed to categorize the transaction. Transformer-based models demonstrated their power in text processing; however, working with the extra attributes was not that straightforward.

The final solution was based on a transformer BERT-like model with a multicomponent prompt as an input. This prompt contained both text input and various features handcrafted from transaction attributes. Working with these features (including feature importance analysis and feature selection) helped improve the system even more in terms of target metrics than typical deep learning model improvements like backbone pretraining or sophisticated loss functions.

11.4 Feature store

Now we have arrived at a powerful design pattern encompassing many techniques mentioned in the chapter into a single entity—a *feature store*. It enables teams to calculate, store, aggregate, test, document, and monitor features for their ML pipelines in a centralized hub.

Imagine investing weeks of effort into engineering sophisticated features only to stumble upon a conversation with a colleague during a coffee break where you discover that another team has already implemented and tested exactly the same features. Alternatively, a colleague approaches you, seeking an implementation of a specific feature. While you confirm its existence, you realize that your code lacks proper documentation and reusability due to heavy dependencies on other code in your repository. Consequently, your colleague decides that an easier way is to reinvent the wheel and develop their own implementation. This inconsistency may lead to each engineer implementing and calculating each feature on their own, causing the company to waste an unacceptably large amount of resources (see figure 11.10).

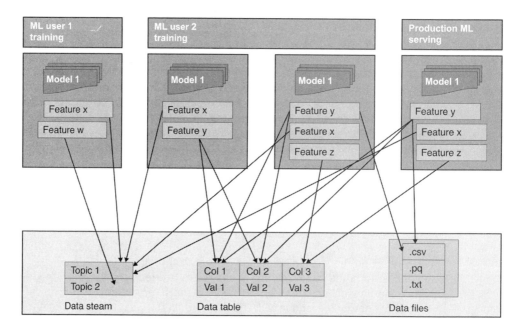

Figure 11.10   Not having a feature store in place can lead to inconsistency and excessive spending.

These scenarios illustrate only a tiny fraction of the challenges that can be addressed by using a feature store. By adopting it, we step away from a fragmented approach where each team independently implements and calculates features. Instead, we embrace a unified system that maximizes the reusability of features, as depicted in figure 11.11.

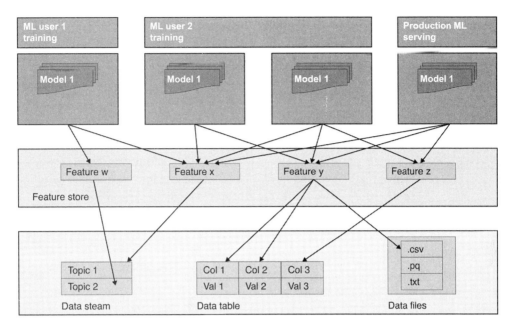

Figure 11.11   A feature store that maximizes the reusability of features implemented in a unified manner

11.4.1 *Feature store: Pros and cons*

Designing, building, and managing a feature store may present certain challenges, but its benefits could far outweigh the drawbacks. Let's explore some of the advantages of having a feature store (figure 11.12 illustrates those ML areas that benefit the most from having feature stores):

- *Reusability and collaboration*—The feature store promotes reusability by enabling teams to share and reuse features across different projects and pipelines. This saves valuable time and effort and fosters collaboration among teams, as they can use each other's work and build upon existing feature implementations.

- *Streamlined workflow*—Rather than starting from scratch with every new project, teams can build upon a foundation of reusable features, accelerating the development process. This streamlined workflow allows for faster iteration and experimentation, leading to quicker insights and improved model performance. The feature store empowers teams to focus on delivering models by minimizing repetitive tasks and providing a structured framework.

- *Consistency and standardization*—With a feature store, there is a unified and standardized approach to feature engineering. This ensures consistency in feature calculation, reducing the risk of inconsistencies or discrepancies across different models, pipelines, or stages of pipelines. By adhering to predefined standards, teams can work together more seamlessly and improve overall system stability.

- *Documentation and transparency*—A feature store facilitates proper documentation (or autodocumentation) of features, including their data sources and methods used for calculation. It enhances transparency, making it easier for teams to discover and assess available features. It also aids in troubleshooting and debugging, as the documentation provides valuable insights into the feature engineering process.
- *Scalability and maintainability*—A well-designed feature store architecture allows for scalability, accommodating large volumes of data and evolving requirements. It simplifies adding new features or modifying existing ones, enabling teams to adapt to changing needs without major disruptions. Additionally, the centralized nature of the feature stores facilitates easier maintenance and monitoring of features, improving the overall reliability of ML pipelines.

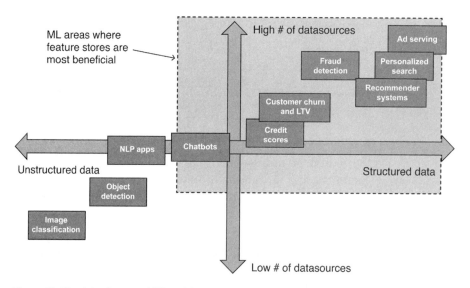

Figure 11.12   A landscape of ML problems with various needs for a feature store

The disadvantages of having a feature store are straightforward:

- It takes time to collect requirements among different teams, design a feature store that meets all the needs, and implement it (or integrate a third-party solution like Tecton, Feast, Feathr, or Databricks Feature Store).
- It reduces flexibility in how we work with features while increasing the dependence of ML teams on each other.
- There is a high cost in the case of development from scratch. We do not recommend reinventing the wheel and suggest resorting to off-the-shelf solutions (e.g., Tecton).
- A feature store may be inappropriate for your particular project.

Let's focus in detail on the last disadvantage. Not all ML problems can be optimized through a feature store. A typical beneficial area for having a feature store is mainly tabular data (structured data) with multiple data sources of various granularity and SLA. Most pure deep learning problems (typically those having one or two sources of unstructured data, like text or images) are less suitable for feature stores. However, given that multimodal data usage is becoming more popular these days, the concept of a feature store has become more universal. Imagine a typical online marketplace; years ago, ML systems would be based on tabular data like the history of sales and clicks, whereas now it is a common pattern to include items' images, descriptions, and user reviews. The simplest way to include such data is to extract embeddings via a pretrained neural network (e.g., CLIP for images or SentenceTransformers for short texts) and treat them as features. This approach closes the loop: such features can be stored in a feature store as well for the same reasons as "classic" features, thus saving processing time and ensuring consistency across the system. As a bonus, storing such features in a centralized storage unlocks additional usage patterns. For example, using a vector database (such as Qdrant or Faiss) for storage allows you to fetch similar items quickly and use them in downstream models.

The best way to start is to analyze the existing extract, transform, and load pipelines of all teams. The following are questions you should be ready to ask:

- Which data sources does each team use? How many of them?
- What are their intersections with features and usage patterns?
- Which kinds of features do they calculate or would they like to?
- Which teams need a real-time response ("online features")?

If we conclude that numerous teams would benefit from having a feature store, it's a sign to invest efforts into designing and building a centralized feature store.

Here we would like to stress once again that building your own custom feature store is a huge and expensive project. That's one of those cases when you should consider reusing an open source solution or a product from a third-party vendor. Some popular options are Feast, Tecton, Databricks Feature Store, and AWS Sagemaker Feature Store.

11.4.2 *Desired properties of a feature store*

In this section, we will touch upon useful patterns and properties in designing feature stores and highlight important problems you must address. Not all of them will necessarily occur in your feature store in particular, but our goal is to make sure each is well covered in the book.

READ-WRITE SKEW

Writing and reading are two essential sides of any feature management system, so during the design stage, we need to know the load size in terms of read and write operations (and the amount of data). What latency of reading is critical for us? How often should we recalculate existing features? Often, calculating a feature in runtime is faster or comparable to fetching one from storage.

Writing is commonly done in batches. We don't prefer to compute a whole dataset when we can do it simultaneously, although this is a widely used antipattern. Moreover, updating the features for the last few days helps us overwrite some temporary corruptions or unavailability on the data warehouse side that may occur just before our daily feature update. It is worth noting that "commonly" is not a common case—features can be appended or updated on different schedules. For example, some are computed by a long job on a daily basis, and some are lightweight enough to be streamed in near real-time.

The critical aspect of reading features is usually latency. We must ensure that the infrastructure we are building for our feature store meets our nonfunctional requirements. Sometimes we can combine precomputed features with real-time features (those that require the most recent events) during read operations, as shown in figure 11.13.

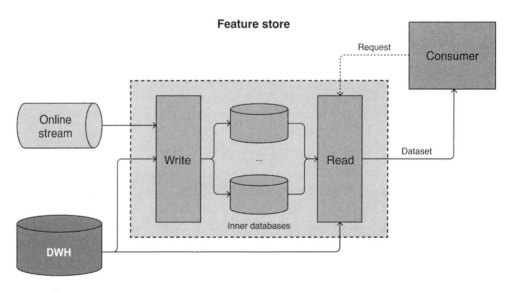

Figure 11.13 Online features and batch features are written in a feature store in different ways but are consumed in the same manner.

PRECALCULATION

The DRY principle in programming stands for "don't repeat yourself." This principle leads us to the fundamental heuristic behind any optimization: if it's possible to avoid computing something, it should be avoided.

In particular, one of the most straightforward patterns is calculating features, which should be done in advance but not when we ask the feature store to gather a dataset. For example, a good time to update features is when our database finishes processing orders for the previous day.

A closely related optimization technique is to split the calculation into multiple steps:

1 We preaggregate raw data (e.g., clicks, prices, revenue) into item-day sums.
2 We aggregate these sums into desired windows (e.g., 7/14/30/60 days).

This approach helps us reuse features calculated yesterday or N months ago (not to run almost the same computation every day) and merge computation of similar features with partly the same lineage or overlapping aggregation windows, as shown in figure 11.14.

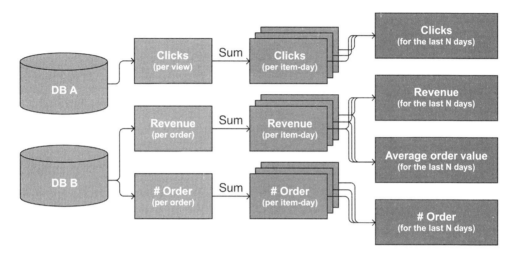

Figure 11.14 A hierarchy of aggregating used in a feature store

FEATURE VERSIONING

A good rule of thumb is that each feature's update should be considered either a new feature (which is not the best solution and will generate many similar features after each tiny optimization and mess up your code) or a new version of an old feature. But why is it important at all?

Suppose some engineer implements a new version of a feature, and your system treats it as if it's the same feature as before, with no differentiaton. You'll be lucky if the calculation is exactly the same but done faster, for example. But if the calculation principle is changed (even a bit)—or worse, if the engineer changes the data source for the same feature—it leads to inconsistency in the precalculated feature. The values of the feature before and after the update can significantly differ from each other, and you don't want to mix values from old and new calculation methods. A well-designed feature store will automatically overwrite the updated feature or, even better, write it to a new table while backfilling all previous values with available history.

Each dataset should capture in its meta info not only which features it contains for a given range of timestamps but also versions of these features at the time of calculation.

It allows us to easily roll back to an old version of a dataset and completely reproduce the results of an old model that was developed, for example, 2 months ago. This pattern is similar to the libraries' version freezing for our application.

FEATURE DEPENDENCIES OR FEATURE HIERARCHY

Not all features are easy to compute from the raw data of our data warehouse. It may cause computationally expensive queries and, again, does not reuse the results of previous computations. This leads us to the concept of feature dependencies, or feature hierarchy, where each feature depends on other features and/or data sources.

A pattern we discussed earlier, preaggregation, can be considered a parent feature for the final features. We highlight them (level 1 features) along with their child features (level 2 features, etc.) in figure 11.15.

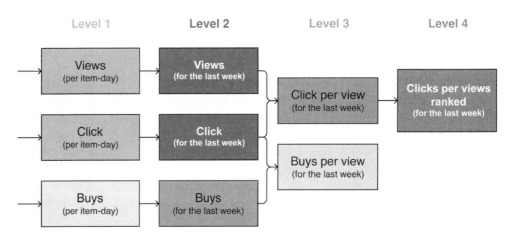

Figure 11.15   A graph of feature dependencies

The way we obtain each feature from its data sources is called a *lineage*, which is effectively a directed acyclic graph (we discussed them in chapter 6). We track the lineage of each feature to know which order to run feature calculations in, whether we need to update its child features after changing the implementation of one of their parents (which triggers a wave of feature version updates), or whether there is a need for any kind of other feature version update, corruption, or deletion.

Lineage tracking also helps engineers and analysts rapidly explore the source of each feature, thus simplifying debugging and improving their understanding of the origin of outliers or other surprising behavior.

FEATURE BUNDLES

We often apply the same transforms and filters to closely related columns from the same data sources (e.g., price before discount, price after discount, and price after applying promo). These similar features have the same key and the same lineage.

It means there is no need to work with features as isolated columns and write a separate data pipeline for each. We naturally prefer to implement our feature store in such a way that it consolidates computations for features derived from the same data sources. Thus, a single entity of computations would be a batch of features, not a single one:

```
<day, user_id, item_id, f1, f2, f3, f1 / f2, ...>
```

Despite merging their computational graphs, we prefer to operate on sets of similar features as a whole in API (or UI) to add them to the dataset simultaneously.

11.4.3 Feature catalog

In relation to the UI, the final secret ingredient for a feature store is a feature catalog. A feature catalog is a service with a web UI where ML engineers, analysts, or even your nontechnical colleagues can search for features and examine their implementation details.

Other things that can be shown to users are feature importance, value distribution, category, the owner, update schedule (daily, hourly), key (user, item, or user-item, or item-day, category-day), feature lineage, ML services that consume this feature, and other meta info.

11.5   Design document: Feature engineering

As we mentioned in the introduction to this chapter, features are the backbone of your ML system's prediction ability, and for this reason alone, they deserve their spot in the design document. We will cover them in both our design documents.

11.5.1 Features for Supermegaretail

After building our baseline solution, we need to determine the next steps for its improvements. One of the primary ways to do this is to use features that will help the model extract useful patterns and relationships from the raw data.

DESIGN DOCUMENT: SUPERMEGARETAIL

VIII. FEATURES

Our key criteria for selecting the right features (outside of prediction quality) are

- *Prediction quality*—The more accurate forecasts we get, the better.
- *Interpretability and explainability*—We prefer features that are easy to describe and explain ("black box" solutions are neither transparent nor trustworthy, especially in the initial phases of the project).
- *Computation time (and computational complexity)*—Features that take a lot of time to compute (as well as features from multiple data sources and with complex dependencies) are less preferred unless the improvement in prediction quality they provide is worth it. That's because they slow down the training cycle and reduce the number of hypotheses we can test.

- *Risks (and feature stability)*—Features that require external/multiple data sources, auxiliary models (or simply poorly designed features), and features based on data sources with low data quality make the pipeline more fragile, which should be avoided.

If a feature adds a statistically significant improvement to the model's performance but violates one of the other criteria (e.g., it takes 2 days to compute), we prefer not to add this feature into a pipeline.

Primary sources of new features are

- Adding more internal and external data sources (e.g., monitoring competitors)
- Transforming and combining existing features

The following is a list of features we will experiment with that will guide our further steps of model improvements after initial deployment:

- Competitors' prices and how they differ from our prices (external sources)
- Special promotion and discount calendars
- Prices (old price, discounted price)
- Penetration (ratio between sales of an SKU and sales of a category)
- SKU's attributes (brand, categories of different levels)
- Linear elasticity coefficient
- A sum/min/max/mean/std of sales of SKU for previous N days
- A median/quantiles of sales of SKU for previous N days
- Predicted weather (external sources)
- Store's traffic (external sources)
- Store's sales volume
- Sales for this SKU 1 year ago
- Economic indicators (external sources)

We formulate them as a hypothesis. For example, using a promo calendar will help the model capture an instant increase in demand during marketing activities, which will decrease overstock in that period.

We will use model-agnostic (SHAP, LIME, shuffle importance) and built-in methods (linear model's coefficients, number of splits in gradient boosting) to measure feature importance. The main goal is to understand the contribution of each feature to the model's outcome. If a feature doesn't contribute much, we drop it.

For automatic feature selection during the first stages (when we haven't determined the basic feature set yet), we use RFE.

Also, we include feature tests in the training pipeline before and after training the model:

- Test feature ranges and outlier detectors (e.g., $0.0 <= discount < X$)
- Test that correlation between any pair of features less than X
- Test that feature's coefficient/number of splits > 0
- Test that computation time is less than 6 hours for any feature

To compute and access features easier, we can reuse a centralized feature store that collects data from different sources in the data warehouse and, after different transformations and aggregations, merge it into one datamart (SKU, store, day). It recalculates features on a daily basis, making it easy to experiment with new ones and track their versions, dependencies, and other meta info.

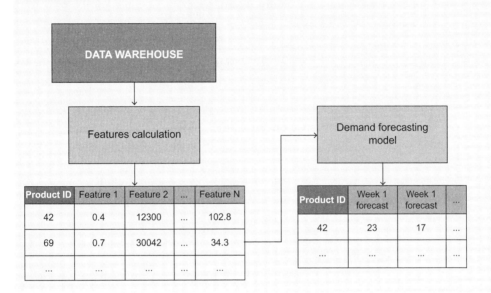

11.5.2 Features for PhotoStock Inc.

A potential set of features for PhotoStock Inc. will be completely different from that for Supermegaretail.

DESIGN DOCUMENT: PHOTOSTOCK INC.

VIII. FEATURES

As stated earlier in the baseline section, we aim to start with a pure content relevancy system by measuring distances between the query and document (image + its description):

relevancy_score = distance(query, image) + distance(query, description)

While it may lead to the conclusion that no feature engineering is involved, that is not exactly correct for at least two reasons:

- Image description and metadata should be somehow transformed to be used as a model input. Thus, we need to suggest a robust and extendable way to do it.
- We may want to introduce additional sources of signal representing users and documents at a later stage. Examples of such document features are document click-through rate, average purchase rate, and time spent on a document page.

Examples of such user features can be aggregates of their click history, explicit settings of their profile, or features calculated by a collaborative filtering-like approach. It is a typical scenario for search engines. Finally, we may want to use features related to photo authors—for example, their average rating or number of items sold to implicitly promote our core contributors. However, it's a significant scope of work, so we don't want to do it right away. Still, we want to design a system that will be easy to extend later.

Given that we expect new types of features to appear, we should design a system that will effectively use signals of multiple origins and output a unified relevancy score—for example:

relevancy_score = distance_function(query_to_image_distance, query_to_

description_distance, user_features, document_features, any_other_

features_we_want_to_add_later)

In this baseline example, we suggested that the distance function is a simple sum of distances. However, it's not the only option. A straightforward option is to use a weighted sum, which effectively suggests training a small linear model on top of the distances.

I. ENCODING THE PHOTO METADATA

Given that we consider a multimodal CLIP-style encoder, we can use the fact it can use any text as input. Thus, we can encode the metadata as text and feed it to the encoder. We suggest gathering all the significant attributes of the photo and concatenating them into a single string—for example, following this template:

"Description: {description}, tags: {tags}, location: {location}"

Generating the prompt like that is a universal approach. We're sure description and tags are vital parts of the metadata, but we can probably craft more. For example, here we suggested using location if coordinates are part of photo EXIF data. There may be more low-hanging fruit like that—for example, crafting features from date (so it reflects season), camera models, etc. Also, we may need to filter tags—for example, by trimming the list of tags to the most informative ones.

As discussed earlier, there is some flexibility in features to be created from the metadata. However, the more features we have, the higher the complexity is. Even if adding a dummy feature doesn't affect the model's performance in terms of metrics, it may increase both training and inference time as transformer-based models are quadratic in terms of the input length. Thus we need to be careful with the number of features we use and apply feature selection techniques to keep the complexity under control. Given the nature of the features, we can't use filtering methods as is, and given a small number of them, we suggest using something precise though slow (e.g., sequential greedy feature selection).

II. FEATURE IMPORTANCE

We need to have access to feature importance at least in two scenarios:

- We need an overall understanding of the model to set priorities for future work. For example, if we see that the model relies heavily on metadata features, we may want to invest more in the metadata feature engineering pipeline. At the same time, we would probably like all the components to contribute to the final score to reduce the chance of overfitting and the chance of the creators exploiting the model weaknesses (e.g., overoptimizing the tags of the photos they upload).
- There will be complaints about the ranking quality, and we need to understand the reason for that. So we need to be able to explain the ranking for a particular query and a particular document. It may reveal new opportunities for future improvements and detect some systematic problems.

Luckily, we don't need a new component like a feature store for the solution described here. However, the need for it may emerge if/when we start using user behavior data as a source of features. In that case, we need to precalculate and store the features somewhere, and a feature store is a natural choice.

Summary

- Running feature importance analysis will help achieve both interpretability and explainability, pinpointing the features that significantly contribute to the model's predictions and signaling whether the model is ready for deployment.
- Thorough feature selection will allow you to sharpen your model's prediction abilities, eventually coming up with a solution that is accurate, is easy to interpret and explain, and boasts faster training and serving time.
- Do not ignore the idea of feature engineering even when working with multimodal data such as images or texts.
- Consider using a feature store, as it enables teams to calculate, store, aggregate, test, document, and monitor features for their ML pipelines in a centralized hub.
- Having a feature store will be especially beneficial if you are working with multiple sources of tabular data. On the other hand, pure deep learning problems are unsuitable for feature stores.

Measuring and reporting results

This chapter covers

- Measuring results
- Benefiting from A/B tests
- Reporting received results

In the preceding chapters, we discussed the building blocks that form the backbone of a machine learning (ML) system, starting with data collection and model selection, continuing with metrics, losses, and validation split, and ending with a comprehensive error analysis. With all these elements firmly established in the pipeline, it's time to circle back to the initial purpose of the system and think about proper reporting of the achieved results.

Reporting consists of evaluating our ML system's performance based on its final goal and sharing the results with teammates and stakeholders. In chapter 5, we introduced two types of metrics: online and offline metrics, which generate two types of evaluation: offline testing and online testing. While offline testing is relatively straightforward, online testing implies running experiments in real-world scenarios. Typically, the most effective approach involves a series of A/B tests, a crucial procedure in developing an efficient, properly working model, which we cover in section 12.2. This helps capture metrics that either directly match or are highly correlated with our business goals.

Measuring results in offline testing (sometimes called *backtesting*) is an attempt to assess what effect we can expect to catch during the online testing stage, either directly or through proxy metrics. Online testing, however, is often a trickier story. For example, recommender systems rely heavily on feedback loops, so the training data depends on what we predicted at the previous timestamps. Moreover, we don't know exactly what would have happened if we had shown item X or Y to user A instead of item Z, which appeared in historical data at timestamp T.

Finally, when the experiment is done, we are ready to report the effect of the model on the business metrics we are interested in. What do we report? How do we present the result? What conclusion should we make about the further steps of system elaboration? In this chapter, we answer questions that might arise during the process.

12.1 Measuring results

Before implementing an ML system, we should fully understand what goal we aim to achieve—that's why our design document should begin with the goal description. Likewise, before running an experiment to check how a change affects our system (in this chapter, we mostly narrow our focus to A/B tests), we design it and outline a hypothesis that covers our expectations of how the given change is expected to affect metrics. This is where offline testing comes into play, as using offline evaluation as a proxy for online evaluation is a valid and beneficial approach. Its objective is to swiftly determine whether the new (modified) solution is better than the existing one and, if so, try to quantify by what margin it is better.

As we already mentioned, metrics are interconnected within a hierarchical structure. There are proxy metrics for other proxy metrics for metrics of our interest (please see chapter 5). Consequently, there are plenty of ways to conduct the offline evaluation.

12.1.1 Model performance

The first layer of evaluation usually involves a basic estimation of ML metrics, which we introduced in chapter 7. We assume that alongside offline metrics (common metrics like root mean square error, mean absolute percentage error, or normalized discounted cumulative gain), we also improve business metrics (average revenue per user or click-through rate [CTR]).

Prediction evaluation is the fastest way to check the model's quality and iterate through different versions, but it is also usually the farthest from business metrics (the relationship between prediction quality and online metrics is often far from ideal).

The offline evaluation procedure is trustworthy and valuable for assessing quality. However, there is rarely a direct connection between offline and online metrics, and learning how an increase in offline metrics A, B, and C affects online metrics X, Y, and Z is a regression problem by itself. To bridge the gap between offline and online metrics and make offline testing more robust, we could gather a history of online tests and online metrics and related offline metrics to calculate the correlation between offline and online results.

12.1.2 *Transition to business metrics*

In some scenarios, we can transition from model predictions to real-world business metrics. To illustrate this, let's consider the example of forecasting airline ticket sales. Often, the fundamental model performance metrics we use for forecasting are the weighted average percentage error (WAPE) and bias:

$$\text{WAPE} = \frac{\sum(|\text{Forecast} - \text{Actual}|)}{\sum \text{Actual}}$$

$$\text{Bias} = \frac{\sum(\text{Forecast} - \text{Actual})}{\sum \text{Actual}}$$

Suppose we have two models, each with a bias of ±10% for predicting ticket sales for a specific flight at a certain hour. In this example, we forecast 110 tickets sold for a given period of time, while the actual number of tickets sold was 100. Also, let's assume we have the actual ticket prices for each day.

Our goal is to avoid overbooking (missed revenue due to offering too many discounted tickets) and minimize unsold seats (lost revenue). Assume the number of tickets sold reflects the passengers' actual demand and that we adjust prices at the beginning of each day based on our forecast. We are okay with this rough estimation for the sake of illustration.

The actual number of tickets sold during the 4 days is [120, 90, 110, 80]. The predicted ticket sales are

- *Model A*—[90, 90, 90, 90]
- *Model B*—[110, 110, 110, 110]

The model biases are

- *Model A*—$\frac{-30 + 0 - 20 + 10}{400} = \frac{-40}{400} = -10\%$
- *Model B*—$\frac{-10 + 20 + 0 + 30}{400} = \frac{40}{400} = 10\%$

The model WAPEs are

- *Model A*—$\frac{30 + 0 + 20 + 10}{400} = \frac{60}{400} = 15\%$
- *Model B*—$\frac{10 + 20 + 0 + 30}{400} = \frac{60}{400} = 15\%$

Both models have the same WAPE and bias, but model A has a negative bias of 10% (and tends to underpredict), while model B has a positive bias of 10% (and tends to overpredict).

The ticket prices for each day are [$200, $220, $230, $210].

The total revenue (we choose the minimum of sold and forecasted tickets for each day) is

- *Model A*—90 * $200 + 90 * $220 + 90 * $230 + 80 * $210 = $75,300
- *Model B*—110 * $200 + 90 * $220 + 110 * $230 + 80 * $210 = $83,900

As you can see, model B generates $8,600 more revenue for a single flight within just 4 days (while the total flight's cost remains unchanged). When multiplied by hundreds of flights and days, this difference will result in a substantial revenue gain.

Certainly, we've oversimplified the real-world context where the model makes forecasts and affects decision-making (e.g., how many tickets to release for sale, how to adjust prices dynamically). Here, the whole transition is done by multiplying by price and, optionally, subtracting flight costs.

Nonetheless, this example illustrates how we can transition from model performance metrics, which may not fully capture the practical effect of predictions, to business indicators like revenue. These business metrics can be reported to the team before running A/B tests.

12.1.3 *Simulated environment*

When the stakes are high, it is reasonable to invest in a more sophisticated, computationally expensive, but more robust offline testing procedure. Building a simulator of the online environment for the problem at hand and running an algorithm against this simulator can become such an investment.

A good example of this kind of environment would be time-series forecasting, which is relatively simple to simulate thanks to the availability of labels, auxiliary information (e.g., historical costs or turnover of goods in stock), and disambiguation in the outcome. That is usually not the case for online recommendation systems, such as news, ads, or product recommendations, where we deal with partly labeled data; we know only impressions of content items (views, clicks, and conversions) that we showed to a particular user, while those that we did not show remain without user feedback as there is always a chance that had we produced an alternative order of impressions, everything might have been very different.

Let's review how such an environment could be created in the case of a recommender system.

Sometimes online recommendation systems are solved via the multi-armed bandits and contextual bandits approaches (usually, this subset of recommender systems is called *real-time bidding*, but in a nutshell, its goal remains the same—to provide the best pick from a variety of options to maximize a specific reward). There is an agent, which is our algorithm, that "interacts" with an environment. For example, it consumes information about user context (their recent history) and chooses which ad banner to show to maximize CTR, conversion rate (CVR), or effective cost per mile (eCPM). This is a typical reinforcement learning problem with a great feedback loop influence: previously shown ads change the future user behavior and give us information about their preferences.

The so-called "replay" algorithm is a simple (but not the most intuitive) way to build a simulation for real-time recommendations, derived from the paper "Unbiased Offline Evaluation of Contextual-bandit-based News Article Recommendation Algo-

rithms" by Lihong Li et al. (https://arxiv.org/abs/1003.5956). Here we summarize
the paper due to its practicality:

1   Suppose we take a historical dataset that consists of user context (user features),
    recommended ads (let's say we can suggest one item at a time), and user feed-
    back (which can be both binary and continuous). Also, for each row of data, we
    know all available items we could recommend for that user at a given moment
    (items are arms for contextual bandits).

2   Also, we have the second dataset, which we'll call the virtual dataset. It is empty
    at the start of the simulation.

3   We split our historical dataset into batches (e.g., 1-hour intervals per iteration).

4   For each row in a single batch, we predict what ad our algorithm could recom-
    mend based on the proposed user context and available items. Our algorithm is
    trained on the virtual dataset, which is initially empty. Hence, we start with ran-
    dom "exploration."

5   Rows, for which the recommendation produced by the model is equal to histor-
    ically chosen ads, are saved to the virtual dataset (with their feedback).

6   We retrain the model based on the updated virtual dataset.

7   We repeat steps 4–6 until we reach the end of the historical dataset.

There is also an optimized version for steps 4 and 5: instead of one item (as in the real
environment), we recommend three or five items for each row, and if the recommended item matches one of them, we append this row to the virtual dataset. This
allows the model to learn more effectively while reducing stochasticity.

A visual example is divided into several pieces in figures 12.1 to 12.5 that demonstrate the work of an unbiased estimator, with figure 12.1 displaying the real history of
events and figures 12.2 to 12.5 showcasing simulated events based on historical data.

Stream of real events

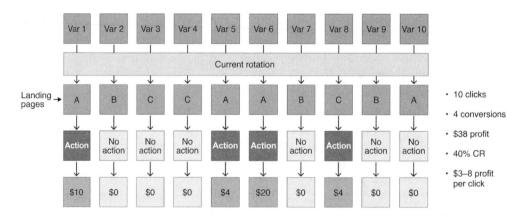

Figure 12.1   Unbiased estimator (offline validation): stream of real events

For the simulated events here, we go through the real history of events and only consider those events in which the output of a new model (chosen landing pages) equals the output of the old model. In figure 12.2, the simulated user behavior implies five transitions from banners to landing pages with two successful purchases and $6 of a predicted profit per click.

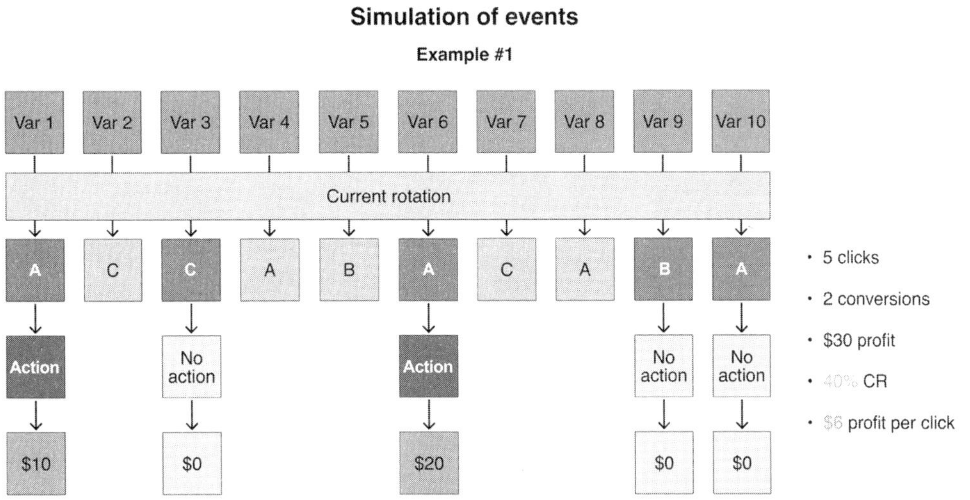

Simulation of events

Example #1

Figure 12.2   Unbiased estimator (offline validation): simulation of events, example 1

Featuring only four goods viewed by users, figure 12.3 suggests the lowest possible profit ($10) and profit per click ($2.5).

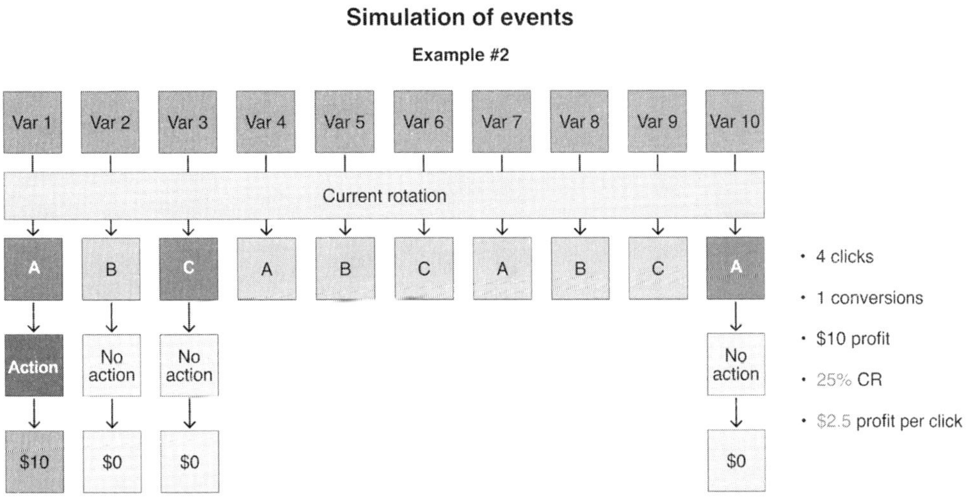

Simulation of events

Example #2

Figure 12.3   Unbiased estimator (offline validation): simulation of events, example 2

Figure 12.4 provides another example of simulated user behavior with a decent conversion rate (50%) but one of the lowest profit-per-click values (only 3%) due to the low cost of purchases.

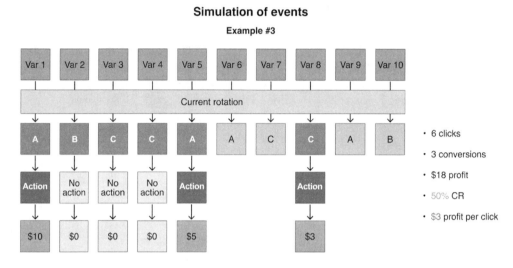

Figure 12.4   Unbiased estimator (offline validation): simulation of events, example 3

Finally, a simulated environment in figure 12.5 suggests the best possible CVR (60%) and profit per click ($7), while the overall profit is only $3 less than that of the stream of real events (see figure 12.1).

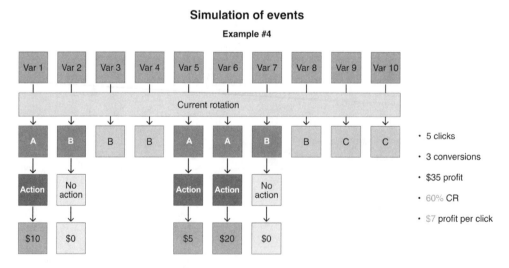

Figure 12.5   Unbiased estimator (offline validation): simulation of events, example 4

We eventually end up with a virtual dataset produced by the interaction of our model with a simulated data flow. Based on it, we can calculate all listed metrics:

- CTR = number of clicks/number of views (total number of rows)
- CVR = number of conversions/number of clicks
- eCPM = revenue/number of clicks * 1000

While not ideal, running different models through this procedure will make it possible to evaluate them from the product metrics point of view and understand the relationship between these estimates of online metrics and the accuracy of predictions and then provide this information to a wider audience.

12.1.4 Human evaluation

Sometimes the final option worth mentioning for measuring results before deploying the system to production is validation by the assessors, or human evaluation. If the simulation is computationally expensive and slow, this can be even worse due to limited bandwidth, longer delay, human-induced ambiguity, and greater costs. However, in cases where human-in-the-loop is applicable, it is usually the most precise and trustworthy way to test the model, except for direct online testing on real data.

For instance, after building a new version of a search engine pipeline, we can either ask a group of experts to estimate the relevance of search results from 1 to 5 for some benchmark queries or choose which output is more relevant, comparing the old and new versions of search results. The second (comparative) formulation tends to produce a more robust evaluation as it excludes the subjectiveness of score estimates. In the case of generative large language models, human evaluation and hybrid approaches (auxiliary "critic" model, trained on human feedback) are the most popular options to measure the quality of generations.

While human evaluation has low throughput and high costs that may impede frequent use, its capacity to yield highly precise and trustworthy assessments (compared to fast but limited automated methods) cannot be downplayed.

12.2 A/B testing

Heavily used in various fields, including marketing, advertising, product design, and many others, A/B testing is a gold standard for causal inference that helps make data-driven decisions rather than relying solely on intuition. You might have a valid question: we have been discussing how to measure and report results, and now we have suddenly jumped on the causal inference boat; how so? In a sense, measuring results is a part of causal inference, as we want to be sure those results are caused by the factor we have influenced (in our case, an ML system). Of course, we can deploy our system in production and measure all metrics of interest as is, but we rarely do so, mainly for the following reasons:

- It is dangerous. If something is broken, deploying it to everyone would lead to further breakage. For this reason, we should deploy it to a small fraction first.

- Even if we don't care about the previous point (probably not, but still), what if something changed outside our control zone, affecting the overall performance, but we thought it was us who caused it and thus made a false conclusion?
- These two points combined lead us to the need for a control group (status quo) and a treatment group (our change), which helps us handle both; on the one hand, we can vary the size of the treatment group, controlling the affected fraction, and on the other hand, we can have the control group to compare the change affecting the treatment group with it.

During A/B experiments, we split entities (in most cases, users) into two groups:

- A control group that uses the existing version of our system
- A testing group that uses the new version

This allows us to isolate the effect of a change on key metrics while controlling external factors that may affect the results (see figure 12.6).

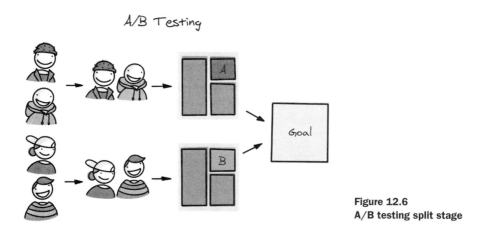

Figure 12.6
A/B testing split stage

12.2.1 Experiment design

Every experiment starts with a hypothesis:

If we do [action A], it will help us achieve/solve [goal/problem P], which will be reflected in the form of an [X%] expected uplift in the [metrics M] based on [research/estimation R].

Let's break down the variables mentioned in the hypothesis:

- *Action* is deploying a new solution to compare it with the existing one. For instance, the goal could be to decrease the number of out-of-stock situations and reduce the gap between predicted and actual sales for Supermegaretail.
- *Metrics* are providing us with a means of quantifying the progress toward our objectives. For example, a "weight loss" metric in a fitness app can demonstrate

a user's progress toward their set target weight. See chapter 5 for further insights.

- *Expected uplift* can be derived from our previous experience, available benchmarks, a rule of thumb, or even wishful thinking (this happens very often!). Additional data provided by offline testing is usually used to make it more precise.

Before running an A/B test, there are at least three hyperparameters we must define:

- *Minimum detectable effect* (MDE), also known as minimum detectable change (MDC), is the smallest disparity between two groups that can be reliably detected given the study's design and sample size. The MDE must be equal to or less than the expected uplift to avoid overlooking it.
- *Type I error* (false positives) is the probability of wrongly concluding that an effect exists when it does not. A typical threshold for this error is 5% (signified by $\alpha = 0.05$).
- *Type II error* (false negatives) is the probability of failing to recognize an effect when it is present. A typically used threshold is 20% (represented by $\beta = 0.2$).

Along with the variation in the data, this affects the number of samples (and therefore the time required to run the test, taking some seasonality into account as well) needed to run the test; all these factors combined result in the following equation:

$$n = \frac{2s^2(Z_\alpha + Z_\beta)^2}{MDC^2}$$

Where n is the required sample size per group, Z_α is the Z-score corresponding to the desired significance level (for type I error rate), Z_β is the Z-score corresponding to the desired power (for type II error rate), s^2 is the estimated variance of the metric, and MDC is the minimum detectable change. As we mentioned before, the very frequent sample unit is *user*, but it could be *session*, *transaction*, *shop level*, and so on.

After formulating the hypothesis and our expectations, we choose a *splitting strategy* determined mainly by the nature of the system we deploy and how it will affect the existing processes.

Next, we decide on the *statistical criteria* and conduct simulation tests, both A/A (where we compare the same system against itself to check type I error rates) and A/B (where we simulate a desired effect through the addition of the noise of a desired magnitude), as a sanity check on historical data. This helps us confirm whether we meet the predefined type I and type II error levels. A comprehensive description of that is beyond the scope of this book, but if you are interested in more details, a great starting point would be *Trustworthy Online Controlled Experiments: A Practical Guide to A/B Testing* (https://mng.bz/86Qz) by Ron Kohavi et al.

Finally, we have everything we need to launch our A/B test. Remember that the design of the experiment is fixed beforehand and cannot be changed on the go. Next we briefly outline the basic stages of A/B testing.

12.2.2 *Splitting strategy*

The question is, how do we split the data? The usual answer is "by user." For instance, we have a control group of users to interact with the existing search engine and an experimental group to use the new version. However, things get more complex when we can't split by users (e.g., there isn't a consistent user ID), or splitting by users is entirely irrelevant to our service.

To zoom in, let's examine hypothetical pricing systems applied in different domains:

- In *offline retail*, it is physically not feasible to show different price tags to customers within the same store. So a more suitable unit for splitting is the store rather than individual customers.
- In *online retail*, while it is technically possible to show different prices to different users, it also can lead to legal problems, as many countries have laws preventing user discrimination in eCommerce.
- In *ridesharing*, users can be separated as the orders are made using the app, but we must consider potential negative user experiences. If we split by user and two users decide to ride scooters together, one user might see a price of $5 per hour in their app, while it will be $6 per hour for the other. This discrepancy could lead to a confusing and negative user experience and feedback.
- When it comes to dynamic pricing applied to *loans and credit rates*, the offered rate is expected to be highly personalized, like a mortgage. Therefore, different "prices" won't raise eyebrows, even if two users are in the same room. In this situation, it's relatively safe to split by user.
- An ideal case for user testing is presented by *advertising networks*, as they offer an abundance of diverse, relatively low-cost data points, and a user-specific cost per click is both common and expected. This type of setup often allows for more traditional user-based splits.

If splitting data by individual users isn't feasible, we can use higher-level entities as atomic units. For offline retail, we could use entire stores; for scooters, trips could be divided based on parking slots, neighborhoods, cities, or even regions. However, this strategy might shift data distribution and create unequal sample sizes or lack of representation, which should be considered when selecting an appropriate statistical test.

When splitting by a nontypical key, aiming for group (bucket) similarity is essential. For instance, if you're compelled to divide geographically, the chosen areas should be similar and possess comparable economic indicators (they should match each other).

Finally, there is a more advanced splitting strategy called *switchback testing*. This technique divides data into region-time buckets and randomly and continuously switches between different models (see figure 12.7). It ensures that each region will be in both the control group and the testing group for an approximately equal amount of time. For further details, see "Design and Analysis of Switchback Experiments" by Iavor Bojinov et al. (https://arxiv.org/abs/2009.00148).

Experiment Bucket

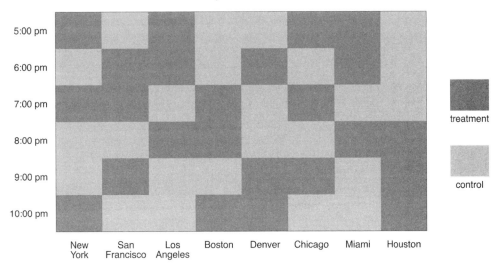

Figure 12.7 **Switchback split pattern, representing time-region cell allocation**

12.2.3 *Selecting metrics*

When designing an A/B test, selecting metrics is a crucial step that can be a deciding factor in the test's success or failure. We prefer trustworthy, sensitive, interpretable metrics with a low feedback delay for online testing.

Every experiment usually has three kinds of metrics:

- *Key metrics* are the primary metrics the experiment aims to improve. These metrics directly affect the success of our business objectives and are used to determine the final outcome of the experiment. For example, the key metric for an eCommerce website could be the CVR, average order value (AOV), or gross merchandise value / revenue.

- *Control metrics* are expected to remain unchanged during the experiment, serving as a check on its validity. For example, if the control metric for the number of visitors to the website (or page loading time) shows a significant decrease (or increase), this could indicate a problem with the experiment design or a change in external factors that could affect the results.

- *Auxiliary metrics* provide additional information about the experiment but are not used to determine the final outcome. These metrics help provide a deeper understanding of the experiment's results and can be used to identify potential problems or opportunities for improvement. For example, an auxiliary metric for an eCommerce website could be the number of product views or the time spent on the website.

All three groups play an important role in the design and execution of an A/B testing experiment. Key metrics determine the success of the experiment, control metrics ensure the validity of the experiment, and auxiliary metrics provide additional information to support the results and inform future experiments.

12.2.4 *Statistical criteria*

The third essential ingredient in any A/B experiment is a statistical test that makes the final decision of whether a significant effect is captured.

In short, statistical criteria are used to quantify the probability of receiving specific results under specific assumptions. For example, the probability of receiving t-statistics equal to or greater than 3 generally will be less than 0.01 (if there's no difference between the groups and assumptions for which the t-test is met).

The most common statistical test used in A/B testing is the t-test we just mentioned. It has many modifications. For example, Welch's t-test is relatively easy to interpret and is similar to Student's t-test, but it can be used even when the variances of two groups are not equal. The statistic for the Welch t-test is calculated as follows:

$$ t = \frac{\mu_B - \mu_A}{\sqrt{\frac{s_A^2}{n_A} + \frac{s_B^2}{n_B}}} $$

The *null hypothesis* (a default assumption under the test's result) for the Welch t-test implies that there is no difference between the means of the two groups; here, the captured difference between the two groups appeared by accident and was caused by noise. The alternative hypothesis is that the captured difference is not caused by noise, and the difference is statistically significant.

By statistical significance, we mean that the probability of capturing a specific value of a statistic or even a more extreme one under the assumption that the null hypothesis is true (we call it *p-value*) is less than *significance level* α (effectively, the same as type I error; typically, $\alpha = 0.05$). P-value, along with the significance level, is a way to standardize the results of any statistical test and map them to a single reference point rather than to define critical values for each test in particular.

While there are many different statistical tests available, the choice of a particular test depends on the context of the experiment and the nature of the data. That said, providing a detailed guide on choosing the most appropriate test is beyond the scope of this book. For a more detailed discussion on selecting the right statistical test for A/B testing, we once again recommend *Trustworthy Online Controlled Experiments: A Practical Guide to A/B Testing* (https://mng.bz/EOKd) by Ron Kohavi et al.

The t-test is widely used because it is a robust test that can handle a variety of situations, it is easy to implement, and it provides results that are easy to interpret. However, the choice of a specific test should always be made considering the type of data you are dealing with, the nature of your experiment, and the assumptions each test requires.

12.2.5 *Simulated experiments*

We can run a simulation to check whether we have succeeded in designing an experiment. We replicate the whole pipeline multiple times on a different set of samples and periods.

A *simulated A/A test* involves randomly sampling two groups with no incurred difference and applying a chosen test statistic. We repeat these actions many times (say 1,000 or 10,000 times) and expect the p-value to follow a uniform distribution (if everything is correct). For instance, in 5% of simulations, the test will reject the null hypothesis for $\alpha = 0.05$. The exact percentage of cases when the test does catch a difference for two groups is a *simulated type I error rate*.

A *simulated A/B test* does a similar thing, but now we add an uplift of a specific size (usually MDE of interest) to the second group B (we assume that groups A and B are the same size as they will be during the real A/B test). Again, we apply our test statistic and run it 1,000 to 10,000 times. After that, we reexamine the distribution of resulting p-values and count how many times we rejected the null hypothesis ("the p-value passed the threshold"). The percentage of cases when the chosen test rejects the null hypothesis is an estimation of sensitivity $(1 - \beta)$, which is the probability that the test catches the difference if there is one. If we subtract sensitivity from 1, we get a *type II error rate* (the probability of ignoring the difference between A and B when there is one). If calculated type I and II error rates fit predefined levels, then the statistical test is picked properly, and the sample size is estimated correctly (see figure 12.8).

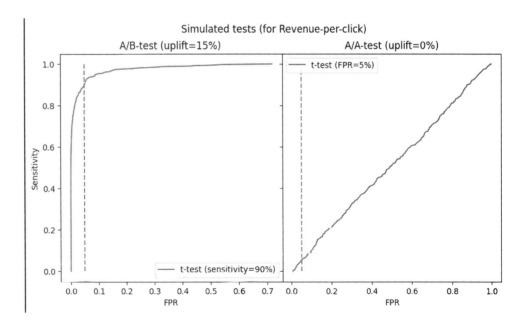

Figure 12.8 Simulation provides a final validation that everything is correct and set up to run an A/B test.

12.2.6 *When A/B testing is not possible*

There are situations where running classic A/B tests is not feasible or desirable—either due to legal restrictions (certain industries, such as healthcare and finance, have strict regulations that prohibit conducting experiments on customers), logistical limitations (it may be difficult to randomly divide the customer base into two groups for testing), or other reasons.

There are different ways to tackle this problem, but since this is a narrow topic that is out of the scope of this book, we will not cover it in detail. For your convenience, however, we list them here so you can use them as keywords for a more in-depth look:

- Casual effect
- Difference-in-difference
- Synthetic control
- Interrupted time-series analysis
- Regression discontinuity design
- Causal inference

12.3 *Reporting results*

Monitoring an ongoing experiment is important for ensuring it runs smoothly and produces reliable results. If something goes wrong during the experiment, it is critical to promptly identify and address the problem to avoid a growing negative effect. Sometimes it is possible to exclude specific users, items, or segments from an experiment and move on. However, this option is not recommended if it was not considered in the initial design. In other cases, we prefer to terminate an experiment entirely and start investigating factors that have caused the failure.

Campfire story from Arseny

Those working in an extra-flexible startup environment may think that all the reporting only applies to big corps, but that is not correct; even in small companies, enough effort should be dedicated to ensure proper reporting and experiment management. I learned this lesson the hard way: once I worked in a relatively small company with only three ML engineers, where I was to improve the core performance of a model. After months of research and experiments, I managed to achieve good results, which were highly appreciated by my manager and the company's CTO. I was into production implementation of the new model when a message from the CTO popped up: "Hey, we have a board meeting tomorrow, and I want to highlight your achievement on the slides. Please give me detailed information on X with the granularity of Y."

I tried to make a report per the request, but suddenly, after careful analysis, the numbers showed that the new model's performance was actually worse than the old one's! It looked awful, but I definitely wasn't going to try to trick the CTO by reporting nonexistent better results. Given that it was my first big project at this company, it looked very suspicious. The group of three—the CTO, my manager, and myself—started digging into the problem.

It was only close to midnight that I found the root cause: while running additional experiments, I accidentally overwrote the results of the best model with some unsuccessful experiments and used this data for the board meeting report. Because I was the only person working on the problem, I didn't pay enough attention to that, and the lack of proper reporting and experiment management (just semirandom chunks of data stored on a dev machine instead) led to this incident.

12.3.1 *Control and auxiliary metrics*

In section 12.2.1, we mentioned control and auxiliary metrics that we should monitor during the test. They can hint if something goes wrong before the key metrics experience a significant drop. For instance, it is important to track user feedback—if you notice a significant drop in user engagement or a spike in user churn, it is a clear indicator of malfunction. In this case, it may indicate that the experimental group is not responding well to the pushed changes. This information can easily lead to an early termination.

Also, when conducting an A/B test, we should consider fairness and biases among different segments of users, which can affect target and auxiliary metrics. This analysis is similar to what we covered in depth in chapter 9. For further reading, we recommend "Fairness through Experimentation: Inequality in A/B Testing as an Approach to Responsible Design" by Guillaume Saint-Jacques et al. (https://arxiv.org/pdf/2002.05819.pdf).

12.3.2 *Uplift monitoring*

The most valuable measurement to track during an A/B experiment is the uplift or the relative difference in the key metric between group A and group B. The longer the experiment runs, the greater the sensitivity of the test and the smaller the effect (either positive or negative) we can detect.

Figure 12.9 shows a funnel representing the range of effects that we cannot detect with statistical significance. If the uplift moves outside this funnel, the effect is significant. Please note that without a specific design, you cannot peek into the test as many times as you wish until you see the desired results. For further reading on the subject, we recommend "Peeking Problem—The Fatal Mistake in A/B Testing and Experimentation" by Oleg Ya (https://gopractice.io/data/peeking-problem/) and "Sequential A/B Testing, Further Reading Choosing Sequential Testing Framework Comparisons and Discussions" by Mårten Schultzberg et al. (https://mng.bz/NBon).

This funnel can be calculated based on the MDC. Here, we need to solve the same equation we saw earlier—however, this time for different time periods—but we cannot make a decision until a period of time that we calculated in advance has passed. You could ask: what's the point of using it then? The answer is to have an emergency stop criterion to abort the experiment if results are outside the funnel and negative—the least expected, desirable, and probable outcome. For any sequential testing frame-

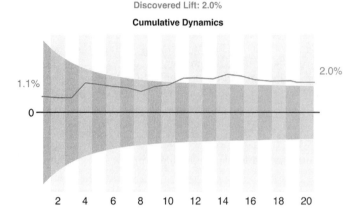

Figure 12.9   **An example of cumulative lift dynamics over time with specific confidence intervals**

work mentioned by the link earlier (e.g., mSPRT), we can make a decision as soon as results are outside the funnel or the experiment time has ended.

12.3.3 When to finish the experiment

It might be tempting to prematurely stop or extend an A/B test based on interim results. However, this can lead to erroneous conclusions due to changes in statistical power and the risk of false positives or negatives if we have not incorporated sequential testing. So when should we stop an experiment if we are not doing sequential testing?

In general, an experiment should run according to the predetermined design unless there's a catastrophic drawdown in key metrics (a significant negative effect) that would result in a meaningful financial loss had the experiment continued.

On the other hand, if you see positive effects in key metrics, the best practice is to stick with the initial plan and let the experiment run its full course. It allows you to confirm that these positive effects are sustained over time and are not a result of short-term fluctuations.

What about those borderline cases where some metrics are positive, some are negative, and others hover around the MDE? It's crucial during the experimental design phase to decide how you will interpret these mixed outcomes and set priorities among the different key metrics.

If you can't wait to see the final results, consider using methods like sequential testing, which allows for repeated significance testing at different stages of the experiment. These methods come with their own assumptions and considerations, so make sure you understand them fully before proceeding.

Deciding whether to stop or continue an experiment is a complex task that requires careful consideration of the metrics, potential outcomes, and their effects. Document these decisions in your experimental protocol, including criteria for possible early termination.

12.3.4 What to report

After finishing the experiment, it is time to start our analysis. Here we need to calculate the required metrics, double-check monitoring, and provide confidence intervals for every measurement.

Not every experiment is successful. According to our experience, it is quite good to have 20% of A/B tests show a statistically significant difference (recall that usually if the false positive rate is 5%, the margin is 15%). And remember: if the test was statistically significant, it doesn't mean that the results are positive or massive.

Suppose we decide that the A/B test is successful and the effect is significant. In that case, we have two options:

- *Report a pointwise effect*—"Effect is significant and equal to X," where X is the calculated difference between metric values on both experimental and control groups.
- *Estimate the confidence interval for effect*—If the pessimistic estimate of the effect is equal to the lower confidence bound of the difference, the conservative estimate is equal to the pointwise difference, and the optimistic estimate is equal to the upper confidence bound.

We have provided the core information of the report (of course, the reported metrics should be understandable to the audience, preferably expressed in earned or saved money, longer user sessions, etc.). In addition, it is good to dive deeper into the change in metrics, analyze how it affected different user or item segments, and outline the further steps (how overall metrics might change if we roll up on 100%). Table 12.1 shows examples of what fields can be included in the reporting table.

Table 12.1 An example of what fields can be included in the reporting table

Metric	Group A	Group B	MDE	Lift	p-value	Conclusion
CVR	75.2%	79.8%	5%	6.12%	0.0472	+4.2–6.9% (significant)
AOV	$232.2	$242.8	11%	4.57%	0.3704	No significant effect
…	…	…	…	…	…	…

Once uplift is reported, the possible positive scenario may include one more experiment on a larger proportion of data or a complete switch to a new system—or a full-scale rollout, pause, and reversed A/B test. A series of successful A/B experiments will provide you with a solid data-driven argument that will serve as adequate support in making decisions on whether to give the green light to further steps.

12.3.5 Debrief document

Writing a debrief document is valuable for transparent communication of A/B experiment results, as well as for improving the quality of future experiments. It should be created during or immediately after the experiment to summarize key findings, including captured insights, detected problems, and recommendations. Sharing this document with the team ensures everyone is on the same page and enables continuous learning and improvement of the system.

If the experiment is successful, a debrief document will include suggestions for similar experiments in other products. In case of failure, it is important to discuss what should be done differently in future tests and what mistakes should be avoided, as well as to develop new control metrics to prevent similar failures in the future earlier during an experiment.

12.4   *Design document: Measuring and reporting*

Because reporting cannot be designed at the preproduction stages when the design document is set to be prepared, it should be skipped by default. However, we've included it for demonstration purposes.

12.4.1   *Measuring and reporting for Supermegaretail*

Measuring and reporting for Supermegaretail as part of the design document have their own peculiarities, and one of the crucial ones is that since we are predicting the future, we can only assess the quality of the system when the future comes; at the end of the day, we want to understand how much profit we will be able to generate, but we can only know this post facto, while the only way to evaluate this is by using certain metrics that are not directly related.

DESIGN DOCUMENT: SUPERMEGARETAIL

IX. MEASURING AND REPORTING

I. MEASURING RESULTS

As a first step to improving the prediction quality of the already deployed sales forecasting model, we plan to experiment with combining existing models (one per category) into one. The reasoning behind this is that we will encode information about the group of items without loss in specificity but will gain more data and, thus, better generalization. Even with no improvement in quality, it is still much easier to maintain one model than many.

As offline metrics, we looked into different quantiles, percentage errors, and biases. But instead of evaluating only the overall score, we checked on metrics and the error analysis of specific categories. These offline tests yielded the following intermediate results:

- The general prediction quality steadily increases across all metrics, and the majority of validation folds when switching to a split model.
- The categories with a small number of products showed an increase in the offline metrics compared to a baseline (multi) model. The amount of data they had was insufficient to learn meaningful patterns. The large categories didn't change many wins when switching to a unified model. The result is reproducible through different seasons and key geo regions.

Previously, A/B tests provided some estimation of what uplift to expect in each major category based on offline metrics. If we reduce metric M for product P by X%, it leads to a decrease in missed profit (out-of-stock) by Y% and cuts losses due to the overstock situation by Z%. According to our estimates, the total increase in revenue for the pilot group is expected to be 0.3% to 0.7%.

II. A/B TESTS

- *Hypothesis*—The experiment hypothesis is that according to the offline metrics improvement, we expect revenue to increase by at least 0.3.
- *Key metrics*—The best proxy metric for revenue we can use in the A/B experiment is the average check. It perfectly correlates with the revenue (assuming the number of checks has not changed). The atomic observation for the statistical test will be a single check.
- *Splitting strategy*—We split by distribution center and, through them, acquire two sets of stores, as each center serves a cluster of stores. From those sets, we pick subsets that are representative of each other and use them as groups A and B.
- *Additional metrics*—Control metrics for the experiment are
  - *Number of checks per day*—Whether the sales volume has no significant drop.
  - *Model's update frequency*—Does the model accumulate newly gathered data regularly?
  - *Model's offline metrics*—Quantile metric, bias, WAPE.
- *Auxiliary metrics*—
  - *Daily revenue*
  - *Daily profit*
- *Statistical criteria*—We'll use Welch's t-test to capture the difference between samples.
- *Error rates*—We set the significant level to 5% and the type II error to 10%.
- *Experiment duration*—According to our calculations, 2 weeks will be enough to check the results. However, given the distribution center's replenishment cadence of 1 week, we will extend this period to one full month.

III. REPORTING RESULTS

A report containing the following chapters is to be provided:

- *Results*—Shown as 95% confidence intervals for primary and auxiliary metrics
- *Graphical representation*—The value of a specific metric at a specific date for all metrics from both control and treatment groups for ease of consumption
- *Absolute numbers*—For example, the number of shops in each group, the total number of checks, and total revenue
- *Methodology*—For example, how groups were picked to be representative of each other, simulations run to check for type I and type II errors, etc. (see the appendix for more details)
- *Recommendation/further steps*—What to do next based on the received results

12.4.2 *Measuring and reporting for PhotoStock Inc.*

We've included this phase as a template for the PhotoStock Inc. case.

DESIGN DOCUMENT: PHOTOSTOCK INC.

IX. MEASURING AND REPORTING

I. MEASURING RESULTS

The following is our baseline list of offline metrics:

- *NDCG@10 (human)*—We use human-labeled relevance scores for each photo in the search engine results page (SERP).
- *NDCG@30 (implicit)*—We use implicit feedback as a relevance score:
  - *3*—Image bought
  - *2*—Image added to Favorites
  - *1*—Image clicked on
  - *0*—Views with no interactions
- *MRR (human)*—The average position of the first photo labeled as relevant.
- *MRR (click)*—The average position of the first photo clicked in SERP.
- *MRR (purchase)*—The average position of the first photo purchased in SERP.

We retrospectively apply these metrics to the current non-ML search algorithm by collecting SERPs displayed for each query. We then measure our online metrics (CTR and CVR) over different time periods. After that, we calculate Spearman's rank correlation coefficient and select an offline metric that correlates most strongly with each online metric. The chosen offline metric is then used in a simple regression model to provide an initial estimate of the MDE in an A/B experiment.

Given that this is the first A/B test, we do not yet have comparative data for more precise MDE estimation. However, for future testing, we propose a systematic approach where we will collect and correlate the differences in offline and online metrics between variations A and B from each A/B test. The ultimate goal is to establish an approximate correlation: for each X% improvement in offline metric C, we see a Y% uplift in online metric D.

Further refinement of our online metrics estimation could involve building a user behavior simulation. However, that would be a more complex task, and we believe the current approach provides a solid foundation for our testing.

Apart from the aforementioned automated offline testing methods, we can also incorporate feedback from assessors. We propose two evaluation tasks:

- Given a query Q and the top 20 photos suggested by the new search engine, assessors would rank the overall SERP from 1 to 5 based on its relevance.
- Presented with a query Q and the top 20 photos from two different search engines (one being the current version and the other the new version), assessors would determine which SERP is more relevant.

The second task allows for a comparative assessment, which generally produces more robust evaluations by reducing the influence of individual scoring biases.

II. A/B EXPERIMENT DESIGN

Let's say we have received approximate estimates of the minimum expected effect in the offline metrics: +5% for CTR and +20% for CVR. Our *experiment hypothesis* is the following:

- If we switch the current search engine to our ML-based solution, it will provide more relevant search results, which will be reflected in an increase in CTR by at least 5% and an increase in CVR by at least 20%.

Consequently, our *key metrics* are CTR and CVR.

Control metrics, which should not change during the experiment, are

- *Views per variation*—If not equal, either there is a problem in splitting strategy, or we greatly affected user experience in the testing group.
- *Response latency*—This should not increase much, or at least fit SLAs.
- *Queries per second*—If the value is low, the search engine seems to become unavailable.
- *A daily number of queries and percentage of sessions started from the search bar*—Both inform user engagement; we expect these numbers to not decrease.
- *A number of customer support reports*—If there is a spike, something is probably broken.

Auxiliary metrics that give additional information but do not participate directly in the decision-making are

- *Average time spent on SERP*—If increased, it can signal that the search engine has become worse and the user needs to spend more time, make more queries, and scroll more pages to find what they are looking for.
- *The total number of clicks and purchases per variation*—Both will report what leads to an increase in conversion rate (the nominator, the denominator, or both with different rates).
- *Total profit and average profit per purchase.*
- *An average position of the clicked photo in SERP and an average number of queries per session*—A tricky metrics that, with a decrease, under some assumptions, indicate that it has become easier for the user to navigate and fewer actions and less time are needed to find what they needed.
- *Percentage of sessions ended with a purchase*—A less sensitive version of CVR.
- *Splitting strategy*—No extra dependencies are added to the user experience by the new search engine, so nothing prevents us from dividing users in a standard way by their unique ID.
- *Statistical criteria*—Considering that we aim to increase CTR and CVR (both are proportion metrics), we choose the proportional Z-test.

We'll use conservative error rates for type I and II errors: $\alpha = 0.01$ and $\beta = 0.05$:

- *Sample size*—Let's analyze what we have before the test:
  - PhotoStock Inc. website has 100,000 visits daily
  - Average search queries: 1.5 per visit
  - Average number of photos viewed after each query: 20
  - Average percentage of viewed photos that were clicked: 10%
  - Average percentage of clicked photos that was purchased: 1%

Therefore, we have $100,000 \times 1.5 \times 20 = 3,000,000$ views daily:

- Baseline CTR is 10% (number of clicks per view)
- Baseline CVR is 10% * 1% = 0.1% (number of purchases per view)

Thus, we have 300,000 clicks and 3,000 purchases daily.

Previously, we discussed that to avoid possible risks, we would like to roll out gradually. So for the first A/B, we will take only 10% for both groups (5% for group A and 5% for group B). That means we have $3,000,000 \times 2.5\% = 150,000$ views per day for each group.

How much time should the experiment take? The following is a formula for sample size estimation based on required MDE and error rates:

$$n = \frac{(Z_1 - \frac{\alpha}{2} + Z_1 - \beta)^2 [p_A(1 - p_A) + p_B(1 - p_B)]}{(p_A - p_B)^2}$$

Here p_A and p_B are old and new proportions (in our case, CTRs or CVRs), and Z_x are critical values of Z-statistic for a given level.

We have 10% and 10.5% as old and new CTR values:

$$n = \frac{(2.57 + 1.65)^2 [0.1(1 - 0.1) + 0.105(1 - 0.105)]}{0.0052}$$

This leads to 131,095 views required, while we have 150,000 views daily for each group. This means that we need only 1 day to collect the necessary amount of data to detect a significant increase (5% or greater) for CTR.

What about the conversion rate? We have 0.1% for the old version and 0.12% for the new version. Applying the preceding formula once again will lead to 978,693 views required. So we need 7 days to collect this data.

Summing up, the experiment will run for a week to satisfy both metrics. A week is also good because it will cover the full cycle of week seasonality, if any (e.g., for PhotoStock Inc., there may be more professional users during working days and amateurs during weekends).

To check whether we did everything right, we will run simulated A/A and A/B tests multiple times, generating samples from the binomial distribution of estimated size and with required CTR and CVR values to ensure that calculated error rates are less than the desired ones.

III. REPORTING TEMPLATE

During an experiment, we primarily monitored MDE dynamics. As expected, the CTR effect was statistically significant on the second day. In contrast, a statistically significant effect in CVR was detected only on the fourth day of the experiment.

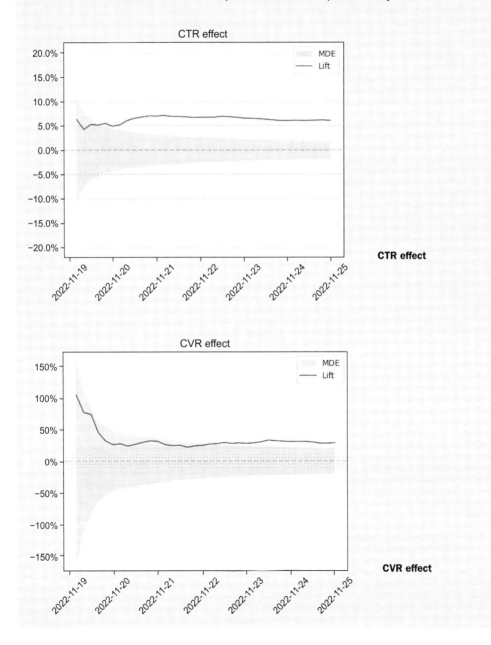

By the end, we collected the following metrics values:

- CTR is 9.91% in group A and 10.51% in group B (+6% difference).
- CVR is 0.10% in group A and 0.13% in group B (+29% difference).

We make the preliminary conclusion:

- The new search engine only slightly increased the number of clicks per view (+6%); however, the clickable photos turned out to be more relevant (+29% more conversions into purchases). Therefore, the A/B experiment was successful.

EXPENDED EFFECT REPORTING

We applied the bootstrap procedure to switch from point-wise effect estimation to distribution. We treat the lower and upper bounds for the 95% confidence interval as pessimistic and optimistic effect estimations. We use the original point-wise effect as a conservative estimate.

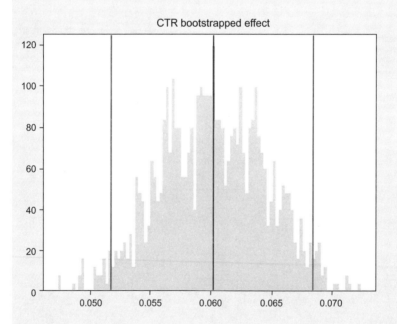

Bootstrapped CTR

We report the following effect for CTR:

- The pessimistic estimate is +5.1% (new CTR is 10.4%).
- The conservative estimate is +6% (new CTR is 10.5%).
- The optimistic estimate is +6.8% (new CTR is 10.6%).

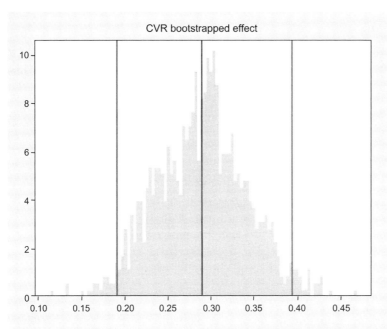

Bootstrapped CVR

We report the following effect for the CVR:

- The pessimistic estimate is +19.2% (new CVR is 0.12%).
- The conservative estimate is +29% (new CVR is 0.13%).
- The optimistic estimate is +39.4% (new CVR is 0.14%).

SCALING UP THE EFFECT

Let's evaluate these gains in terms of revenue when we scale the newly tested ML-based search engine to all traffic, assuming that the average photo profit ($3.0) and amount of daily visits (3 million) are the same.

The baseline CVR was 0.1%. Multiplying by daily traffic and fee, we get $9,000 daily income or $3.3 million yearly:

- The pessimistic estimate gives us $10,800 daily (+$1,800) or $3.9 million yearly (+$600,000).
- The conservative estimate gives us $11,700 daily (+$2,700) or $4.3 million yearly (+$1 million).
- The optimistic estimate gives us $12,600 daily (+$13,600) or $4.6 million yearly (+$1.3 million).

These numbers fully justify all our efforts and time.

Further steps will require running two to three shorter A/B experiments to cover a larger percentage of users (for instance, 20% -> 30% -> 50%) to ensure the system is safe, the effect is reproducible, and the experiment results are trustworthy.

Consider these side notes:

- Control metrics detected no incidents during the experiment.
- The average search time slightly decreased, which is a good sign. This means that the user experience has improved and that users can find what they need faster.
- The number of sessions that ended with purchase grew. SERPs became more relevant.
- The average profit per photo remained unchanged (~$3.0).

After the experiment, we also retrospectively estimated how many overall clicked photos were in the top 1,000 of the new model. It turns out that Recall@1000 for these clicks was 97%. This important finding hints at the further improvement of the system, specifically switching to the two-stage pipeline by adding a retrieval stage (candidate model).

Summary

- Use offline evaluation to get an approximation of the expected effect of your ML system before deploying and running the online testing phase.
- There are various ways to derive a connection between offline and online metrics, including benchmarks and the history of previously run A/B tests and their respective offline metrics.
- To make data-driven decisions about whether a new model is better than the old one (or an ML-based solution is better than a non-ML one), the industry standard is an A/B test (however, there are other options to derive a causal relationship).
- To run an A/B test smoothly and safely, we need to formulate a plausible hypothesis, pick the right key/control/auxiliary metrics, estimate expected lift and experiment duration, and sometimes perform simulated A/A and A/B tests before conducting real testing.
- While reporting the experiment results to stakeholders and teammates, we need to communicate the captured effect, what effect to expect if we roll out the service, what effect is seen in different segments, what problems were found during the experiment, and what the next steps and suggestions for further improvements are.

Part 4

Integration and growth

This is the final part of the book, dedicated to integration and growth. Chapter 13 covers integration, from API design and release cycle to operating the system and turning to fallbacks in case of malfunctioning. In chapter 14, we discuss monitoring and reliability, software system health, data quality and integrity, and model quality and relevance. Chapter 15 overviews serving and inference optimization, the challenges that may arise during the serving and inference stage, preferred tools and frameworks, and such topics as optimizing inference pipelines. Finally, chapter 16 reviews ownership and maintenance, accountability as one of the key factors in having a healthy ML system, tradeoffs between teams' efficiency and redundancy, the fundamental importance of properly arranged documentation, and the deceptive appeal of complexity.

Integration

As we claimed earlier, the worst thing you can do is build a system, only to put it on a shelf instead of going live. Both of us have faced such problems at least once in our careers, and it is not an experience we recommend.

A rookie mistake would be to think that integration is a one-time event or a single phase of a project. That is an antipattern: you cannot just dedicate some weeks to future integration and start building a system in a vacuum. In reality, it is a continuous process that starts from the very beginning of the project and ends only when the system is decommissioned. Even more, when the system's life cycle comes to an end, it requires certain deintegration efforts, making sure none of the direct or indirect users will be affected by switching it off. Proper integration is the key to the success of your system, making it much easier to get feedback on and improve.

The smoother various elements are integrated into your system, the shorter the feedback loop and the faster the iterations you can implement.

In this chapter, we discuss how to efficiently integrate your system, with a focus on technical aspects.

13.1 API design

API design is a crucial part of the integration process. It may be perceived as a contract between your system and its users, but it is a contract you need to read through thoroughly before signing. The is that is your API design will be costly to change once it has been set up, even if it's not set in stone and the system is still in development.

If you are a reader who is experienced in machine learning (ML), you may feel tempted to skip this section, simply because you know how to design APIs and have done it many times. That is a fair claim, as we are not going to teach you the difference between REST and RPC or how to design APIs in general. Besides, there are myriads of great books and articles on this topic (e.g., a nice collection of recommended materials can be found at https://news.ycombinator.com/item?id=24383180). Instead, we will focus on the key aspects and highlight pitfalls specific to ML systems in particular.

If we were to pick just two properties of a good API, we would choose *simplicity* and *predictability*. There is a classic software quote by Butler Lampson, which is even referred to as the "fundamental theorem of software engineering": "We can solve any problem by introducing an extra level of indirection."

A variation of this quote is that any programming problem can be solved with a layer of abstraction except for a problem of too many abstractions. So the simplicity of an API is the art of finding the right abstraction that is not leaky. An abstraction is considered leaky when it exposes too many underlying implementation details.

The vital role of *simplicity* lies in its ability to make an API easier to learn and use without a deep understanding of internals. A typical ML system often has many handlers and parameters, and it is always tempting to expose them to the external user. This leads to overcomplicated solutions where calling methods requires providing multiple parameters, and at the end of the day, it is hard to understand their meanings and how they are interconnected. A better approach implies hiding the complexity behind a simple interface and offering a few methods with a small number of parameters. Users will be grateful for that.

However, hiding all the parameters is not the best idea either (see figure 13.1). It is important to provide a way to customize the system's behavior, especially for debugging purposes. Imagine yourself debugging a system that has a dozen parameters during a late-night on-call shift, and you cannot modify any of them. Not a pleasant experience! In these cases, it always makes sense to suggest reasonable defaults and provide a way to override them.

**Figure 13.1
Overconfiguration vs.
underconfiguration**

Campfire story from Arseny

I used to work for a company that provided an API for external developers. I was in charge of building a brand-new endpoint that would mirror a classification system under the hood. In the early stages, the API seemed to be very straightforward—just accepting an object as input and delivering a label from a predefined taxonomy as output.

The accuracy of the baseline was not perfect, though, and one of my colleagues suggested returning a list of labels instead of a single label. It was a reasonable suggestion, which I implemented with no hesitation. However, practice showed that users only needed a single label even when it was incorrect (their usage patterns could not use the second label or further). The bad news was that the list of labels had already been exposed in the API, and it would be hard to remove it without breaking compatibility. So the API became overly complicated for no reason, and many users shared their frustration about that: "Why do you return a list of labels if it always contains a single item?" Too quick a decision about the API design led to a suboptimal solution that was hard to fix later.

Predictability is another crucial property of a good API. We've already talked about how ML systems tend to be nondeterministic unless they are forced to intentionally (please see chapter 10). This is an even more critical factor for APIs, as they must be deterministic and predictable. It is important to make sure that the same input will always produce the same output. Of course, there are algorithms that are nondeterministic by design (e.g., text generation with temperature sampling), but this is an exception that proves the rule.

There is always a possibility of forcing *deterministic behavior*. One simple example would be taking a random seed from the parameters (and choosing your own seed if not specified). By the way, while many ML libraries use random seeds from a global state, it is not possible in JAX, a new numerical computing library by Google that emerged recently. Its design suggests that you have to pass the random state explicitly exactly for this reason—to force full reproducibility. See https://mng.bz/lrQ2 for more information.

Another source of nondeterminism would be input data, including some implicit data like the current time (it should be provided via parameters as well).

Let's look at two implementations of a predict function that uses time as input and returns somewhat stochastic results with different random states. The following listing has the only explicit argument, while its output depends on three parameters, meaning that the output is not reproducible.

Listing 13.1   A mediocre design for a `predict` function

```
def predict(features):
    time = datetime.now()
    return model.predict(features, time, seed=42)
```

Unlike the previous example, the function caller shown in the following listing controls all the parameters affecting the output.

Listing 13.2   A better design for a `predict` function

```
def predict(features, time=None, seed=42):
    if time is None:
        time = datetime.now()
    return model.predict(features, time, seed)
```

> **NOTE** While we use Python in these examples, the fundamentals for higher-level abstractions remain unchanged. Imagine that this function is part of an HTTP API where `time` and `seed` are newly introduced query parameters. In this case, the same principles will be applied.

A specific aspect of predictability is *compatibility*. When talking about compatibility, engineers usually imply either backward compatibility or forward compatibility. Backward compatibility means that the new version of the API is compatible with the old one (the old code can be used with the new version of the API without any changes). Forward compatibility implies that the old version of the API is compatible with the new one (the new code can be used with the old version of the API without any changes).

In the context of ML systems, compatibility is also related to versioning the underlying model. There is a common practice to version the model and provide a way to request a specific version of the model during initialization.

Listing 13.3   Adding a model version to the API

```
class Model:
    def __init__(self, version):
        self.version = version
        self.model = load_model(version)
```

```
def predict(self, features, time=None, seed=42):
    if time is None:
        time = datetime.now()
    return self.model.predict(features, time, seed)
```

This example is oversimplified, and you may need a much more advanced solution for a complicated system. Read materials about the model registry pattern (e.g., https://neptune.ai/blog/ml-model-registry) if you want to learn more.

Versioning is tricky. One antipattern can be updating the model without bumping the version, which leads to changes in the behavior of the system without any notification. There are a lot of scenarios in which updating the model is considered a breaking change, and it must be reflected in the version. Even more, this is applicable not only for the model but for any aspect of the pipeline—data input/output (IO), preprocessing, postprocessing, etc. Some changes are not even intended: you can update the dependencies and get a different result, thus breaking the compatibility implicitly.

> **Campfire story from Arseny**
>
> How long might it take to update a Python version? This seems like a simple question, but once I had to learn the hard way that, in fact, it is not. And the reality slap was so hard that it sent me down a rabbit hole.
>
> The system I worked on required full compatibility. And, boy, was I surprised when bumping a Python version (while keeping everything else static!) led to a mismatch in several outputs. After a few iterations of bisection, I realized the problem was related to the image reading library. The same version of the library built for Python 3.5 had slightly different behavior from the version for Python 3.6, and therefore, the files readable with one version of the library were not compatible with the other.
>
> But how could that even happen? It appeared that the library used a low-level JPEG library implemented in C; at the same time, different builds of a Python library—even with the same version—used different versions of the underlying C library as they used one installed globally on a build machine. Finding which one was used in every given case was not easy and required some hardcore software archeology (digging into 6-year-old build logs of the open source library, finding the clues from there, and finally reproducing the very same build).
>
> Once again, the difference was not significant at all; still, it was enough to break compatibility because the models were trained on the images read with one version of the library, and their sensitivity to the input was too high. It was not likely that the users would notice the difference, but it was still a breaking change—a thing that was not supposed to happen due to the user agreement.

While Arseny's experience demonstrates the challenges of maintaining compatibility within a single system, the following story from Valerii highlights how versioning problems can become an even bigger difficulty when versioning is broken not within a system but at the point of our interaction with a third-party solution.

Campfire story from Valerii

One time I needed to implement a KYC (know your customer) solution for a financial organization. A part of this solution required verifying ID documents uploaded by users and ensuring a user's face wasn't present among existing users. In other words, it was a regulatory required constraint on user uniqueness. As a person familiar with a build-or-buy tradeoff (please see chapter 3), I used a face recognition solution from a big popular vendor.

The system was simple: take documents as input, find a face, calculate a vector, make sure there were no similar vectors in the database, and let the user sign up; otherwise, make customer support verify the case manually. The system worked fine until one unlucky day when the customer support team got overloaded with false positives. After the investigation, it appeared that the vendor's API version had been fixed—unless it was unset by mistake. As a result, a newer version of the API returned implicitly incompatible results that led to the incident.

This kind of failure is dangerous because of its implicit nature. An external API suddenly changing the field name may lead to an outage, which, luckily, is easy to catch and fix. When the model's version is changed, you may not notice it at first—it has returned a vector of floats before it returns a similar vector now, and the outage can be detected either by a properly configured testing/monitoring setup or after the downstream task (customer verification in this case) degradation.

Nothing helps to catch things like that better than a proper set of tests running on continuous integration (CI).

13.1.1 API practices

Over the years, the industry has developed multiple practices for working with APIs. We mention a few that we consider efficient. They may not be necessarily specific to ML systems, but they are often relevant to them (see figure 13.2):

- *Design at least two layers of the API.* Here, we are talking about the external and internal layers, where the former is logically a subset of the latter while not necessarily following the same protocol. The external API is exposed to users or other components, and the internal API is used by the external one. As long as the internal API is not exposed to users, it can be changed without breaking compatibility. The external API, in its turn, is a subset of the internal API and should be designed with compatibility in mind. It helps separate the concerns and make the external API simpler and easy to maintain in terms of compatibility while leaving the internal API flexible and easy to change.

- *Try separating the ML and IO components of the API when possible.* An ML service is easiest to maintain when it is stateless and thus idempotent. It's not always possible, but it's a good practice to strive for. This approach is useful not only for maintenance but also for scalability: IO and ML components can be scaled independently, which is a great property given that they have different requirements (e.g., an ML component is usually CPU- or GPU-bound). On top of that, it simplifies the evolution of the system: you can deploy a new version of the ML component without touching the IO component and use both ML components simultaneously for some time during A/B testing or a gradual rollout.

- *Build a client library for your API for simpler usage.* Whether it is for external users or your teammates, having a client library lowers the entry barrier, so it smooths the debugging process and speeds up experiments. It is also a good place to implement practices that are not parts of the API directly, such as recommended retries, timeouts, and so on.

- *Consider embedding feature toggles* (also known as feature flags) or any other alternative used in your organization. ML systems often operate in risky environments, and it will always be beneficial to have a way of disabling a new version of the model or switch to a fallback solution in case of arising problems. Feature toggles are not part of the API, but they effectively serve as a workaround to control the behavior of the system without redeploying it or changing the API/ client behavior.

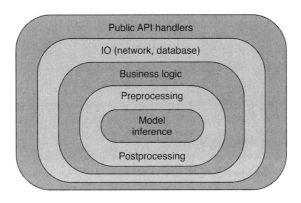

Figure 13.2   Layered API structure is simpler to maintain, test, and develop.

13.2   Release cycle

The release cycle of an ML system is usually similar to that of regular software. However, there are two main differences:

- ML systems are trickier to test.
- Training a new model (even with a fully automated pipeline) usually takes way more time than compiling code and building other artifacts.

Let's elaborate on these points.

Due to testing complexity, running tests alone is not always enough, and regressions may occur anyway. Let's talk about software for a moment. Once regular software is updated, it is usually enough to run tests to ensure everything works as expected. But if we are talking about ML models, the situation is quite different, as many improvements come with a price. When the ML model is updated, even if we have a representative dataset for tests and a good test coverage of software-related parts, we still cannot guarantee that the changes won't provoke harmful outcomes. For example, say there are 100 samples in the final test set, and the new model improves performance on 3 samples that have been labeled errors before but introduces two new errors on other samples. The overall performance is better, but is the change good enough to be released?

Real-life scenarios are full of similar examples, and this means that many releases require a human in the loop. It is similar to testing user experience changes, where an employee should check if the changes bring sufficient benefits. And evaluating the tradeoffs between improvements and regressions is usually more complicated than just checking if the UI animation works as expected. The human-in-the-loop method may vary depending on the system. In some cases, an ML engineer is responsible; in others, it can be a product manager or an external domain expert, or the job can even be delegated to crowd-sourcing platforms providing a large pool of users with aggregated feedback.

There are simpler cases where some kind of AutoML allows for the model (not the whole system—just the model) to be released automatically without additional reviewing. Imagine you are building an advanced text editor with a powerful feature: an autocomplete that mimics the author's style (oh, we wish we had one while writing this book!). This software needs to run a custom model (probably on top of a large foundational model) for each user. Gathering new users' writings and regularly updating the model without human involvement seems a good practice here; otherwise, it is not scalable. Such scenarios need an even higher paranoid level of testing to cover as many pessimistic paths as possible and disable model updates once there is a chance of a malfunction.

Okay, let's assume testing is not a problem. Say you have found a bug in the preprocessing code; you are confident fixing it is a good solution that won't make things worse, and an advanced testing toolset can help you make sure that is really the case. For regular software, it would mean that you can just fix the bug, run the tests, and deploy a new version; usually, it does not take too long. But it will not work this way for ML systems because you need to retrain the model. We will not use extra-large-scale examples here, but even based on our experience, models that were trained for weeks are not uncommon, so releasing the fix the next day is not possible at all.

In practice, it means the release cycle for ML systems is usually longer than for regular software; still, it may vary a lot—from multiple times a day to once a year with multiple variations in between. Make sure to take this into account when designing your system. A long release cycle implies that the system should be more reliable and tested extensively, while a short release cycle allows it to be more agile and allows for more experimentation.

Multicomponent systems can have and use different release cycles for different components. Imagine a simple search engine that contains four components: an index containing the documents to be searched across, the lightweight filter for preliminary selection, a heavy model for the final ranking, and an API layer to expose the search results. Documents may be added to the index all the time (with no release required), the index codebase is rarely touched, and the filterer and API layers are pure non-ML software that is easier to test and build, so they can be released more frequently. In its turn, the ranking model is trained and released biweekly with additional verification. It allows us to be more agile with the non-ML components and more stable with the ML component.

There is a family of release-related techniques, including blue-green deployment (see figure 13.3) and canary deployment (see figure 13.4). They may slightly differ, but the core idea behind them is to have two or more systems in production at the

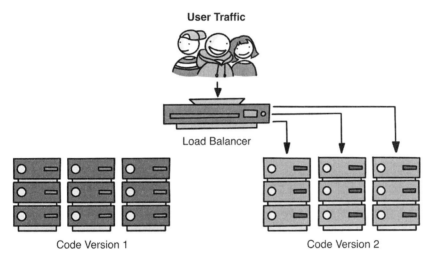

Figure 13.3   Blue-green deployment

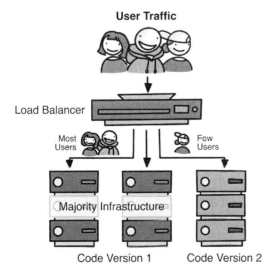

Figure 13.4   Canary deployment

same time. New users are sent to a new version once it is deployed while the old version is still functioning. In the blue-green deployment, changes are discrete (all users are switched to either the blue or green version), while in canary deployment, the rollout is granular, and the new version is used for a small portion of the existing users. It allows us to test the new version in production and roll back more easily if something goes wrong. It is not specific to ML systems, but it can be applied for them as well. Another technique ML systems can use is decomposition (e.g., some components like a model can be released with canary deployment; in contrast, other components like API layers can be released in a more traditional way).

Canary deployment should not be confused with the A/B tests we discussed in chapter 12. While technically they may look like similar concepts (multiple instances of a system are live, and traffic is sent toward them in a proper split), their intent is different. A/B tests are used to evaluate the performance of different versions of the system, while canary deployment is used to test the new version of the system before switching to it completely. In A/B tests, we want to compare the performance of the system across different versions, and the time of the test is decided based on statistical significance; it is fine to end up keeping either option A or option B. With canary deployment, we want to make sure the new version is good enough to be used by all users, and we aim to switch to it completely as soon as possible.

While large enterprises usually tend to have stricter policies and longer release cycles, this is not always the case: aiming to reduce the time gap between iterations using both technical and organizational approaches is a noble goal. It is also an important aspect of the DevOps culture, and ML systems are not an exception here. If you're interested in this topic, we recommend checking out the book *The Phoenix Project*. It is not about ML systems, and it's not even a very technical book (more like a "business fable"), but it is a great read about the DevOps culture and how it can be applied in the real world.

Startups and mature big-tech companies are usually more agile and have shorter release cycles, but that can vary as well. Arseny once worked for a startup where deploying late on Friday night was a common practice (sometimes it led to outages that had to be solved by engineers who were already enjoying a solid pint of beer). In the other, more established startup, the release cycle was very flexible; every engineer could deploy their component at any time, but a simple guardrail warned before deployment if the time was imperfect (e.g., Friday after lunch).

Those who are blessed to schedule releases should be aware of all the dependencies: how the system influences other systems and how others can affect it. The biggest outages usually happen either on the infrastructure level or between the systems or components that are not owned by the same team. Having proper communication with other teams to avoid such problems is a must-have skill for any senior engineer. Unfortunately, this skill and the understanding of its importance often come at a certain cost (usually after a big outage).

Arseny's biggest outage was related to a logger configuration (not something you expect to care much about while building an ML system). Some ML-related load happened in threads, and when aiming to track the behavior, he overengineered a complicated logger to keep requests' IDs between the threads. It worked fine in one environment and was later deployed to another, where engineers had way less control. It was a dark moment when the defect revealed itself: the problem could only happen after 1,000 requests of a certain type that never happened in previous environments. It took a while to understand the root cause or roll back the new version, so the incident came to be a good lesson to introduce more checks in the release process.

13.3   Operating the system

It is never enough to build the system and integrate it directly with other components that need its output in terms of product logic. Any system requires additional connections for healthy operations, both tech and non-tech related. Some are required to smooth the maintenance and operations (from both the engineering and product perspective); others are caused by implicit nonfunctional requirements related to the system (such as legal or privacy concerns). Let's name a few.

13.3.1   Tech-related connections

CI is usually the first element of the whole infrastructure to be set up. It helps identify and resolve integration problems while facilitating smoother and faster development processes. Typical tasks for CI are running tests (unit or integration) and building artifacts that will be used down the stream (e.g., for further deployment). However, there may be other needs covered on the CI level, such as security testing, performance testing, cost analysis ("Does this release require us to spin out more cloud servers?"), deployment to test environments, linting the code style, reporting key metrics, and many more.

Two main things that are not part of the system's data but need to be stored are logs and metrics. Usually, there is a common approach to how logs and metrics are stored, aggregated, and monitored in a company, and you just need to follow the common way. We'll elaborate a bit more on this topic in the next chapter.

The system's performance may be prone to malfunctions, and it should not come as a surprise. Thus, the system should be connected to the alerting and incident management platform used in the company, so the person on call will be aware of a potential incident and react appropriately.

But how do they react, exactly? Here you may need to prepare specific cookbooks describing what expected failure modes are and how to approach them. Also, there may be an additional toolset to help with firefighting, like an admin panel for configuration, system-specific dashboards, and so on, which we will cover in chapter 16. Again, usually there is a company standard shared between ML and non-ML systems, so it is very likely that you will only need to adapt the software toolset already in use without reinventing the wheel.

Designing a system requires considering the whole life cycle of the system, not just the happy path, and being a little paranoid helps.

13.3.2   *Non-tech-related connections*

Other than purely technical aspects of operations, there are some non-tech aspects that should be considered. They are often related to customer success or compliance, and they are not always obvious. What should we do if the user wants all their personal data to be purged as allowed by the General Data Protection Regulation (recall chapter 11 and imagine how deeply their data can propagate)? Is there a regulation forcing the model to be explainable, and what is the best way to follow it without sacrificing the model's performance? What if a high-level executive or a startup investor faces a bug in the system and gets mad? How do we debug the system's behavior in hard-to-reproduce scenarios (e.g., a defect can be only reproduced by an aforementioned executive's user account)? All these questions should be answered before the system is released, and the answers should be at least briefly reflected at the design stage. Otherwise, the changes may be too expensive to implement later. Often it requires building additional components, like some user impersonation mechanism or an admin panel for data management or model explainability, and it may take a lot of project time and require help from other teams (e.g., Legal or Compliance to understand the regulations or Web Development to build the required dashboard).

From our experience, all these additional connections and considerations usually take more time than the core system itself, and the bigger the company, the more effort it takes. Given current trends, it's not likely to improve in the near future as even more regulations related to ML and privacy are being applied globally.

13.4   *Overrides and fallbacks*

Your system may have a legit reason to fail. An example of such a reason could be an external dependency: you pull out a chunk of data from a third-party API, and at some point, it's just not available. That is one of the situations where you may want to have a fallback solution.

A *fallback* is a backup plan or an alternative solution that can be used when the primary plan or solution fails or is not available. We use it to ensure that the system can still function and make decisions even if the primary ML model has failed for whatever reason.

This can be particularly important in systems used for critical tasks or in industries where even the shortest downtime can lead to significant consequences. For example, a fallback can be crucial for a model used to predict equipment failures in a manufacturing setting, ensuring that production can continue even if the primary model experiences problems.

Another reason to use a fallback is to provide an alternative solution when the primary system is unable to provide a satisfactory answer or a confident prediction or when the primary model's output is outside the acceptable range.

There are quite a few different approaches that can be used for implementing a fallback. One common approach is to use a secondary ML model, which can be trained on a different set of data or using a different algorithm. It might be a simpler baseline solution as we reviewed in chapter 8 or a dual-model setup. In this setup, the first model is built using only stable features, while the second model is used to correct the output of the main model using a larger feature set. The models can be used together, with the output of one model chosen over the other based on the input data or a predetermined rule. Alternatively, input feature drift monitoring (see chapter 14) can be set up for the "core" model to detect crucial shifts.

Another option is to use a rule-based system as a fallback, which can provide a stable and predictable response when the model is unavailable or is performing poorly. It is also possible to use a combination of these approaches, such as using a rule-based system to handle simple cases and the ML model for more complex scenarios (however, this alone introduces additional complexity and breakpoints).

As with baselines, a simple constant can be our fallback as well. Finally, sometimes a fallback solution is to reply with an explicit error message.

A fallback solution should always have a plan in place for activating the fallback and switching between the ML model and a fallback system. It can be either automatic (triggered by a monitoring event), manual, or hybrid, depending on the use case.

One custom type of fallback is an override. It is a way to manually override the model's output when it is signaling a bad prediction. One example may be dropping the model's output and using a constant instead when the model's prediction is beyond the acceptable range or when the model's confidence is too low. Another reason to use an override is related to a release cycle. For example, a customer complains about the model failing in a very specific scenario. Ideally, we need to ensure this scenario is represented in the training data, retrain the model, run all the checks, and deploy it. But, as we discussed earlier, it may take a while. So we can override the model's output for this particular scenario using a rule-based approach, keep the customer happy, and address it properly in the following release.

The downside of overrides is that they are not transparent and can be easily forgotten. For this reason, it is important to have a way to track them and to have a plan for how to address them properly; otherwise, they may turn into a technical debt. The positive side effect of having many overrides is that collections of overrides can be used to improve the model via *multisource weak supervision*—a technique when unlabeled data is labeled with "labeling functions" (these heuristics are not perfect but are cheap to implement). The labeling functions provide a noisy dataset that becomes a foundation for model training. More details on this technique can be found in papers by Alexander Ratner et al., "Data Programming: Creating Large Training Sets, Quickly" (https://arxiv.org/abs/1605.07723) and "Training Complex Models with Multi-Task Weak Supervision" (https://arxiv.org/abs/1810.02840). The concept of multisource weak supervision has gained recognition in the industry thanks to the popular library named Snorkel (https://www.snorkel.org/).

Arseny's colleague once implemented a more elegant solution that helped address the limits of a long release cycle. He worked on a named entity recognition problem, and sometimes the model was not able to recognize some entities that were important to customers. However, training a new model after the problem had been found was not an option because of the long training time. So he implemented a solution based on the knowledge base: before running the model, the input text was checked against the knowledge base, and if the possible entity was found there, it was used as a hint for the model. It allowed the team to fix the problem without retraining. Adding a sample to the knowledge base could be done in a minute by a nontechnical person, so the problem could be addressed promptly. The solution is described in more detail in a blog post (https://mng.bz/BgG1). This case was somewhat similar to overrides, but it augmented the model's inputs, not outputs.

13.5 *Design document: Integration*

Approaches to integration for both Supermegaretail and PhotoStock Inc. aim at creating user-friendly, fast, and efficient mechanisms for either inventory predictions or search results.

13.5.1 *Integration for Supermegaretail*

Supermegaretail's integration strategy is tailored to offer a seamless, dynamic, and highly responsive prediction system that helps manage inventory.

DESIGN DOCUMENT: SUPERMEGARETAIL

X. INTEGRATION

I. FALLBACK STRATEGIES

Fallbacks are crucial for maintaining operational efficiency in the face of unforeseen circumstances. Supermegaretail has adopted a multitiered fallback system:

- *Primary fallback*—The primary model is trained on a subset of the most significant features. It will be used if no feature drift/problems are detected within this subset.
- *Secondary fallback*—Our next layer of fallback involves time-series models like SARIMA or Prophet, which we explored in section 4.4. These models are less dependent on external features, allowing for more robust predictions if drift occurs.
- *Tertiary fallback*—As a last resort, we would predict sales akin to the previous week's data, with modifications for expected events and holidays.

The system monitors for data drifts and quality problems, triggering alarms that automatically switch to the appropriate fallback to ensure the most accurate predictions possible.

II. API DESIGN

- *HTTP API handler*—This component will manage requests and responses, interfacing with users in a structured JSON format.
- *Model API*—This will extract predictions directly from the model.

The request format is

```
GET /predictions?query=<query_string>&parameters=<parameters>&version=
➡<version>
&limit=<limit>&request_id=<request_id>&sku=<sku>&entity_id=<entity_id>
&group=<group_type>
```

The response format is

```
{
    "predictions": [
        {
            "sku": <sku_id>,
            "demand": <demand>,
            "entity": <entity_id>,
            "period": <time_period_for_demand>,
        },
        ...
    ]
}
```

III. RELEASE CYCLE

A. Release of the wrapper vs. release of the model

Within our integration strategy, the release of the wrapper and the release of the model represent two distinct processes. The following are the nuances for each.

For the release of the wrapper (infrastructure), we should consider the following:

- *Frequency and timeline.* The release typically happens less frequently than that of the model. As demand patterns can shift over the night, it is important to be able to incorporate them into the model through training.
- *Dependencies.* Infrastructure releases are mostly dependent on software updates, third-party services, or system requirements. Any changes in such areas may necessitate a new release.
- *Testing.* Comprehensive integration testing is a must to ensure all components work harmoniously. It is also crucial to ensure backward compatibility, so existing services are not disrupted.
- *Rollout.* This usually employs standard software deployment strategies. Depending on the nature of the changes, a blue-green deployment might not always be necessary, especially if the changes are not user-facing and do not affect batch jobs.
- *Monitoring.* The focus will be on system health, uptime, response times, and any error rates.

For the release of the model, we should consider the following:

- *Frequency and timeline*—Model releases are more frequent and are tied to the availability of new data, changes in data patterns, or significant improvements in modeling techniques.

- *Dependencies*—These predominantly rely on the quality and quantity of new training data. Any drifts in data patterns or introduction of new data sources can trigger the model's update.
- *Testing*—Before rolling out, the model undergoes a rigorous offline validation. Once validated, it might be tested in a shadow mode, where its predictions run alongside the current model but are not used. This helps in comparing and validating the new model's performance in a real-world scenario without any risks.
- *Rollout*—When introducing a new model, it's not just about deploying the model file. There's also a need to ensure that any preprocessing steps, feature engineering, and other pipelines are consistent with what the model expects.
- *Monitoring.* The primary focus remains on model performance metrics. Also, keeping an eye on data drift is essential. See chapter 14 for more details.

B. Interplay between wrapper and model releases

In cases where the infrastructure has updates that would affect the model (e.g., changes in data pipelines), coordination between the two releases becomes vital. Additionally, any significant changes to the model's architecture might require updates to the wrapper to accommodate the changes. By treating them as separate processes yet ensuring they're coordinated, we maintain the system's stability while continuously improving its capabilities.

IV. OPERATIONAL CONCERNS

Feedback is integral for continuous improvement. A feedback mechanism, inclusive of an override function, should be available to internal users. Not only does this aid in refining the predictions, but it also gives business users a sense of control and adaptability based on real-time insights.

V. NONENGINEERING CONSIDERATIONS

The integration strategy will also take into account nonengineering factors—for instance

- *Admin panels*—Crucial for managing the system and obtaining a high-level overview
- *Integration with company-level dashboards*—For company-wide visibility and decision-making
- *Additional reports*—Essential for deeper insights and analysis
- *Overrides*—A necessary feature to account for manual adjustments based on unforeseen or unique circumstances

Furthermore, standard CI tools used in the company, along with a typical scheduler, will be integrated to maintain consistency and optimize workflow.

VI. DEPLOYMENT

Given that our audience primarily consists of internal customers and the frequent batch jobs, there's no immediate need for green-blue or canary deployment. The absence of end-user traffic eliminates the need for such staggered deployments, simplifying our rollout strategy.

13.5.2 *Integration for PhotoStock Inc.*

The integration strategy for PhotoStock Inc. is focused on providing the most relevant search results regardless of the complexity of search queries while maintaining prompt responses.

DESIGN DOCUMENT: PHOTOSTOCK INC.

X. INTEGRATION

I. API DESIGN

Our search engine needs to expose one HTTP API handler, which takes a query string + optional additional filters (e.g., price, collection, resolution, author, etc.) and returns a list of IDs of the photos that match the query sorted by relevance. Besides these product-focused parameters, we need to pass more technical ones, like `version`, `limit`, and `request_id`.

The handler will be only used internally and will not be exposed to the public, so we don't need to worry about authentication and authorization, given that it's operating within a private network.

We can't keep the service fully stateless (we need to own index and overrides), but all the query-related metadata should be handled by the backend service as they already store other users' metadata.

Under the hood, we will use a simple cascade to narrow the search results. We will first filter by the optional filters, then fetch the nearest neighbors of the query string in the embedding space, and finally sort the results by relevance with the final model.

We consider using Qdrant (https://qdrant.tech/) as a rapid vector database capable of filtering + fetching candidates at scale; however, it has not been used in the company before, so we may need to test it properly before using it in production. Alternatively, we can consider using other vector databases if needed.

The request format is

```
GET /search?query=<query_string>&filters=<filters>&version=<version>
&limit=<limit>&request_id=<request_id>
```

The response format is

```
{
    "results": [
        {
            "id": <photo_id>,
            "score": <score>
        },
```

```
        ...
    ]
}
```
~~~

Both the request and response are in the JSON format, as that's the default format we use in our internal APIs. Structures of the request and response are simple and straightforward for now but can be extended in the future if needed.

The underlying API should be layered in the following way:

- The HTTP API handler only serves as a proxy to the underlying API and does not contain any business logic; it just parses the request, passes it to the underlying API, wraps the response into a JSON format, and handles errors.
- The vector DB API is responsible for filtering and fetching candidates given the embedding of the query string.
- The model API is responsible for extracting the embeddings from a string and scoring the candidates.
- The ranking API is responsible for sorting the candidates by relevance and applying possible overrides.

II. RELEASE CYCLE

We assume that model updates will be relatively rare as training takes a lot of time, and we don't expect the data to change significantly over time. We can expect releases of a new model and relevant APIs every 1 to 2 months, while most hot updates will be related to index and overrides only.

The index is the core of the search engine, and it will require regular updates (for data, not software). We can add new items on a daily basis (e.g., with a batch job running every night) and be ready to update the index on demand if needed (e.g., removing banned images or adding a new image by special requests from VIP users).

III. OPERATIONAL CONCERNS

Many internal users can provide a lot of feedback on search results, so we need to provide them with appropriate tools. For a start, we can just add a "Report bad match" button to the search results page for internal PhotoStock Inc. users. It will send a request to the data gateway, so we save an event with the photo ID, search engine results page position, and query string to the data lake. We can then use this data during the model retraining stage and error analysis and for manual overrides. In the future, we can consider providing similar functionality to some external authenticated users (e.g., top buyers we trust).

IV. OVERRIDES AND FALLBACKS

As a fallback, we're going to use the existing search engine, which is based on Elasticsearch. While it's not as good as the new one is set to become in terms of relevance, it's still a decent search engine.

As for overrides, we may have manual overrides for certain queries, which we can store in a separate database. It may happen in case of poor relevancy for popular/critical queries, which we cannot fix with the model promptly enough. For now, it can be a simple key-value store where the key is a regex of the query string, and the value is the list of photo IDs, which we will use in the search engine results page. This solution is not very scalable, but it's solid enough for the first version. We may want to make a simple UI for managing these overrides in the future.

There is another possible type of override related to "bad photos" that we want to hide from the search results (e.g., photos with nudity/violence that passed moderation). However, if we suddenly realize a given image is no longer welcome in our search results, we can simply remove it from the index.

Summary

- Remember that integration is not a one-time event or a phase of the project but rather a continuous process that starts from the beginning of the project and ends only when the system is decommissioned.
- When selecting an API for your system, the two main qualities you should look for are simplicity and predictability.
- The API practices we consider effective with regard to ML systems are designing at least two layers of an API, separating the ML and IO components of an API when possible, building a client library for an API, and embedding feature toggle or its alternatives.
- Having a fallback provides you with a backup plan or alternative solution that can be used when the primary plan or solution fails or is not available.

Monitoring
and reliability

Traditional software development is based on a simple principle: a quality-built product will perform with high stability, efficiency, and predictability, and these values will not change over time. In contrast, the world of machine learning (ML) is more complex, and working on an ML system does not end at its release. There is a practical explanation for this; while in the first case, a solution performs strictly within predesigned algorithms, in the second case, functionality is based on a probabilistic model trained on a limited amount of certain input data.

This means that the model will inevitably be prone to degradation over time, as well as experience cases of unexpected behavior, due to the difference between the data it was trained on and the data it will receive in real-life conditions.

These are risks that cannot be eliminated but that you need to be prepared for and able to mitigate so that your system remains effective and valuable to your business over the long term.

In this chapter, we'll cover the essence of monitoring as part of ML system design and the sources of problems your ML model may encounter as it operates. We will also explore how you want to monitor typical cases in system behavior change and how you need to respond to them.

14.1 Why monitoring is important

Having an operating ML solution in production is an excellent feeling. Having a proper validation schema, test coverage, and working continuous integration and continuous delivery CI/CD is an even better (although rarer) feeling. Unfortunately, this does not guarantee your system will remain stable without going crazy. By craziness here we mean any unexpected, illogical, wholly wrong, and unexplainable output from the model that can severely affect the system output—anything you would not expect to see from a healthy, reliable system (at least without notifying its maintainers and switching to fallback).

Without proper monitoring, even the most well-trained and accurate models can begin to degrade over time due to changes in the data they are working with. This is especially evident during times of significant change, such as the recent COVID-19 pandemic, where models used for tasks like predicting item availability, credit risk, and many more had to face enormous challenges. By implementing monitoring systems, we can identify and address problems with data quality and ensure that our models continue to make reliable predictions.

If somebody asks us to make a simplified high-level review of a generic ML system, it will most likely look like figure 14.1.

Figure 14.1   A simplified structure of a regular ML system

We can expect deterministic (e.g., reproducible) output only if all stages are fixed, exactly the same sample of data goes through precisely the same model (the same structure and the same weights), and this model is nonprobabilistic (some of the most popular models in the world, e.g., generative AI champions ChatGPT and Midjourney, are probabilistic; however, to be completely pedantic, we can fix a random

generator or seed and improve the reproducibility) with precisely the same postprocessing, and then we could expect that the results would be identical. Actually, this is
among the primary reasons for designing a proper training pipeline, which helps create and maintain these conditions for reproducible iterations and thus provides for
improvement and experimentation.

However, the probability that such a combination of factors can happen is
extremely low, as we are always dealing with a multitude of inputs that can change
with varying degrees of probability and effects on the model. Let's break down all four
components from figure 14.1 to understand what challenges we may encounter.

14.1.1 *Incoming data*

Unfortunately, the more complex the system we have, the smaller the chances that
data inputs will be repeatable (if that were the case, we could use a simple cache
instead), meaning that we can assume every input is unique. In addition, the distribution of specific features in data might change over time, affecting downstream stages.
Another possibility is that something will break in the data pipeline and corrupt the
data or someone will try to tackle the input in a way that will affect the output in the
desired and sometimes malevolent way (this, however, is usually more related to planting backdoors; see, for an overview, "Planting Undetectable Backdoors in Machine
Learning Models" (https://arxiv.org/pdf/2204.06974.pdf). If the system is not robust
to these perturbations, things can backfire at any moment in time.

14.1.2 *Model*

Unlike the incoming data, the model's structure (or architecture) and weights can be
stable. That, of course, depends on the presence of online training (e.g., updating the
model based on incoming data in a real-time/quasi-real-time fashion) and scheduled
updates (e.g., retraining every week on the latest batch of data). After any update,
regardless of this being a batch learning on online learning, it is not entirely the same
model as before. If the model is not the same, output from the same data might
change, which is essentially the reason why we retrain the model. Still, we want to be
sure that retraining/updating affected the model adequately and was a necessary
thing to do (recall section 13.2).

Another thing is that the system we have might be probabilistic/generative by
nature. The dialogue with ChatGPT (as of July 2024) shown in figure 14.2 is a rather
illustrative example.

The screenshot shows four different (though similar) replies from ChatGPT. While
behaving within a specific range is something we would expect, not having the same
output for the same input makes it more challenging to check the health of the system. Which reply is acceptable, and which is not? As of January 2023, our experience
with ChatGPT showed that it is not rare to receive several answers in a row that are
completely different or contradict each other, although this was partially fixed in later
versions.

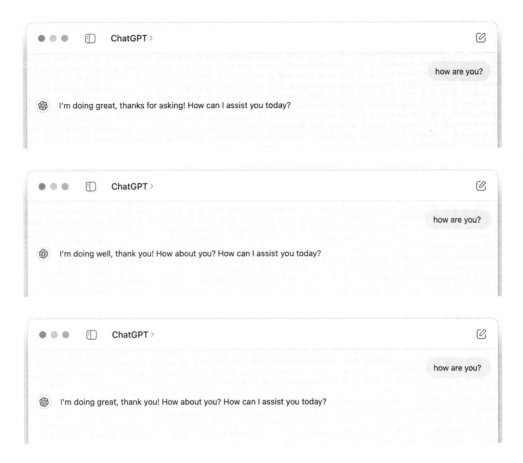

Figure 14.2   Annoying ChatGPT to ensure it is a fairly nondeterministic model. Although responses are similar, they are not identical.

14.1.3 Model output

It might be a relatively rare thing, but the model's output can become irrelevant due to so-called *concept drift*—for example, a change of the underlying dependencies between input data and the resulting output, making dependencies built by the model obsolete and inadequate. This is different from input data distribution shifts in the sense that while incoming data distribution remains the same, the labels, previously correctly allocated to them, are now different. For example, according to a recent tax change in the UK, which took place in 2022, the highest tax bracket is now applied to people with an income of 125,000 pounds per year, with the previous threshold being 150,000 pounds. Now imagine you have a marketing campaign to promote tax service assistance and a model set to pick the most probable users for this service to remain within the marketing budget. Such a change in the legislation would immediately trigger a lot of refinements to your model.

Another example would be a lag in time, causing shifts in understanding of the world to happen much later than the event that prompted these shifts. A good example here is the *Madoff investment scandal*, which was revealed only decades after the original shenanigans. For many years, signals coming from it were reviewed as signals of a successful hedge fund, but later, it turned out to be a Ponzi scheme. In other words, for many years, the incoming data was labeled as benevolent, only eventually turning out to be fraudulent.

14.1.4 Postprocessing/decision-making

It is important to be aware of the potential for a mismatch between the quality of the ML model and the business value it is expected to deliver. Several factors can contribute to this mismatch, including changes in the environment in which the model is used, as well as changes in how the model is being utilized.

If the model was designed to support a specific business process, it may no longer be effective if the process changes over time. For example, say the model was set up to prioritize customer support for the incoming tickets based on the future revenue of those users, and the new process is to focus on the quickest tickets to solve. Similarly, if the model is not being used in the way it was intended or is not being used at all, it may not be able to deliver the expected business value. To mitigate these risks, it is important to continuously monitor the performance of the ML model and the business value it is delivering and to make adjustments as needed to ensure that the model is able to support the desired business objectives.

In the following sections, we cover the most common cases of what can go wrong, focusing primarily on the first three stages. We discuss how to monitor and detect them, what to do if something has changed, and how to incorporate this into the design document so that you are able to plan beforehand and not after something terrible happens. Before we dive into potential malfunctions and ways to handle them, let's talk about the main components of monitoring ML systems. In her article "Monitoring ML Systems in Production. Which Metrics Should You Track?" (https://mng.bz/86B2), Elena Samuylova highlights four integral components of ML system monitoring, represented as a pyramid in figure 14.3.

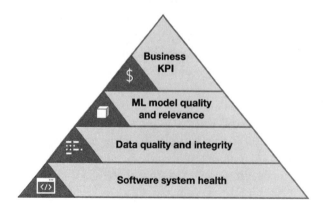

Figure 14.3   Core components of ML system monitoring (source: https://mng.bz/86B2)

The foundation of proper monitoring is the software backend, topped subsequently with data quality and integrity, model quality and relevance, and business key performance indicators (KPIs). The last point may seem irrelevant at first sight, as it is not part of an ML system per se, but the way a corrupted system may affect our KPIs and, eventually, the business itself cannot be underestimated. Let's break down every layer of the pyramid in reverse order.

14.2 Software system health

It is crucial to think of the software backend as the foundation of the design. This includes monitoring software performance to ensure it is functioning properly, executing tasks efficiently, and responding quickly to requests. Failing to prioritize the stability and performance of the software backend can have detrimental effects on the overall effectiveness of the ML system. Because this book covers the principles of ML system design and there are many books out there dedicated to "regular" software system design and its reliability, we are not covering this extensively. However, it naturally has to be addressed, as any system is only as strong as its weakest link. For a more in-depth analysis of system health, see the article by Chris Jones et al. (https://mng.bz/EOAl).

Monitoring the health of an ML system is an important aspect of production deployment. It is essential to ensure that the system is up and running and to track its performance characteristics to meet service-level objectives. Many of the same monitoring practices used in traditional software systems—such as application and infrastructure monitoring, alerting, and incident management—can also be applied to ML systems. These practices can help ensure the health and performance of the ML system and allow for timely intervention if any problems arise. By using the tools and practices developed for traditional software systems, it is possible to effectively monitor and manage the health and performance of an ML system in production.

There are various metrics that can be monitored, depending on the deployment architecture of the ML system. These can include service usage metrics such as the total number of model calls, requests per second, and error rates, as well as system performance metrics such as uptime, latency, cold start time, error rate, and resource utilization metrics such as memory and GPU/CPU utilization. It is important to carefully select a few key metrics that quantify different aspects of service performance, often referred to as *service-level indicators*. These metrics can help identify problems with the system and allow for timely intervention to prevent failures or degraded performance.

It is important to log events and predictions with their timestamps to monitor and debug your ML system. In the context of an ML system, we recommend recording data on every prediction if this is feasible and fits the budget (there are cases when storing every intermediate model output may drastically affect the profit margin), including the input features and the model output. This will allow you to track the performance of the model and identify any problems that may arise. As a general rule, you should log every prediction unless there are specific circumstances, such as privacy regulations or the use of edge models on a user's device, that prevent you from doing so. In these cases, it may be necessary to develop workarounds to collect and label some of the data.

In addition to prediction logs, it is also important to have software system logs—time-stamped events that provide information on what is happening within your ML-powered application. Having access to these logs can be helpful for debugging problems that may arise and for improving the model's performance. There are multiple tools available to help you centralize and analyze these logs, like Prometheus and Grafana among open source tools or AWS Cloudwatch or Datadog among cloud services.

> **NOTE**   You can always remove logs that you later consider unnecessary, but you can't retroactively add them back. Don't log if it doesn't add new context; in other words, make sure logs contain proper values and IDs, not just static statements.

The following shows examples of a poorly written log message and a good log message:

✗ `logger.info("Fraud probability calculated")`
✓ `logger.info(f"Fraud probability = {score:.3f} for user id {user_id}")`

The model health assurance platform at LinkedIn (https://mng.bz/dZEo) can provide some ideas on this topic. Service Level Objectives by Google can provide a necessary vocabulary to ensure system health (https://mng.bz/r1eJ).

Logs and metrics should be stored in systems, allowing for exploration and alerting. There are multiple software solutions for this matter. Good examples of self-hosted systems are the ELK stack (Elasticsearch, Logstash, and Kibana) for logs and Prometheus or Victoria Metrics for metrics. Similar systems are often provided by all-in-one cloud providers (e.g., AWS Cloudwatch) and more dedicated companies like Datadog. As we mentioned in chapter 13, connecting your ML system to a proper logs/metrics toolset is a must, though inexperienced engineers often underestimate the importance of this step.

14.3   *Data quality and integrity*

Data quality monitoring is essential for ensuring that the data used to train and make predictions with an ML model is accurate and reliable. Working with faulty data will inevitably lead to faulty predictions by the model. To maintain trust in the data, it may be necessary to stop and use a fallback until the data quality is restored or to investigate and resolve problems as they arise. Next we will touch on the most common possible situations that can require a fallback.

14.3.1   *Processing problems*

It is common for the system to rely on various upstream systems to provide input data. However, these data sources can trigger problems that will affect the performance of your ML system. For example, data may not be received or may be corrupted, which can be caused by problems in the data pipeline. Imagine an ML system that personalizes promotional offers for clients and may rely on data from an internal customer database, clickstream logs, and call center logs, which are merged and stored in a data warehouse. If any of these data sources experience problems, it can affect the functioning of the entire system.

One of our favorite examples is when a job processes zero rows and reports success (expected green square in the UI reporting the successful execution of the extract, transfer, and load job), so everyone is happy—until 1 week passes and we find out that there was a problem in the upstream data sources.

In addition, the data processing stage of an ML pipeline can also be prone to problems. This can include problems with the data source, data access problems, errors in the SQL or other queries used to extract the data, infrastructure updates that change the data format, and problems with the code used to calculate features. In batch inference systems, detecting and correcting these problems is possible by rerunning the model. However, in high-load streaming models, such as those used in eCommerce or banking, the effect of data processing problems can be more severe due to the large volume of data being processed and real-time decisions made based on model outputs.

14.3.2 *Data source corruption*

In addition to changes, data can also be lost due to problems with the data source. This can occur due to bugs, physical failures, or problems with external APIs. It is essential to monitor data pipelines closely to catch these problems early, as they can lead to irreversible loss of future retraining data.

Sometimes, these outages may only affect a subset of the data, making the problem harder to detect. Additionally, a corrupted source may still provide data, but it may be incorrect or misleading. In these cases, it is crucial to keep track of unusual numbers and patterns to identify potential problems. These failures can be both gradual and instant. Let's imagine two computer vision systems used for industrial needs: one is used on sterile assembly lines where photos of half-assembled devices are taken and analyzed, and the other is used on gigantic ironworks where it monitors how metal scrap turns into new alloys. The first could have an instant failure of lighting, and thus, the datastream suddenly becomes dark. The second is affected by dust and temperature; thus, the camera lens degrades over time.

If a data source problem is detected, it is important to assess the damage and take appropriate action, such as updating, replacing, or pausing the model if necessary.

Some data source problems are, unfortunately, inevitable. Imagine building a recommendation system for a marketplace where some merchants fill in every attribute of their goods and others ignore optional fields. In this case, a smart choice is to think about it in advance during the feature engineering stage to make the model ignore such cases.

Let's take a look at a more concrete example:

```
def get_average_rating(item):
    # return average rating across all item reviews, 1 - 5 stars
    try:
```

```
      # happy case, read from DB and return the number
      ...
except Exception:
    return -1
```

This function is not the best way to approach potentially missing or corrupted data if
-1 is not replaced downstream. While returning some impossible value is a common
practice in low-level programming, for ML purposes, it would be more suitable to
return something like the median value across other items.

14.3.3 *Cascade/upstream models*

In more complex ML systems, there may be several models that depend on each
other, with the output of one model serving as the input for another model. This can
create a loop of interconnected models, which can be vulnerable to problems (see figure 14.4).

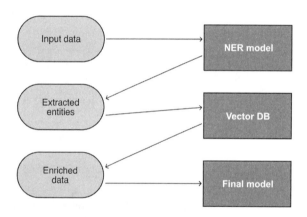

Figure 14.4   **Input data is processed
by a chain of models; even a small drift
in the first one can lead to
accumulated error downstream.**

Arseny worked for a company that used a chain of models; first, the named entity recognition model extracted core entities; later they were enriched with multiple internal
and external datasets, and finally the result was used for classification. Components of
the system were developed and maintained by different people, and sometimes it could
lead to situations when the named entity recognition model demonstrated improvements on its own metrics while the downstream classifiers' performance dropped.
Luckily, after the first catch, engineers implemented cross-stack checks, so it was no longer possible to deploy a new release upstream without running proper checks across
downstream models, and thus potential failures were caught in advance.

For example, in a content or product recommendation engine, one model may
predict the popularity of a product or item. In contrast, another model makes recommendations to users based on the estimated popularity. If the popularity prediction
model is incorrect, this can lead to incorrect recommendations provided by the second model.

A similar problem can occur in a car route navigation system, where a model predicts the expected time of arrival for various routes, and another model ranks the options and suggests the optimal route. If there is a problem with the model that predicts the expected time of arrival, this can lead to incorrect route recommendations, which in turn can affect traffic patterns.

These types of interconnected systems can be at risk for problems if something goes wrong with one of the models, leading to a chain reaction of negative actions throughout the system. It is essential to carefully design and monitor these types of systems to ensure that they are functioning correctly.

14.3.4 Schema change

Changes in data schemas, where the format, type, or structure of data is altered, can be a major challenge for ML systems. These changes can cause the model to lose signal, as it may be unable to match new categories with old ones or process new features. This can be particularly problematic in systems that rely on complex features based on a category type, as changes to categories can require the model to relearn how to interpret the data.

For example, in a demand forecasting or e-commerce recommendation system, changes to the product catalog can affect the model's understanding of the data. Similarly, updates to business systems or the introduction of new data sources or APIs can also cause problems for the model if it has not been trained on new data. (See chapter 6 for more information.)

To mitigate the affect of data schema changes, it is vital to design the model with this possibility in mind and to educate business users about the potential consequences of these types of changes. Data quality monitoring can also help identify and address these problems as they arise.

14.3.5 Training-serving skew

Training-serving skew is a situation where an ML model performs poorly on real-world data because it was trained on an artificially constructed or cleaned dataset that does not accurately represent the data it will be applied to. This can happen when the training data is incomplete or does not adequately capture the diversity and complexity of the real world (see chapter 6 for detailed information).

One example of training-serving skew is a model trained on a limited set of crowd-sourced images that performs poorly when applied to real-world images with a wide range of data formats and image quality. Similarly, a model trained on high-quality images in a lab setting may struggle to perform well on real-world images taken in poor lighting conditions (see figure 14.5).

Figure 14.5 Such a drastic difference between sandbox sets of images and real-life photos can lead to significant drops in the model's performance.

> **Campfire story**
>
> This story was told by one of our friends. There was a company developing an augmented reality application based on computer vision on top of camera data; the company office was in St. Petersburg, a Russian city located by the Baltic Sea. St. Petersburg is famous for its cloudy weather—the average annual number of sunny hours is about 1,600. That was where engineers gathered most of the data and tested their product.
>
> The company's lead investors were located in Cyprus, a Mediterranean country with 3,400 sunny hours annually. So when they tested the prerelease version of the product, they were terrified—the ML component worked so poorly! After a short investigation, the engineers realized the problem was caused by a data distribution mismatch: outdoor scenes they used were captured in the cloudy and rainy environment of a Russian winter, while investors tested the product under the blazing sun of the Cyprus summer.

To address training-serving skew, it may be necessary to continue developing the model by collecting and labeling a new dataset or adapting the existing model based on the data from an unsuccessful trial run. Sometimes the trial run may generate enough data to train a new model or adapt to the existing one. There's a great article by Will Douglas Heaven on Google's medical AI published in *Technology Review* (https://mng.bz/V2ay). Note that this is somewhat close to the data drift scenario we will review in the following section.

14.3.6 *How to monitor and react*

Danger foreseen is half avoided, so the first and most crucial step in monitoring is knowing beforehand what might go wrong. In addition to that, though, we attempt to provide some actionable advice.

Data quality monitoring is somewhat specific to ML, as it involves ensuring that the data we use to train and make predictions with an ML model meets specific expectations. However, it is also necessary for other analytical use cases; here, existing approaches and tools can be reused.

Traditional data monitoring is often performed at a macro level, such as monitoring all data assets and flows in a warehouse, but ML requires monitoring to be more granular, focusing on particular model inputs. In some cases, you can rely on existing upstream data quality monitoring. Still, additional checks may be required to control feature transformation steps, real-time model input, or external data sources.

Various metrics can be monitored to ensure the quality of the data that is being used in an ML model. Some common types of metrics and checks are as follows:

- *Checking missing data* implies a search for lost data in particular features and the overall share of missing data in the model's inputs. It is generally acceptable to have some missing values, but it is important to ensure that the level of missing data stays within an acceptable range, both for the entire dataset and for individual features. You should also check for different expressions of missing data, such as "N/A," "NaN," or "undefined," as a simplistic check for missing values may not catch all cases. You can use a visual aid like a plot to identify missing data with your own eyes and set a threshold for when to pause the model or use a fallback if there are too many missing values. It is also helpful to identify the key driving factors in your dataset based on model feature importance or SHAP values (see chapter 11 for more details) and ensure these are not missing. This will allow you to set up different monitoring policies for critical and auxiliary features.

- *Duplicated data* is a problem that is the opposite of the previous one, and it can be dangerous, too. Duplicates often happen for a subset of the whole dataset, which changes the data distribution, affecting downstream models.

- *Data schema validation* verifies whether the input schema matches expectations to detect erroneous inputs and track problems like the appearance of new columns or categories.

- Constraints on individual feature types assert the specific feature type, such as *ensuring that a feature is numerical.* This approach can catch input errors, such as a feature arriving in the wrong format.

- It is important to *check the number of model calls* to ensure that the model is functioning properly. This is particularly useful if the model is expected to be used on a regular basis, as it can help you identify any sudden changes or deviations from the typical usage pattern. Additionally, checking the number of model responses can help you detect if the model is experiencing problems or if there is a problem with the service itself. This can help prevent disruptions in service and ensure the system continues to operate smoothly. Last but not least, this check is very easy to implement.

- With *constraints on individual feature ranges*, expectations about "normal" feature values can be formulated, such as sanity checks (e.g., "age is less than 100") or domain-specific checks ("normal sensor operating conditions are between 10 and 12"). The violation of a constraint can be a symptom of a data quality problem. It may start with common-sense checks, but for more complicated domains it requires a deep understanding of the problem.

- Feature statistics track particular features' mean values, min-max ranges, standard deviation, the correlation between features, percentile distribution, or specific statistical tests. This can help *expose less obvious failures*, such as a feature behaving abnormally within the expected range. Histograms/class distribution for categorical features can be used for manual checks; however, they are not easy for automatic data quality monitoring

- With *anomalous effects*, you can use the anomaly and outlier detection approaches to detect "unusual" data points and catch corrupted inputs. This will allow you to focus on detecting individual outliers or tracking their overall rate.

For nonstructured data like images, texts, or audio, similar principles may be applied. We cannot apply a primitive check like "customer age should be in the range between 12 and 100," but we can introduce simple features on top of data that will be tested.

These features don't have to be directly used in the models (so we still directly apply a deep learning model to images) but are used only for data quality monitoring. It could be brightness or color temperature for images, length (number of characters) for texts, and distribution of wave frequencies for audio.

In most cases, it may be useful to *validate inputs and outputs separately for each step in the pipeline* to identify the source of the problem more easily. This can be particularly helpful if your pipeline is complex and involves multiple steps, such as merging data from different sources or applying multiple transformations. By running checks at different stages of the pipeline, you can locate the source of any problem and debug them more quickly. On the other hand, if you only validate the output of the final calculation and notice that some features are incorrect, it may be more difficult to identify the source of the problem, and you may need to retrace each step in the pipeline.

The choice of metrics to monitor will depend on various factors such as the model's deployment architecture (e.g., batch, live service, or streaming workflows), the specifics of the data and real-world process, the importance of the use case, and the desired level of reactivity. For example, if the cost of failure is high, more elaborate data quality checks may be necessary, and online data quality validation with a pass/fail result may be added before acting on predictions. In other cases, a more reactive approach may be sufficient, with metrics like average values of specific features or the share of missing data tracked on a dashboard to monitor changes over time.

One of the challenges of data quality monitoring in ML is the execution of the monitoring process itself. Ensuring the quality of data fed into ML pipelines is critical, but setting up a monitoring system can be time-consuming. This is especially true if you need to codify expert domain knowledge outside the ML team or if you have many checks to set up, such as monitoring raw input data and postprocessed feature values.

Another challenge is managing a large number of touchpoints in the data quality monitoring process. It is important to design the monitoring framework to detect critical problems without being overwhelmed. If your monitoring system sends tens of false alerts daily, at some point you will just ignore its signals, so finding the right balance of sensitivity is crucial.

Finally, tracing the root cause of a data quality problem can be difficult, especially if you have a complex pipeline with many steps and transformations. Data quality monitoring is closely connected to data lineage and tracing, and setting this up can require additional work.

We highly recommend reading a paper from Google called "Data Validation for Machine Learning" (https://research.google/pubs/pub47967/).

The following is a highly condensed summary of the paper that features a list of actions that we recommend to effectively monitor your system:

- Identify *key data quality dimensions* that are critical to the ML use case, such as completeness, accuracy, timeliness, and consistency.
- Set up data quality *constraints* for each dimension and define the acceptable range for each constraint. For example, you might set a constraint that the data must be complete, with no more than 5% missing values.

- Implement a *data validation pipeline* that regularly runs to check the data against the defined constraints. The pipeline should produce a report indicating the data quality status for each dimension.

- Set up *reliable alerts and notifications* for when the data quality falls outside of the acceptable range. This will allow you to take timely action to fix any problems. Reliability is the balance between false positives and false negatives, which is context-dependent.

- *Continuously monitor* and improve the data quality over time. This might involve updating the constraints or adding new ones as you learn more about the data and the ML use case.

For a detailed review, see the previously mentioned Google paper.

We recommend setting up a data governance framework to ensure that the data validation system is properly maintained and aligned with business objectives. This might involve establishing roles and responsibilities for data quality management, as well as establishing processes for data quality improvement and problem resolution.

14.4   Model quality and relevance

Even if the software system is functioning correctly and the data is of high quality, this does not guarantee that the ML model will perform as expected. One problem that can arise is model decay, which occurs when the model begins to perform poorly—either out of the blue or gradually.

Model decay, also known as *model drift* or staleness, refers to the phenomenon of a model's performance degrading over time. This can occur for a variety of reasons, such as changes in the data or the real-world relationships that the model was trained on. The speed at which model decay occurs can vary widely; some models can last for years with no need for updates, while others may require daily retraining on fresh data. One way to monitor for model decay is to regularly track key performance metrics and compare them to historical baselines. If the metrics start to degrade significantly, it could be an indication of model decay (see figure 14.6).

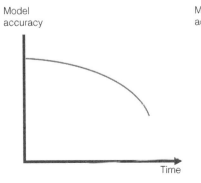

Model decay over time

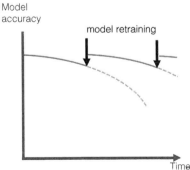

Regularly updated model

**Figure 14.6
Regular retraining can
help with model drift.**

There are two main types of model drifts (see figure 14.7):

- *Data drifts* occur when the model is applied to inputs that it has not previously encountered, such as data from new demographics. It means the original dataset was not representative enough for the model to generalize.
- *Concept drifts* occur when the relationships in the data change, such as when user behavior evolves. It is important to continuously monitor for model drift and take appropriate action. One of the solutions is to retrain the model to maintain its accuracy and efficiency.

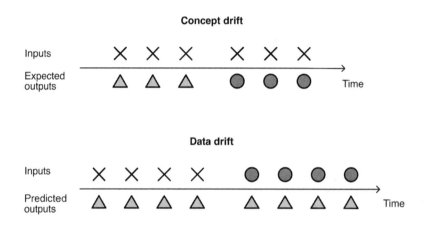

Figure 14.7   With a concept drift, identical inputs may lead to new expected outputs; with a data drift, incoming data changes while the model is not adapted.

Possible causes of model drift include

- Shifts in the global environment, such as the start of a pandemic/war/crisis/ legislation change.
- Deliberate business changes, such as launching an app in a new location or for a new user segment.
- Adversarial adaptation when bad actors try to adapt to the model's behavior.
- Model feedback loop where the model itself influences reality. For example, a recommendation system uses current item popularity as a feature and recommends it often, so the item becomes even more popular, thus becoming self-reinforced.
- Model decay can sometimes occur when there is a mismatch between the design of the model and how it is being used. For example, if a lead scoring model is designed to predict conversion probabilities but users start using it for scenario analysis by feeding it different input combinations to understand the effect of different factors on the model's decisions, this could lead to poor

model performance. Such cases may require a different analytical tool that is better suited to the intended use case. Arseny made a similar error in his career: at a ride-hailing company, his team built a model to estimate how long it could take for a taxi driver to reach the destination. The model was fine, but they tried to apply it for a slightly different scenario (estimating the overall duration of the ride), and the model performed poorly. The initial problem was about short rides (a free driver picking up a passenger), but the latter one can involve long rides as well.

Some people distinguish *output drift*, which refers to a change in the predictions, recommendations, or other output produced by an ML model. This change can be detected by comparing the "new" output data to the "old" output data using statistical tests or descriptive statistics. For example, if a model that rarely recommended that shoppers buy sunglasses is now pushing them into every recommendation block, this could indicate output drift.

We review output drift as one of the markers to monitor and detect model drift, as it can indicate a change in the model's performance or a change in the relationship between the input and output data, which either belongs to concept drift or data drift. By identifying and addressing output drift, you can help ensure that the model continues to produce reliable and accurate results.

Model drift can lead to increased model error or incorrect predictions, and in severe cases, the model can become inadequate overnight. It is important to continuously monitor for model drift and take appropriate action to maintain the accuracy and effectiveness of the model (see chapter 8 for more context).

14.4.1 Data drift

Data drift, also known as *feature drift* or *covariate shift*, refers to a situation where the input data for an ML model has changed in such a way that the model is no longer relevant for the new data. This can occur when the distribution of variables in the data is significantly different from the distribution the model was trained on. As a result, the model may perform poorly on the new data, even though it may continue to perform well on data that is similar to the "old" data.

One example of data drift is when an ML model trained to predict the likelihood of a user making a purchase at an online marketplace is applied to a new population of users who were acquired through a different advertising campaign. If new users come from a different source, such as Facebook, and the model did not have many examples from this source during training, it may perform poorly on this new segment of users. Similarly, data drift can occur if a model is applied to a new geographical area or demographic segment or if the distribution of important features in the data changes over time.

To address data drift, it may be necessary to retrain the model on the new data or build a new model specifically for the new segment of data. Monitoring the data and the model's performance can help identify data drift early on and take corrective action before the model's performance deteriorates significantly. As data drift is not something inherently wrong with the data, it has to be fixed on the model level instead.

14.4.2 Concept drift

Concept drift occurs when the patterns that the model has learned are no longer valid, even if the distributions of the input features remain unchanged. Depending on the scale of the change, concept drift can result in a decrease in the model's accuracy or make the model entirely obsolete.

There are several types of concept drift: *gradual concept drift, sudden concept drift,* and *recurring concept drift. Gradual* or *incremental drift* occurs when external factors change over time, leading to a gradual decline in the model's performance (see figure 14.8). This type of drift is usually expected and can be caused by a variety of factors, including changes in consumer behavior, changes in the economy, or wear and tear on equipment when the data is coming from physical sensors.

Figure 14.8
Gradual concept drift

To address gradual concept drift, the model may need to be retrained on new data or even rebuilt entirely. To determine if that is needed, it is essential to monitor model performance over time to ensure it continues to make accurate and reliable predictions. The rate at which a model's performance degrades, or "ages," can vary greatly depending on the specific application and the data being used.

To estimate how quickly a model will age, it is helpful to perform a test using older data and to measure the model's performance with different frequencies of retraining. This can give an indication of how frequently the model should be updated with new data to maintain its accuracy. It is also essential to consider the effect of external factors, such as changes in the market or the introduction of new products, which may affect the relationships between the model's inputs and outputs and cause concept drift.

Monitoring the performance of ML models and regularly retraining them as necessary is a critical aspect of maintaining their effectiveness in a production environment.

Sudden concept drift usually happens due to external changes that are sudden or drastic and can be hard to miss. These types of changes can affect all sorts of models, even ones that are typically "stable." For example, the COVID-19 pandemic affected mobility and shopping patterns almost overnight, causing demand forecasting models to fail to predict surges in certain products or the cancellation of most flights due to border closures. In addition to events like the pandemic or stock market crashes, sudden concept drift can also occur due to changes in interest rates by central banks, technical revamping of production lines, or major updates to app interfaces. These changes can cause models to fail to adapt to unseen patterns, become obsolete, or become irrelevant due to changes in the user journey.

In an ML system, it is common for certain events or patterns to recur over time. For example, people may display different behavior during the holiday season or on certain days of the week. These repeating changes, also known as *recurring drift*, can be anticipated and accounted for in the design of the system (see figure 14.9). For example, we can build a group of models to be applied in certain conditions or incorporate cyclic changes and special events into the system design to account for such recurring drift and prevent a decline in model performance.

**Figure 14.9
Recurring concept drift**

14.4.3 How to monitor

Monitoring model quality serves two primary purposes:

- To give you confidence in the model's reliability
- To alert you if something goes wrong

An effective monitoring setup should provide enough context to efficiently identify and fix any arising problems with your model. This may involve three main scenarios:

- Retraining the model
- Rebuilding the model
- Using a backup strategy

Data drift may be more significant for tabular data compared to other data modalities, such as images or speech. If there is a delay between prediction and the availability of ground truth data, this may be the signal for monitoring proxy metrics including data and prediction drift. For high-risk or critical models, you will likely use more granular monitoring and specific metrics (e.g., fairness). Low-risk models may only require monitoring of standard metrics relevant to the model type.

There are hundreds of different metrics that can be calculated to evaluate the performance of an ML model (see chapter 5). We will cover several categories into which these metrics can be grouped.

Model quality metrics evaluate the actual quality of the model's predictions. These metrics can be calculated once ground truth or feedback is available and may include

- Mean absolute error and root mean squared error for regression models
- Accuracy, precision, and F1-score for classification models
- Top-k accuracy and mean average precision for ranking models

Model quality by segment involves tracking the model's performance for specific subpopulations within the data, such as a geographical location. This can help identify discrepancies in performance for specific segments.

Prediction drift occurs when the model's predictions change significantly over time. To detect prediction drift, you can use statistical tests, probability distance metrics, or changes in the descriptive statistics of the model's output. We recommend reading a post by Olga Filippova (https://mng.bz/x60d) for more details.

Input data drift refers to changes in the input data used by the model. This can be detected by tracking changes in the descriptive statistics of individual features, running statistical tests, using distance metrics to compare distributions, or identifying changes in linear correlations between features and predictions. Monitoring for input data drift can help identify when the model is operating in an unfamiliar environment.

Outliers are unusual individual cases where the model might not perform as expected; it is important to identify these and flag them for expert review. Please note that this is different from data drift, where the goal is to detect the overall distribution shift. Outliers can be detected using statistical methods and distance metrics.

> ### Campfire story from Valerii
>
> While I was working at a prominent crypto company, I turned into a fervent user of its services, among which, of course, was a basic opportunity to buy crypto using fiat money. One day I tried to do that and was successful until I was blocked by the anti-fraud system.
>
> Why was I blocked? Because I did too many transactions. And why is that? Because the transaction limit introduced by the same team forced me to do more transactions than I would do otherwise. This is one of the possible ways to handle outliers—in that case, relying on the single feature (people who did too many transactions)—but it is probably not very user-friendly and results in losing the revenue of those users. Fortunately, we were able to improve this system further and make a multistage outlier detection and specific flow (that sometimes could include manual review) to handle them.

Fairness is also key. For certain use cases, you should make sure that the model performs with equal efficiency for different demographic groups. Metrics such as demographic parity and equalized odds can be used to evaluate model bias.

The monitoring process can't be done without covert challenges, though. These include

- *Lack of blueprints*—This belongs to a list of problems that still do not have a solid out-of-the-box solution, as appropriate metrics and heuristics depend on a given context and goals of the model. Thus, it is important to understand the model and data to choose the right monitoring approaches.
- *Monitoring without ground truth*—The actual quality of the model's predictions is often difficult to evaluate without access to ground truth labels. In these cases, a

solution would be to use proxy metrics while carefully considering how to set thresholds and trigger alarms.

- *Computing metrics at scale*—Calculating complex metrics at a large scale can be computationally expensive, particularly when working with distributed systems. It is essential to find a fast, efficient, and scalable way to compute metrics.

14.4.4 How to react

It would require a separate book to cover all the possible scenarios and ways to address data drifts and concept drifts, but we discuss some of the scenarios next.

DATA DRIFT

Facing a data drift leaves you with two options. The first option is to monitor the model's performance and look for changes in metrics like accuracy, mean error, and fraud rates. If there is a decline in performance, you may need to reevaluate the model and determine whether it is still appropriate for the current data. The second option is to incorporate additional data or features into the model to capture the changed patterns in the data more accurately. In some cases, you should consider retraining the model from scratch using the updated data.

If new labels are available and the training pipeline is up and running, it is very tempting to hit the retrain button (you can find more information in an article by Emeli Dral, https://mng.bz/AaYo). But there are things we can do prior to that if we dig deeper.

Check whether the problem is related to data quality or if it is a genuine change in the patterns the model is attempting to capture. Data quality problems can arise from a variety of sources, such as data entry errors, changes to the data schema, or problems with upstream models. It is important to have separate checks in place to monitor for data quality problems and to address them as soon as they are detected (see section 14.3).

If data drift is genuine, try to investigate the cause of the shift. This can help us understand how to address the problem in an optimal way and maintain the model's accuracy and effectiveness.

One way to start this process is to plot the distributions of the features that have experienced drift, as this can provide insights into the nature of the change. Another helpful step would be consulting with domain experts who may have insights into the real-world factors that could be causing the shift.

In cases where concept drift is also detected, there is a chance that the relationships between features and the model output may have changed, even if the individual feature distributions remain similar. Visualizing these relationships can provide further insights into the nature of the drift. For example, plotting the correlations between features and model predictions can highlight changes in these relationships. Additional insights may also come from plotting the shift in pairwise feature correlations.

It is important to *determine whether the observed drift is meaningful and warrants a response*. This can involve setting drift detection thresholds tailored to a given use case and set to be alerted to potentially significant changes.

However, it is often necessary to iterate on these thresholds through trial and error, as it can be difficult to predict in advance exactly how data will drift over time. When a drift alert is triggered in production, we need to carefully assess its nature and magnitude, as well as the effect it may have on the model's performance. This may involve consulting with domain experts or conducting further analysis to gain a deeper understanding of the changes. Based on this assessment, you will be able to decide whether to address the drift. In some cases, you may be able to understand the causes of the drift and decide to (temporarily) accept the changes rather than take action to address the problem.

For example, suppose additional labels or data are expected to become available in the near future. In that case, it may be worth holding off on taking action until this information can be taken into account. If it was a false alert, we can change the drift alert conditions or the statistical tests, as well as discard the notification to avoid receiving similar alerts in the future.

In some cases, the model may still perform despite the drift. For example, if a particular class becomes more prevalent in the model's predictions but this is consistent with the observed feature drift and the expected behavior, there may be no need for any further action. In these situations, it may be possible to continue using the model as is without the need to retrain or update it. However, given the potential consequences of this decision, monitoring the model closely to ensure it remains effective is crucial.

Adapt the preprocessing used in the pipeline. For example, say your system uses images captured by a camera in a factory. At some point, the factory manager decides to upgrade the light bulbs, so the assembly line is now well lit, and so are the images. Once it affects the model performance due to drift, one solution can be applying an artificial "darkening" function to mimic the original data distribution.

Retrain the model using updated or new data. This is often the most straightforward approach and can be effective if the necessary data is available. By retraining the model using updated or new data, you should improve its performance and adapt to changing patterns in the data (if nothing is broken in the data pipelines). If you follow the good practices from chapter 10, retraining the model should be relatively simple.

Instead of hitting the retrain button, you can *consider developing an ML model that is more robust to drift.* This could involve applying more robust model architectures (e.g., those designed for online learning) or using techniques such as domain adaptation to make the model more resilient to changes in the data distribution. The following are some additional details on options for addressing data drift:

- *Reweighting samples*—This involves giving more weight to more recent samples in the training data to prioritize newer patterns. It can be a simple way to address data drift, but it may not always be effective, especially when the drift is significant.
- *Creating separate models for different segments*—If the model is failing for certain segments of the data, you can consider creating a separate model specifically for those segments. Alternatively, you can use an ensemble of models, where

each model is responsible for a different segment of data. (In our experience, one model is almost always better than many, as it incorporates more data, but context is the king.)

- *Changing the prediction target*—You may be able to improve the model's performance by changing the prediction target. For example, switching from weekly to daily forecasts may allow the model to better capture short-term changes in the data. Alternatively, you could change the type of model you are using, such as switching from a regression model to a classification model (to some extent, it might be considered reviewing the problem coarser).

- *Incorporating human expert knowledge into the model training process*—You can use expert features or active learning techniques to guide the model's training data selection. Ultimately, the most effective approach will depend on your data's specific characteristics and the requirements of your application.

- *Introducing more regularization*—Include techniques that can implicitly address the drift. Let's recall augmentations; they're a popular regularization practice, and you can design them keeping in mind possible drifts that may happen in the domain. For example, for image data, it may be useful to imitate different weather conditions.

- *Using a more powerful pretrained model as an initializer*—Empirically, in the deep learning world, training custom models works better if the initial model is trained on a larger and more diverse dataset and thus tends to generalize better.

One strategy for dealing with changes in the data distribution is to *identify and isolate the low-performing segments of the data*. This can be especially useful when the change is not universal and affects only a specific subset of the data.

To do this, you can start by analyzing the changed features of the data and identifying any potential correlations with the model's performance. For example, if you see a shift in the distribution of a feature (e.g., location), you might try filtering the data by that feature to see if it is causing the low performance.

Once you are able to identify low-performing segments of the data, you can decide how to handle them. One option is to route your predictions differently for these segments, either by relying on heuristics or by manually curating output. Alternatively, you can single out these segments and wait until you have collected enough new labeled data to update the model.

Finally, processing outliers in a separate workflow can also help limit errors under data drift. Outliers are individual data points that are significantly different from the rest of the data, and processing them separately can help to ensure that the model can continue to operate effectively.

Another option to address data drift is to *apply additional business logic on top of the model* by either making an adjustment to the model prediction or changing the application logic. This approach can be effective but difficult to generalize and can have unintended consequences if not done carefully.

A good example of this approach is manually correcting the output, which is common in forecasting demand. Business rules for specific items, categories, and regions can be used to adjust the model's forecast for promotional activities, marketing campaigns, and known events. In case of data drift, a new correction can be applied to the model output to account for the change.

Another example is setting a new decision threshold for classification problems. The model output is often a probability, and the decision threshold can be adjusted to assign labels based on a desired probability. If data drift is detected, the threshold can be changed to reflect the new data.

Alternatively, you can consider using a hybrid approach where you combine ML with non-ML methods, especially if you have a small amount of data or if you need to make predictions in a dynamic environment where relationships between variables are constantly changing. In some cases, using a non-ML solution can be more robust and easier to maintain because it does not depend on data patterns and can be based on causal relationships or expert knowledge. However, it may not be as flexible or able to adapt to changing circumstances as ML models. It's important to carefully consider the tradeoffs and choose the appropriate solution for a given problem. See section 13.4.

CONCEPT DRIFT

With concept drift, there are several approaches to retrain the model, including using all available data, assigning higher weights to new data, and dropping past data if new data that has been collected is enough. In some cases, simply retraining the model may not be sufficient, and there is a chance you will have to tune the model or try new features, architectures, or data sources as the new patterns to be captured are too complex for an existing model.

Retraining the model may mean either full retraining for a smaller model or some kind of finetuning for a larger one, depending on how serious the drift is and what the computational budget is.

You may have to modify the model's scope or the business process (this can be done by shortening the prediction horizon, postponing the predictions to have more time for data accumulation, or increasing the frequency of model runs). With this approach, it is important to maintain effective communication with business owners and other system consumers, ensuring that everyone is prepared for changes and is able to handle them.

Additional attention should be paid to recurring drift or seasonality. There are many possible reasons for it, such as increased shopping on Black Fridays or altered mobility patterns on holidays or payday at the end of the month. Consider incorporating these periodic changes or building ensemble models to take them into account. This can help prevent a decline in the model's performance, as these predictable changes (recurring drift) are expected and can be accounted for.

To effectively handle seasonality in a ML system, it is important to train the model to recognize and respond to these periodic changes. For example, if an ML model is used to forecast loungewear sales, it should be able to recognize and anticipate an increased demand on weekends. In this case, the model correctly predicts the known pattern of increased shopping on weekends. A predictable change like that will not require an alert, as it is a regular occurrence.

DRIFT DETECTION FRAMEWORK

When dealing with drift, the first thing to do is to consider possible actions and then design a drift detection framework to monitor potential changes. This allows you to define the degree of change that will trigger an alert and how to react to it.

To design it effectively, consider ways in which the model and the real-world process behind the data are likely to change. Depending on the needs and constraints of the model, there may be a variety of approaches to detecting and responding to drift.

For instance, if the model's quality can be directly calculated using timely obtained true labels, you can ignore distribution drift. Instead, you can focus on identifying and addressing problems such as broken inputs using rule-based data validation checks.

On the other hand, if the model is being used in a critical application with delayed ground truth and interpretable features, you may need to switch to a more comprehensive drift detection system. This might include a detailed data drift detection dashboard and a set of statistical tests to help identify changes in data distribution and correlations between features. If you know the model's key features and the business value they provide, you can assign different weights to those features and focus on detecting drift in those. If not, you can consider the overall drift of multiple weak features but increase the threshold for defining drift in this case, compared to a few key features to avoid false positives.

Ultimately, the best approach to drift detection will depend on the specific needs and constraints of the model and may involve a combination of different methods and metrics. So carefully keep in mind the potential for false-positive alerts and the consequences of the model's failure and design a system that can effectively detect and respond to drift while minimizing disruption and downtime.

A NOTE ON BUSINESS KPIS

Monitoring business KPIs can be challenging due to the complexity of isolating the effect of the ML system and the difficulty in measuring certain metrics. In these cases, it is important to find a proxy or interpretable checks that can provide insight into the ML system's performance. It is also worth noting that monitoring business KPIs may not always provide the required context in case of model decay. In these circumstances, it may be necessary to investigate other factors such as the model, data, and software to determine the root cause of any problems.

However, there is a reason why business KPIs are taking their place at the top of the pyramid in figure 14.5. Monitoring business metrics and key performance indicators is crucial for understanding the business value of your ML system. Tracking metrics such as revenue and conversion rates (if your model revolves around user acquisition, for example) allows you to determine whether the ML system meets its goals and exerts a positive effect on the business.

It is also important to involve both data scientists and business stakeholders in the monitoring process to ensure that the ML system is meeting the needs of the business. We also advise tracking both absolute and relative values to gain a more comprehensive understanding of the ML system's effect.

Most importantly, whatever technically honed metrics you define for your ML system, they are nothing but the result of gradual cascading of business KPIs. And it is for this reason that ultimately the effectiveness and sustainability of any system directly or indirectly affects the success of your employer or even your own business.

14.5   Design document: Monitoring

The ways to monitor your ML system may vary depending on its goals, properties, and architecture. The two design documents we provide as examples display their unique approaches to monitoring, as the systems we are designing have essential differences and features.

14.5.1   Monitoring for Supermegaretail

We have dedicated certain sections of this chapter to the peculiarities of monitoring forecasting systems and are now ready to delve into the practical part focused on monitoring the Supermegaretail's model.

DESIGN DOCUMENT: SUPERMEGARETAIL

XI. MONITORING

I. EXISTING INFRASTRUCTURE ANALYSIS

Unfortunately, demand forecasting is among the pioneering ML projects for Supermegaretail, meaning that there is no proper ML monitoring infrastructure in place. Luckily, quick preliminary research proved to be fruitful, and we found Evidently AI—an open source Python library (https://github.com/evidentlyai/evidently) that helps with monitoring. The motto "We build tools to evaluate, test and monitor machine learning models, so you don't have to" perfectly suits our goals until and if we decide to build our own platform (see section 3.2). According to the description, Evidently AI covers model quality, data drift, target drift, and data quality. This means that we still have to build some foundations for this to implement.

II. LOGGING

We will keep model prediction logs in a column-oriented database management system. We should record data on every prediction: the features that went in and the model output + timestamps. We will use an open source such as ClickHouse as it is already used for other similar needs in the company.

In addition, we will log basic statistics: requests per second, resource utilization, error rate, p90, p99, p999 latency, and error rate, as well as a number of model calls per hour, day, and week and average, median, min, and max prediction from the model on the same aggregation level. We will use Kafka + Prometheus + Grafana for that. We will keep the last month of data. We will use this stack as well for real-time ML monitoring and visualization (https://mng.bz/ZVOR).

III. DATA QUALITY

In addition to basic extract, transform, load and data quality checks, we will monitor for the following:

- *Missing data*, as a percentage from the whole dataset and separately as a percentage from the most important features according to the feature importance (see section 11.2). We will use historical data (cleaning out occurrences with broken pipelines) to calculate the z-score. We will set an alarm of three z-scores for important features and four z-scores for the rest. In addition, we will use several test suite presets from the Evidently AI library. There is a preset to check for data quality and another for data stability.
- *Schema compliance.* Are all the features there? Do their types match? Are there new columns?
- *Feature ranges and stats.* To ensure that the learning model is being fed good-quality data, we will manually define expected ranges for each important feature, as three z-scores + checks for invalid stats (e.g., negative data for the amount of sales, min $>= 0$).
- *Correlations.* To detect any abnormalities in the data, we will plot the correlation matrix between features and compare the difference between the two plots. A basic alarm will be set for residuals higher than $|0.15|$.

IV. MODEL QUALITY

We are very fortunate to have the availability of true labels with a very minor delay. We receive daily sales information 15 minutes after they happen. With that in mind, we will monitor quantile metrics for quantiles of 1.5, 25, 50, 75, 95, and 99, both as is and with weights equal to the SKU price. In addition, we will monitor the root mean squared error and mean absolute error to track the mean and median. We will set up final thresholds after we receive the first 3 months of the data; we will pick initial thresholds based on the historical data and model performance on the validation.

In addition, we set up alarms for negative values and max values. An alarm will fire if the new max value is 50% higher than the previously seen max value.

We will set up prediction drift monitoring. We will use it as an early alarm for the next day, week, and month predictions. We will test two approaches: Population Stability Index > 0.2 and Wasserstein distance > 0.1. For Wasserstein distance, we will apply growth multiplayer to the control dataset. For example, when comparing April 2021 to April 2022, knowing that overall growth is expected to be 15%, we multiply everything in 2021 by 1.15. We will further adjust this based on historical data experimentation.

V. DATA DRIFT

While we have true data available with a minor delay, we don't need to track input drift as a proxy for understanding the model relevance. However, it would still help us detect upcoming change before it affects the model quality. After reading a post titled "Which Test Is the Best? We Compared 5 Methods to Detect Data Drift on Large Data-sets" (https://mng.bz/2g5g), we decided to pick Wasserstein distance to alert us in case of data drift. We start from the threshold of the mean drift score. We can later try to apply the paper titled "Feature Shift Detection: Localizing Which Features Have Shifted via Conditional Distribution Tests" (https://mng.bz/RNQZ).

VI. BUSINESS METRICS

Business metrics of interest remain the same as we describe in section 2.1.1: revenue (expected to increase), level of stock (expected to decrease or remain the same), and margin (expected to increase), which we will monitor through a series of A/B tests, switching and swapping control groups over time.

14.5.2 Monitoring for PhotoStock Inc.

The set of actions within the system monitoring for PhotoStock Inc. will differ from the previous example, as here we are dealing with the design of a model for a "smart" stock photo search engine.

DESIGN DOCUMENT: PHOTOSTOCK INC.

XI. MONITORING

I. SOFTWARE HEALTH

We need to be sure the following logs are available:

- Original query
- Candidate document IDs
- Top 20 of final ranking

Other than that, all negative scenarios and fallbacks should be logged.

Logs should be traceable via three IDs:

- *user_id*—Could be empty as not all users are logged in
- *session_id*—Handled by backend; may contain multiple queries in a row
- *request_id*—A batch of logs related to a single search/query

We will use the same log storage provider as used across the company (AWS Cloudwatch).

We should report metrics related to latency as we assume it is important for user experience, and some of the components can be somewhat slow. A sample (not necessarily comprehensive) list is

- Fetching candidates
- Final ranking
- Overrides application

Metrics should be reported to AWS Cloudwatch as well.

II. DATA HEALTH

Given the origin of our data, we can be very confident about the image data (photos are carefully reviewed by our internal moderation team and their AI tools as well) but less confident about search queries (obtained from users) and ranking scores (obtained via crowdsourcing).

Search queries should be filtered to reduce the amount of total garbage (e.g., a cat walking across the keyboard). Other than that, some silly queries are possible and should be present in the training set as that's the real input from our users. Too aggressive filtering here may lead to training-serving skew.

Ranking labels used for the model training are our bread and butter. They should be as correct as possible, and we should invest in their quality together with the labeling platform vendor. That must include cross-checks and honeypots to filter out inaccurate labelers. Additionally, we can consider using some algorithmic validation of the labeled data with the help of foundational models—for example, prompt GPT API if image description + tags can be relevant to the query or prompt self-served multimodal image + text model like LLAVA (https://llava-vl.github.io/). In the future, we can consider using the model as the main source of labels and people as validators, depending on the labels' accuracy by both parties.

III. MODEL HEALTH

To the best of our understanding, the image search problem is not too sensitive to drift problems. However, there may be some changes in both user preferences and photos we host: new topics may emerge, new types of images, and so on. Also, we don't output anything other than ranking, so it's hard to imagine any catastrophic failure (in the worst case, we can switch back to the previous non-ML search engine).

Given that, we don't have to include specific model health monitoring in the first version with the assumption that model quality is assured in the previous steps (validation, testing). However, there are already existing monitors used by the current search engine: average clicked position, average first clicked position, and so on. Keeping them as is should be the first line of defense. In the future, we can consider an open source solution like Deepchecks (https://deepchecks.com/) for the proof of concept if we realize drift-related problems are causing us real harm.

Summary

- Even the most well-trained and accurate models can start degrading over time without proper monitoring. This can happen due to changes in incoming data, model architecture, or even model output.
- The foundation of proper monitoring is software backend, topped subsequently with data quality and integrity, model quality and relevance, and business KPIs.
- Make sure to monitor the software health of your system, as it is essential to provide efficient task execution and prompt responses to requests. Failing to

prioritize the stability and performance of the software backend can have detrimental effects on the overall effectiveness of the ML system.

- Many monitoring practices used in traditional software systems—such as application and infrastructure monitoring, alerting, and incident management—can also be applied to ML systems.

- Monitoring data quality implies problems at the data processing stage (from access problems to changes in data format) or potential corruption of data sources, which can occur due to bugs, physical failures, or problems with external APIs.

- In case of cascade models where you have to deal with a loop of interconnected models, the output data of the preceding model will force invalid predictions by the next model, thus breaking the whole system.

- Some models are able to last for years with no need for updates; others may require daily retraining on fresh data. Track key performance metrics and compare them to historical baselines regularly to avoid model decay or detect it at the earliest stage.

- Data drift occurs when the distribution of variables in the data is significantly different from the distribution the model was trained on. To address data drift, it may be necessary to retrain the model on the new data or build a new model specifically for the new segment of data.

- Concept drift occurs when the patterns that the model has learned are no longer valid, even if the distributions of the input features remain unchanged and can result in the decrease of the model's accuracy or make the model entirely obsolete.

- You have two options while facing data drift: you can either monitor the model's performance and look for changes in metrics like accuracy, mean error, or fraud rates or you can incorporate additional data or features into the model to capture the changed patterns in the data more accurately.

- When concept drift occurs, you may want to retrain the model, including using all available data, assigning higher weights to new data, or dropping past data if new data that has been collected is sufficient.

Serving and inference optimization

This chapter covers

- Challenges that may arise during the serving and inference stage
- Tools and frameworks that will come in handy
- Optimizing inference pipelines

Making your machine learning (ML) model run in a production environment is among the final steps required for reaching an efficient operating lifecycle of your system. Some ML practitioners demonstrate low interest in this aspect of the craft, preferring instead to focus on developing and training their models. This might be a false move, however, as the model can only be useful if it's deployed and effectively utilized in production. In this chapter, we discuss the challenges of deploying and serving ML models, as well as review different methods of optimizing the inference process.

As we mentioned in chapter 10, an inference pipeline is a sequence (in most cases) or a more complicated acyclic graph of steps that takes raw data as input and produces predictions as output. Along with the ML model itself, the inference pipeline includes steps like feature computation, data preprocessing, output postprocessing, and others. Preprocessing and postprocessing are somewhat generic terms, as they can be built differently depending on the specific requirements of a given system. Let's take a few examples. A typical computer vision pipeline often starts with image resizing and normalization; a typical language processing pipeline, in turn, initiates with tokenization, while a typical recommender system pipeline kicks off by pulling user features from a feature store.

The role of properly tuned inference may vary from domain to domain as well. High-frequency trading companies or adtech businesses are on a constant hunt for the brightest talents to refine their systems of extremely low latency. Mobile app and Internet of Things (IoT) developers put efficient inference at the top of their priority list, chasing more efficient battery consumption and thus improved user experience. Those who utilize high-load backend in their products are interested in keeping the load without spending a fortune on the infrastructure. At the same time, there are many scenarios when the model prediction is not a bottleneck. For example, once per week, we need to run a batch job to predict the next week's sales, generate the report, and distribute it to the procurement department. In those cases, if the report is required to be in corporate emails by Monday morning, it doesn't make much of a difference if it will take 10 minutes or 3 hours to compile, as long as it's scheduled for Sunday night.

In general, this chapter is mostly focused on deep learning-based systems. And it shouldn't come as a surprise, as heavy models require more engineering efforts before production deployment, while serving some lightweight solution like a logistic regression or a small tree ensemble is not too complicated as long as your feature infrastructure (described in chapter 11) is in place. At the same time, some principles and techniques described here apply to any ML system.

15.1 Serving and inference: Challenges

As always happens in system design, our first step lies in defining the requirements. There are several crucial factors to keep in mind, and we touch on each of them next:

- *Latency*—This defines our expectations of how prompt the system is in providing predictions. For real-time applications that require an immediate response, latency is generally measured in milliseconds (there are extreme cases where even 1 ms is too long!), while in some scenarios, waiting for hours or even days is totally acceptable.

- *Throughput*—This refers to the number of tasks or amount of data that a system can process in a given time frame. In the world of ML, it implies the total number of predictions the model can produce per unit of time. Optimizing for throughput is often crucial in cases when you need to process large volumes of data over a short period, such as batch processing of large datasets.

- *Scalability*—We need to understand the number of predictions the system may face and how this number can either increase or decrease. Load patterns are often seasonal and may vary depending on the industry. For retail, it is common to see a spike in sales during the holiday season or on days of huge discounts such as Black Friday or Cyber Monday. For the adtech industry, the load may be higher due to higher activity on the internet. While some spikes, as mentioned here, are predictable, others can come out of the blue; the viral popularity of an app or a sudden usage burst by a large customer is not something we can prepare for in advance. The system should possess sufficient scalability to handle the peak load without compromising latency and throughput.

- *Target platforms*—Your models can run on CPU-only or GPU-accelerated servers; in serverless environments like AWS Lambda or Cloudflare Workers; on desktop, mobile, or IoT devices; or even in the browser. Along with advantages, each platform has its own limitations and requirements, and we must have a deep understanding of those before building the system. If we are building a mobile app, we'll need to consider the model's size, as it should be small enough to fit into the app package yet efficient enough to run on a user's device without draining the battery. If we are developing a backend system, there's more freedom in choosing the hardware, which provides a vast array of opportunities in terms of the system's complexity and size. If our target platform is exotic IoT hardware, there is a chance we can't design a fancy model with all the bells and whistles, so sticking to the simplest architectures becomes the major technical requirement.

    Things can get more complicated when we have to use more than one platform for our product. In certain cases, we may decide to run small batches on user devices and send the rest to the backend or load the backend with finetuning before sending the model to a user's device for inference. This way, the combined requirements of both platforms are followed. Furthermore, we may need to use various computing units within a single platform. Arseny once needed to speed up a system that ran on devices with low-end GPUs. Under the hood, the system used a small model to process multiple concurrent requests, which led to those cheap GPUs failing to handle the load. The solution Arseny came up with introduced a pool of mixed-device sessions: every time the GPU was overloaded, the following request was processed by a CPU, thus providing a more balanced load across devices and meeting the latency requirements.

- *Cost*—ML systems are often the most resource-intensive solutions in a company, and with heavy generative models gaining more and more popularity, costs are standing out as a crucial factor like never before. With the cost of an ML infrastructure becoming an ever-growing concern, businesses are forced to look for smart decisions for inference pipelines, which can lead to massive financial benefits. It is important to understand the cost of the infrastructure and how it will scale based on an increasing load before building the system. It may even lead to scenarios when the infrastructure cost ends up being higher than the revenue generated by the system. In other cases, it will not be a concern if inference is performed on a user's device. For mobile apps or IoT devices, for example, a growing user base will not affect the infrastructure cost in any significant manner (we can't claim it will not affect it at all; if users download the models from your content delivery network, every new 1,000 users will cost you extra cents).

- *Reliability*—Reliability can become a problem when you settle for a cheap option in your choice of inference platforms. Opting for the least expensive hardware vendor only to go through a sudden failure in the middle of a hot season may be at times worse than investing more in a time-tested, reliable solution. Think of all the disasters that may happen during an unexpected spike in the load, a bug in the model, or a hardware failure and, most importantly, how (and if) the system will tackle them.

- *Flexibility*—Even if a newly released system shows stable performance and efficiency, we can't be certain about future requirements and ideas we'll need to implement. Thus, the system should be flexible enough to digest changes and improvements. Those may include a new model (which may even be trained with a different framework!), additional preprocessing or postprocessing, new features, additional APIs, etc. Always keep in mind that the system will evolve and should be easy to modify without affecting the existing functionality.

- *Security and privacy*—This subject spreads much farther than just one paragraph of text, but within the scope of this chapter, we can only mention that security requirements rely heavily on the target platform. For example, when your system operates fully within your backend, and the predictions never leave the perimeter of the organization, you barely need to think about security beyond your current protocols. On the other hand, if you are building a mobile app that will run on a user's device, you need to heavily consider protecting the model from reverse engineering. In some cases, the model should be protected from users themselves, with one of the most notable examples being jailbreaks for large language models (LLMs) that became popular in 2023, when users tried to outsmart them to get answers to sensitive questions.

15.2 Tradeoffs and patterns

The factors mentioned here are often conflicting and even mutually exclusive. For this reason, it is not possible to optimize for all of them simultaneously, meaning we'll have to find compromises between those factors. However, there are certain patterns we can lean toward in finding a fair balance in various scenarios.

15.2.1 Tradeoffs

Let's start with *latency* and *throughput*. Both are very popular candidates for optimization, and improvements in one of them may lead to either improvements or degradation in the other.

Real production systems are often optimized for the best throughput for a given latency budget. The latency budget is dictated by the product or user experience needs (do users expect a real-time/near-real-time response, or are they tolerant of delays?), and given this budget, the aim is to maximize throughput (or minimize the number of required servers for expected throughput) by changing either the model architecture or inference design (e.g., with batching, as we describe later in section 15.3).

Let's go through some examples. Imagine a simple deep learning model—a convolutional network like Resnet or a transformer like BERT. If you just reduce the number of blocks, it is very likely both your latency and throughput numbers will improve no matter what your inference setup is, so things are very straightforward (the model's accuracy can drop, but that's not the case in the current example). But imagine having two models with the same number of blocks and the same number of parameters per block but utilizing two different architectures: model A runs them in parallel with further aggregation (similar to the ResNeXt architecture), and model B runs every block sequentially. Model B will have a higher latency compared to model A due to the sequential nature of its architecture, but at the same time, you can run multiple instances of model B in parallel or run it with a large batch size, so the throughput of model A is not any worse than that of model B. Thus, parallelism is one of the internal factors that can affect latency and throughput in different ways. In practice, it means that the number of parameters or the number of blocks cannot be the definitive factor in comparing models, and our understanding of the architecture in the context of the inference platform is what helps us identify the bottlenecks, as seen in figure 15.1.

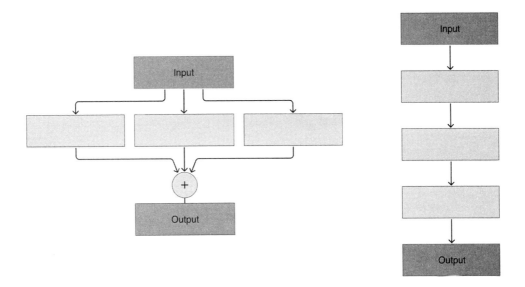

Figure 15.1 An example of wide versus deep models. While they have the same number of parameters, the deep one is more limited in terms of parallel computation

Another tradeoff is related to model accuracy (or other ML-specific metrics used for the system) and correlated latency/throughput/costs. ML engineers are often tempted to solve the model's imperfection by upgrading to a larger model. This can provide eventual benefits occasionally, but it is an expensive and poorly scalable way to fix the problem in the first place. At the same time, trying to solely optimize for cost by choosing the simplest model is not a good idea either. A dependency between compute costs and the value of the model is not linear, and in most cases, there is a sweet spot where the model is good enough, and the cost is relatively low, while radical solutions on the edges of the spectrum are less efficient. If we revisit section 9.1, one can be built with the same idea in mind: we can plot the model's accuracy as a function of the compute costs and find a proper balance for our particular problem (see figure 15.2 for details).

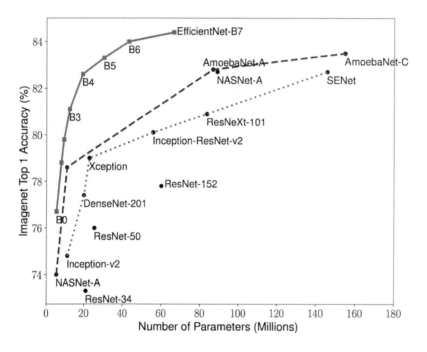

Figure 15.2   Different sizes of models belonging to the same families and their respective accuracy values on the Imagenet dataset. The chart illustrates that larger models tend to have higher accuracy, but this effect tends to saturate. (Source: https://mng.bz/QVzG.)

Finally, a tradeoff that might not be that obvious but is still worth mentioning is based on a link between research flexibility and production-level serving performance. On the one hand, we can benefit from building a model that is easy to migrate from the experimental sandbox directly to production. On the other hand, having a clear separation between research and production will allow the research team to experiment with new ideas without affecting the production system. But as we go further down the stretch, the difference between experimental code and real system inference will amplify, thus increasing the chance of facing a defect caused by the difference in the environments, which is hard to track without proper investments in monitoring and integration tests (please see chapter 13 for deployment aspects and chapter 14 for observability).

There are certain tools and frameworks that you may want to consider when facing the choice between either option. Because the route you take will significantly affect the sustainability of your system, the following section is fully dedicated to this very important subject.

15.2.2 Patterns

Once we have determined the tradeoffs we need to make for optimizing our model, it's time to choose the right pattern to implement. We will once again limit ourselves to a small list and mention three diverse patterns. Although this list is not complete, it is highly likely that you will use one of these patterns in your system.

The first pattern worth mentioning is *batching*, a technique used to improve throughput, which needs to be considered in advance. If you know that the system can be used in a batch mode, you should design it accordingly. Batching is not just a binary property (to use or not to use) and features multiple nuances. Imagine a typical API for a web page: the client, whom we can't control, sends some data, and the backend returns a prediction. That's not a typical offline batch mode prediction, but there is room for dynamic batching: on the backend side, we wait for a short period (e.g., 20 ms or, say, 32 requests, whichever comes first) and collect all the requests that landed during this period, and then run a batch inference on them. This way, we can reduce the latency for the client but still keep the system responsive. This approach is implemented in frameworks like the Triton Inference Server by Nvidia and Tensorflow Serving. Another example of smart batching is related to language models: the typical input size for the model is dynamic, and running a batch inference on multiple inputs of various sizes requires padding to the size of the longest input. However, we can group inputs by size and run batch inference on each group separately, thus reducing the padding overhead (at the cost of smaller batches or a longer batch accumulation window). You can read more about this technique at Graphcore's blog (https://mng.bz/XVEv).

The second pattern we'd like to talk about is *caching*, which has earned the status of the ultimate level of optimization (we'll discuss inference optimization later in the chapter). Cache usage comes from the obvious idea: never compute the same thing twice. Sometimes it is as simple as in more traditional software systems: input data is associated with a key, and some key-value storage is used to keep previously computed results, so we don't run expensive computations twice or more.

> **Listing 15.1   Example of the simplest possible in-memory cache**

```
class InMemoryCache:
    def __init__(self):
        self.cache = {}
```

```
def get(self, key: str, or_else: Callable):
    v = self.cache.get(key)
    if v is None:
        v = or_else()
        self.cache[key] = v
    return v
```

In reality, the distribution of inputs for an ML model may have a long tail, as most requests are unique. For example, according to Google, 15% of all search queries are totally unique (https://mng.bz/yoeB). Given that cache time to live is typically way lower than the whole Google history, the share of unique (noncacheable) queries would be high within any reasonable window. Does it mean the cache is useless? Not necessarily. One reason is that even a low percentage of saved compute can provide a great benefit in terms of saved money. Another concept is the idea of using fuzzy caches: instead of checking the direct match of the key, we can relax the matching condition. For example, Arseny has seen a system where the cache key was based on a regular expression, so the result could be shared by multiple similar requests matching the same regex. Even more aggressive caching can be built based on the semantic similarity of the key (e.g., https://github.com/zilliztech/GPTCache uses such an approach to cache LLM queries). As practitioners who care about reliability, we recommend thinking twice about using such caching: its level of fuzziness is huge, and thus the cache would be prone to false cache hits.

A third pattern has recently emerged in the LLM world: *routing between models*. Inspired by the "mixture of experts" architecture (https://mng.bz/M1qW), it proved to be a good step for optimization: some queries are hard (and should be processed by expensive in serving but advanced models); some are simpler (and thus can be delegated to less complex and cheaper models). Such an approach is mostly used for general LLMs, machine translation, and other—mostly natural language processing-specific—tasks. A good example of the implementation is finely presented in the paper "Leeroo Orchestrator: Elevating LLMs Performance Through Model" by Alireza Mohammadshahi et al. (https://arxiv.org/abs/2401.13979v1).

A variation of this pattern is to *use two models* (one is fast and imperfect; the other is slow and more accurate). With this combination, a quick response is generated by the first, smaller model (so it can be rendered with low latency) to be later replaced with the output of the second, heavier model. Unlike the previous pattern, it does not save the total compute required, but it does optimize a special kind of latency, which is time to initial response.

15.3 Tools and frameworks

The inference process is heavily engineering focused. Luckily, there are many tools and frameworks available for use. Following the approach taken for this book, we don't aim to provide a comprehensive overview of every framework you might need to construct a reliable inference pipeline; instead, we focus on the principles and mention popular solutions for illustrative purposes.

15.3.1 Choosing a framework

One common, although not immediately apparent, heuristic is to separate your training and inference frameworks. It is typical to use tools like Pandas, scikit-learn, and Keras as they offer flexibility and simplicity during research, prototyping, or training. However, they are not ideal for inference due to the inevitable tradeoff between flexibility and simplicity. This is why it's a popular practice to train models in one framework and then convert them for further inference in another. Additionally, it's essential to decouple the training framework from the inference framework as much as possible so that if you need to switch to a different training framework with new features, it won't affect the inference pipeline. This is especially crucial for production systems expected to be operational and evolve for years.

From the other perspective, some research-first frameworks like Torch tend to close the gap between research and production. The compilation functionality introduced in Torch 2.0 allows for making a fairly optimized inference pipeline from the same code used for training and relevant experiments. So, whether you want to use a universal framework or a combination of two or even more solutions for different purposes, both paradigms are viable, depending on which approach you choose (see figure 15.3 for information on the most popular frameworks).

How to choose a framework

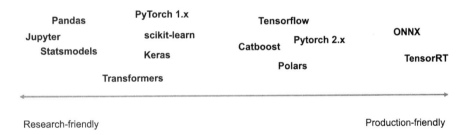

Figure 15.3 A wide spectrum of tools with their focus on either research or production serving goals

Achieving a balance between research flexibility and high performance in the production environment may require an interframework format. A popular choice for this purpose is ONNX, which is supported by many training frameworks for converting their models to ONNX. On the other hand, inference frameworks often work with the ONNX format or allow the conversion of ONNX models into their own format, making ONNX a common language in the ML world.

Here it should be mentioned that ONNX is not just a representation format but rather an ecosystem. It includes a runtime that can be used for inference and a set of tools for model conversion and optimization. ONNX Runtime is well-suited for a variety of backends and can run on almost any platform with specific optimizations for each of them. This makes it an excellent choice for multiplatform systems. Based on our experience, ONNX Runtime strikes a popular balance between flexibility (although less flexible than serving PyTorch or scikit-learn models directly) and performance (although less performant than tailoring a highly custom solution for the specific combination of models, hardware, and usage patterns).

For the server CPU inference, a popular engine is OpenVINO by Intel. For CUDA inference, TensorRT by Nvidia is commonly used. Both of them are optimized for their target hardware and are also available as ONNX Runtime backends, which allows them to be used in the same way as ONNX Runtime. Two more honorable mentions are TVM (https://tvm.apache.org/), which is a compiler for deep learning models capable of generating code for a variety of hardware targets, and AITemplate (https://github.com/facebookincubator/AITemplate), which can be used even for running models on the less common AMD GPUs via the ROCm software stack.

Those familiar with iOS model deployment may be aware of CoreML, an engine for iOS inference that uses its own format. Android developers usually opt for TensorFlow Lite, although there are more options available on Android thanks to its greater fragmentation. This list is far from complete, but it provides an idea of how large the variety of available options is.

When we say something like "engine X runs on device Y," it may not be precisely accurate. For example, even when the overall inference is meant to run on a GPU, some operations may be forwarded to the CPU because it produces more efficiency. GPUs excel at massively parallel computing, making them ideal for tasks like matrix multiplication or convolutions. However, some operations related to control flow or sparse data are better handled by the CPU. For instance, CoreML dynamically splits the execution graph between the CPU, GPU, and Apple Neural Engine to maximize efficiency.

Various inference engines often come with optimizers that can be used to improve the model's performance. For example, ONNX Runtime offers a set of optimizers that can reduce the model's size by trimming unused parts of the graph (e.g., those only used in training for loss computation) or by reducing the number of operations after fusing several operations into one. These optimizers are typically separate tools used to prepare the model for inference but are not part of the inference engine itself.

By the time this book is published, there's a chance this section will be outdated, as the field is evolving rapidly. For example, when we started writing the book, few people paid attention to LLMs, and now they are ubiquitous. People often debate which is a better inference engine for them—whether it's VLLM (https://github.com/vllm-project/vllm), TGI (https://mng.bz/aVG7), or GGML (https://github.com/ggerganov/ggml). LLM inference is overall a kind of specific topic—unlike most of the more traditional models, LLMs are often bound by large memory footprint and autoregressive paradigm (you can't predict token $T + 1$ before token T is predicted, which makes parallelization barely possible without additional tricks). If you're interested in LLM

inference, we recommend reading the blog post at https://vgel.me/posts/faster-infer
ence/ and some truly profound pieces of research (e.g., at the moment of polishing
this chapter, we were impressed with "PowerInfer: Fast Large Language Model Serving
with a Consumer-grade GPU" by Song et al. (https://arxiv.org/abs/2312.12456).

While the terms *inference engine* and *inference framework* are often used interchangeably, they are not completely identical. An inference engine is a runtime used for
inference, while an inference framework is a more general term that may include an
engine, a set of tools for model conversion and optimization, and other components
that assist with various aspects of serving, such as batching, versioning, model registry,
logging, and so on. For example, ONNX Runtime is an inference engine, while Torch-
Serve (https://pytorch.org/serve/) is an inference framework.

There is no single answer to the question of whether you need a fully featured framework or just a small wrapper on top of the inference engine. From our experience, once
your needs reach a high level of certainty and you generally tend to work with more
advanced machinery while having enough human resources to maintain it, frameworks
are the way to go. On the other hand, once you're in a startup and need to ship the system somehow but know that your needs will only be formulated in the next several
months, it makes sense to opt for the leaner way, which is to deploy the model with a
simple combination of an inference engine and some communication layer (e.g., web
framework) and postpone a more reliable solution for the next version.

15.3.2 Serverless inference

Serverless inference is an emerging approach that stands out from traditional server-
based models. Popularized by AWS Lambda, this serverless paradigm has now found
representation in multiple alternatives from major cloud providers such as Google
Cloud Functions, Azure Functions, and Cloudflare Workers, as well as from startups
like Banana.dev and Replicate. As of the current writing, major providers primarily
offer CPU inference with limited GPU capabilities, although this is likely to change as
startups continue to push the boundaries in this field.

More advanced products by major cloud providers like AWS Sagemaker jobs can
be viewed as serverless as well. They share core serverless properties (managed infrastructure, pay-as-you-go pricing, autoscaling) but aim for another level of abstraction:
slower functions and more containerized jobs running for extended periods.

It's important to note that the term *serverless* can be somewhat misleading. It
doesn't imply the absence of servers in the system. Rather, it means that engineers
have no direct control over the servers, as they are isolated from them by cloud providers, so they don't need to concern themselves with server management.

Attitudes toward serverless inference are generally either strictly positive or strictly
negative due to its notable advantages and disadvantages. Let's highlight some of them:

- *No need to manage infrastructure or pay for idle resources*—You pay only for what you
  use. While serverless advocates emphasize this, the reality is that some level of

infrastructure management may still be required, although likely at a higher level and with reduced complexity.

- *Ease of scaling, especially for sporadic loads*—However, it's not a universal solution. Cloud providers may impose limitations on concurrent requests, preventing infinite and swift scaling. Additionally, the problem of "cold start," where it can take several seconds for a large model to initialize, is a concern for applications with low latency requirements. Some serverless providers, like Runpod, offer more control in this regard, allowing you to set minimum and maximum numbers of workers and customize scaling rules. Cold start is viewed as a significant problem of serverless computing, so providers develop specific solutions to address it, like SnapStart by AWS (https://mng.bz/gAWV) and Flashboot by Runpod (https://mng.bz/eV9Q). When aiming for serverless inference, cold start time also becomes a factor when choosing the inference engine, as we should aim for slimmer artifacts (like Docker images) and lower load time.

- *Cost-effectiveness for low loads*—Yet, for moderately low but consistent and predictable workloads, dedicated machines might be more cost-efficient than a serverless solution. The pricing and latency combination can also be perplexing. For instance, if a model takes 100 ms to process when warm and 5,000 ms when cold (i.e., right after a break), and the pricing is based on processing time, the cost for the cold request would be 50 times higher. Optimizing such scenarios isn't always straightforward. A special case of low load is various testing environments: it is nice to avoid costs associated with more traditional architecture and only pay for rare test calls happening in your staging environment.

- *Harder to test locally*—The overall complexity of the dev infrastructure tends to increase for the serverless inference, even though it can be cheaper, as mentioned earlier. It is not just "I can't test it without an internet connection anymore." Once the serverless inference is deep in our system, it may bring additional problems (e.g., there's a need to redeploy test artifacts for trivial changes, make sure the test environment has proper permissions, etc.)

Some serverless providers, like Replicate, offer a wide range of pretrained foundation models that can be used out of the box. This is particularly advantageous when starting new projects, especially for prototyping or research purposes.

We've observed both successful and failed cases of serverless inference in small pet projects and high-load production environments. It's unquestionably a viable option, but careful consideration and a thorough cost-benefit analysis are crucial before fully embracing it. The rule of thumb that we follow is as follows: consider using serverless inference when the autoscaling is a significant advantage (e.g., high variance in the number of requests) and the model itself is not excessively large (although even LLMs can sometimes be deployed in CPU-only serverless environment; https://mng.bz/pxnz). Another good idea is to consider serverless inference when you are uncertain about the future load: it can somewhat fit multiple load patterns at the beginning of the project, giving you enough time to redesign the inference part once the situation becomes clearer.

15.4   Optimizing inference pipelines

> *Premature optimization is the root of all evil.*
>
> — Donald Knuth

Optimizing inference pipelines is a wide topic that is not a part of ML system design per se; still, it's a crucial part of ML system engineering that deserves a separate section, at least for listing common approaches and tools as a landscape overview. At its core, optimizing inference pipelines often boils down to a tradeoff between the model's speed and accuracy and the required resource capacity, which implies numerous optimizing techniques that mainly depend on the model's characteristics and architecture.

A reasonable question that may pop up here is, "What would be the starting procedure for optimizing?" We asked a similar question of a number of ML engineers during job interviews and received a variety of answers that mentioned such terms as *model pruning, quantization* (see "Pruning and Quantization for Deep Neural Network Acceleration: A Survey" https://arxiv.org/abs/2101.09671), and *distillation* (see "Knowledge Distillation: A Survey," https://arxiv.org/abs/2006.05525), with references to the state of the papers (we only mention a couple of surveys so you can use them as starting points). These techniques are widely known in the ML research community; they're useful and often applicable, but they are only focused on model optimization without letting us control the whole picture. The most pragmatic answer was, "I would start with profiling."

15.4.1   Starting with profiling

Profiling is a process of measuring the performance of the system and identifying bottlenecks. In contrast to the techniques mentioned earlier, profiling is a more general approach that can be applied to the whole system. Just like strategy comes before tactics, profiling is a great starting point that allows for the identification of the most promising directions for optimization and the selection of the most appropriate techniques.

You might be surprised by how often the seemingly most obvious factors may not be the model's weakest links. Let's take latency as an example. There are cases when it is not the bottleneck (especially when the served model is not a recent generative thing but something more conventional), and the problem is hiding somewhere else (e.g., data preprocessing or network interactions). Furthermore, even if the model is the slowest part of the pipeline, it doesn't automatically mean it should be the target for optimization. This may seem counterintuitive, but we should look for the most optimizable, not the slowest, part of the system. Imagine that a full run takes 200 ms, 120 ms of which is required for the model. But the fact is, the model is already optimized; it runs on GPU via a highly performant engine, and there is not much room for any more improvement. On the other hand, data preprocessing takes 80 ms, and it is an arbitrary Python code that can be optimized in many ways. In this case, it is better to start with data preprocessing, not the model.

Another example comes from Arseny's experience; he was once asked to reduce the latency of a system. The system was a relatively simple pipeline that ran tens of simple models sequentially. The first idea to improve timing was to replace the sequential run with a batch inference. However, profiling proved the opposite: the inference itself was insignificant (around 5%) compared to the time spent on data preprocessing, and a batch inference would not help. What helped was optimizing the preprocessing step, which could not benefit from batching and was eventually coupled with the initially designed sequential run. In the end, Arseny managed to speed up the system by 40% without touching the core model inference, and such elements as thread management, IO and serialization/deserialization functions, and cascade caching were the real low-hanging fruit.

Here we should mention that profiling ML systems differs slightly from profiling regular software for reasons like extensive use of GPUs, asynchronous execution, using thin Python wrappers on top of high-performance native code, and so on. And since the whole process may include a larger number of variables, you should be careful when interpreting the results of profiling, as it is easy to get confused by the tricky nature of the problem.

GPU execution can be especially confusing. Typical CPU load is simple: the data is loaded into memory, and the CPU executes the code: done. There may be nuances related to CPU cache, single instruction, multiple data instructions, or concurrent execution, but in most cases, it is straightforward. Although the GPU is a separate device, it usually comes with built-in memory, and the data has to be copied to the GPU memory before the execution. The copying process itself can be a bottleneck, and it's not always obvious how to measure it. The highly parallel nature of the GPU execution also makes for nonlinear effects. The simplest example is that if you run a model on a single image, it may take 100 ms, but if you run it on 64 images, the processing time will increase only to 200 ms. That is because the GPU is not fully utilized when processing just one item, which leads to a significant overhead of copying the data to the GPU memory. The same happens on a lower level of model architecture: reducing the number of filters in a convolutional layer may not reduce latency, as the GPU is not fully utilized and uses the same CUDA kernel under the hood. Overall, programming for CUDA and other general-purpose GPU frameworks is a separate and extremely deep rabbit hole; the only takeaway we would like to focus on is that the typical programmer's intuition on what is fast and what is slow can be totally irrelevant for GPU-based computing.

So a proper approach to profiling requires keeping a wide mix of tools at hand, starting from basic profilers like cProfile from a Python standard library, more advanced third-party tools like Scalene (https://github.com/plasma-umass/scalene), memray (https://github.com/bloomberg/memray), py-spy (https://github.com/benfred/py-spy), and ML framework-specific tools (like PyTorch Profiler) and ending with low-level GPU profilers like nvprof (https://mng.bz/OmqE). Finally, when working with exotic hardware like tensor processing units or IoT processors, you may need to use vendor-specific tools.

After interpreting the profiling results, we can start optimizing the system, addressing the most visible bottlenecks. Typical approaches are arranged across various levels:

- *Model-related optimizations* like architecture changes, pruning, quantization, distillation, feature selection, etc.
- *Serving-related optimizations* like batching, caching, precomputation, etc.
- *Code-related optimizations* like more effective low-level algorithms, using more effective paradigms (like vectorized algorithms instead of for loops), or rewriting in a faster library/framework (e.g., numba for numeric computation) or even language (e.g., replacing Python bottleneck with a faster wrapper on top of C++ or Rust alternative).
- *Hardware-related optimizations* like using more powerful hardware, vertical/horizontal scaling (please refer to chapter 13), etc.

15.4.2 The best optimizing is minimum optimizing

If we step away from the operating level and give an overview of optimizing from the overall design perspective, some of the problems that arise during the maintenance stage can be avoided if the system has been given a thorough treatment in accordance with the original requirements during the design stage. If we are aware of strict latency requirements, we should initially choose a model that is fast enough for the target platform. Of course, we can reduce the memory footprint with quantization or pruning or reduce latency with distillation, but it is better to start with a model close to the target requirements rather than trying to speed it up when the system is ready. From our experience, an urgent need for optimization is a result of poor choices at the beginning of the system's life cycle (e.g., heavy models were used as a baseline), an unexpected success case (a startup built a quick prototype and suddenly needs to scale), or a planned tech debt ("Okay, we've built something really suboptimal but fast for now; if it survives and helps us finding the product-market fit, we will clean it up").

Choosing the level of optimization is a crucial decision for effective inference. A founding engineer in a startup who needs to extend their minimal viable product to the second customer should usually just scale via straightforward renting of additional cloud computing resources. On the other hand, a platform engineer in a big tech company would likely benefit from reading "Algorithms for Modern Hardware" (https://en.algorithmica.org/hpc/) and applying low-level optimizations at scale.

15.5 Design document: Serving and inference

A separate section of the design document dedicated to inference optimization should cover the anticipated actions during the maintenance stage. Let's examine the commonalities and differences in inference optimization for the two rather divergent ML systems.

15.5.1 *Serving and inference for Supermegaretail*

Based on the key features and requirements of retail-focused ML systems, the solution for Supermegaretail will not require real-time involvement, allowing modification of the model in batches; still, it will involve a large scope of work.

DESIGN DOCUMENT: SUPERMEGARETAIL

XII. SERVING AND INFERENCE

The primary considerations for serving and inference are

- Efficient batch throughput, as forecasts will be run daily, weekly, and monthly on large volumes of data
- Security of the sensitive inventory and sales data
- Cost-effective architecture that can scale batch jobs
- Monitoring data and prediction quality

I. SERVING ARCHITECTURE

We will serve the batch demand forecasting jobs using Docker containers orchestrated by AWS Batch on EC2 machines. AWS Batch will allow for the definition of resource requirements, dynamic scaling of the required number of containers, and queuing of large workloads.

The batch jobs will be triggered on a schedule to process the input data from S3, run inferences, and output results back to S3. A simple Flask API will allow on-demand batch inference requests if required.

All data transferring and processing will occur on secured AWS infrastructure, isolated from external access. Proper credentials will be used for authentication and authorization.

II. INFRASTRUCTURE

The batch servers will use auto-scaling groups to match workload demands. Spot instances can be used to reduce costs for flexible batch jobs.

No specialized hardware or optimizations are required at this stage, as batch throughput is the priority, and the batch nature allows ample parallelization. We will use the horizontal scalability options provided by AWS Batch and S3.

III. MONITORING

Key metrics to track for the batch jobs include

- Job success rate, duration, and failure rate
- Number of rows processed per job
- Server utilization: CPU, memory, disk space
- Prediction accuracy compared to actual demand
- Data validation checks and alerts

This monitoring will help ensure the batch process remains efficient and scalable and produces high-quality predictions. We can assess optimization needs in the future based on production data.

15.5.2 *Serving and inference for PhotoStock Inc.*

Search engine optimization includes two main components:

- Real-time processing of user requests, where the overall number of users is prone to seasonal drifts (e.g., the day/night difference) with possible drastic spikes.
- The index used for the photo search itself, which should be regularly updated. Similar to the Supermegaretail case, a real-time approach is not required but will require processing large amounts of data.

DESIGN DOCUMENT: PHOTOSTOCK INC.

XII. SERVING AND INFERENCE

Given that our search engine is based on vector similarity, there are two aspects we need to care about: generating vectors for searchable items (updating the index) and searching for user queries (querying the index). Those two aspects have different requirements and constraints, so we will design them separately.

I. INDEX UPDATE

Updating the index is a batch process that happens once a day (as mentioned in chapter 13). Other than regular updates, we also need to support the initial index creation or re-creation if the core model is updated. Although it's a relatively rare event, it is important to have a process that can be run on demand.

Both cases share the same characteristics:

- Mild latency requirements
- Strict throughput requirements

We need to be able to process a large number of items in a reasonable time at a reasonable cost. For the rough estimates, we should support reindexing ~10e5 items per day within several hours. We also need to be able to reindex ~10e8 items within a reasonable time if the core model is updated.

II. INDEX QUERY

Querying the index is a real-time process that engages every user query. We need to minimize the latency of the query so that our throughput requirements are not too high, as our average number of searches is 150,000 per day (please see chapter 12), which is about 2 queries per second. However, the number of queries is not evenly distributed, and we need to be able to handle peak loads of ~100 queries per second, as well as upscale and downscale quickly in cases of traffic spikes.

We suggest using the same model converted to ONNX for both batch and real-time inferences. It is not a requirement, but it will simplify the design and maintenance of the system. However, the inference process is different for each batch, and real-time should be separated given the different requirements.

III. FRAMEWORK AND HARDWARE

From a software perspective, we will use Nvidia Triton Inference Server as a serving framework. It is a high-performance open source inference serving software that supports ONNX and has a lot of features that simplify the serving process. We will use the HTTP API of Triton Inference Server to communicate with it from our application. We will use the same model for batch and real-time inference, but the real-time inference will use a more latency-optimized version of the config (e.g., dynamic batching's parameter `max_queue_delay_microseconds` should be under 10 ms).

For batch inference, we will use a default solution by our cloud provider: AWS Sagemaker. It is a managed service that allows us to run the batch inference on configurable instances, it is easy to scale if needed, and it is integrated with other AWS services we use. We can consider using spot instances under the hood to reduce the cost of the batch inference. The batch job itself will be a simple script on top of the real-time inference that adds an IO layer, reading the data from the queue and writing the results to both S3 and the database.

For real-time inference, it would be nice to have a serverless solution that can scale to zero when there are no queries. However, given our high load and low latency requirements, this may be hard to achieve using major providers like AWS Lambda; thus, we will use a more traditional approach with a pool of servers behind our load balancer. We will use AWS EC2 instances for the servers and AWS Application Load Balancer for the load balancer. We can use spot instances under the hood to reduce the cost of the real-time inference because each worker will be stateless, and we can easily replace it with a new one if it is terminated by AWS. We need to make sure that the system has a reasonable number of available workers guaranteed and enable additional scaling if needed.

An exact hardware configuration for both batch and real-time jobs is a subject of future experiments; obviously, we need to use GPU instances for both, but the exact type of GPU and other resources is not clear yet. We don't expect heavy CPU usage given that the preprocessing is relatively simple, but we need to ensure we have enough CPU and avoid it becoming a bottleneck; thorough monitoring of resource usage (CPU/RAM/GPU) is required. The exact number of instances under the balancer is also subject to future experiments.

IV. AUXILIARY INFRASTRUCTURE

We will start model serving with a default float32 precision, but we will experiment with lower precision (e.g., float16) later to reduce the serving cost. Optimizing the model itself for latency can be done later as well, although at the moment we don't expect specific bottlenecks, as the CLIP model is relatively simple.

Because queries are more popular than others, we can use a cache to reduce the load on the inference servers. We can use AWS Elasticache for that; it is a managed service that supports Redis and Memcached. We can use a simple key-value cache with a low time to live (the exact number is subject to data analysis). Caching is useful for the runtime inference, not for the batch inference; the batch inference should be responsible for updating the cache, though, if the key has changed.

We need to make sure that the system can scale to handle the peak load. This part of the design should be refined further with the site reliability engineering team and

AWS experts. At the initial stage, we want to ensure autoscaling is enabled for the real-time inference and all relevant metrics (e.g., resource usage, # of requests, # of active instances) are monitored + alerts are configured.

No additional security measures are required for the serving system, given that it is not exposed to the internet and is only accessible from our application. We need to make sure that access to the serving system is restricted to our application only and that access is granted only to the required resources (e.g., we don't need to give the serving system any access to the database).

Summary

- While it may be tempting to limit your efforts to developing and training your system, inference optimization is just as important a step that will ensure stable performance when you hit the operation stage.
- There are key factors that affect the way you will design the inference optimization process for your system. These include latency, throughput, scalability, target platforms, cost, reliability, flexibility, and security and privacy.
- The aforementioned factors can be conflicting or even mutually exclusive. Hence, it would be impossible to optimize for all of them simultaneously, which will inevitably force you to go for tradeoffs to finetune your model in the best way possible.
- Remember to train your model on one framework and then convert it for further inference in another. This step is especially important, as it won't affect the inference pipeline once you need to switch to a different framework with new features.
- One of your primary goals will be achieving the balance between research flexibility and high performance in the production environment. Bear in mind, however, that it will require an interframework medium.
- The most important point is that the best optimizing is minimum optimizing. Some of the problems that arise during the maintenance stage can be avoided if the system has been properly designed in accordance with the initial requirements.

Ownership and maintenance

> *The competent programmer is fully aware of the limited size of his own skull. He therefore approaches his task with full humility and avoids clever tricks like the plague.*
>
> — Edsger Dijkstra

Throughout the last 15 chapters, we have tried to keep this book organized as an extended, in-depth checklist that you can always refer to at any stage in the design of your machine learning (ML) system. But these seemingly obvious recommendations are harder to follow than you may think.

Building an ML system from scratch and especially operating an existing solution is a process so complex and all-demanding, we're guaranteed to stumble, blunder, hit a few bumps, and compromise some of the principles on our road to bringing value to a business. Being imperfect humans, we are also aware that sometimes we may allow ourselves to ignore some of our own tips.

Indeed, sometimes you may see or end up with a system that is not following the principles we advocate in the book, and reasons for that may vary in a vast number of ways: some details could have been missed, the company may have changed priorities and constraints, the system really needs some refresh because its original assumptions are not valid anymore, and so on.

Usually, it's even more mundane, as the people who originally designed and built the systems tend to change jobs. More than that, they may leave the company before they finish building the system; this is the nature of things. With that in mind, ownership and maintenance is not something we only need to think about later but rather is the cornerstone of the whole system to be ingrained from the very beginning. In this process, however, there is the possibility and risk of becoming too attached to your creation, and this is something that should be avoided. The system should not be viewed as part of its author, and you should detach yourself and your ego from your design to deliver the best possible solution.

To put that in three bullet points, it is essential to know the following at any moment in time:

- What is the area of responsibility behind every person involved in the project? Do we have any gaps in accountability/ownership?
- How many people have specific knowledge? Do we have enough redundancy?
- Where is available documentation, and what components of the system are documented? Will anyone outside of the responsible team be able to run the system?

To some extent, the design document helps answer (although only partially and not always directly) these questions. That means only one thing: we must focus on these aspects to avoid any woeful consequences in the future. After all, the most important thing is to build and maintain a product that will meet your demands and bring value.

In this chapter, we cover the essential basics of making the system long-lasting and robust to human-induced changes.

16.1   Accountability

In earlier chapters of this book, we mentioned the importance of involving a variety of stakeholders in the information-gathering process who will provide critical input into the preparation stage of ML system development.

As the project grows, enriches with new inputs, and evolves from a simple constant baseline to a series of tightly interconnected complex models, it will be gradually joined by new participants. Some of them will only join you for a short period of time and leave once their participation is no longer necessary (e.g., data labelers are vital at the dataset processing stage but fall off by the time of deployment), some of them will turn into permanent contributors until the system's release, and a handful of people will eventually become what can be called the "core team" (i.e., your closest people on the project). These colleagues of yours (or representatives of external vendors, if that's the case) will become the ones accountable for the end result and the stability of your system. And it is you who should keep in touch with them on a regular basis, or at least know them personally.

Knowing the areas of responsibility and the people assigned to these roles is crucial for the successful launch and future of any project or system. It may sound absurd, but it's even more important for team members who are actually responsible for specific components to be aware of that. You would be surprised to know how many times person A was convinced that person B was accountable for a certain part of a project, while person B, in turn, was sure of the opposite. A classic illustration of such a case can be seen in figure 16.1.

Figure 16.1 Explicit versus implicit approaches to involving people in the project

Being redundantly explicit is much more valuable than being implicit in the hopes that everyone is on the same page, and based on our experience, this approach is applicable as soon as there are three people on the project, let alone more team members involved. One of our favorite quotes on the subject comes from the Nobel Prize-winning physicist Richard Feynman. In his book *Surely You're Joking, Mr Feynman!*, he wrote

> *One of the first interesting experiences I had in this project at Princeton was meeting great men. I had never met very many great men before. But there was an evaluation committee that had to try to help us along, and help us ultimately decide which way we were going to separate the uranium. This committee had men like Compton and*

Tolman and Smyth and Urey and Rabi and Oppenheimer on it. I would sit in because I understood the theory of how our process of separating isotopes worked, and so they'd ask me questions and talk about it. In these discussions one man would make a point. Then Compton, for example, would explain a different point of view. He would say it should be this way, and he was perfectly right. Another guy would say, well, maybe, but there's this other possibility we have to consider against it.

So everybody is disagreeing, all around the table. I am surprised and disturbed that Compton doesn't repeat and emphasize his point. Finally, at the end, Tolman, who's the chairman, would say, "Well, having heard all these arguments, I guess it's true that Compton's argument is the best of all, and now we have to go ahead."

It was such a shock to me to see that a committee of men could present a whole lot of ideas, each one thinking of a new facet, while remembering what the other fella said, so that, at the end, the decision is made as to which idea was the best—summing it all up—without having to say it three times. These were very great men indeed.

If you don't have a bunch of geniuses working on a national priority project, you better not rely on their internal understanding and say (or write!) things three times, sharing it with everyone and putting it where it is hard to miss them. Things like meeting minutes, follow-ups, updates, and syncs are essentially done for this sake.

However, we have seen plenty of people abusing these principles, spending too much on meaningless syncs, turning the very concept of meetings into an industry-wide boogeyman. Those rituals, artifacts, or whatever you call them don't require much time and don't have to be done just because it's written in the textbooks but rather serve the specific goal of maintaining focus. Not using them, as well as using them too much, might seriously affect performance and sustainability in the long run. We are convinced documentation is very undervalued, and its importance is severely underestimated.

Areas of accountability should be written down for explicit and unambiguous understanding across the team. There may be various levels of formality—from the startup-friendly "Alice is fully responsible for making system X work" to a complex multipage hierarchy. A fairly balanced approach will involve using the simple yet powerful RACI matrix that splits involved people into four groups:

- *Responsible*—The individual(s) who actually perform the task. Usual suspects: ML engineers.
- *Accountable*—The person ultimately answerable for the completion of the task, typically a manager or team leader. It is recommended that a single person accountable for every component should also have the authority to approve or reject the work. Usual suspects: a project lead or a senior engineer.
- *Consulted*—Those whose opinions are sought, usually subject matter experts or stakeholders with a particular interest in the task. Usual suspects: subject matter experts or legal representatives.
- *Informed*—People who need to be kept up-to-date on the progress or decisions but do not directly contribute to the overall input. Usual suspects: front-end engineers.

For better or worse, there's always room for gaps in accountability; thus, it makes sense to describe an explicit way of escalation—what can be done if the situation doesn't match the matrix or other accountability-related artifact?

One final and probably least favorite part about accountability is an on-call rotation. Being on call means that a specific person is responsible for responding to any critical incidents during their shift. They must be ready to react quickly in case of emergency, usually within 30 to 60 minutes. The rotation part implies this duty is typically shared among team members and changes on a regular basis. For example, one person might be on call for a week and then pass the duty to the next person for the following week (see figure 16.2).

Figure 16.2   On-call shifts are a necessary measure against team burnout.

An on-call schedule usually emerges over the company's growth. Those who started their careers or had experience in smaller companies may recall that there's no need for rotation in those environments, as everyone is on call all the time, with incidents being handled by whoever is available at the moment. However, at some point, this approach becomes unmanageable, when the responsibility is blurred between team members, leading to incidents being managed by everyone and no one at the same time. As soon as you start to pick up signals of such behavior, it's time to formalize an on-call rotation. Later, there might be a need to have a dedicated on-call team structuring the rotation into tiers like L1/L2/L3 and so on.

But even if your on-call schedule is up and running, there may be other reasons for overloading the whole team. Arseny worked for a company during its early evolution stage, where he faced system incidents that couldn't be solved at all simply because he had no clue what systems were even affected. This was a frustrating experience until the engineers who had built and maintained those systems finally wrote solid cookbooks with recommendations on typical problems. Some tech debt was cleared, and on-call shifts transformed from endless nightmares to a regular duty—not the most comfortable one but at least tolerable. When L1 incidents became owned by a dedicated team, the amount of time spent on call by the ML team was reduced even further.

Obviously, being pinged at 3:00 AM on a Saturday is not ideal, which probably creates additional incentives to build a robust and well-monitored system, which could help minimize problems and build a schedule in a way that people know in advance the on-call "roster" and shift times. Any engineer who doesn't see the value in proper logging and observability should be put on call for a long enough period to change their mind.

We believe that a person responsible for system design and implementation is also responsible for the system's maintenance and support. They know the details better than anyone else, and they can forecast corner cases and suggest shortcuts to fix them. It doesn't mean they have to be the only person on call, but they should prepare the system for the on-call rotation and provide the on-call team with the necessary tools and documentation.

Typical tools include

- Logs, metrics, alerts, and dashboards
- System and related infrastructure configuration
- System source code and documentation

Access to production data is a bit trickier. It's not always necessary to have access to production data to fix a problem; we have witnessed cases when privacy policies limit access. However, it's usually good to have access to the production data to investigate the problem and find the root cause. Otherwise, logs and metrics should be detailed enough to help with that.

There should always be a runbook containing comments on how to fix the most common problems and a list of people to escalate the problem to if needed (e.g., there may be an outage on the vendor's side, and an on-call engineer has to reach the CTO who can communicate with the vendor). Many problems occur with some cadence; they are reflections of either the tech debt or usage pattern. For example, imagine having a big customer with a spiky usage pattern, which causes the system to struggle with the load. For such a scenario, an on-call engineer may need a recipe on how to spin up additional instances of the system and how to scale it down when the load is back to normal.

Arising production problems provoke two derivatives: solving and learning. To avoid facing the same mistake repeatedly, make sure to set up a process of learning from failures. This can be arranged through retrospectives and postmortems. We recommend following the principle of *proportional response*—a set of postincident actions that should be sized similarly to the failure effect adjusted for a chance of a similar failure in the future. Some incidents are only worth a 10-minute discussion and adding a paragraph in the runbook. Arseny once triggered an outage so large that a CTO had to start an initiative named "Race for Reliable Releases," which involved every engineering team in the company and improved the reliability across all systems, not only the ML system Arseny successfully broke.

16.2   *Bus factor*

The bus factor is a measure of the risk of a project being disrupted by the loss of a single team member. The term *bus factor* comes from the hypothetical scenario of a team member being hit by a bus, which would suddenly and unexpectedly remove them from the project.

The CAP theorem states that any distributed data store can only offer two of the following three characteristics:

- *Consistency*—Every read request receives the most up-to-date response or an error.
- *Availability*—Every request receives a valid response, but with no assurance that it contains the most recent data.
- *Partition tolerance*—The system continues to operate even if communication between nodes is disrupted or lost.

When a network partition failure occurs, a decision must be made between canceling the operation to enhance consistency at the cost of availability or proceeding with the operation to maintain availability while potentially compromising consistency.

We consider the team structure very close to that but with different criteria: efficiency and redundancy. As computer science describes, redundancy means having extra or duplicate resources available to support the primary system. It is a backup or reserve system that can step in if the primary system fails. The reserve resources are redundant as they are not being used if everything is working correctly.

> **NOTE** Engineers often tend to solve organizational problems with technical solutions (in other words, treat people like software) just because that is what they excel at. Sometimes it is a good enough call because building software may indeed be simpler than getting along with people and aligning toward a challenging goal. However, a senior engineer should not be like a hammer seeing nails everywhere—they should choose the right tool for the problem, and sometimes one that is not technical at all.

How can this redundancy/efficiency problem affect the team structure? From what we have seen, the company/team/project scheme usually evolves from being efficient to becoming redundant. However, neither being too efficient nor too redundant is beneficial.

16.2.1   *Why is being too efficient not beneficial?*

If you are too efficient and cover multiple factors with only a few people, you are at risk. Every single person on the team is irreplaceable, not only thanks to their experience but, unfortunately, also because they work at full capacity. If anything happens to at least one of your team members, the company (or a project) is in trouble. The only way to handle problems that arise with no drops in overall efficiency is by acts of heroism that are not in any way scalable and thus are considered an antipattern (https://mng.bz/YVyA; see figure 16.3).

Figure 16.3   The downside of ultraefficiency is extremely high vulnerability to external factors.

16.2.2 *Why is being too redundant not beneficial?*

As opposed to efficiency, the main advantage of redundancy is extra capacity that provides reliability, security, room for improvement, and a margin to outlast a crisis. However, too much redundancy creates sloppiness, reduces trust between team members, and repels top performers, as it impairs the overall vibe and feeling of doing a meaningful and impactful job.

The two examples here are obvious corner cases that should be avoided. As soon as you feel that the team is approaching its capacity limit, it is worth thinking about expanding, which will be the right solution in the long run, despite the increased costs at the current moment.

The same rule will work the other way around: have just enough capacity to avoid working to exhaustion on the one hand but to be well-armed for potential crunching at peak load times.

16.2.3 *When and how to use the bus factor*

We need to keep the right balance between efficiency and redundancy, and the first step to controlling something is the ability to measure; one of the very simple and well-known metrics is the bus factor.

The bus factor is calculated by counting the number of team members that would need to be lost before the project would be unable to continue. For example, a project with a bus factor of 1 would be in serious trouble even if one (specific) team member was lost.

Obviously, a bus factor of 1 is less than desirable, while a bus factor of 10,000 might be too much (though this might happen if you need many people with relatively similar scope, e.g., customer support); the final number depends on many variables: project importance, budget constraints, deadlines, expected turnover, and project owner's anxiety/confidence. But as soon as you have a list of people accountable for different parts of the system/project, you have everything you need to calculate a bus factor, which includes areas and people accountable for them. The next thing you need to do is to find out how many other people know this area well enough. As a rule of thumb, a person accountable for the area knows everybody else who can (to some extent) replace them. With that in mind, you can calculate the bus factor, assess potential risks, and make the necessary decisions on hiring, moving, or collaboration activities to cross-pollinate the knowledge and address the fragility you might have on the project.

Of course, we can't label people in a discrete manner as "they know how the system or its component works" versus "they don't." Typically, there are shades of knowledge within a system, and even when it is not possible to keep many engineers informed about everything, it is possible to spread this knowledge partially. This usually manifests through design/code/documentation review, pair programming sessions, and open hours where key members share their expertise.

This reasoning describes the balance between two criteria. Real decision-making, though, may and will require more criteria to take into account (e.g., not just team size but also its seniority balance and exposure to particular technologies).

For those who are interested in a simple yet practical framework on how to see the tradeoff between costs, system performance, and human capacity, we recommend getting familiar with the Rasmussen model for failures, nicely explained in this post: https://mng.bz/GNqO. Unlike the previous text, which focused on the team structure, the post reflects SRE's perspective on the system tradeoffs: while people and hardware are very different, there are similar patterns in finding an optimal tradeoff.

16.3 Documentation

We have already mentioned the importance of documentation. Unfortunately, documentation is usually highly underestimated and does not always receive the level of care and attention it deserves. Ironically, the word "documentation" often stands next to such words as "later," "not now," and "not urgent." And when documentation is needed, it is usually either too late to prepare or extremely outdated.

The significance of documentation cannot be overstated. It serves as a means of knowledge transfer and onboarding new team members, helping to smooth the learning curve for newcomers and ensuring the system's longevity. Comprehensive documentation allows someone outside of the responsible team to understand and run the system effectively.

Campfire story from Valerii

I have worked in different companies: offline and online food retail, eCommerce marketplaces, social network companies, and fintech. One thing I am very proud of is that—regardless of the company size, market, and maturity—the systems and organizations I built were able to withstand my departure and continued successful operation. Cornerstones to this were a smooth learning curve for newcomers, extensive documentation and thorough integration with other departments, and people knowing who was accountable for specific parts.

Once I received a message from my former peer at a big tech company asking how to reproduce a specific system component (a language model capable of generating synthetic reviews for sold items). My answer was brief—the documentation for that project is available under a specific tag, and it was! (Frankly, he didn't even need me to find that out.) And not only was it available, but you could use it to reproduce the whole deployment process with a single command or inspect the code repo and datasets if needed.

Here is a very different example. Once I worked at a company where we had to re-create an on-chain analysis of the Bitcoin blockchain, which had initially been done 2 years ago, but some sources had changed and had to be replaced/updated. Unfortunately, there was almost no documentation, and what should have taken 2 weeks at most consumed almost 3 months (on-chain analysis is not very straightforward; for example, you might send 0.1 BTC, but it will look like you sent 1 and received 0.9, which is very different from the actual situation). A short time after this project was finished, most of the team members working there were laid off, alongside 30% of the company's workforce. That was the second layoff within 6 months. Combined, they shrank the company's population by almost 60%. It is hard to say if the primary reason for that was the lack of documentation, but I am sure that reinventing the wheel (in this case, retaking the same step anew) repeatedly is not the most efficient way of spending resources. That is why caching is so widespread in computer science. Unfortunately, the layoff happened when the project was finished, but the documentation wasn't yet done.

Documentation also helps to achieve higher reliability by enabling smoother transitions when team members leave (bus factor) or new members join. Moreover, documentation facilitates collaboration across different departments and stakeholders, fostering a shared understanding of the system (accountability) and keeping each engineer more autonomous, thus agentic and productive.

While it may require additional time and effort upfront, documentation ultimately saves resources in the long run. It reduces the reliance on tribal knowledge, prevents the repetition of work, and minimizes the risk of costly errors and delays due to a lack of information. Documenting processes, procedures, configurations, and best practices empowers the team to work more efficiently and provides a foundation for continuous improvement. It should be prioritized from the beginning and not considered an afterthought. By acknowledging the importance of documentation and dedicating the necessary resources, teams can build resilient systems that can adapt to changes and continue to deliver value over time.

To some extent, our whole book is dedicated to why and how to write a particular sort of documentation, which captures important information about the system's design, architecture, implementation details, and operational procedures. But a design document is a very specific piece of documentation and does not aim to become a holistic text covering all aspects of the system but rather an overview that helps to sync the team of system builders and stakeholders. That said, there is always space for other documents, including

- *User manuals and guides* that explain how to use a system and provide step-by-step instructions for common tasks, such as data preparation, model training, and prediction

- *Cookbooks* that suggest simple ways to reach a goal using the system and provide code snippets, data examples, and specific steps to reach a target outcome

- *Low-level technical specifications* and *API documentation* for developers that describe the underlying technical details of an ML system and give guidance on how to interact with the system on a programming level using functions and APIs

- *Installation and configuration guides* that give instructions on how to set up and finetune ML environments, as well as explain dependencies, installation steps, and options for configuring software

- *FAQs and troubleshooting guides* that address frequently asked questions related to using ML tools and suggest solutions or workarounds for common problems you may face during training, testing, or deployment

- *Release notes* that detail changes applied in new software versions; explain new features, bug fixes, performance improvements, or known problems; and inform users about new releases and their impact on the general workflow

- *Previous incident investigation reports* that analyze and document root causes of past problems or failures, share lessons learned and measures to avoid similar incidents, and improve system reliability and user confidence

Investing time and effort in creating and maintaining documentation from the outset helps teams mitigate risks associated with knowledge gaps and dependencies on specific individuals. In the course of the book, you have seen two design documents that we hope have given you a good overview of the described systems.

16.4 Complexity

Make everything as simple as possible, but not simpler.

— Attributed to Albert Einstein

According to the second law of thermodynamics, the entropy of an isolated system left to spontaneous evolution cannot decrease with time. While originally *entropy* was a term used for physics, it was later adapted by information theory with almost the same meaning: entropy quantifies the amount of uncertainty or randomness.

Metaphorically speaking, software and ML systems follow the very same law: during time, entropy can only increase. At some point, it becomes too hard to handle, and that's why old systems are often decomposed into sets of smaller systems (remember the fundamental theorem of software engineering from section 13.1) to be maintainable by teams of decently intelligent people, not generational talents. Adding a new level of abstraction "hides" the entropy but doesn't really reduce its level across the whole stack.

There are many pieces of collective consciousness stating similar ideas: the YAGNI ("You aren't gonna need it") approach from the extreme programming culture, the

KISS ("Keep it simple, stupid") principle that originated in the US Navy in the middle of the 20th century, and even Occam's razor from as far back as medieval ages. All these ideas pursue the same goal: limit complexity.

At the same time, the software engineering culture tends to land on the opposite side of the spectrum, as expressed in acronymic proverbs like DRY ("Don't repeat yourself"). At first glance, those are controversial: following DRY suggests introducing more layers of abstraction, and that is exactly one of the (or rather the only) sources of complexity.

Imagine writing a simple code snippet computing a well-known metric across multiple datasets. A typical code set would contain maybe three functions: one reads the data, the next one calculates the metric, and the final one orchestrates the execution, running both functions in a loop and saving the result.

Now, let's imagine two sides of the spectrum: too-simplistic code on the one hand and overcomplicated code on the other hand, which execute the same thing. The former could be written by a person who doesn't know much about loops and functions; they would just write it by instruction: read file A, calculate metric for A, save metric for A, read file B, etc. Overcomplicated code would contain some metaprogramming and other complex patterns. While they are completely different in nature, both would make the code readability worse.

This is a trivial example you can find in almost every software engineering textbook that teaches how to write clean code. But the same principle is applicable on a larger scale. Imagine solving the following problem: your company wants to help the customer support team prioritize the most urgent cases to help the most unhappy customers first.

A typical solution for this problem these days would be to use a foundation large language model with a tailored prompt to classify messages into several urgency buckets. Before the large language model revolution, the proportional baseline would be to make a simplistic model (like a logistic regression on top of a bag of words) to run the classification so it covers the majority of urgent messages. It would also need some engineering efforts (e.g., building data pipelines to fetch the training set and labeling it with the customer support team, connecting the model with customer service software to propagate these labels and visualize them in the UI, etc.).

A deviation into unreasonable simplicity would be to build a baseline with several ifs and regular expressions. This solution will definitely work for a while, but relatively soon your colleagues will be as unhappy as a customer who paid for the product twice because a glitch requested the company to roll back the transaction, and for some unclear reason, your model classified the ticket as "low priority."

An overcomplicated solution can include many components united by the same word: *irrelevant*. You can bring multiple complicated natural language understanding models trained from scratch, cover them with some research to make them work in a few-shot scenario, and polish them with a calibration layer. Complexity can be not ML-specific but skewed into engineering as well: instead of having a couple of simple

APIs, an engineer can use all the buzzwords they know of to make the system as fault-tolerant as spaceship firmware and as scalable as Google's search engine, ignoring the fact it should only process dozens of messages per day.

All kinds of systems—including nonsoftware ones—suffer from complexity. The additional layer of software complexity is its constant evolution. When you're building a house, you won't be adding extra rooms on top of it a month after finishing the roof. Adding new features to a software system, though, is a much more commonly applied practice. The complexity of data-focused systems increases because of constant problems related to data drifts. ML systems are even more complex—some models are nonlinear black boxes by design, and this doesn't make things easier.

At the very end of the book, we'd like to once again refer to chapters 2 and 3, covering problem understanding and preliminary research. Some complexity is unavoidable, but a big share of excessive complexity is caused by misses on these stages: poor understanding of the problem, surface-level research, setting irrelevant goals, and not covering obvious risks from the very beginning. These can lead to a snowball of poor decisions and increased complexity.

When you need to cross a river, a reliable paddle boat can be enough. You could even equip it with a motor to speed up your cross-river journeys, but there is no way of evolving this boat for transporting thousands of people across the ocean (see figure 16.4). At the same time, those who start assembling a cruise ship when the traveling distance does not exceed a couple of miles can never reach the goal. Many ML systems are doomed for reasons related to this metaphor: their designers either try to evolve a primitive system with bells and whistles to meet rather challenging goals or start building a spacecraft with no good reasoning and get fired even before the first phase of construction is ready.

Figure 16.4 Just like a basic model will end up underperforming and failing to meet the project goals, an overkill solution will devour valuable resources of a business.

Campfire story from Arseny

I failed the deadline of finalizing this chapter because I was too busy with my main job and because of my own smarty-pants decision in the past. Three years ago, I needed to test a part of the system that was supposed to run the model in two environments: locally and cloud-based. The test was straightforward: run the same thing in both spaces and assert the results are equal. But I was chasing to save some milliseconds and thus made two calls run concurrently in separate threads. That was smart and effective! Years passed, the codebase evolved, new features were shipped, the infrastructure changed a lot, and one of these infrastructural changes changed the way things are supposed to work in the cloud. So you could expect this test to start failing. However, Python exceptions in threads are not implicit, so a test failure in this situation leads to a barely relevant message. As a cherry on top, these tests were also executed concurrently, which hid the real problem even further. An unnecessary complexity took a full day of my work to uncover this problem.

This story omits some engineering details like non-typical CI configuration, but even when simplified, it demonstrates that there is no single root cause of this wasted time—it is more like death by a thousand cuts. As a popular list, "How Complex Systems Fail" (https://how.complexsystems.fail/), says, "Post-accident attribution to a 'root cause' is fundamentally wrong." There was not a single poor decision but a combination of suboptimal choices. The combinatorics is not on your side: even when most of the decisions related to the system are optimal, an enormous number of combinations in a complicated system will lead to a growing number of incidents. All you can do is reduce this number together with the effect of each small failure.

16.5 Maintenance and ownership: Supermegaretail and PhotoStock Inc.

Throughout the book, we have concluded each chapter with a case study illustrating the chapter's relevant design-document section for Supermegaretail and PhotoStock Inc. This makes little sense in this case, as it would have required making up a couple dozen fake first and last names. We limit ourselves to general considerations about how maintenance would go in both examples.

Since Supermegaretail is a large corporation with thousands of employees and has a high level of bureaucratization and complex work processes, while its key business units are predominantly nontechnical, an important role in a project's success lies in the successful coordination of all stages with stakeholders at each level of the hierarchy. Thus, the basis for the effective postrelease operation of the system would be a detailed RACI matrix that would include the company's employees involved in the project, as well as lists of sign-offs from the delivery team and executive and business teams.

On the other hand, PhotoStock Inc. is a fairly small, purely tech-based company, and the specificity of custom search engines working with millions of images implies continuous load on the system with regular peak loads. The search engine is both an ML-heavy and infrastructure-heavy project. As highlighted before, it requires extensive cross-team collaboration. Given that there are four core components (API handlers, index, ranking models, internal tools), we would want to make sure that

- There is a senior engineer directly responsible for each component.
- Those engineers have a fair visibility of other components.

With that in mind, two levels of on-call rotation would be the optimal solution:

- The primary on-call engineer is first to respond to any incident.
- The primary on-call engineer can escalate specific problems to component on-call engineers.

As we said back in chapter 4, the design document is a living thing, and the maintenance section is to be added and filled in last, not only because, at this stage, you have a complete vision of your ML system but also because by this point you have managed to build connections with representatives of other teams and units and have an understanding which personalities will be included in the working group of your project.

Summary

- A person responsible for system design and implementation is also responsible for the system's maintenance and support.
- Be sure to know the areas of responsibility and the people assigned to these roles. Even more importantly, be explicit in reminding those people of their respective roles, as it is much more valuable than being implicit in the hopes that everybody is on the same page.
- To follow the growing reach of your system, remember to provide an on-call rotation to respond to any critical incidents.
- Always look for a tradeoff between the efficiency and redundancy of your team to avoid working to exhaustion and, at the same time, maintain enough capacity to withstand peak load times.
- Keep every piece of documentation for your system updated and available to any engaged parties. While it may require additional time and effort up front, documentation ultimately saves resources in the long run.
- Start small, improve a thing or two, build trust, and then continue with higher-effect changes. It's very likely you will get more support from your colleagues and gather more implicit knowledge about the system while doing so, which will help you to make better decisions.
- Try to avoid overcomplicating your solution. Excessive complexity either can be a result of personal ambitions or can indicate a poor understanding of the problem, surface-level research, setting irrelevant goals, and not covering obvious risks from the very beginning.

index

RELATED MANNING TITLES

Managing Machine Learning Projects
by Simon Thompson

ISBN 9781633439023
272 pages, $49.99
May 2023

Machine Learning Engineering in Action
by Ben Wilson

ISBN 9781617298714
576 pages, $59.99
March 2022

Designing Deep Learning Systems
by Chi Wang and Donald Szeto
Forewords by Silvio Savarese and Caiming Xiong

ISBN 9781633439863
360 pages, $59.99
June 2023

Design a Machine Learning System (From Scratch)
by Benjamin Tan Wei Hao, Shanoop Padmanabhan,
and Varun Mallya

ISBN 9781633437333
325 pages (*estimated*), $59.99
Spring 2025 (*estimated*)

For ordering information, go to www.manning.com